Outbreak

Foodborne Illness and the Struggle for Food Safety

TIMOTHY D. LYTTON

The University of Chicago Press
Chicago and London

The University of Chicago Press, Chicago 60637
The University of Chicago Press, Ltd., London
© 2019 by The University of Chicago
All rights reserved. No part of this book may be used or reproduced in any manner
whatsoever without written permission, except in the case of brief quotations in
critical articles and reviews. For more information, contact the University of Chicago
Press, 1427 E. 60th St., Chicago, IL 60637.
Published 2019
Printed in the United States of America

28 27 26 25 24 23 22 21 20 19   1 2 3 4 5

ISBN-13: 978-0-226-61154-9   (cloth)
ISBN-13: 978-0-226-61168-6   (paper)
ISBN-13: 978-0-226-61171-6   (e-book)
DOI: https://doi.org/10.7208/chicago/9780226611716.001.0001

Library of Congress Cataloging-in-Publication Data

Names: Lytton, Timothy D., 1965– author.
Title: Outbreak : foodborne illness and the struggle for food safety / Timothy D.
    Lytton.
Description: Chicago ; London : The University of Chicago Press, 2019. |
    Includes bibliographical references and index.
Identifiers: LCCN 2018034311 | ISBN 9780226611549 (cloth : alk. paper) |
    ISBN 9780226611686 (pbk. : alk. paper) | ISBN 9780226611716 (e-book)
Subjects: LCSH: Food adulteration and inspection—United States. | Food handling—
    United States. | Consumer protection—United States.
Classification: LCC HD9000.9.U5 L988 2019 | DDC 363.19/260973—dc23
LC record available at https://lccn.loc.gov/2018034311

♾ This paper meets the requirements of ANSI/NISO Z39.48-1992
(Permanence of Paper).

To my children, Medad, Margalit, and Asher

And to Rachel Anisfeld
Many women have acted virtuously,
but you surpass them all.
Proverbs 31:29

Contents

Trouble in the Fields:
An Introduction to the Food Safety System

The family farms of Rocky Ford, Colorado, enjoy a well-deserved reputation for producing exceptionally flavorful cantaloupes. The surrounding Arkansas River Valley offers ideal conditions for melon cultivation—hot days and cool nights that enhance the plants' sugar production. But in 2011, cantaloupes from this region attracted attention for a different reason. They were the source of one of the deadliest food poisoning outbreaks in US history.

Eric and Ryan Jensen, two hardworking brothers in their mid-thirties, raised and packed cantaloupes ninety miles east of Rocky Ford. Fourth-generation melon farmers, the brothers inherited 160 acres from their father and expanded their operations to 6,000 acres. During the 2011 harvest, Jensen Farms produced three hundred thousand cases of cantaloupes, labeled "Sweet Rocky Fords," which were sold through a distributor to leading retail supermarkets, such as Walmart, Kroger, and Safeway. Many of these melons were contaminated with a virulent bacterial pathogen, *Listeria monocytogenes*, and they caused 147 reported cases of serious illness and thirty-three deaths in twenty-eight states.[1]

No one has ever conclusively identified the source of the contamination. One possibility is organic fertilizer. At the time of the outbreak, the brothers were in the midst of a three-year process of converting their operations from conventional to organic production, which requires replacing mineral fertilizers and chemical pesticides with alternatives derived from plants and animals. From a business perspective, the brothers sought to profit from the growing consumer demand for organic fruits and vegetables. They also had a deeply personal reason for the shift. Their father, Robert Jensen, had died in March 2010, at the age of fifty-nine, from cancer, which the brothers suspected might have been caused by pesticide or other chemical exposure. They believed that organic production would redeem Jensen Farms from decades of synthetic fertilizer and pesticide application. However, organic fertilizers also pose risks to human health. If not properly treated, they can harbor microorganisms, including bacterial pathogens such as *Salmonella*, *E. coli*, and *Listeria*.[2]

The Jensen brothers were not unmindful of the risk of bacterial contamination. They began post-harvest processing by immersing the melons in a dunk tank filled with chlorinated water to remove dirt and reduce harmful bacteria on the surface of the fruit. The melons were then dried, packed into crates, placed in cold storage, and later shipped to a distributor for sale to retail stores. In August 2010, a private food safety auditor inspected the fields and packinghouse operations, awarding Jensen Farms a score of 95 percent and a "superior" rating. When one of the brothers asked how they could improve their processing, the auditor responded that the dunk tank, with its recirculating water, was a potential food safety "hot spot" and that they should consider replacing it.[3]

The following spring, with advice from a local equipment supplier, the brothers purchased and installed spray-washing equipment originally designed to clean potatoes and modified for melon processing. The new equipment used non-recirculating city water to wash the melons as they passed along a conveyer belt. A subsequent July 2011 audit awarded Jensen Farms a score of 96 percent and another "superior" rating. The audit report noted that the spray wash system "does not have anti-microbial solution injected," but this was not characterized as a deficiency, nor did it detract from the audit score. To the Jensens, the new non-recirculating spray wash system appeared more sanitary than the old dunk tank, which became increasingly dirty during the course of each production run. However, without antimicrobial solution added to the wash water, the spray wash spread bacterial contamination from melon to melon and dispersed it all over the processing equipment.[4]

By late August, Colorado health officials began receiving reports of individuals suffering from listeriosis. On September 2, they notified the federal Centers for Disease Control and Prevention (CDC) of seven cases in the state. Within a week, state and federal investigators traced the source of the outbreak to Jensen Farms cantaloupe. Four investigators arrived at the farm on September 9 and 10 to collect samples. Tests confirmed that samples taken from Jensen Farms melons, equipment, and facilities contained the same pathogenic strains of *Listeria* as those found in recently reported cases of listeriosis. The Jensens immediately ceased shipment of their cantaloupes and destroyed their remaining crops, and on September 14, the company voluntarily ordered a seventeen-state recall of its melons.[5]

The recall came too late for forty-eight-year-old Shelly Occhipinti-Krout, who left behind a husband and three children when she died from listeriosis, which she contracted from eating Jensen Farms cantaloupe. "It started with just flu-like symptoms," her daughter Tiffany recalls. "Then she collapsed . . . and was taken to the hospital. While she was getting a CAT scan, she went into cardiac arrest, and doctors put her into a medically induced coma." After three weeks in the hospital, her body was so swollen from the infection that she was unrecognizable. "I kept thinking that she was going to come home," says Tiffany. "She went like a normal person to the grocery store, got her stuff, came home, and ate it. From that my mom got sick, and I'm never going to see her again."[6]

Eighty-seven-year-old William Beach also died of listeriosis from eating Jensen Farms cantaloupe. "He was in and out of the hospital several times," remembers his wife, Monette. "About a month before he died, we were in the living room watching TV one night, and he said, 'Honey, we've got trouble; there is something wrong with me, and I don't know what it is.'" In the hospital, when doctors attempted to insert a feeding and medication tube, he began to hemorrhage through his mouth and nose. William eventually succumbed to the infection. "The bottom line here is that my father died because somebody didn't do their job," says William's daughter Debbie, expressing a view held by many victims and their families. "I think it's unconscionable. All of us hope that when we go it's quick. But never, ever, do we ever think that it's going to come with us spewing blood out of our mouth and our nose in terror because we don't know what's going on but we know it's over. Somebody's responsible for it."[7]

In the end, public health authorities attributed 147 reported cases of listeriosis to tainted cantaloupes from Jensen Farms. Thirty-three victims died within weeks of consuming the melon, and another ten died months later, possibly as a result of the infection. Some of those who survived sustained brain injuries and other long-term disabilities. Victims and their families were left with large medical bills—in several cases exceeding a million dollars.[8]

Researchers at the CDC in Atlanta estimate that "48 million people get sick, 128,000 are hospitalized, and 3,000 die from foodborne diseases each year in the United States." (For a detailed account of how researchers estimate the number of cases and the economic costs of foodborne illness, see appendix A.) These statistics have led many commentators to declare the food safety system "broken" and in need of significant reform. A report by the US Public Interest Research Group analyzing outbreaks and recalls in 2011 and 2012 concludes that foodborne illness caused by microbial contamination "has stayed stagnant and potentially grown worse, taking a substantial toll on public health and the economy," and that "the rules and inspection systems we have now are not up to the task."[9]

Not everyone agrees that outbreaks signify that the system is broken. Even highly effective regulatory programs tolerate a certain amount of risk. There will always be some residual risk in the food system—zero risk is simply not possible. As one food safety professional with more than thirty years of experience in the poultry sector puts it: "People who demand bacteria-free eggs just don't understand where they come from—there's only one way out of the chicken." Nor is zero risk a desirable goal, because at a certain point, the costs of additional risk reduction would outweigh the benefits. Tom Vilsack, secretary of agriculture in the Obama administration, expressed a view widely shared within the food industry when he boasted in 2012 that, although there is admittedly room for improvement, the United States has the world's "safest food supply—an achievement made possible by a wide range of skilled, dedicated people."[10]

Leaving aside for the moment the question of how well the food safety system performs, available data suggest that foodborne illness in the United States is a problem of noteworthy magnitude comparable to other common sources of illness and injury that have attracted the attention of public health authorities. (The analysis that follows relies on data drawn from a variety of sources, collected using various methods, and covering different years. Some

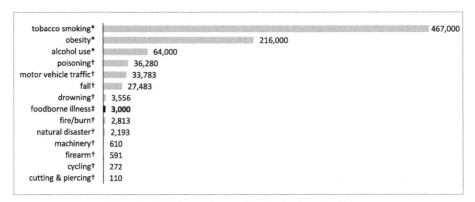

tobacco smoking*	467,000
obesity*	216,000
alcohol use*	64,000
poisoning†	36,280
motor vehicle traffic†	33,783
fall†	27,483
drowning†	3,556
foodborne illness‡	**3,000**
fire/burn†	2,813
natural disaster†	2,193
machinery†	610
firearm†	591
cycling†	272
cutting & piercing†	110

FIGURE 1.1. Leading causes of death annually from illness and unintentional injury.

* Estimates from 2005 data: Goodarz Danaei et al., "The Preventable Causes of Death in the United States Comparative Risk Assessment of Dietary, Lifestyle, and Metabolic Risk Factors," *PLOS Medicine* 6, no. 4 (2009): https://doi.org/10.1371/journal.pmed.1000058.

† Based on census of medical records: CDC, "20 Leading Causes of Unintentional Injury Death, United States 2011," WISQARS Leading Cause of Death Report, archived at http://perma.cc/U828-3VDH.

‡ Estimate from Elaine Scallan et al., "Foodborne Illness Acquired in the United States—Unspecified Pathogens," *Emerging Infectious Diseases* 17, no. 1 (January 2011): 20.

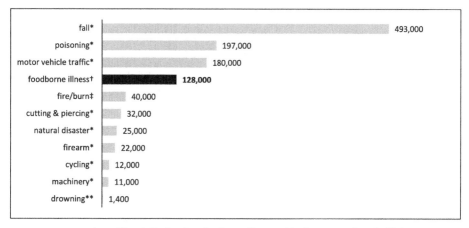

FIGURE 1.2. Annual hospitalization from foodborne illness and leading causes of nonfatal injury.

* Average annual hospital discharges 2004–2005, from G. Bergen, L. H. Chen, M. Warner, and L.A. Fingerhut, *Injury in the United States: 2007 Chartbook* (Hyattsville, MD: National Center for Health Statistics, 2008), 126, https://www.cdc.gov/nchs/data/misc/injury2007.pdf, archived at https://perma.cc/D99P-M9WT. The figure for firearms includes intentional injuries.

† Estimate from Elaine Scallan et al., "Foodborne Illness Acquired in the United States—Unspecified Pathogens," *Emerging Infectious Diseases* 17, no. 1 (January 2011): 20.

‡ Based on hospital discharge data from 2010, American Burn Association, "Burn Incidence and Treatment in the United States: 2016, http://ameriburn.org/who-we-are/media/burn-incidence-fact-sheet/, archived at https://perma.cc/P3A3-MNMA.

** Estimate based on reports of emergency department visits for 2010 from CDC, "Data and Statistics (WISQARS): Cost of Injury Reports" (2,646 emergency department visits), archived at https://perma.cc/284C-DYHC; CDC, "Unintentional Drowning: Get the Facts" (stating that more than 50 percent of drowning victims treated in emergency departments require hospitalization), https://www.cdc.gov/homeand recreationalsafety/water-safety/waterinjuries-factsheet.html, archived at https://perma.cc/TQY4-3PJT. Compare Stephen Bowman et al., "Trends in US Pediatric Drowning Hospitalizations, 1993–2008," *Pediatrics* 129, no. 2 (February 2012) (2000 annual hospitalizations from drowning for children age 0–19).

of the numbers represent direct tallies from health records, while others are estimates that rely on surveys and statistical models. The aim is to provide general perspective not precise comparisons.) By using the CDC estimate, figure 1.1 shows that annual deaths from foodborne illness are far fewer in number than those caused by tobacco smoking, obesity, and alcohol use; considerably fewer than those caused by poisoning, motor vehicles, and falls; comparable to those caused by drowning, fire, and natural disasters; and significantly greater than those caused by machinery, firearms, cycling, and cutting and piercing.

Figure 1.2 compares the estimated number of hospitalizations from foodborne illness to those from leading sources of injury.[11] Although hospitalizations from foodborne illness are fewer than those of the top three sources of nonfatal injury—falls, poisoning, and motor vehicle accidents—they exceed several other leading sources, such as burns, cutting and piercing, natural disasters, firearms, cycling, machinery, and drowning.

Figure 1.3 suggests that the estimated number of foodborne illness episodes involving acute illness far exceeds that of other leading forms of unintentional injury.[12]

Using estimates from researchers at the US Department of Agriculture (USDA) Economic Research Service, figure 1.4 compares the cost of medical care due to foodborne illness and leading forms of illness and unintentional injury. The medical costs of foodborne illness rank below those of tobacco smoking, obesity, falls, cycling, alcohol use, motor vehicle accidents, and poisoning, but they exceed those of burns, drowning, and firearms.

The burden of foodborne illness falls most heavily on the elderly, who are at greatest risk of death or severe complications. Half of the reported listeriosis cases in the Jensen Farms melon outbreak were among individuals older than seventy-seven years, and most who died were older than eighty. In a 2011 report on foodborne illness caused by major pathogens, the

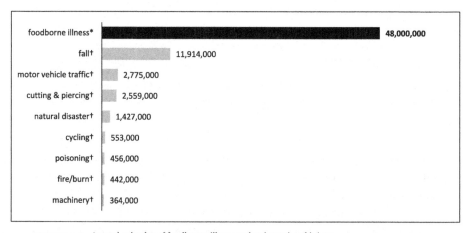

FIGURE 1.3. Annual episodes of foodborne illness and unintentional injury.
* Estimate of episodes of illness from Elaine Scallan et al., "Foodborne Illness Acquired in the United States—Unspecified Pathogens," *Emerging Infectious Diseases* 17, no. 1 (January 2011): 20. The definition of an episode of foodborne illness includes only acute illness, for example, gastroenteritis involving three or more loose stools in twenty-four hours or vomiting, lasting more than one day or resulting in restricted daily activities (see Scallan et al., 17).
† Average annual injury episodes 2004–2005, from G. Bergen, L. H. Chen, M. Warner, and L.A. Fingerhut, *Injury in the United States: 2007 Chartbook* (Hyattsville, MD: National Center for Health Statistics, 2008), 127, https://www.cdc.gov/nchs/data/misc/injury2007.pdf, archived at https://perma.cc/D99P-M9WT. The definition of an episode of injury includes only acute injury, defined as a fatal or medically attended injury (see *Chartbook*, 8).

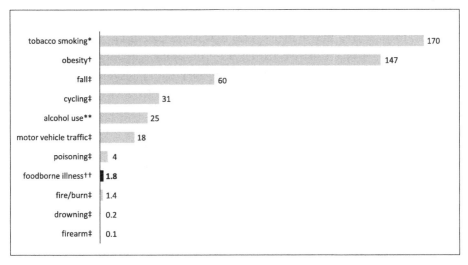

FIGURE 1.4. Annual cost of medical care for leading causes of death, illness, and unintentional injury ($ billion).

* Estimate for 2014 from CDC, "Smoking and Tobacco Use, Costs and Expenditures," https://www.cdc.gov/tobacco/data_statistics/fact_sheets/fast_facts/, archived at https://perma.cc/S6KB-QQDE.

† Estimate for 2008 from CDC, "Adult Obesity Facts," https://www.cdc.gov/obesity/data/adult.html, archived at https://perma.cc/XQE4-T77C.

‡ Estimates for 2010 from CDC, "Data and Statistics (WISQARS): Cost of Injury Reports," archived at https://perma.cc/R8RX-YWGC.

** Estimate for 2006 from CDC, "Excessive Drinking Is Draining the U.S. Economy," https://www.cdc.gov/features/costsofdrinking/, archived at https://perma.cc/VM45-GQFN.

†† Estimate for 2013 from Sandra Hoffmann, Bryan Maculloch, and Michael Batz, "Economic Burden of Major Foodborne Illnesses Acquired in the United States," Economic Research Service of the USDA, *Economic Information Bulletin*, no. 140, May 2015, 11 (includes cost of medical care for fifteen leading foodborne illnesses, which constitute approximately 95 percent of the total).

CDC found that 13 percent of infections, 24 percent of hospitalizations, and 57 percent of deaths occurred among adults sixty-five or older. Thus, the elderly not only face a higher risk of infection; they are also far more likely to suffer serious illness and death as a result. Young children and those who are immunosuppressed—for example, cancer patients receiving chemotherapy—also face a higher risk.[13]

Another way to evaluate the significance of foodborne illness is to consider public perceptions. Survey data suggest that consumer concern about food safety may be growing. A 2012 survey of US consumers by an industry-funded organization called the International Food Information Council found that 18 percent of respondents reported that they were "not too" or "not at all confident in the safety of the US food supply," a number that rose to 30 percent in a subsequent 2014 survey. In this latter survey, the council also found that "two out of five Americans [38 percent] have changed the foods they eat as a result of food safety information" and that a "third [34 percent] of Americans consider getting sick from something they eat as their most important food safety issue." A 2010 survey by the federal Food and Drug Administration (FDA) found that 35 percent of respondents characterized contamination of food by microorganisms as a "serious food safety problem."[14]

Of course, there may be a gap between perceived and actual risk. Public concern may be driven more by media coverage of outbreaks than by careful risk analysis. Nevertheless, in the context of democratic politics and competitive markets, if voters and consumers believe something is a big problem, then for elected officials and companies it is. Moreover, even leading food safety experts, who frequently lack hard data to support their policy prescriptions, rely on their risk perceptions, which are influenced by dramatic outbreaks, value-laden choices about priorities, and general views about the proper role of government in risk regulation. Food safety, says Marion Nestle, a leading voice on food policy, "is a highly political issue."[15]

This book attempts to describe how the US food safety system works. The topic is large and unwieldy for a number of reasons. First, food safety encompasses a broad array of issues, including concerns about microbial pathogens, food additives, pesticide exposure, antibiotics in animal feed, chemical contamination, foreign objects, and genetically modified organisms. Second, the food industry is not one but many different industries, each with its own history, culture, modes of production, and methods of distribution. Making broad generalizations about "the food industry" on the basis of the production of fluid milk, ground beef, or leafy greens is likely to obscure more than it illuminates. Third, efforts to reduce the risk of foodborne illness involve a dizzying array of government officials at the federal, state, and local level; industry managers in farming, animal husbandry, transportation, food processing, product distribution, retail supermarkets, and food service operations; and assorted consumer advocates, lawyers, and insurance companies—all of whom bring a wide variety of perspectives from agriculture, veterinary science, microbiology, biochemistry, food technology, management, law, and underwriting, and who employ multiple tools, including law enforcement, supply chain management, and civil litigation.

The book focuses exclusively on efforts to reduce foodborne illness caused by microbial pathogens such as bacteria and viruses. Concentrating on this slice of the food safety system allows for exploration of the system's complexity without getting overwhelmed by it. The aim is not to discount the importance of other food safety issues but to avoid biting off more than one can digest. For the same reason, the book focuses on the US food safety system rather than adopting a global or comparative perspective. The book discusses global institutions where they directly influence the US food safety system, and readers will find much in this analysis of the US system that is useful in understanding food safety regulation in other countries.

Each chapter of the book presents a case study of an outbreak in a different sector of the food industry as a means of exploring a particular aspect of the food safety system. Each chapter drills down in one place into the system with the hope that, by the end of the book, they will together support a broad perspective on the system as a whole. A closer look at the story of the Jensen Farms cantaloupe listeriosis outbreak—from three different angles—will introduce readers to the various actors and their roles within the system. After fleshing out more details of the story, this first chapter introduces some general themes of the book and offers a brief overview of the chapters that follow.

Government Regulation

Indications of the listeriosis outbreak eventually traced to Jensen Farms cantaloupe first appeared in late August 2011. Alicia Cronquist, a Colorado health department epidemiologist in charge of foodborne illness investigations, received reports from doctors' offices and medical labs of seven cases of *Listeria* infection within one week. State law requires physicians and labs to report all cases of certain medical conditions, including listeriosis, to state public health authorities. Typically, the state health department receives reports of one or two listeriosis cases per month. "Clearly, we were on high alert," recalls Cronquist. She immediately commenced an investigation.[16]

Bacterial samples collected from patients' blood and cerebrospinal fluid were sent to a state laboratory specially equipped to identify the particular subtype, or strain, of *Listeria* using a process that reveals the bacteria's DNA profile. When two patients are infected with the same strain, this suggests a common source of infection. Lab results revealed that each of the seven listeriosis patients was infected with one of three strains. As it is possible for the same food item to harbor multiple strains, it remained unclear at that point whether the investigators were dealing with one outbreak from a single source or simultaneous outbreaks from different sources. The labs uploaded test results from all the samples to PulseNet, a national database administered by the CDC, which catalogs the DNA profiles of bacterial infections throughout the country. CDC epidemiologists matched the three *Listeria* strains from patient samples in Colorado with identical strains from cases reported concurrently in several other states, including Nebraska, Texas, and New Mexico.

While the laboratory analysis was under way, Cronquist dispatched local health department officials to interview patients and their families in order to gather information about possible causes of the infection. Using a detailed fifteen-page standardized questionnaire for investigating listeriosis outbreaks, officials asked patients to recall the foods that they had consumed in the weeks before falling ill and the sources of those foods. All the patients reported having consumed cantaloupe. Colorado investigators collected melons from one patient's refrigerator and three stores where patients reported having shopped. Lab tests revealed that the melons from the patient's refrigerator and two of the stores tested positive for all three *Listeria* strains found in patients' blood samples.

Although the cantaloupes that tested positive for *Listeria* bore no labels, several patients recalled that the cantaloupes they had consumed said "Rocky Ford" on them. Using patients' grocery store receipts and purchase records, investigators identified specific lots of contaminated melons on store shelves, linked them to distributors, and traced them back to Jensen Farms. A team of federal and state investigators visited Jensen Farms to collect microbiological samples from packinghouse equipment and cantaloupes in cold storage. Several of these samples yielded *Listeria* strains identical the three strains associated with the outbreak. Thus, by mid-September, two weeks after the outbreak was first detected, investigators had traced the outbreak to Jensen Farms processing equipment. The evidence was "very, very strong in this case," recalls the FDA's chief investigator on the case, James Gorny, "some of the strongest evidence I've ever seen." At that point, federal officials issued public statements identifying Jensen Farms cantaloupe as the source of the outbreak and warning consumers not to eat it. Jensen Farms and several retailers immediately initiated product recalls.[17]

On September 22 and 23, a team of FDA and Colorado health department investigators conducted a second, more thorough inspection of Jensen farms to identify possible root causes of the contamination. Their report noted that a truck used to haul damaged cantaloupe for animal feed to a nearby cattle operation was parked adjacent to the packing facility and suggested that contamination from manure on the wheels of the truck could have been tracked by personnel into the packing facility. The report also speculated that the processing equipment, previously used for handling raw potatoes, could have introduced *Listeria* into the facility. Samples of soil, water, and cantaloupes in the growing fields tested negative for *Listeria*, although the report did not exclude the possibility that *Listeria* in the fields from organic fertilizer, decaying vegetation, or animal droppings on cantaloupe might have been the initial source of the bacteria.[18]

The report cataloged a number of significant food safety problems in the packinghouse. Investigators found that the facility design allowed for standing water to accumulate on the floor directly under packing equipment and that the drain was not accessible for adequate cleaning. In addition, the investigators stated that the machines used to wash and dry the cantaloupe were not designed to be easily or routinely cleaned and sanitized—they observed dirt and product buildup on some areas of the equipment even after it had been disassembled, cleaned, and sanitized. The report also stated that, at the Jensens' request, the machines were equipped with a system to inject antimicrobial solution into the wash water but that they did not use it. Finally, according to the report, after harvest, the cantaloupes were not precooled to remove field heat before being placed in cold storage, allowing for the formation of condensation on the rind, which created cold and damp conditions conducive to the growth of *Listeria*. Samples collected from standing water on the floor, processing equipment, and cantaloupes in cold storage all tested positive for outbreak-related strains of *Listeria*. "It was a very tragic alignment of poor facility design, poor design of equipment and very unique postharvest handling practices of those melons," the FDA's Gorny concluded. "If any one of those things would have been prevented, this tragedy probably wouldn't have occurred."[19]

By all accounts, the Jensen brothers cooperated fully with local, state, and federal health official throughout the crisis. They welcomed inspectors, ceased production, recalled products, accepted all recommendations for improvement, and agreed to refrain from resuming production until receiving FDA approval. "We are deeply saddened that there's a possibility that our family's cantaloupe could have gotten somebody sick," Eric Jensen told a television news reporter as events unfolded. Colorado agriculture commissioner John Salazar stated at a press conference that the Jensens were working "wholeheartedly" to correct the problems noted by the FDA. Despite their willingness, however, the brothers never had the chance to improve their operations. In May 2012, overwhelmed by civil lawsuits, Jensen Farms filed for bankruptcy.[20]

Shortly following the conclusion of its investigation, the FDA sent the Jensens a warning letter demanding that they remedy the deficiencies discovered by investigators. Ultimately, however, agency officials decided that a mere warning was not a sufficient response to a food safety failure that produced a death toll of thirty-three—the deadliest foodborne illness outbreak since the 1920s and the second deadliest in US history.[21] Admittedly, the Jensens never intended to harm anyone, nor were they aware of the widespread *Listeria* contamination of their processing equipment and melons. Nevertheless, from the FDA's perspective, serious and elementary food safety failures—standing water on the packinghouse floor, absence of an antimicrobial agent in wash water, and no system for precooling melons prior to cold storage—unleashed a deadly pathogen with devastating consequences.[22]

In September 2013, two years after the outbreak, the FDA teamed up with the US Department of Justice to bring criminal charges against Eric and Ryan Jensen on six counts of selling contaminated food in violation of the Federal Food Drug and Cosmetic Act—a misdemeanor carrying a maximum sentence of one year in prison and a fine of up to $250,000 for each count. Under the act, conviction does not require intent or even knowledge of the contamination; it merely requires that the defendant sold a contaminated food product. Facing the possibility of six years in prison and $1.5 million in fines, the brothers pled guilty, and a federal judge sentenced them each to five years of probation, six months of home detention, and payment of $15,000 restitution to victims.[23]

Clearly the FDA sought to make an example of Eric and Ryan Jensen. Although *Listeria* was a pathogen previously associated with processed meat and dairy products, microbial contamination of cantaloupe was not a new problem. Since the mid-1980s, nearly two dozen foodborne illness outbreaks had been attributed to cantaloupe infected with *Salmonella*, *Campylobacter*, and *Norovirus*. The netted rind of cantaloupe, which can harbor pathogens, is difficult for consumers to effectively sanitize, making proper farm processing essential for consumer safety. "As this case tragically reminds us, food processors play a critical role in ensuring that our food is safe," explained John Walsh, the former US attorney for Colorado, when he filed criminal charges against the Jensens. "They bear a special responsibility to ensure that the food they produce and sell is not dangerous to the public. Where they fail to live up to that responsibility . . . this office and the Food and Drug Administration have a responsibility to act forcefully to enforce the law." Patrick Holland, who directed the Kansas City field office of the FDA's Office of Criminal Investigations at the time of the Jensen Farms case, asserted that "US consumers should demand the highest standards of food safety and integrity. The filing of criminal charges in this deadly outbreak sends the message that absolute care must be taken to ensure that deadly pathogens do not enter our food supply chain." After the Jensens pled guilty, Holland declared that criminal prosecution is an effective way to heighten awareness "among food growers, processors and distributors and demonstrate the critical role they play in the health and safety of every American."[24]

Civil Litigation and Consumer Advocacy

Attorney Bill Marler first learned of the outbreak before it was publicly announced. He received a call from a state public health official informing him that a significant foodborne illness outbreak was about to blow up. Marler, based in Seattle, is the nation's most widely known lawyer representing victims of foodborne illness. After successfully representing victims of the landmark 1993 *E. coli* outbreak caused by contaminated hamburgers sold by Jack in the Box restaurants—a devastating episode resulting in four deaths and 171 hospitalizations—Marler founded Marler Clark LLP, a law firm dedicated to representing victims of foodborne illness. In the twenty years since the Jack in the Box litigation, Marler has become a ubiquitous advocate for improving food safety—he writes a leading blog on food safety policy, underwrites the widely read *Food Safety News* website, regularly addresses food industry groups, testifies before Congress, and provides advice to government agencies. He also continues to file lawsuits on behalf of victims.[25]

In this case, as victims became aware that Jensen Farms cantaloupe was the source of their illnesses, they began calling the Marler Clark law firm, whose staff quickly assessed their claims by obtaining state health department records. On September 15, the day after Jensen Farms ordered a recall of its melons and the FDA issued a consumer advisory not to eat Jensen Farms cantaloupe, Marler filed the first lawsuit related to the outbreak. Marler has been at the forefront of litigation in every major foodborne illness outbreak since Jack in the Box. He is typically the first to file, handles the largest number of cases, and dominates media coverage. As Jensen Farms victims contacted his office, Marler filed a steady stream of lawsuits. Of the sixty-six claims eventually filed, Marler Clark litigated forty-six of them and provided assistance to several more.[26]

From a purely legal point of view, victims' claims against Jensen Farms were a slam dunk. A food manufacturer who sells contaminated food is liable for any resulting injury to consumers. This rule applies even if there is no evidence of negligence. Manufacturers who are unaware of the contamination are nevertheless subject to liability. This is known as *strict liability*. The term *manufacturer* in this context includes farmers who harvest and process fresh produce. (For further details on the legal doctrines governing liability for foodborne illness, see appendix B.) Jensen Farms was clearly liable for the injuries and deaths of victims who consumed the *Listeria*-tainted cantaloupes that it sold. Medical and public health records provided all the evidence necessary to prove the victims' claims.[27]

Practically, however, Jensen Farms lacked the money to pay more than a small fraction of the claims against it. Shortly after Marler began filing lawsuits, the attorney representing Jensen Farms contacted him and explained that the company had $2 million in liability insurance coverage. Marler estimated the total value of victim claims at more than $50 million.[28]

Seeking additional sources of compensation, Marler sued companies involved in the distribution and retail sale of Jensen Farms cantaloupes, including distributors Frontera Produce and FreshPack, and retail giants Walmart and Kroger, all of which settled for undisclosed amounts. In an unusual move, Marler also sued Primus Labs, the private food safety auditing firm that had awarded Jensen Farms a "superior" rating. In twenty years of litigating foodborne illness cases, Marler had never sued an auditor. He alleged that the company's auditors were negligent in awarding Jensen Farms a passing score in light of the serious food safety problems subsequently documented by the government investigation following the outbreak. Primus, like many private food safety auditing firms, offers a variety of different audits, some of which include greater levels of scrutiny, higher standards, longer duration, and return visits to verify correction of problems cited in the audit. The audits that Primus provided to Jensen Farms were inexpensive audits that did not include any of those features.[29]

When food safety failures occur, lawsuits enable victims to obtain compensation from the corporations that sold the food that sickened them. With Marler's firm on their side, victims and their families can hold big companies like Walmart accountable. A seasoned trial lawyer, Marler is intimidated by no one. "Between strict liability, big damages, and our financial wherewithal, we can crush these people. I can go against Walmart, Kroger, and Frontera. It's not your typical litigation where there is an asymmetrical power structure—it's pretty evenly matched." Marler does not, however, pick fights unnecessarily. After twenty years litigating foodborne illness cases, he has cordial relations with most of his counterparts in the food industry. "I've got a great relationship with most of the defendants," he explains. "They don't necessarily do what I want them to do—at least not without beating them up a bit—but for the most part, I have pretty good relationships with all these guys." Marler explains that his primary goal in each case is to secure adequate monetary compensation for victims left with large medical bills or long-term complications. "At the end of the day," he says, "that's what's driving the litigation."[30]

In addition to compensation, some victims and their families are also interested in advocating for stricter food safety regulations, and Marler connects them to public health officials, politicians, and the media to tell their stories. In this way, Marler has converted some of his litigation awards into lobbying muscle. He recalls that by the early 2000s, "I had been in the food safety world for over a decade and had taken much from the food industry on behalf of their customers. I had money, and I made use of it to secure access to the offices of politicians." He lobbied vigorously for passage of the Food Safety Modernization Act of 2011—the most ambitious reform of federal food safety laws in seventy years—by "shepherding clients to hearings to explain the devastation of being poisoned by food." In their efforts to advance food safety reforms, Marler and his clients work alongside a number of prominent consumer advocacy organizations—including the Center for Science in the Public Interest and the federation of Public Interest Research Groups—that conduct independent research, publish reports, and lobby legislatures and regulatory agencies.[31]

Marler does not believe that litigation is the best way to safeguard consumers from the deadly risk of foodborne illness. But until both industry and government can improve their regulatory performance, lawsuits are necessary to compensate victims and create pressure for reform. "Civil litigation in America is a blunt instrument for change," Marler told the House Energy and Commerce Committee in 2008, and "it is better for the government and business to work together to eliminate the need for lawsuits and lawyers." Marler looks forward to the day when filing lawsuits is no longer needed to achieve these ends. "I am a trial lawyer who has built a practice on food pathogens," he wrote in a 2002 *Denver Post* op-ed. "Since the Jack in the Box *E. coli* outbreak in 1993, I have represented hundreds of families who were devastated for doing what we do every day—eating food. This may prompt some readers to consider me a blood-sucking ambulance chaser who exploits other people's personal tragedies. If that is the case, here is my plea: *Put me out of business, please.*"[32]

Industry Supply Chain Management

No one feels more sorely misunderstood in the Jensen Farms fiasco than Primus Labs, the private food safety auditing firm that awarded the company a 96 percent audit score and a "superior" rating six days before the first outbreak victim fell ill from *Listeria*. As accounts of food safety failures at Jensen Farms emerged, Primus was singled out for especially sharp criticism. "It's just disgusting to me," Stephen Patricio, chair of the California Cantaloupe Advisory Board, told *USA Today*. "I think of the damage that they've done to our industry as a result of this oversight. No, I won't even talk about it as oversight; it's abuse." CNN asserted that, to "some food safety experts, the

third-party audit system the Jensens relied on is a joke." Mansour Samadpour, a well-known food safety consultant, was especially caustic. "They are
not food safety audits. They have nothing to do with food safety," he told
CNN. "If this industry is sincere and they want to have their products be of
any use to anyone, they should be printing their audit reports on toilet paper.
. . . People who are commissioning these audits don't seem to understand that
they are . . . not worth the paper that they're written on."[33]

Congressional investigators also focused blame on Primus and the private auditing system. In a letter to FDA commissioner Margaret Hamburg,
members of the House Committee on Energy and Commerce asserted that
their "investigation identified problems with the third-party inspection system used by growers and distributors to ensure the safety of fresh produce."
Committee members criticized Primus for failing to audit Jensen Farms'
compliance with FDA guidance and industry best practices. In addition, they
faulted the company for not requiring correction of the deficiencies that it
found or reporting them to the FDA or state officials. Committee members
further chastised Primus for providing advance notice of the audit to Jensen
Farms, conducting the packinghouse audit in four hours, and employing an
inexperienced subcontractor to perform the audit. More broadly, they denounced the "inherent conflict of interest" in a system in which auditors are
paid by the companies they audit. The committee members' most stinging
rebuke came when they questioned the 2010 auditor's suggestion that the Jensens consider replacing the dunk tank with an alternative washing system. "It
appears that the auditors who inspected Jensen Farms did more than simply overlook egregious food-safety practices: they specifically recommended
those practices."[34]

Primus has characterized these attacks as grossly unfair. Jensen Farms
contracted with Primus to conduct an announced audit of its operations to
assess compliance with FDA regulations and conformity with standard industry practices. The audit score of 96 percent indicated that Jensen Farms
was not in full compliance with FDA regulations and that its operations fell
below industry standards. The auditor's report identified specific problems:
no hot water at hand-washing stations, wooden processing equipment that
was difficult to sanitize and prone to splintering, open doors during operating hours, inadequate documentation regarding the maintenance of pest
control equipment and the calibration of thermometers, absence of records
regarding corrective action taken since the previous audit, and noncompliance with federal food security regulations regarding personnel background
checks and training. Notably, on the first page of the detailed twenty-one-
page report—in the first comment on the facility—the auditor wrote: "This

is a packing facility for cantaloupes which are washed by a spray bar roller system, graded, sorted by size, packed into cartons and stored in dry coolers. No anti-microbial solution is injected into the water of the wash station." The auditor mentioned the lack of antimicrobial or sanitizing solution in wash water four more times in different sections of the report. Thus, the Primus audit accurately identified specific regulatory compliance shortcomings and aspects of the packinghouse operations that fell below standard industry practices.[35]

According to Primus, critics have mischaracterized the scope of the audit that the company was paid to perform. The audit that Jensen Farms requested was explicitly designed to detect noncompliance with FDA regulations, not adherence to voluntary FDA guidance, and conformity with standard industry practices, not industry best practices. Moreover, Jensen Farms requested an announced half-day inspection. It did not request unannounced or multiple inspections or follow-up visits to verify remediation of problems. Nor did Jensen Farms request that Primus collect microbiological samples to test for bacterial contamination. Jensen Farms scheduled the audit on July 25, 2011, the first day of production that season, when Primus estimates that the packinghouse was operating at less than 10 percent capacity and the facility and equipment were in very different condition from what they were more than a month later—after processing three hundred thousand cases of melons—when state and federal investigators arrived. Had Jensen Farms requested a more rigorous audit against more stringent standards using more sophisticated methods, Primus would have conducted one. From Primus's perspective, blaming the audit firm for failing to provide a service beyond what the client paid for is like purchasing a Chevrolet and blaming the car dealer for not delivering a Cadillac.[36]

Primus and its defenders argue that critics misunderstand the proper role of audits in the food safety system. Auditors do not purport to certify that food is safe. Instead, they provide a snapshot of the food safety policies and practices in a facility at the time of the audit. Whether the facility consistently implements these policies and practices every day is beyond the scope of an audit, which is merely a diagnostic tool designed to assist a company in an ongoing process of evaluation and improvement. To be effective, regular audits must be part of a broad commitment on the part of both company managers and workers to making food safety a top priority, to fostering what experts call a "culture of food safety."[37]

Moreover, auditors do not set audit standards; they merely audit against standards determined by a supplier in accordance with buyer specifications. For example, a fresh produce supplier will typically request an audit of its operations against food safety standards dictated by its distributors, which are, in turn, based on retailers' product specifications. To simplify the process of reviewing audits, buyers generally require that audits be scored and that scores be presented on a one-page audit certificate. Buyers set thresholds that define a passing score. Primus worries, as do many audit firms, that scores divert attention from the detailed analysis of a facility's food safety policies and practices that its audits provide. Nevertheless, audit firms reduce their findings to scores because—in the highly competitive market for food safety audits—buyers demand them.

In addition, auditors typically translate scores into ratings, such as "superior," "excellent," "good," "satisfactory," and "unsatisfactory." Primus rates a score between 95 percent and 100 percent as "superior," even though any score below 100 percent reflects that a facility has significant deficiencies. Auditors and buyers believe that framing audit results exclusively in critical terms will lead to defensiveness and resignation among suppliers, whereas positive-sounding ratings are likely to encourage transparency, cooperation, and improvement over time.[38]

In lawsuits against Primus, retailers Walmart and Kroger, seeking to recoup their payments to outbreak victims and their litigation costs, claimed that they were misled by the 96 percent score and "superior" rating that the audit firm awarded to Jensen Farms. Primus and its defenders have denounced these claims as hypocritical. The audit certificate, to which the full report was attached, states in bold type: "Please refer to the audit report to read scope, scoring and commentary details." The "superior" rating appears on the first page of the report, six lines above the first mention of the absence of antimicrobial solution in the wash water. No one who read even the first page of the audit report could have been ignorant of food safety problems at Jensen Farms. Retailers' professed surprise concerning food safety problems at Jensen Farms suggests either that they did not read the audit report or that they read the report but chose to overlook the food safety problems that it documented.[39]

Moreover, both Walmart and Kroger accepted what they knew to be a relatively less rigorous audit of Jensen Farms. Upon request, Primus could have provided an audit that included additional buyer specifications beyond regulatory compliance and standard industry practices, detailed evaluation of risk management in the facility, and a requirement that the supplier take corrective action to address any problems as a condition of certification. Indeed, both Walmart and Kroger required audits that include all of these elements for suppliers of their store-brand products. If audit standards are too low, argues industry expert Jim Prevor, then retailers are responsible. When it comes to audit standards, "Wal-Mart gets exactly what it wants and what it is willing to pay for."[40]

Although food safety officials at Walmart and Kroger have been tight-lipped about the Jensen Farms cantaloupe outbreak, one might speculate on their behalf that they rely on third-party private audit ratings precisely because they lack the capacity to scrutinize the details of audit reports from thousands of fresh produce suppliers, some of whom may be submitting multiple audits for different products. Moreover, retailers cannot be expected to have in-house expertise in the complex details of so many different types of food production. Although their suppliers pay for the audits, retailers depend on reputable auditing firms to provide reliable advice about the food safety practices of their suppliers, not unlike how a person might place their trust in a doctor or a lawyer to advise about complex medical issues or legal matters. When the doctor or the lawyer commits malpractice, it is hardly the client's responsibility for any resulting bad outcomes.[41]

Primus and its defenders reject allegations about its competence and integrity. Academic research published several years before the first Jensen Farms audit cautioned that immersion of melons in a dunk tank heightens the risk that bacteria on the rind of a melon will penetrate into the melon or spread to other melons. Thus, the 2010 auditor's characterization of the dunk tank as a potential food safety "hot spot" rested on state-of-the-art science. Moreover, Prevor and others argued that, government assertions notwithstanding, FDA guidance did not require antimicrobial solution in non-recirculating wash water or precooling melons before placing them in cold storage.[42]

Prevor also accused the FDA of inaccurately portraying Jensen Farms as a rogue operation and Primus as a feckless inspector. "When the FDA goes into a facility, it has the gift of 20/20 hindsight and unlimited time and resources to solve a food safety issue such as this one," explained Prevor. "It is thus able to identify many ways in which this facility falls short of the ideal. It would be a terrible mistake for the industry, though, to think that this means that this was some horrid facility. It was not. It was a perfectly mainstream facility, better than many. The flaws the FDA found at Jensen Farms could be found in the vast majority of produce packing facilities with a team there day and night swabbing and looking for days and weeks on end." The Produce Marketing Association similarly commented: "It is often interesting and frustrating to read FDA investigative reports following a foodborne illness event where conditions in the field or packing facility are described. Observations are included and cited as potential contributing factors to potential contamination even though those same observations could be made at hundreds or perhaps thousands of production operations around the world. For example,

water on floors of packinghouses, cracks in concrete floors, animals in prox-
imity to fields and other observations of a similar nature are reported, yet
these conditions are common to many fruit or vegetable production operations." As for assertions that Primus should have reported deficiencies to government authorities—even if its auditor had discovered regulatory violations
(which he did not), under accreditation standards for auditors, an auditor
owes a strict duty of confidentiality to the entity being audited not to report
any findings to third parties without written authorization.[43]

Uncertainty and Complexity

Taking into account these different perspectives, it is hard to figure out who
was ultimately responsible for the Jensen Farms cantaloupe outbreak. The
original source of contamination remains a mystery. Subsequent failure to
disinfect the melons during the sorting and packing process resulted from
multiple interconnected factors—the Jensen brothers' food safety practices,
the Primus auditors' evaluation, Walmart's specifications, and the FDA's guidance. No one seems entirely to blame, yet everyone seems partially at fault.

The Jensen Farms episode illustrates that it can be hard to assign responsibility for foodborne illness outbreaks because of uncertainty regarding the
root cause of contamination and the complexity of interconnections among
the many individuals and institutions concerned with food safety. In later
chapters, additional case studies show how uncertainty and complexity also
make it difficult to evaluate the effectiveness of current food safety efforts or
to identify cost-effective reforms that are likely to reduce the risk of foodborne illness. Although the past two decades have been a time of rapid and
dramatic advances in outbreak investigation, uncertainty remains a persistent and pervasive challenge to identifying the sources and reducing the risk
of foodborne illness. Meanwhile, the complexity of the food safety system
has grown steadily. An expanding number and variety of professionals offer
increasingly sophisticated analyses and hold specialized positions in growing
bureaucracies within business operations, trade organizations, and government agencies.

In addition to uncertainty and complexity, competing assumptions about
the duties of farmers, auditors, retail stores, and government regulators to
prevent foodborne illness generate different views about responsibility for
outbreaks and the desirability of particular reforms. Rival interpretations of
the interests and motives of these various participants in the food safety system also shape opinions about whether, for example, industry-led initiatives
are designed to promote public health or protect profits. As the case stud-

ies make clear, one can typically find sufficient facts to support divergent perspectives.

In the face of all this ambiguity, this book aims to clarify the nature and sources of uncertainty about microbial contamination of food. Along the way, the book maps the complexity of the food safety system—its multiple institutions, its diverse approaches to regulating industry, and its various dynamics. The analysis also exposes the competing assumptions that support different views about how the system works and how to improve it.

The Food Safety System

The case studies in each chapter offer examples of food safety efforts in particular segments of the food industry. To obtain a sense of what the food safety system as a whole looks like, it will be helpful to employ a number of abstract concepts. The Jensen Farms cantaloupe outbreak reveals that food safety regulation encompasses more than merely legal requirements on industry enforced by government agencies. For practical purposes, the rules of food safety include nonbinding FDA guidance and industry standards. These rules are enforced by public authorities, such as government agencies, as well as by private entities, such as plaintiffs' attorneys pursuing civil claims and buyers who require their suppliers to pass third-party audits. Scholars have coined the term *governance* to describe this diversity of regulatory activity. Criminal prosecution, civil litigation, and industry supply chain management are all forms of governance.[44]

The Jensen Farms cantaloupe outbreak also illustrates the importance of feedback in the development of food safety. The Jensen brothers experimented with what they considered a new and improved system of washing melons using non-recirculating wash water. The outbreak investigators' report, the civil lawsuits, and the criminal prosecution that followed provided feedback to the produce industry about the advisability of adding antimicrobial solution to all wash water, even non-recirculating wash water. One definition of a *system* is an interconnected set of elements that relies on feedback to achieve something. Under this definition, the actors and institutions engaged in food safety efforts constitute a system.[45]

In addition, the Jensen Farms cantaloupe outbreak suggests that the food safety system can be organized into three interacting components: (1) government regulation, (2) civil litigation and consumer advocacy, and (3) industry supply chain management. Each of these components is itself composed of interacting components. For example, government regulation is made up of federal, state, and local efforts. Each of these subcomponents can be further divided. Thus, federal efforts include the work of the FDA, the CDC, and the Department of Justice, each of which, in turn, consists of multiple interacting divisions, such as the FDA's Office of Food Safety, Office of Compliance, and Office of Regulations, Policy, and Social Science. Staff members in each of these offices, depending on their training and duties, participate in a variety of professional networks that create links throughout the system. For instance, FDA officials are members of the International Association for Food Protection, which fosters collaboration among food safety professionals in government, consumer advocacy, and industry. This same type of structural analysis can be applied to the other two major components of the system. The structure of the food safety system is *complex* insofar as it consists of diverse individuals and institutions interconnected in a network of networks.[46]

Finally, as subsequent case studies illustrate, food safety governance has evolved over time on the basis of feedback following outbreaks like the one caused by contaminated Jensen Farms cantaloupes. Food safety experts use the lessons learned from these tragic events to design and implement new approaches to reducing the risk of foodborne illness. Leaving aside the question of whether these new approaches reduce the risk of foodborne illness, this process of feedback and learning nevertheless makes the food safety system *adaptive* to new information and conditions.

When one steps back from case studies, which afford a detailed but incomplete view, to get a sense of the whole, one sees that food safety efforts can be conceptualized as a *complex adaptive system of governance*.[47] In the chapters that follow, case studies set the groundwork for the further elaboration of these abstract concepts that, with some patience on the part of the reader, will prove helpful in categorizing and organizing what would otherwise be an overwhelming volume and variety of details—an interesting but ultimately incoherent exercise in drilling down in particular places without looking up to take in the entire landscape.

Improving Feedback and Learning

This book advocates two reforms to improve the food safety system. First, it recommends focusing government investment in food safety primarily on improving the infrastructure of outbreak investigations rather than on hiring and training more agency inspectors. Dedicating more public resources to outbreak investigations would reduce uncertainty about the root causes of foodborne illness. Second, the book argues for improving the reliability of food safety auditing by greater reliance on buyer-funded audits carried out by government inspectors on a fee-for-service basis and, when buyers insist on private auditors, subjecting private auditors to civil liability for negligence. These auditing arrangements would foster more reliable oversight to ensure rigorous implementation of food safety efforts.

In addition to these reforms, the book applauds two promising trends. Technological advances in digitizing supply chain management information are likely to improve the capacity of investigations to identify the root causes of an outbreak and the ability of responsible companies to effectively recall contaminated products to stem the spread of infection. In addition, the maturation of product contamination and food safety liability insurance promises to disseminate advice and incentives that will help food companies more effectively and efficiently manage the risk of microbial contamination.

The book endorses these reforms and trends because they will generate information likely to enhance feedback and learning. Uncertainty and complexity make it hard to identify weaknesses in the food safety system and to prescribe workable solutions. As the case studies that follow show, government and industry have undertaken many ambitious food safety efforts on the basis of limited data and speculation about their effectiveness. Food safety governance is experimental, and better feedback and learning can generate more robust data and replace speculation with more reliable statistical inferences. The result will be a more evidence-based approach to food safety regulation.

Before proceeding further, it may be helpful to offer a clarification concerning the underlying aims of this book. Highlighting the role in food safety governance of private actors—supply chain managers, private auditors, trade association experts, plaintiffs' attorneys, and insurance underwriters—is not intended to undervalue the contribution of government officials. This book is not a pitch for reducing government regulation; it does not advocate a less prominent role for government in food safety regulation. Instead, the book argues that government regulation is only one part of a much larger system working to advance food safety, a system in which private actors play an essential part. The origins of this system lie in late nineteenth and early twentieth century efforts to clean up the nation's milk supply—a story that is the subject of the next chapter.

The Gospel of Clean Milk:
Dairy Sanitation, Pasteurization,
and the Origins of the American Food Safety System

At age thirty-three, inspired by divine visitations during prayer, Robert Milham Hartley joined the Temperance Society. He threw himself fervently into the battle against alcohol consumption—conducting investigations, giving speeches, distributing pamphlets, and publishing newspaper articles. Rising quickly in the ranks, he was elected the organization's secretary in 1833. During the course of his investigations, Hartley discovered a widespread practice among breweries and distilleries of selling mashed and fermented grains left over from beer and whiskey production as feed for dairy cows. The cows that consumed this repurposed industrial waste produced a thin, bluish milk with little nutritional value, to which dairymen typically added chalk and plaster of Paris to make it appear creamy, and molasses to give it a yellow color. The ensuing campaign that Hartley launched against "distillery slop dairies" and the "swill milk" that they produced represents the pioneer effort in American dairy sanitation—the first stage of a decades-long effort to clean up the milk supply, which established the institutional structure, regulatory techniques, and political dynamics that characterize the US food safety system.[1]

The Campaign against Swill Milk

Distillery slop dairies first emerged in the 1820s. Brewery and distillery owners discovered that the by-products of their operations could be used as cattle feed, and dairy operators discovered that cows fed on distillery slops produced more milk, although with a much lower fat content and an unappealing color. Urban growth throughout the nineteenth century in cities such as New York, Boston, and Philadelphia decreased available pasturage for dairy herds while simultaneously increasing the demand for fresh milk. With no

system for quickly transporting large quantities of cooled milk from suburban and rural farms to meet this demand, urban distillery dairies proliferated
and grew in size—some containing as many as two thousand head of cattle.
Hartley estimated that the distillery slop dairies of New York City housed and
fed eighteen thousand cows and produced more than five million gallons of
swill milk each year. By the 1850s, these operations dominated urban milk
markets.[2]

Production involved considerable cruelty to the animals. Grains left over
from alcohol production are not an unhealthy supplementary feed for cattle
(they are still used today), but distillery slop dairies frequently used them as
the predominant or sole feed. This diet caused the cows' teeth to rot, rendering them unable to chew any hay or raw grains that the owners might provide
in addition to the slop. Large tanks of swill were delivered by cart throughout the day to the dairies. To reduce transportation costs, some dairies were
located adjacent to breweries and distilleries, and the slop was conveyed
through a system of wooden sluices to the feeding troughs. One newspaper
account depicted how the "swill comes rushing and foaming down into the
troughs from an upper duct . . . boiling hot . . . and the cows, at risk of scald-
ing their mouths, thrust their heads into it. At first the cows revolt against the
swill, but after a week or two they begin to have a taste for it, and in a short
time we find them consuming from one to two, even three barrels of swill a
day." Hundreds of cows were densely packed into low, unventilated sheds,
confined permanently to three-foot-wide stalls, which were rarely, if ever,
cleaned, leaving the animals to stand up to their bellies in piles of their own
excrement. The filth bred severe fungal infections and painful deformities in
the animals' hooves. In such conditions, the animals were prone to infectious
disease. Crude efforts to inoculate the animals against bovine tuberculosis by
inserting matter from a diseased cow's lungs into a slit made in a living cow's
tail resulted in sores that spread all over the animal's body and, frequently,
the loss of its tail. So common was this condition that distillery dairy cows
were popularly called "stump tails." Most animals did not survive for more
than a year. According to one report, among 1,841 cows housed in a Brooklyn
distillery dairy, 230 died in a ten-week period. When cows died, their diseased
carcasses were sent to a local butcher and the meat sold to the public.[3]

Hartley disapproved of distillery slop dairies not only because they supported the beer and liquor industries and brutalized animals but also because swill milk threatened public health. The unsanitary conditions of the
stables presented multiple opportunities for contamination. The workers
who milked the miserable cows took few, if any, sanitary precautions. Hartley described how dairy workers at one facility strained out visible dirt from

the milk with dirty dish towels, which they hung up to dry on the stable door, and used straw from the stable floor to clean out milk pails. In a long treatise on the evils of swill milk, he recounted how a dairyman milked a cow with an infected and badly swollen teat that had been recently lanced and was oozing puss. "But the dairyman, unwilling to lose the milk, was carefully stripping three of the teats, while at every pressure of the fingers, bloody and yellow corrupt matter was forced from the wound, ran trickling down over the back of his hands, and mingled with the mess of milk in the pail." To increase sales, dairies diluted their milk with water, which provided an additional source of contamination.[4]

Hartley attributed significant increases in infant mortality between 1815 and 1840 to the rise of swill milk. When his wife was unable to nurse their eldest son, she was forced to feed him cow's milk. Hartley recounted how the child's health declined steadily as a result: "The eyes were sunken, and his appearance unnaturally pale and haggard; he lost strength and vivacity; gradually fell away in flesh; so that at the age of fifteen months, his weak and emaciated body would scarcely sustain itself without bolstering." Upon investigating, Hartley discovered that the milk was produced at a local distillery dairy. Hartley obtained higher-quality milk, and the child's condition improved, although he remained "frail and sickly" and his growth was permanently "stinted." Hartley denounced the production of "whiskey milk" as a "grievous offense against God and high treason against humanity . . . by which the health and lives of multitudes are annually destroyed."[5]

After a direct appeal to dairy owners to end the use of distillery slops in milk production was rebuffed, Hartley published a series of scathing exposés about the swill milk industry in 1836 and 1837, for which he was physically attacked by thugs hired by the dairy owners. Undeterred, he published a book in 1842 further detailing the industry's corruption of the milk supply. Hartley's calls for reform resulted in resolutions presented to the New York City Board of Aldermen in 1841 and 1842 calling for a special commission to investigate the swill milk industry, but the board took no action. Although he was unsuccessful in prompting government regulation, Hartley's efforts did inspire market competition—rural famers formed groups and began shipping "country" milk into New York City by rail.[6]

Hartley's campaign against swill milk was taken up by Dr. Augustus Gardner, a prominent physician, who, in 1847, published a critique of the city's distillery dairies in the *New York Tribune* and chaired a committee of the New York Academy of Medicine charged with investigating them. When the committee presented its report in 1848, the academy tabled its recommendations for reform and did not release its findings until 1851. In 1853, journalist John

Mullaly published a widely circulated book detailing the unsanitary conditions in New York's distillery dairies and the adulteration of the milk that they sold, especially the dilution of milk with water by unscrupulous dealers. So common was this practice that industry insiders referred to the typical hand pump used to add the water as "the cow with the iron tail." Mullaly advocated increasing rural milk production to supply the city and requiring milk dealers to be licensed, with stiff penalties for those found selling injurious milk. However, Mullaly's efforts to whip up public outrage failed to produce government intervention. In the years following publication of Mullaly's book, several of the city's newspapers published similar attacks on the distillery dairies and called for reform. A *New York Times* article estimated that two-thirds of the city's milk came from distillery dairies and asserted that swill milk caused "the deaths of no fewer than 9,847 children under the age of two."[7]

When city government finally took action, its response did more to reveal the political muscle of the dairymen than to advance the agitators' public health agenda. In 1856, the Brooklyn Common Council passed an ordinance prohibiting anyone from keeping more than four cows on a half-acre lot, more than six cows on an acre lot, or more than twelve cows on any lot, with a $10 fine per cow over the legal limit—effectively outlawing distillery slop dairies. H. L. Husted, a local distiller with a large dairy operation, convinced the Common Council to meet in special session and amend the ordinance to exempt distillery owners and milkmen already in business, preserving their operations and protecting them from new competitors. When Husted's stables burned down later that year, he purchased existing stables from a neighbor, recommenced production, and approached the Common Council once again to make another exception for his operations.[8]

Husted's machinations ignited the righteous indignation of publisher Frank Leslie, whose popular illustrated weekly newspaper launched a barrage of critical articles attacking Husted and his fellow distillery dairymen, including gruesome accounts and shocking images of conditions in the stables. The public outrage generated by Leslie's media campaign, which was joined by the *Times* and the *Tribune*, pressured the Common Council of Manhattan in 1858 to appoint a committee to investigate the conditions at distillery dairies. According to press accounts, councilman Michael Tuomey's committee visited only one distillery dairy, giving the owner advance notice and time to clean up his stables, took a cursory look around, shared a drink of whiskey with him, and returned to City Hall.[9]

Media criticism and public outrage at the inadequacy of the Tuomey committee's investigation prompted the New York City Board of Health to launch a second, more thorough, inquiry. However, the Board of Health at that time consisted of the mayor and the Common Council, and they appointed a Select Committee consisting of four councilmen—including Tuomey and E. Harrison Reed, who had served alongside him on the previous committee—to examine the milk industry. The Select Committee held hearings, during which committee members aggressively questioned physicians testifying about the harmful effects of swill milk while being more cordial to industry supporters, including a distiller "who testified that he had once saved the life of a child by feeding him swill milk." A three-member majority of the committee found the stables acceptably "clean," the cattle "in good condition," and both the swill and the milk uncontaminated by any "deleterious or poisonous element." The committee noted that it had not uncovered a single case of death or illness caused by drinking swill milk. Its report merely recommended better ventilation in stables and greater stall space for the cows. The one dissenting member of the committee produced a minority report condemning the distillery dairies and calling for their abolition. Charges of whitewashing and political corruption from the press failed to move the Common Council.

The mayor, however, turned to the Academy of Medicine to further investigate the swill milk issue, and the academy appointed a five-man committee, led by Dr. Samuel Rotton Percy. Unlike previous investigators, Percy and his fellow committee members went undercover to see the real conditions of the distillery stables, and two members of the team actually ate distillery slops. "They were rewarded with diuretic and laxative outpourings far beyond their most sanguine fears or expectations," according to one account. The committee also documented cases of illness among children attributable to milk. The resulting report—known as the Percy Report—recommended banning the sale of swill milk and licensing of milk distributors. The academy endorsed the report and its recommendations and sent them to the mayor and the Common Council, which, despite further agitation from Leslie and other media outlets, did not publish the report for a year and took no further action.[10]

At the same time, however, the report, as well as lobbying by the Academy of Medicine, the Association for Improving the Condition of the Poor, and the New York Sanitary Association, prompted enactment in 1862 of a New York State law banning the sale of "impure, adulterated or unwholesome milk" and making it a crime to keep cows in "crowded or unhealthy conditions" or feed them food that produces "impure, diseased or unwholesome milk." Enforcement of the law initially proved difficult when distillery dairy owners mounted successful legal challenges to the law, in which courts found that the phrase "impure, adulterated or unwholesome milk" did not include milk diluted with water. Moreover, the statute's restrictions on keeping and feeding cows covered only the production, not the sale, of swill milk. Consequently, the state legislature amended the statute to specify that "the addition of water or any substance other than a sufficient quantity of ice to preserve the milk while in transportation is hereby declared an adulteration. Any milk that is obtained from animals fed on distillery waste, usually called swill, or upon any substance in a state of putrefaction or fermentation is hereby declared to be impure and unwholesome."[11]

New York State's law marked the beginning of the end of the swill milk trade. By 1866, there were no more distillery dairies in Manhattan. Other states followed New York's lead in passing legislation outlawing the sale of milk from cows fed distillery slops, although distillery dairies survived in many cities until the end of the first decade of the twentieth century. In Brooklyn, where local officials refused to enforce the law, swill milk production continued until 1904.[12]

The campaign against swill milk presents a familiar story of regulatory politics. Activists like Hartley, Gardner, Mullaly, and Leslie used the media to arouse public outrage and mobilize a reform movement to regulate a powerful industry. The leaders of that industry used their wealth to influence key politicians. This special interest group "captured" the regulatory process—they distorted investigations, blocked legislation, and hindered enforcement. Eventually, mounting public pressure compelled legislators to impose mandatory restrictions on the industry.

With a growing understanding in the late nineteenth century that infectious disease was transmitted by bacteria came a realization that the most significant dangers from milk came not from unwholesome cattle feed, or even from adulterants like plaster of Paris, but from the many sources of bacterial contamination in the journey from teat to table. The prevailing mid-nineteenth-century theory that disease was transmitted by miasma—noxious, foul-smelling vapor that emanated from decomposing organic matter (*miasma* means "pollution" in Ancient Greek)—had encouraged the anti–swill milk crusaders to focus on the unsanitary conditions of distillery dairies. Cleaning up stables was a good start, even if the underlying science was erroneous. The bacteriological revolution brought greater sophistication to efforts to make the milk supply safer, and it stimulated a dramatic expansion in regulatory activity.[13]

The Certified Milk Movement

Dr. Henry Leber Coit married Emma Gwinnell in 1886. They settled down to start a family in Newark, New Jersey, where the young physician developed a general practice. When Emma was unable to breastfeed their infant son, Henry "poured over the scanty scientific literature on infant dietetics" and scrupulously searched the city and surrounding region to obtain clean cow's milk. The baby thrived, and his parents took pride in his "perfect bodily development." At age two, however, little John Summerfield Coit contracted diphtheria from contaminated milk and died.[14]

Looking back years later, Coit recalled searching for milk to feed the child. "I was driven from one source of impoverished and contaminated milk to another until, in desperation, I sought a small suburban dairyman who kept, cared for, and delivered the milk of four cows. An honest and industrious man, but without knowledge of hygiene, he became unwittingly a dangerous element in my family life." Upon visiting the farm after his son fell ill, Coit found that the dairyman alternated between caring for three family members stricken by diphtheria and milking his cows. The tragic loss of his infant son motivated Coit to specialize in pediatrics and preventive medicine and to play a vital role in a decades-long effort to clean up America's milk supply.[15]

Physicians, public health officials, and social reformers from the middle of the 1800s to the early decades of the 1900s invested a great deal of time and energy attempting to resolve "the milk problem." Harvard Medical School professor Milton J. Rosenau, a widely respected public health expert, opened a series of endowed lectures on the subject in 1912 by declaring that "clean milk is a vital problem touching humanity in every phase of its social fabric. It is a live and burning topic of the day." A contemporary bibliography of publications on the milk problem included 8,375 entries.[16]

Milk posed an especially high food safety risk. Conventional wisdom considered it an essential food for infants and a staple for adults. At the same time, milk was prone to bacterial contamination from unsanitary practices during production, distribution, and consumption. Milk is also a very hospitable medium for germ growth, and the inability to keep country milk cool during its long journey from rural farms to urban markets fostered the multiplication of bacteria in contaminated milk, a problem that was exacerbated during hot summer months. Whereas cooking kills bacteria in other foods susceptible to contamination, milk was consumed raw.[17]

High rates of infant mortality generated increasing public concern, and many blamed contaminated milk as the cause of unidentified intestinal illnesses and the carrier of well-known infectious diseases such as tuberculosis, diphtheria, scarlet fever, and typhoid. The increasingly common practice of "hand feeding" using cow's milk instead of exclusive breastfeeding—a result of economic pressures on poor women to return to work quickly after giving birth, social expectations on middle-class women that competed with the demands of nursing, and erroneous medical advice—increased the exposure of infants to these milk-borne risks. Throughout the late 1800s and early 1900s, children less than one year old accounted for a quarter of all deaths in New York City, and children between the ages of one and five years old, another fifteen percent. These data were typical of the situation throughout the country. Rosenau lamented in his 1912 lectures that "during the last ten years over two million babies less than a year old have died in the United States," and he asserted that, although "the fundamental causes of infant mortality are poverty, ignorance, and neglect," "there is no doubt that many an infant is sent to an early grave through drinking dirty or infected milk." Children were not the only victims of contaminated milk. Adults, too, suffered from milk-borne illness, which could, especially for the elderly, be fatal. A 1912 study by federal public health authorities counted five hundred reported epidemics of typhoid fever, diphtheria, and scarlet fever within the previous fifty years in which infection was transmitted by contaminated milk. Summing up the problem, Rosenau declared, "We are dealing with an essential article of food: one that is probably accountable for more sickness and more deaths than all other foods put together."[18]

For several years following the death of his son, Henry Leber Coit traveled the countryside surrounding Newark, visiting dairy farms, discussing with farmers the challenges they faced, and compiling copious notes with ideas on how to improve the sanitation of their operations. During this time, Coit attended an annual meeting of the New Jersey State Medical Society and proposed the creation of a committee of two physicians from each county to investigate the relationship between infant mortality and contaminated milk. After two years of work, the committee issued a report with recommendations, which served as the basis for lobbying the state government to improve dairy sanitation through stricter standards and regular inspections. The committee could not muster sufficient support for its efforts, and it disbanded. State officials considered the committee's proposed reforms too expensive. "Such a radical reform as you desire in the production and handling of milk may not be accomplished in our generation," wrote the state dairy commissioner in a letter to Coit.[19]

Determined, Coit shifted his energies from advocating statewide government regulation to establishing a local voluntary effort. At a meeting of the Practitioners' Club of Newark, Coit presented a plan for the sanitary produc-

tion and certification of milk according to strict guidelines under the supervision of a group of physicians for clinical use to feed infants, convalescents,
and pregnant mothers. The plan attracted a number of Coit's colleagues, and
in 1893, they formed the Essex County Medical Milk Commission to further develop and implement it at once. The plan required regular veterinary
examination and tuberculosis testing for cows, medical checkups for dairy
employees, sanitary inspections of farming operations, and chemical and
bacteriological analysis of milk at the points of production and distribution.
It specified sanitary production practices, such as frequent hand washing,
cleaning cows' udders before milking, sterilization of equipment by steam
or dry heat, immediate cooling of milk to forty-five degrees Fahrenheit, and
bottling and sealing at the point of production—as opposed to the standard
practice of selling milk in forty-gallon containers to distributors (milkmen),
who ladled it out to customers at the point of retail sale. The plan also included standards regarding the character of the land used for pasturage and
cultivating fodder; the construction, location, ventilation, and drainage of
buildings; clean water sources and proper drainage; separation of milking
operations from other animals; proper grooming, feeding, and stabling of
animals; and waste removal. In addition, the plan set quality standards, requiring that milk remain in its natural state—unheated, no additives such as
coloring or preservatives, and without extracting cream or any of its other
elements—and that it contain an average of 4 percent butter fat and a bacterial count of not more than ten thousand bacteria per cubic centimeter at the
time of delivery to the consumer.[20]

Members of the commission agreed to volunteer their time to inspect
dairy operations and check personnel and to arrange for veterinary examinations and laboratory testing of milk, the cost of which would be borne by the
farmer in exchange for certification by the commission and the purchase of
certified milk at a premium by local physicians for their patients. Stephen
Francisco, a well-to-do owner of one of New Jersey's largest dairy farms, entered into a contract with the commission to produce milk under the terms
of the plan. Several members of the commission agreed to underwrite Francisco's dairy for three years to cover any additional expenses that could not
be recouped from sales. However, revenues more than covered the costs of
enhanced sanitation. Francisco, described as a "staunch Methodist; honest,
hard-headed, straight thinking," quickly became a champion of certified
milk. Looking back years later, he asserted that "there is nothing that has
happened in the last decade to help the needs of the human race, to sustain
life, to instill strength, and to assist the conservation of child life more than
the production of Certified Milk." Francisco's certified milk marked a revolu-

tion not only in the content of milk but also in the packaging: it was the first milk sold in bottles.[21]

"It was a gala-day in Dr. Coit's home," wrote Emma Gwinnell Coit, when the first bottle of certified milk, tied with a blue ribbon, was delivered to their two-year-old daughter. In the early years, monthly meetings were held at the office of a Dr. Pierson, recalled a member of the commission: "Dr. Coit would come with a great pile of papers and every subject had to be considered before we were allowed to drink any of the Certified Milk that Francisco frequently brought to the meetings. I must acknowledge, however, that the rest of us except Coit and Francisco, preferred Dr. Pierson's sherry."[22]

Francisco's dairy sold its certified milk for twelve cents per quart, twice the price of normal milk. His customers included not only doctors but also consumers willing to pay a substantial premium for a safer product. To maintain the integrity of the certified milk label, the commission attempted to copyright it, but the federal government would not grant a copyright to a professional body. So instead, Francisco copyrighted the label with the commission's blessing, under an agreement that he would protect the term *certified milk* on behalf of the commission and that he would not object to its use by other milk commissions that adhered to the same standards.[23]

In 1896, the New York County Medical Society appointed a commission to certify milk in New York City, and a third commission was established in Philadelphia the following year. By 1906, there were thirty-six medical milk commissions, and in 1907, Dr. Otto Geier, of Cincinnati, convened a meeting of medical milk commissions, which led to the establishment of the American Association of Medical Milk Commissions. The members of the association elected Coit their first president and Geier secretary. At annual meetings, association members discussed a wide variety of technical questions and policy matters related to improving dairy sanitation. By 1912, the association included sixty-three medical milk commissions in the United States, two in Canada, and several in Europe and Asia.[24]

The certified milk movement developed a rigorous and professional system of private third-party food safety inspection. Individual medical milk commissions and committees of the American Association of Medical Milk Commissions elaborated increasingly detailed standards. In 1912, the association promulgated ninety-seven detailed standards covering dairy hygiene—including pasture drainage, stable construction, pest control, cattle grooming, bedding, manure removal, feed, hand washing, clothing, strainers, temperature control, bottle sterilization, water supply, and toilet facilities—as well as guidelines for transportation, veterinary testing of herds, bacteriological and chemical testing of milk samples, and medical examination of employees.[25]

Association members also discussed and endorsed best practices for commissions. Typically, commission members were physicians. Most commissions consisted of five to twelve members, although size ranged from three to one hundred. Members received no remuneration and held no financial interest in any dairy business, which allowed the commissions to maintain independence from the dairies they certified and to avoid even the appearance of a conflict of interest. Commissions met monthly or every other month to review the results of inspections and tests and to grant certification. They subjected certified dairies to weekly bacteriological testing, monthly facility inspections and chemical testing, and annual tuberculin testing of herds. The professionals who performed these tasks—physicians, veterinarians, bacteriologists, and chemists—worked for the commissions, which paid their salaries. Some commissions received funds from the local medical society; others obtained funds from certified dairies by charging fees for inspection and testing services, collecting bottle taxes, or selling certification labels.[26]

The certified milk movement's rigorous inspection regime and stringent testing standards produced high-quality milk for clinical use and for consumers willing to pay a steep premium—roughly double the price of uncertified milk—but certified milk never developed a sufficiently robust market to rise above 2 percent of sales in any major city. Medical milk commissions were ultimately unable to scale up their model of sanitary milk production to meet the demands of a national mass market. That distinction belongs to a rival approach, which quickly outgrew and long outlasted certified milk.[27]

Pasteurization

Nathan Straus used to say that he had "milk on the brain." Fueled by righteous indignation over high infant mortality and government inaction, he spent nearly forty years and a considerable portion of his large fortune fighting "the white peril" of milk-borne disease. "The tragedy of needless infant slaughter, desolating so many homes and wringing so many hearts, lies like a dark shadow on our boasted civilization. It is nothing more than permitted murder, for which the responsibility must lie at the door of the agencies of government that fail to recognize its existence and demand its prevention," he wrote in an 1897 letter to the presidents of health boards in American and Canadian cities. Like Robert Hartley and Henry Coit, his passion for pure milk was also rooted in personal loss—the tragic death of a two-year-old daughter, which Straus attributed to a lack of good milk.[28]

Undeterred by the inadequate government response to the milk problem,

Straus—a successful businessman who was co-owner with his brother Isidor of Macy's department store—established an "infant milk depot" in New York City that pasteurized and sold bottles of milk in the summer of 1893, the same year that Coit founded the first medical milk commission. Straus sold his pasteurized milk at subsidized prices to make it affordable, and he printed coupon books that were distributed by hospitals and charitable agencies to make his milk accessible to those without the means to pay for it. He located the depot at the East Third Street Pier in Manhattan, where he erected a large canvas-topped pavilion with benches and tables to make a "free fresh-air resort" where mothers could purchase milk and their children could play. The depot also provided twice-a-week lectures by physicians on childcare and free medical examinations for all children. For sick or malnourished children, the attending physician could prescribe a special formula of modified milk also sold by the depot.[29]

Straus operated his first depot from June through November, when summer heat caused an increase in milk-borne disease and infant mortality rose. That first season, he distributed 34,400 bottles of milk. The following summer he opened six depots and distributed 306,446 bottles. In 1898 Straus purchased a pasteurization plant to increase his production. By 1906, he was distributing 3,140,252 bottles annually through seventeen depots throughout the city. In these and the following years, he also helped launch milk depots throughout the United States and abroad. In 1907, there were 159 infant milk depots distributing milk in twenty-two American cities.[30]

Straus frequently presented data to demonstrate the effectiveness of his pasteurized milk in reducing infant mortality. "As the infantile death rate of New York City went steadily down from 96.2 per 1,000 in 1892 to 55 per 1,000 in 1906, coincident with the increase in the use of pasteurized milk, the significance of my work became apparent," he declared at an international congress in Brussels in 1907. A few years later, he cited a further reduction of 45.8 deaths per 1,000 in 1910, concluding, "I can state with certainty that excessive infantile mortality has been immediately checked whenever I have supplied pasteurized modified milk, and the rate has been cut down at least to half of the average for the preceding five years." Straus pointed proudly to his success at an asylum for abandoned children on Randall's Island, New York, where mortality rates among the children dropped dramatically from more than 40 percent to less than 20 percent following his establishment of a pasteurization plant on the premises.[31]

Not everyone shared Straus's enthusiasm for pasteurization. Commercial dairies and milk dealers in America, starting in the 1890s, originally heated milk to postpone spoiling, sometimes reheating it a second or third time to make it last even longer. Early commercial boiling and pasteurization techniques often adversely affected the taste of the milk. Companies did not disclose that their milk had been pasteurized, and consumers began to view the process with suspicion, as a form of adulteration. A developing medical critique of pasteurized milk suggested that heating milk destroyed microorganisms vital to milk's nutritional value and even that pasteurization caused scurvy and rickets. To overcome these concerns Straus established stands in public parks where he sold his pasteurized milk by the glass to allow consumers to verify for themselves its rich, sweet flavor. In the summer of 1906, Straus's popular stands sold 1,078,405 glasses of milk. Straus also cited and in return received endorsement of his efforts from medical experts such as Abraham Jacobi, a leading physician and pioneer in pediatrics who, as early as 1873, had advocated heating milk for infant feeding.[32]

Certified milk advocates feared that reliance on pasteurization would encourage lax sanitary standards in production and handling. Initially, certified milk advocates conceded the utility of pasteurization as a temporary, second-best solution to protect public health while production and handling practices improved with growing adoption of the medical milk commissions' protocols. For their part, pasteurization advocates praised the efforts of medical milk commissions and the superior quality of certified milk while also noting the limited scale of these efforts as a solution to the milk problem. Eventually, however, as certified milk advocates raised questions about the healthfulness of pasteurized milk and pasteurization advocates pushed for universal government-mandated commercial pasteurization of the milk supply, relations between the two camps soured. Certified milk was a high-priced luxury that cultivated the "patronage of the well to do" and favored the "classes" over the "masses," declared an advocate of pasteurization at the 1911 meeting of the American Association of Medical Milk Commissions. "I prefer raw milk without pathogenic organisms in it to a pasteurized milk with dead bacteria in it," retorted a well-known chemist in the certified milk camp. Straus described unpasteurized milk as "worse than the plague," and he concluded an address to an international child welfare congress with the declaration: "Use no raw milk." Coit accused Straus of excessive egotism and insisted that the certified milk movement "must have no relation with him whatever." After an outbreak of tuberculosis was traced back to a certified dairy in 1914, Straus asserted that Coit had been "thoroughly discredited." Coit shot back, bitterly asserting at the 1915 meeting of the American Association of Medical Milk Commissions that the "medical profession and the public are menaced by a bacillus far more vicious and virulent than the tubercle bacillus [and] its name is Commercialism, its genus is greed and its species is milk. It sometimes infects health officers, newspapers, self-constituted authorities on pure food and even infects well known milk crusaders."[33]

Despite their bitter rivalry, Coit's certified milk movement and Straus's pasteurization campaign shared an important feature: both were private philanthropic ventures borne out of frustration with the inadequacy of industry and government responses to the public health crisis of milk-borne illness. "Private philanthropy has led the way," wrote Assistant Surgeon-General John Kerr in a 1909 report on the certified milk movement and infant milk depots. But as the Gilded Age's laissez-faire ideology gave way to the Progressive Era's enthusiasm for government regulation, Kerr expressed the widely shared view that "the public, through its official representatives, should assume its share of responsibility."[34]

Straus, who had himself held public office as a New York City park commissioner from 1889 to 1893 and president of the New York City Board of Health in 1898, welcomed government regulation of the milk supply. From the beginning, he viewed his personally funded pasteurization plant and milk depots as a temporary, and ultimately unsustainable, demonstration project. Even as his operations were just beginning to expand in 1897, he foresaw that "there will come a time" when the increasing expense of subsidizing pasteurized milk "will outrun the ability of any private individual to supply it at . . . a nominal price." By 1907, he wrote that "the limit of the capacity of my present establishment is being rapidly reached, and, to be at all adequate to the demands made upon it, must very shortly reach a point where it belongs to the sphere of municipal rather than private effort." He insisted throughout that "the municipality and the State are primarily responsible for the milk supplies."[35]

In 1911, New York City began establishing municipal milk depots, and Straus began scaling back his operations. The quality of the municipal milk supply gradually improved as the city expanded its inspection of dairies and distributors and passed an ordinance requiring that all milk sold in the city be either pasteurized or certified. By 1916, 90 percent of the milk sold in New York City was pasteurized, and the city began to convert its milk depots into baby health stations dedicated to educating parents in childcare. In 1920, Straus donated his pasteurization plant and remaining eight milk depots to the city.[36]

Coit's model of private regulation by volunteer medical milk commissions also proved financially unsustainable and was eventually replaced by a larger system of government inspection and licensing. As the certified milk movement proliferated, it proved difficult to enforce uniform standards, and fraudulent certification became a growing problem. Moreover, the American Association of Medical Milk Commissions suffered from lack of funds soon after its launch in 1907. By 1911, more than half of its member commissions failed to pay their dues, and the growing administrative burdens of the organization fell on the shoulders of Coit and Geier. In addition, certified milk producers bridled at the association's rigid adherence to even the smallest details of its official standards without regard to cost. Coit dismissed such concerns as "commercialism," which, he insisted, should play no role in safeguarding the milk supply. Consequently, certified milk could not compete with less expensive pasteurized milk, which was increasingly dominating the market. Although the certified milk movement gradually declined, its standards shaped the more extensive government regulation that eventually eclipsed it.[37]

Government Inspection

Like a handful of American cities in the 1890s, Rochester employed one or two milk inspectors "with whom sobriety was not a strong point" and who "were known to 'borrow' money occasionally from milkmen." Although the earliest municipal testing of milk samples dates back to 1859, and municipal dairy inspection to 1882, neither became widespread until after the turn of the century. Early government milk regulation aimed primarily at reducing fraud rather than preventing contamination. Moreover, before the bacteriological revolution in the 1890s, efforts to improve dairy sanitation focused on visible dirt and filth, which did not necessarily protect consumers from the germs that caused disease. City health departments were chronically understaffed and corruption was widespread. State boards of health during this period were underfunded, powerless, and inactive.[38]

Frustration with the inadequacy of government regulation gave rise to private initiatives. But it quickly became apparent that private efforts like Coit's certified milk movement and Straus's milk depots, though instructive and inspiring, were too small to solve the milk problem. Writing in 1917, J. Scott MacNutt, a leading public health scholar at the Massachusetts Institute of Technology, characterized these private efforts as merely "a drop in the bucket." In a lengthy treatise, he opined that "the certified milk idea was, until recent years, undisputedly predominant in the clean milk movement and so has served its purpose. In the solution to the general milk problem, however, certified milk plays little part. Its market will continue to be restricted and its quantity small because of the high price at which it must be sold." Similarly, MacNutt recognized the value of milk depots as models but observed that they served a limited population and could not produce sufficient volume to supply "the general market."[39]

In the early decades of the 1900s, government programs emerged that adopted the inspection, testing, and pasteurization techniques developed by medical milk commissions and private milk depots. In 1905, New York City health commissioner Dr. Thomas Darlington instituted the first systematic inspection of the city's milk supply. New York City had first appointed milk inspectors decades earlier, and both the city and the state had passed laws setting sanitation standards for milk production. Before Darlington's efforts, the city had made significant progress in combatting economic adulteration, but it had made less headway in improving dairy sanitation and reducing bacterial contamination. Darlington launched an aggressive campaign within the city limits. Citing "revolting conditions," his inspectors shut down dozens of dairies in Brooklyn and Staten Island. He then extended his reach to dairies and distribution centers in the countryside. Although such operations were beyond his jurisdiction, Darlington relied on an 1896 provision of the sanitary code requiring all persons selling milk in the city to obtain a permit, and he threatened to revoke the permits of milk dealers whose out-of-town suppliers did not permit inspections and adhere to the city's standards. The efforts aimed to cover farms in New York State, New Jersey, Pennsylvania, Connecticut, Massachusetts, Vermont, and Ohio that supplied the city with six hundred million quarts of milk in 1906.[40]

Darlington's inspectors gradually overcame initial resistance from rural farmers. "It is hard to teach people who toil all day and never see a newspaper except on Sunday, and who know nothing whatever about such matters as germs, but when you teach them that when they don't wash up and obey the Board of Health requirements, their milk cannot be received in the city, they begin to understand," Darlington explained in a speech at an annual conference of the American Association of Medical Milk Commissions. "Few, if any, contracts are now made between dealers and farmers for milk, without a stipulation that all milk and dairy farms come up to the requirements of the New York City Department of Health."[41]

In addition to farm inspections, the department reported conducting more than one thousand unannounced inspections annually of 542 production plants throughout the state and more than eight thousand licensed milk dealers in the city. The department also conducted chemical and bacteriological testing, responded to consumer complaints, and traced milk-borne illness outbreaks back to their sources. In one 1905 case, department inspectors traced fifteen cases of typhoid to an unsanitary creamery in a town with eight typhoid cases, four of them on farms that supplied milk to the creamery. In 1906, the department claimed that it found not a single case of typhoid traceable to milk. Darlington declared triumphantly, "Not a drop of impure milk can now break through the cordon of inspection guarding every entrance to the city, not a drop can reach the consumer which has not been tested, nor can a drop get to the table of which we have not a complete history."[42]

Not everyone shared Darlington's view that the Department of Health had finally solved the city's milk problem. Social critic John Spargo, in *The Common Sense of the Milk Question*, wrote in 1908 that the city's inspection resources were inadequate to regulate the daily milk supply of 1.6 million quarts of milk. Eighteen inspectors assigned within the city were responsible for inspecting railroad terminals, depots, trains, trucks, retail wagons, and stores that transported and sold milk, as well as the condition of the cans and bottles in which it was shipped. Another fifteen country inspectors were charged with overseeing the thirty-five thousand farms and seven hundred creameries scattered across seven states that supplied the city with milk, leaving many facilities uninspected and few resources for reinspection when corrective action was required. Others believed that inspection alone was not enough, and they lobbied for legislation that would require mandatory pasteurization. A series of typhoid outbreaks in the city between 1910 and 1912 led Darlington's successor to require milk intended for infants and children to be either certified or pasteurized, and after another typhoid outbreak in 1913, the city extended this requirement to all milk, although the provision was not strictly enforced until the 1920s.[43]

Although municipal milk regulation efforts in New York City during this time were more extensive than in other cities, they were not unique. By 1914, most major cities had inspection and testing programs. The City of Rochester went even further—it provided on-site technical assistance to dairy farmers to teach them sanitary production and bottling methods, and the city operated several dispensaries that distributed high-quality milk. Cities also mandated pasteurization and tuberculosis testing of dairy herds. In 1909, Chicago required pasteurization of all milk not from tuberculin-tested herds, and within the next few years, many other cities passed pasteurization ordinances and instituted tuberculin-testing programs.[44]

State governments also passed laws, promulgated regulations, fielded inspectors, established laboratories, analyzed samples, and tested dairy herds —although generally on a smaller scale than municipal efforts. State regulation was typically constrained by limited funding and, in many states, fierce opposition to government regulation from powerful farm lobbies. In states with active municipal milk regulation, states complemented municipal efforts. New York State deputized city inspectors and fielded a dozen of its own inspectors. In more sparsely populated states, milk regulation was exclusively carried out—to the extent that it was carried out at all—by the state board of health or a state dairy commissioner. In small towns and rural communities, without a municipal or county health department, there was typically no one to enforce state regulations.[45]

Federal regulation also emerged during this period. In 1906, Congress passed the federal Pure Food and Drug Act, which authorized the USDA's Bureau of Chemistry to institute prosecutions and seizures through the Justice Department for the sale of adulterated or misbranded food. Although primarily focused on harmful additives and fraudulent misrepresentations, federal officials also used the statute to prosecute cases involving bacterial contamination. The statutory definition of adulteration included any food consisting "in whole or in part of a filthy, decomposed, or putrid animal or vegetable substance . . . or if it is the product of a diseased animal."[46]

In one early landmark prosecution, government inspectors purchased a pint bottle of milk from the wagon of a milk dealer in Washington, DC, and took it to the city health department's laboratory, where it was analyzed and found to be heavily contaminated with bacteria associated with cow feces. When the defendant objected that it was practically impossible to produce milk free from bacteria and that the statute imposed an impossibly high standard on the dairy industry, the court responded that "the dividing line between pure and impure or adulterated food is in each instance a question of fact" to be decided by the court on a case-by-case basis and that fecal contamination of milk presented a clear case of adulteration.[47]

These federal efforts were limited. Federal regulation covered only milk sold in interstate commerce or sold in Washington, DC, and the Bureau of Chemistry's small inspection force relied heavily on cooperation with state and municipal health departments. Moreover, federal officials lacked the legal authority to inspect food facilities until Congress passed the Federal Food, Drug, and Cosmetic Act of 1938.[48]

Aside from enforcement of the Pure Food and Drug Act, the federal government conducted research, disseminated information, and provided advice to support state and local regulators. The USDA's Dairy Division conducted research in collaboration with the National Association of Dairy Instructors and Investigators to develop and disseminate a uniform scorecard for dairy inspection, and the USDA went on to develop a similar scorecard for dairy processing plants. These scorecards were widely adopted by state and local health departments. In 1907, President Roosevelt created a commission to examine the milk problem. The commission's final report endorsed pasteurization as a way to "prevent much sickness and save lives," lending a weighty federal endorsement to state and local efforts to mandate pasteurization. In 1909, the US Public Health and Marine Hospital Service published an eight-hundred-page volume, *Milk and Its Relation to the Public Health*, of contributions by the nation's leading authorities on milk in the fields of chemistry, bacteriology, infectious disease, pediatrics, epidemiology, sanitation, and public health.[49]

Industry Initiatives

Harvey Perley Hood started out in the dairy business with a one-horse delivery operation in Boston in the 1840s. After a few years, he purchased a farm in Derry, New Hampshire, from which he shipped a daily rail car full of milk to Boston. By the end of the century, H. P. Hood and Sons had become one of the nation's most prominent dairy companies. Greatly impressed by the work of Nathan Straus, Hood began pasteurizing his milk in 1895, more than a decade before Boston passed an ordinance mandating pasteurization. Hood was not alone in this respect. By 1900, many large companies supplying major cities openly pasteurized their milk. Some emphasized this in their advertising and charged a premium. These large firms developed a market for pasteurized milk, which helped overcome public resistance to pasteurization and made possible, eventually, government regulations mandating it.[50]

Dairy companies also developed their own systems of inspection and testing that contributed to solving the milk problem. In contracts with the farmers who supplied them milk, these large firms imposed detailed production and quality specifications, and they enforced them through company inspectors and laboratory analysis. Borden, the nation's largest milk company, which served New York and Chicago, sent inspectors to visit its suppliers "once or twice a week" as well as veterinarians to examine herds "at least twice each month." Large companies also tested milk samples both before and after pasteurization.[51]

Companies encouraged compliance with their specifications in a number of ways. They paid premiums to suppliers who earned high inspection scores and whose milk had low bacterial counts. Company inspectors also provided coaching to suppliers. In a 1906 magazine article, a bacteriologist who worked for a leading Boston dairy company described how "having been country-bred, and therefore knowing the characteristics of the New England farmer, I undertook to visit personally every farm sending milk, to talk with the farmer and explain the reasons for our inspections, and to suggest whatever means of improvement in his methods and appliances seemed to me sensible and practicable." In addition, he directed a company program that collected samples for bacteriological testing. Trained assistants collected samples at receiving stations from each supplier "at least once a month, sometimes twice, or three or four times if it is necessary." These collections were unannounced, so that there was "no chance for a farmer to be especially careful on the day his milk is sampled." Farms with poor testing results received warnings: "A card is sent directly from my laboratory to the farmer . . . telling him that on a certain date his milk contained a given number of bacteria, and suggesting that greater care and cleanliness will probably remove the difficulty. If his record has been a good one hitherto, a statement is written in to that effect, together with the statement that the lapse is probably accidental. If, on the other hand, the record of the farm has not been satisfactory, the full force of the warning is expressed, viz.: that unless improvement takes place at once the company will be forced to exclude his milk. It is interesting to note that after a warning card is received, milk from that particular farm is generally of excellent quality."[52]

Brand competition motivated the emergence of these efforts by companies to manage their suppliers. One contemporary commentator noted that "it is true that this course is not followed by all companies, but the laggards are being gradually forced toward this standard." "Milk-borne disease is a bugbear of the large dealer," explained another commentator, "and, to avoid it, he has been willing to go to considerable trouble and expense and to adopt pasteurization and other precautions." Although some commentators believed that supply chain management was more effective than government regulation and that it would eventually eclipse it, others perceived a permanent role for government inspection and testing as a necessary form of oversight of private efforts. Dairy companies may also have been motivated by a desire to avoid penalties for noncompliance with government regulations or fear of civil liability.[53]

Supply chain management was not cheap, and the emerging market for safer milk favored large firms. Many public health advocates cheered growing consolidation among retail milk dealers. Social critic John Spargo saw consolidation as the key to effective supply chain management and government regulation. "There is no good reason why New York should have from twelve to thirteen thousand places where milk is sold. True, there would be some objection to any attempt in the direction of lessening the number, on the ground that it crushed out small dealers and tended to the centralization of the trade. But that is the law of progress, in distribution as well as in production. The small farmer and the small retailer must go!"[54]

Standardization

"I believe the milk problem, as a problem, is being rapidly settled," announced Dr. Charles E. North at the Milk Dealers Association annual conference in 1912. North was a physician, public health officer, inventor, and agricultural scientist who was widely respected as a leading authority on milk production. Although it was certainly too early to declare victory, North had reason to be optimistic. By the end of the first decade of the twentieth century, a variety of promising approaches to eliminating bacterial contamination in milk had emerged. Private philanthropists, government agencies, and industrial firms developed and implemented these approaches, which included sanitary production practices, medical examination of workers, tuberculin testing of cows, laboratory analysis of milk samples, and pasteurization.[55]

The concurrent efforts of diverse actors and the proliferation of different approaches—not to mention the increasingly hostile division between certified milk supporters and pasteurization proponents—made some observers less optimistic. Leslie C. Frank, a sanitary engineer at the US Public Health Service, writing fifteen years after North's address, lamented the "chaotic state of milk control in the Nation as a whole." Frank blamed decentralization and lack of uniformity in milk regulation for the persistence of communicable disease outbreaks caused by contaminated milk. He also believed that conflicting regulatory approaches in different jurisdictions led dairy farmers and companies to have a low opinion of health officials, whom they perceived as incompetent. Frank worried that the failure to establish effective, uniform milk regulation resulted in lower milk consumption "than is desirable from a public health point of view."[56]

Keenly aware of these concerns, North spearheaded efforts to standardize milk production. In 1909, the New York Milk Committee—a private philanthropic group established in 1906 by the Association for the Improvement of the Condition of the Poor, which anti–swill milk crusader Robert Milham Hartley had founded sixty years earlier—established a model milk receiving station in upstate New York called the New York Dairy Demonstration Project and appointed North to oversee it. The goal was to create a system of commercially produced high-quality raw milk on a larger scale and at a lower cost than certified milk. The project avoided the cost of on-farm inspection by relying instead on financial incentives. It paid famers more for milk produced in accordance with its strict production standards, and it conducted in-house laboratory testing to verify the quality of the milk it purchased. After a year of operation, the committee was not convinced that its vision of affordable high-quality raw milk offered a comprehensive solution to the milk problem. It abandoned its former opposition to pasteurization and took the position that milk should either be produced under sanitary conditions by tuberculin-tested cows or pasteurized. North became an even more ardent proponent of pasteurization. "I finally became convinced that in pasteurization lay the only absolute safeguard," he declared.[57]

In 1910, the New York Milk Committee convened the Conference on Milk Problems, where experts from around the country made presentations and debated the merits of different approaches. At the end of the conference, the participants passed a unanimous resolution to form a national commission to develop uniform standards for milk production. The National Commission on Milk Standards—consisting of twenty members chosen from a field of two hundred nominees and financed by the New York Milk Committee— convened in May 1911. Under the leadership of North, who served both as secretary of the New York Milk Committee and as a consultant to the Milk Dealers Association, the National Commission on Milk Standards developed standards for dairy sanitation, pasteurization, chemical and bacteriological testing, and a uniform system for grading milk, which was adopted by New York City, Newark, and Boston, as well as other cities and the State of California. In subsequent years, the commission held annual, and sometimes semi-annual, meetings at which it discussed, adopted, and revised standards. Regular commission reports were published by the US Public Health Service.[58]

The National Commission on Milk Standards was part of a larger constellation of professional and trade associations that emerged in the late nineteenth and early twentieth centuries. The professionalization of many fields of work—including medicine, public health, and chemistry—was characterized by the development of expertise and the organization of associations to share and standardize that expertise, initially on a local, and then regional, and eventually national level. These associations published journals, disseminated reports, issued policy statements, and supported professional education and training. They included practitioners, public officials, industry professionals, and academics. Among the earliest national professional associations was the American Medical Association (1847), followed by the American Veterinary Medicine Association (1863), the American Public Health Association (1872), the Association of State and Territorial Health Officials (1879), the Association of Official Agricultural Chemists (1884), the Association of Food and Drug Officials (1896), the National Association of Dairy Instructors (1906), and the International Association of Milk and Food Sanitarians (1911). Trade associations included the Milk Dealers Association (1909), as well as other organizations dedicated to various areas of the dairy industry, such as butter, evaporated milk, and ice cream.[59]

The experts who participated in these professional and trade associations constituted a complex network that knit together philanthropic, government, and industry efforts to solve the milk problem through the development of national standards. Many of them held positions in more than one sector during their careers. For example, North started his career working in the dairy industry, went on to work for a number of municipal health departments, and later served as secretary to the New York Milk Committee, convener of the National Commission on Milk Standards, and consultant for the Milk Dealers Association. When, in 1912 the National Commission on Milk Standards issued a report endorsing pasteurization for all milk except for certified milk or its equivalent, the report incorporated standards promulgated by the Association of Official Agricultural Chemists, and it was subsequently endorsed by the American Medical Association, the American Public Health Association, and the American Veterinary Medicine Association.[60]

The operation of this complex network in the drive for national standards is also evident in the evolution of dairy scorecards. In the late 1900s, industry leader Borden and the Board of Health in Montclair, New Jersey, replaced written dairy inspection reports with printed forms, which helped organize record keeping and encouraged greater uniformity in inspections. Others in industry and government soon developed printed forms. In 1904, W. C. Woodward, the health officer of the District of Columbia, developed a dairy scorecard, which not only itemized the different aspects of dairy operations to be inspected but also weighted them by relative importance and allowed the inspector to assign a score on a one-hundred-point scale. In 1905, R. A. Pearson, a professor of dairy science at Cornell University and later New York State commissioner of agriculture, independently developed a similar dairy scorecard based on his experience for a year in industry overseeing dairy production and for seven years in government as assistant chief of the Dairy Division at the USDA. In 1906, C. B. Lane, an official in the Dairy Division at the USDA, developed a scorecard. That same year, the newly founded National Association of Dairy Instructors and Investigators established a scorecard committee, which included both Pearson and Lane. In 1908, the committee published a scorecard that was immediately endorsed by the USDA and became known as the "official" dairy scorecard. The card covered cattle, production methods, and equipment. By 1914, more than two hundred cities and twenty-five states had adopted this official scorecard. Scorecards were also widely adopted by medical milk commissions.[61]

Dairy scorecards advanced milk regulation in a number of ways. Itemizing the various aspects of an inspection helped inspectors do a thorough job, and adoption of a standard scorecard promoted greater consistency between inspectors by enabling them to compare notes and calibrate their judgments. Weighting the items educated farmers about the relative importance of different sanitary measures. Some municipalities published scores, which provided dairies a powerful incentive to maintain high standards to protect their reputations among milk companies and consumers, who were often willing to pay a premium for the milk of higher-scoring dairies or avoid the milk of lower-scoring dairies. Record keeping allowed both inspectors and farmers to track trends in dairy sanitation over time. Enthusiasm for scorecards led to the development of new cards designed for processing plant inspections. Henry Coit even developed a scorecard for medical milk commissions to assess their own performance in order to promote greater uniformity within the certified milk movement of inspection standards and methods.[62]

Cities that adopted the scorecard system saw steady improvements in dairy conditions. Skeptics pointed out, however, that more uniform inspection standards and increased regulatory compliance did not necessarily produce safer milk. Dairy sanitation, it seemed, was a poor proxy for milk purity. In a widely cited 1915 study, James Brew, a bacteriologist at the New York State Agricultural Experiment Station in Geneva, New York, found "no correlation whatever" between scores earned by dairies and the purity of the milk based on laboratory testing of bacterial counts. Brew showed that this lack of correlation was equally true of the official scorecard developed by the National Association of Dairy Instructors and endorsed by the USDA, the card developed by Pearson at Cornell, and the card used by the New York City Board of Health. "There exists no relationship between the quality of milk and the dairy score on the score cards now in use," Brew concluded. "Milk of all grades, ranging from the finest quality to the poorest, is produced in barns which would be excluded [from the market by regulators] on account of low scores. All grades of milk are likewise produced in high-scoring barns." Brew attributed the failure of the existing scorecard systems to produce safer milk to "a large number of items included on the score card that have little or no effect upon the number of bacteria present in the milk." As a result of Brew's study, North launched an effort to reform the scorecard by including only those items of dairy operations demonstrably related to reducing bacterial contamination.[63]

Scorecards improved the reliability, consistency, and usefulness of inspections. However, no matter how carefully designed and executed, inspections provided only a snapshot of the conditions of a dairy or processing plant at the time of inspection. Proponents of laboratory testing argued that regular sampling provided an efficient means of ongoing monitoring. But testing measured only the bacterial count of a sample; it could not distinguish different types of bacteria. Thus, a milk sample with a low bacterial count could still harbor small but sufficient amounts of deadly typhoid or diphtheria bacteria. Gradually, a general consensus emerged in favor of an integrated approach to milk regulation that relied on a combination of inspection, laboratory testing, and pasteurization. Consequently, professional and trade associations promulgated national standards not only for scorecards but also for laboratory testing, pasteurization, equipment, and many other aspects of milk production.[64]

Efforts to develop an integrated approach to the milk problem based on national standards gained momentum in 1924, when Alabama health officials requested help from the US Public Health Service in drafting a voluntary sanitation and pasteurization program. In response, the Public Health Service developed model legislation that became the Standard Milk Ordinance, a detailed set of guidelines for herd testing, employee health, sanitary inspection, bacteriological analysis, chemical composition, pasteurization, grading, bottling, labeling, storage, and transportation. The ordinance was quickly adopted by ten states, and in 1926, the Association of State and Territorial Health Officers adopted a revised version. However, the refusal of roughly a dozen states, including California and many northeastern states, to adopt the ordinance resulted in a patchwork of different regulatory regimes, which impeded the free flow of milk between states just as advances in refrigeration and transportation enabled the emergence of a national market in the 1930s.[65]

To address this problem, the Association of State and Territorial Health Officers and the Public Health Service in 1950 convened the National Conference on Interstate Milk Shipments (NCIMS), which established a voluntary program, still operating today, to certify interstate shippers whose milk is in compliance with the requirements of the Standardized Milk Ordinance. Under the program, a cooperative state-federal effort administered by NCIMS in conjunction with the FDA, states agree to maintain regulatory standards at least as strict as the ordinance and to allow the sale of milk within their jurisdiction by any certified shipper. A shipper can obtain certification only if the farms and processing plants that supply its milk pass regular state inspections. Occasional FDA inspection of some of these same facilities provides federal oversight. Certified shippers are included in an Interstate Milk Shippers List maintained and published by the FDA.[66]

NCIMS has provided a forum for regular revision of the ordinance, which was limited in 1965 to standards for pasteurized milk and renamed the Grade "A" Pasteurized Milk Ordinance (PMO). The revision process allows for input from committees that include members from government, industry, independent laboratories, and academia. Proposed revisions are submitted to a body of delegates consisting of state representatives, with each state allowed one vote, and subject to final approval by the FDA. State delegates successfully resisted efforts in the 1970s by the FDA to make the PMO into a binding federal regulation, and the Interstate Milk Shippers Program, which today includes all fifty states, remains voluntary. "The Grade 'A' PMO adopted and uniformly applied will continue to provide effective public health protection without being unduly burdensome on either Regulatory Agencies or the dairy industry," boasts the FDA in the preface to the current revision. "It represents a 'grass roots' consensus of current knowledge and experiences and as such represents a practical and equitable milk sanitation standard for the nation."[67]

A Prototype of the US Food Safety System

Solving the milk problem was a matter of life and death. Bacterial contamination of milk was a leading cause of the highest infant mortality rates the United States has ever seen, and it occupied the top of the nation's public health agenda for decades. Efforts between the 1830s and the 1920s—the campaign against swill milk, the certified milk movement, the push for pasteurization, municipal milk inspection, industry initiatives, and the quest for national standards—all contributed to solving the milk problem. These efforts are significant for another reason as well: they laid the foundations of the US food safety system. From the various strategies to solve the milk problem emerged a complex system of public and private institutions employing a combination of laws, market incentives, and social norms.

Efforts to solve the milk problem illustrate how food safety governance involves a variety of professional experts working in multiple public and private institutions employing an array of regulatory tools. Regulation involves a great deal more than government rule making and enforcement. In some cases, government regulation merely complements private initiatives. Authority and activity are dispersed. Private and public efforts are intertwined. To achieve a clearer understanding of this prototype of the food safety system, it will be helpful to break down all of this complexity into three categories: the institutional structure of milk regulation, the dynamics that motivate the individuals involved, and the array of governance techniques that the institutions and individuals employed.

THE STRUCTURE OF MILK REGULATION

The system of milk regulation that emerged during this period was made up of government regulation, industry supply chain management, and social activism (the forerunner of civil litigation and consumer advocacy, which would arise in the twentieth century). Government regulation was carried out by a network of officials working in local, state, and federal agencies. Industry supply chain management was implemented by a network of milk company managers, their private inspectors, and their suppliers. And social activism was conducted by a network of reformers—a group made up of protesters like Hartley, physicians like Coit, and philanthropists like Straus. Academics and independent consultants comprised a fourth network that provided expert advice and assistance throughout the system.

Professional organizations and trade associations promoted communication and fostered relationships in each of these networks. The Association of State and Territorial Health Officials and the Association of Food and Drug Officials knit together a nationwide network of government regulators. The Milk Dealers Association was one of many trade associations that nurtured cooperation among dairy companies. Organizations like the American Association of Medical Milk Commissions and the New York Milk Committee brought activists together. The National Association of Dairy Instructors and the International Association of Milk and Food Sanitarians provided regular opportunities for academics and independent consultants to exchange information about the latest advances in dairy science and to develop professional training programs.[68]

Interaction between members of these different networks occurred through diverse channels. Organizations invited outsiders to speak at their meetings. For example, annual meetings of the American Association of Medical Milk Commissions regularly featured presentations by government officials, industry representatives, academics, and independent consultants. Media also facilitated information sharing across networks, through newspapers, association newsletters, government reports, academic journals, and books. Not only information but also individuals moved between the different networks. Examples include Nathan Straus, a private philanthropist who served as president of the New York City Board of Health, and R. A. Pearson, who started his career in industry, spent many years in academia, and became the New York State commissioner of agriculture. Charles North worked in industry, served as a public health official, staffed the New York Milk Committee, and advised the Milk Dealers Association. Some organizations, like the National Commission on Milk Standards and the National Conference on Interstate Milk Shippers, were founded for the express purpose of bringing together stakeholders from different networks to develop national standards and coordinate efforts. Emerging professional networks among physicians, sanitarians, public health experts, chemists, bacteriologists, and veterinarians—each with their own associations, like the American Medical Association or the American Public Health Association—created ties across the different regulatory networks of government officials, reformers, industry managers, and academics and consultants.[69]

THE DYNAMICS OF MILK REGULATION

The history of milk regulation from the 1830s to the 1920s illustrates a number of dynamics typical of the US food safety system. It will be helpful to organize these dynamics into the politics, economics, and administration of regulation.

Public concern about contaminated milk propelled the politics of regulation. Outbreaks of illness associated with contaminated milk heightened public anxiety and increased pressure for reform. This was part of a general pattern in the development of urban sanitation and public health. Periodic disease epidemics in the seventeenth, eighteenth, and nineteenth centuries—the most notorious were smallpox, yellow fever, and malaria—spurred the formation of volunteer committees and the appointment of local health boards, which established sanitary regulations, quarantine laws, and inoculation programs. Outbreaks of diphtheria, cholera, typhoid, and tuberculosis in the nineteenth and early twentieth centuries had a similar catalyzing effect on milk regulation. A series of typhoid outbreaks in New York City during the summers of 1910–1913 led municipal authorities to institute mandatory pasteurization. Such outbreaks provided what public policy scholars call "focusing events"—dramatic events that generate media coverage, increase public attention to an issue, and create pressure for change.[70]

Media coverage disseminated information about the risk of contaminated milk. It raised public awareness, magnified fears, moved reformers to take action, pushed industry to respond, and increased pressure on government officials to institute new regulations. In turn, growing public anxiety encouraged ongoing coverage of the issue by media outlets eager to satisfy readers. In this way, the concerted media campaign against the distillery dairies by the *New York Tribune*, the *New York Times*, *Leslie's Weekly*, and *Harpers* played a key role in advancing the cause of reform. For decades, the media intensively covered the milk problem. Throughout much of the 1930s, the *New York Times* ran a story about milk every other day and published an editorial every two months.[71]

Expert opinions both reflected and fueled anxiety about the milk supply. These opinions invoked the new science of bacteriology to offer lurid descriptions of contamination. "We have been told of the countless millions of bacteria which we have been drinking daily," wrote Herbert William Conn, a leading bacteriologist of his day, in an 1899 essay, published in *Popular Science Monthly*. "This has somewhat disturbed us, and no sooner have we become reconciled to this idea than we are told of the great amount of filth that finds its way into milk—two hundred pounds of cow dung being the daily ration of New York city, someone tells us. The matter appears more serious still when we are told by the public press that there are more bacteria in city milk than in city sewage." When Rosenau delivered his 1912 lectures on the milk question, anxiety about contaminated milk was still running high. "After discussion upon the subject of bacteria in milk we often hear it said, 'The wonder is that any of us are alive.'"[72]

Popular anxiety about the milk supply was bound up with a more general unease about industrialization of food production. Industrialization replaces face-to-face relationships—in which small producers and local consumers interact directly—with mass markets characterized by large-scale production, long supply chains, and impersonal standards. The enormity, opacity, and anonymity of industrial production frequently prompt fear and suspicion. This is especially true in the case of food. Consumers who lack information about where their food comes from, what is in it, and the conditions under which it was produced are prone to anxiety about the purity and safety of food.[73]

Emphasis on infant mortality also intensified anxiety about the risks of contaminated milk. Social critic John Spargo echoed the sentiments of activists like Coit and Straus when he wrote in 1908 that "our cities today are directly responsible for a considerable proportion of the awful yearly loss of babies—that, to put it plainly, our civic authorities stand in the position of murderers and accessories to the murder of thousands of infants every year." The vulnerability of children increased the salience of the risk associated with contaminated milk.[74]

The moral zeal of social activists kept the issue of milk industry regulation in the public eye and on the agendas of politicians and government officials. In early battles against distillery dairies, religious reformers like Hartley pursued the cause of dairy sanitation as part of their efforts to preach temperance and fight poverty. As the movement gained momentum, it attracted medical professionals such as Augustus Gardner and Samuel Rotton Percy and their colleagues at the New York Academy of Medicine, who increasingly took on leadership roles. Although this new breed of Progressive Era reformers spoke more of public health than of personal salvation, they were motivated by a religious fervor similar to that of their pietistic predecessors. Coit, was referred to as the "apostle of certified milk" who "spread the gospel of clean milk," and he claimed that he was guided in his work by "a spirit of trust and confidence in a higher power." Straus, the "famed missionary of pasteurized milk depots for infants," similarly declared that "devotion of a part of our wealth to those less fortunate than ourselves is demonstrated by Justice, dictated by conscience, and expressly commanded by Mosaic law."[75]

Professionalization played an important role in the politics of milk regulation. Experts in the emerging professions of medicine, public health, bacteriology, and chemistry exercised increasing influence in government, industry, and philanthropy. Sociologist Andrew Abbott explains that the process of professionalization entails harnessing new forms of abstract knowledge, such as scientific theories, to exert claims of authority and to exercise power. As Abbott puts it, professionals assert exclusive "jurisdiction" over certain issues. Professionals working in government agencies, dairy companies, and academia, and as independent consultants, increasingly dominated policy discussions about the milk problem. By the early twentieth century, the most prominent voices were no longer those of religious reformers like Hartley, journalists like Leslie, philanthropists like Straus, or industrialists like Hood, but rather medical and scientific experts like Rosenau, Pearson, and North. The ambition to advance public health and safety through a combination of moral zeal and professional expertise reflected the ideals of Progressive Era reform.[76]

Opposition to reform also shaped the politics of milk regulation. Many farmers had little faith in new scientific theories of dairy sanitation promoted by professional experts, who typically had little actual experience in the day-to-day operation of a dairy farm. With the rise of large-scale competitors and the concentration of increasingly powerful milk companies, many smaller dairies operated on a very thin margin, and they worried that additional regulatory burdens would put them out of business. Larger milk companies also worried about the additional costs of production that increased regulatory demands would impose. Within government, opposition to increased regulation came from politicians who feared having to raise taxes to pay for it or incurring blame for having caused an increase in milk prices. Sometimes, industry opposition took the form of corruption and capture—as when powerful distillery dairy owners hired thugs to intimidate reform advocates and

journalists, or when they controlled specific city council members who ma-
nipulated official investigations and stymied reform legislation. Opposition
to increased government regulation also took the form of legitimate interest
group politics—typically with farm and business lobbies on one side and
public health and consumer advocates on the other.[77]

Technological advances shook up the politics of milk regulation by creating new technical possibilities, changing business models, and reconfiguring
interest-group alliances. For example, the new science of pasteurization at
the turn of the century realigned the interests of several key groups. Powerful
public health advocates, like Straus, backed by influential professional associations promoted mandatory pasteurization as a solution to the milk problem.
Farmers favored pasteurization because they did not have to pay for it. Large
milk companies saw pasteurization as a way to build their brands and create
fair standards of competition for industry. Because pasteurization equipment
required significant capital investments, it offered the added bonus of excluding their smaller competitors from the market. For politicians and government officials, pasteurization offered a means of protecting consumers
without having to raise taxes to pay for extensive government inspection.[78]

In addition to political interests, economic incentives also shaped responses to the milk problem. Consumer demand for cheap milk created pressure on farmers and milk companies to keep their production costs down to
maintain low prices. This demand for cheap milk fueled the proliferation of
distillery dairies, which relied on inexpensive feed and avoided the cost of
transporting milk from rural farms to urban markets. The demand for cheap
milk also ultimately doomed certified milk as a solution to the milk problem because consumers were unwilling or unable to pay a higher price for it.
"Probably the chief obstacle in the way of . . . reform lies at the consumer's
end of the problem," wrote Conn in a 1913 article in *Harper's Weekly*. "It is
still unusual to find even educated people willing to pay a cent a quart more
for good milk when they find they can get an ordinary kind cheaper. . . . Reform will come just as soon as the public is ready for it, and that will be just
as soon as the consumer is ready to pay for quality."[79]

Frustrated public officials chided consumers. "Until you are willing to
pay for clean milk, until you are willing to pay for having milk inspected
as it should be inspected, you will get a product having high fertilizer and
low hygiene value, and you and your children will suffer disease and death
as a consequence," wrote George W. Goler, the health officer of Rochester,
New York, in a 1906 magazine article. "To demand food that is entirely free
from suspicion of carrying disease to ourselves and our children, and then to

quarrel because we must pay more for it is utterly childish," declared a 1913 newspaper editorial in exasperation.[80]

Some milk companies developed brands based on higher quality, for which consumers were increasingly willing to pay a modest premium. Because an outbreak traced to a company's milk could destroy the value of its brand, larger companies invested in pasteurization equipment and promoted mandatory pasteurization laws to secure a competitive advantage over smaller rivals who could not afford the equipment. Brand competition led companies to advertise "pure" milk with pictures of country maids milking cows in pastoral settings—aimed at consumers anxious about the perils of city milk—and to tout their state-of-the-art pasteurization and bottle sanitizing equipment. The widespread adoption of pasteurization by large milk companies and the passage of mandatory pasteurization laws was thus due not only to the political alignment of various interest groups but also to the fact that it struck the right economic balance between consumers' demands for safety and their desire for low prices.[81]

Along with political interests and economic incentives, administrative considerations shaped responses to the milk problem. Incompetence, inconsistency, conflicts of interest, corruption, insufficient resources, and scientific uncertainty were constant challenges to effective regulation. When the city of Geneva, New York, sought to hire a dairy inspector in 1907, it had to settle for "a railroad baggage-master whose technical acquaintance with dairying was restricted to hazy recollections of his boyhood on a fruit farm." Dairies received inconsistent evaluations from different inspectors. Public officials supplemented their government incomes by accepting payments from companies that they were responsible for regulating—sometimes in exchange for consulting and laboratory testing services and sometimes as explicit bribes. In New York City, a criminal investigation in the mid-1920s uncovered that the city's dairy inspectors were part of an organized ring in the health department that extorted more than $3 million each year from milk dealers, slaughterhouse operators, and restaurant owners. States routinely passed ambitious mandates to clean up milk production but then failed to provide sufficient funds for inspection and enforcement. City health departments never had enough inspectors to regulate the vast market that supplied milk to large urban populations, and smaller local health authorities typically received little funding. In the early decades of dairy sanitation, the etiology and nature of milk-borne diseases were poorly understood, and, even as the disciplines of medicine, epidemiology, and bacteriology emerged, the increasingly sophisticated scientific theories and new technologies that they developed did not provide complete information. For example, while the ability to measure the bacterial count of milk samples represented an advance over examining milk only for visible dirt, early bacteriological tests could not distinguish between harmless and pathogenic bacteria. A number of administrative responses emerged to meet these challenges.[82]

Formal professional training improved the competence of inspectors and laboratory personnel. The University of Wisconsin established the first dairy school in 1891, and shortly thereafter, the University of Michigan, Cornell, and the Massachusetts Institute of Technology established courses and programs in dairy science and applied bacteriology. Increasingly, inspectors were required to possess specialized knowledge of dairy sanitation, milk processing, medicine, chemistry, bacteriology, or veterinary science.[83]

Standardization and better record keeping promoted greater consistency among inspectors. Detailed model scorecards reduced variation in how different inspectors evaluated the same conditions. In upstate New York, Pearson instituted a system in which inspectors merely recorded responses to factual questions concerning the conditions of a dairy, then managers evaluated the findings and assigned a score. "Thus the work of a number of inspectors may be unified by one mind and the quality of uniformity imparted to the work of all." Professional and trade associations supported greater consistency by setting national standards for inspection, laboratory testing, and pasteurization and publishing them in model codes. States similarly published model codes for municipalities. Public health departments developed filing systems to keep track of scores and test results, which further enhanced their capacity to track consistency among inspectors.[84]

Management oversight improved the quality and integrity of inspections. Some local health departments employed chief inspectors. The New York City health department was reorganized several times to root out corruption and improve the quality of supervision. Medical milk commissions closely supervised the certified milk inspectors whom they employed to inspect dairies. To add an additional layer of oversight, in some places, state health boards supervised the work of the commissions. Coit proposed that the Association of Medical Milk Commissions institute a peer-review system to periodically audit the work of member commissions using a scorecard to assess commissions' oversight of their own inspectors.[85]

Administrative routines aimed to reduce conflicts of interest and corruption. For example, in the 1880s, the New York City health department rotated its milk inspectors every three weeks to a different district to deter collusion between inspectors and the dairies, processors, and distributors whom they inspected. For similar reasons, New York State passed a law in 1887 requiring milk inspectors to work in pairs. Cities increasingly insisted that inspectors work full-time rather than divide their time between working for the city and consulting privately with industry.[86]

Government agencies developed a number of ways to cope with limited resources. They prioritized inspection of farms and producers with histories of regulatory violations. They also relied on private inspection systems, like the medical milk commissions. Finally, they supported regulatory approaches that required fewer inspections, such as mandatory pasteurization.[87]

Regulators coped with the limits of scientific knowledge by regulating what they could detect and measure. For example, government and industry standards relied heavily on bacterial counts in the absence of any way to test for particular pathogens in milk samples, although it was well understood that such counts provided incomplete information. Regulators also combined multiple regulatory approaches—testing, inspection, and pasteurization—to compensate for the shortcomings of each.[88]

Feedback and learning were essential to the evolution of these administrative advances. Agricultural experiment stations, funded by the federal and state governments, conducted research on the efficacy of government regulatory programs and published their results, which were widely cited and provided the basis for reforms and new initiatives. Academics conducted similar studies of milk depots funded by private foundations. Medical milk commissions shared annual reports with peers at their annual meetings, and traded ideas about how to improve performance. Scorecards provided feedback to company managers and to regulators, which they could use to assess their own performance.[89]

Finally, a shared sense of mission, which gradually spread from social activists to government and industry, greatly enhanced the administration of efforts to address the milk problem. Mutual suspicions and recriminations during the early campaigns against distillery dairies steadily gave way to collaboration on committees and commissions that brought together public officials and company executives. Dr. C. Hampton Jones, assistant commissioner of health in Baltimore, asserted in a 1906 article that this shared sense of mission was the key to successful regulation of the milk industry, emphasizing "relations of trust and confidence between the producer, dealer, and health department, thereby producing a hearty cooperation."[90]

Cooperation among government, industry, and activists took various forms. One form of coordination was mutual support. Government sometimes supported private efforts, for example by passing statutes granting medical milk commissions the exclusive right to certify milk and prosecuting unauthorized certification, and by providing laboratory space for bacteriological testing. Conversely, the efforts of private groups often generated support for government regulation, and private groups frequently helped with implementation by conducting their own regulatory compliance inspections and reporting violations to public health authorities. Another form of cooperation was borrowing and feedback. Government regulators frequently adopted milk sanitation standards and inspection practices developed by private efforts, sometimes improving on them, leading private groups, in turn, to revise their original standards and practices. Dairy inspection, laboratory testing, pasteurization, and milk depots all benefited from this kind of borrowing and feedback between government, industry, and social activists, with input from academia and private consultants. A third form of cooperation was collaboration, as when the National Association of Dairy Instructors and the USDA together developed the official dairy inspection scorecard.[91]

Relations between the different regulatory efforts were not always harmonious. For example, the Louisville medical milk commission reported that it had been "considerably antagonized by the City Health Department," which viewed the commission as a rival. The multiplicity of sources of regulation sometimes generated redundancy and confusion. Farmers grumbled about having to endure time-consuming inspections by local and state officials as well as their buyers, who frequently used different standards and sometimes issued contradictory demands.[92]

THE GOVERNANCE TECHNIQUES OF MILK REGULATION

The various public and private efforts to address the milk problem employed a number of different techniques. These can be organized into rule making, information gathering, and enforcement.

Rule making by government took the form of legislation and agency regulations. As early as the mid-nineteenth century, state laws and city ordinances regulated various aspects of milk production from farm to table. Private standard setting also played a significant role in milk regulation. For example, the Association of Medical Milk Commissions and the National Association of Dairy Instructors and Investigators developed detailed sanitary standards for dairy inspection, and the Association of Official Agricultural Chemists and the American Public Health Association established standards for chemical analysis and bacteriological testing. Industry associations such as the International Milk Dealers, the Milk Industry Foundation, and the Dairy and Food Industries Supply Association set standards for the cleanability of processing equipment. Lawmaking and private standard setting did not occur in isolation—government regulators frequently adopted private standards into legal rules, and private standards typically required compliance with the law. Some procedures were a hybrid of public and private rule making. For example, the standards in the Grade "A" Pasteurized Milk Ordinance were developed by committees that included stakeholders from government, industry, independent laboratories, and academia; ratified by a body of delegates from state health and agricultural departments; and subject to final approval by the FDA, after which they were incorporated into federal regulations, adopted by state legislatures, and included in suppliers' product specifications.[93]

Rule making produced different types of rules. Some specified that regulated entities achieve particular outcomes—for example, acceptable levels of bacteria in milk samples. Others prescribed particular processes, such as hand washing, equipment cleaning, and pasteurization. Regulatory efforts frequently combined outcome rules and process rules, for example, by testing samples to verify the effectiveness of process controls.[94]

Information gathering techniques enabled regulators to monitor the conduct of regulated entities, such as dairy farms and milk companies. These techniques included inspections of production facilities using itemized checklists and scoring, laboratory analysis of milk samples, and tuberculin testing of herds. Other information gathering techniques helped regulators learn more about patterns of contamination. Public health authorities in the late nineteenth century developed new systems for reporting communicable diseases that allowed for ongoing surveillance of the population. They also evolved epidemiological investigation techniques that enhanced their ability to trace outbreaks back to the source of contamination.[95]

Enforcement techniques varied in terms of how coercive they were. Educational efforts were the least coercive. Government issued nonbinding guidance in the form of US Public Health Service and USDA bulletins on milk production and testing. Government inspectors and private certifiers frequently coached dairy farmers and milk producers. Writing in 1917, the Massachusetts Institute of Technology public health scholar J. Scott MacNutt noted the emergence of this phenomenon: "Inspection seems to have been originally regarded as a species of policing, often with elements of detective work. The object was to 'catch' the bad milkman. This idea has been largely superseded by that of advice, of 'education of the dairyman.'" According to social critic John Spargo, "The most efficient worker for reform is not the sharp-nosed inspector who catches the occasional culprit, but the man who can win the confidence of the farmer; the man who can successfully appeal to his good sense and show him the practical advantages which arise from the observance of certain elementary rules of hygiene."[96]

In enforcing the Pure Food and Drug Act, USDA officials "adopted an advisory-before-the-fact attitude by offering constructive suggestions which should enable manufacturers to keep their products in compliance with the law," according to an agency report. "The Federal food and drugs act [*sic*] is administered on the theory that more is to be accomplished by acting in an advisory capacity under such conditions as will ensure legal products than by accumulating a record of successful prosecutions with attending fines." According to one scholarly account, the USDA's Food Research Laboratory "developed a reputation for its role in educating food manufacturers and distributors in the best methods of cold storage, transportation, and factory sanitation." Medical milk commissions similarly emphasized educating over policing the dairies under their supervision. Professor Rosenau, while serving as president of the American Association of Medical Milk Commissions, told annual meeting attendees that "the Medical Milk Commission should cooperate in a friendly and helpful spirit with the producer, help the producer over his perplexity and out of his trouble[,] . . . give him a helping hand."[97]

Federal, state, and local governments promoted education by sponsoring contests and exhibitions, at which they awarded prizes for the best milk to farmers and milk companies. Experts gave lectures on the latest advances in sanitation, processing, and testing. Entrepreneurs demonstrated new technology and equipment. Medical milk commissions and the Certified Milk Producers association hosted certified milk contests around the country at which samples were scored and winners were awarded "valuable silver cups."[98]

Information disclosure—a second type of enforcement tool—exerted pressure on farmers and milk companies through reputational effects. State and local health departments in some places disclosed inspection results, which were frequently published in local newspapers. In the late 1890s, the Massachusetts Dairy Commission published a "white list" of dairies that complied with state sanitary standards. Private consumer groups also published such lists. Publication of inspection results incentivized farmers and milk companies to improve their sanitary practices. Farmers with low reported scores often found that their milk company clients would switch to other suppliers, and low-scoring milk companies lost consumers to their higher-scoring competitors. Milk grading and labeling laws created similar incentives for brand-sensitive companies, because consumers were willing to pay more for higher-grade milk and increasingly avoided low-grade milk.[99]

Contracts provided a third type of enforcement technique, which governments and private entities used to manage supply chains. Government procurement contracts for public institutions such as hospitals, orphanages, and prisons included sanitary and testing requirements for milk. Medical milk commissions required certified farms to sign contracts that they would comply with the commission's standards and to post bonds in case of breach. Milk company contracts with suppliers imposed dairy sanitation and storage specifications.[100]

Civil enforcement actions were a fourth type of enforcement technique. Starting in the late 1800s, local and state governments in many places required milk producers and sellers to obtain a license, which required them to follow mandatory rules regarding sanitation and to submit to regular inspection and testing. The power to revoke a license provided substandard operations incentive to take corrective measures, and it enabled government regulators to eliminate those who refused. New York City health commissioner Dr. Thomas Darlington used the city's licensing power to carry out his aggressive 1905 campaign of systematic dairy inspections, and he revoked the licenses of dozens of low-performing dairies. Aside from license revocation, the power to seize and destroy contaminated milk provided a powerful means of civil enforcement. New York City's Sanitary Code granted the city this power starting in 1883, and subsequent legislation provided for the seizure and destruction of tubercular cows. The FDA seized and destroyed milk with excessively high bacterial counts under the Pure Food and Drug Act starting in 1915.[101]

Criminal prosecution was the most coercive type of enforcement technique. City health departments in Washington, DC, and Rochester on occasion brought criminal charges against the most recalcitrant milk regulation offenders at the turn of the century. In 1904, New York State made it a misdemeanor to sell milk as certified that was not certified by a medical milk commission or health board.[102]

As the range of enforcement tools available emerged, public and private regulators typically started with less coercive approaches and responded to resistant dairy farmers and milk companies by gradually increasing incentives and penalties—a pattern known among regulatory scholars as "responsive regulation." Describing the efforts of George W. Goler in Rochester, Spargo wrote that "moral suasion is the force upon which the greatest reliance is placed. Dr. Goler has wisely recognized all the conditions resulting from the ignorance of milk producers and retailers, and set himself to teach all who are teachable how to produce a better class of milk. In order to do this, he has had to show them the importance of cleanliness in producing and handling milk to the public health, a gigantic task in which he has been splendidly aided by his assistants. When moral suasion fails, as it sometimes

---

Structure
- government regulation: federal, state, local
- industry supply-chain management: buyers, private inspectors, suppliers
- social activism: protesters, journalists, philanthropists

Dynamics
- politics: public concern, reformers' moral zeal, professional expertise, industry resistance, technological advances
- economics: market demand for cheap milk, market demand for safe milk, company brand sensitivity
- administration: professionalization, standardization, management oversight, administrative routines, coping with limited enforcement resources, regulating what you can measure, feedback & learning, shared sense of mission

Governance Techniques
- rulemaking: legislation, regulations, standard setting
- information gathering: inspection, testing, surveillance, investigation
- enforcement: education, information disclosure, contract, civil actions, criminal prosecution

---

FIGURE 2.1. Analysis of efforts to solve the milk problem.

does, then resort is made to sterner measures, such as arrests, fines, and revocation of licenses." Figure 2.1 summarizes this analysis of efforts to solve the milk problem.[103]

Assessing the Public Health Impact

A study published in 2007 concludes confidently that reducing microbial pathogens in the milk supply was "the single most important contributor to [a] decline in both diarrheal and overall infant mortality in the United States during the first part of the 20th century." The author first attributes high infant mortality rates from diarrheal disease to contaminated milk by citing data indicating that, in the late nineteenth and early twentieth centuries, diarrhea was a dominant cause of infant mortality and that feeding infants cow's milk rather than breast milk was associated with increased infant mortality from diarrhea. The author then links decreases in infant mortality to efforts to solve the milk problem by presenting data showing that infant mortality, particularly diarrheal mortality, declined steadily in the first decades of the twentieth century and pointing out that this "decline in infant mortality largely correlates with the cleaning of the market milk supply between 1840 and 1940."[104]

The study considers and rejects several alternative explanations for the decline in infant mortality. These include a resurgence of breastfeeding (the author presents data reflecting a continuing decrease in breastfeeding during the first decades of the twentieth century), water purification (the author surveys studies from the period, which found no perceptible reduction in infantile diarrhea associated with filtration of local water supplies), and medical advances (the author points out that new medical treatments for infantile diarrhea did not emerge until the 1930s). The study also asserts that the purity of the milk supply had a greater impact than living standards on infant mortality by presenting data from Baltimore in 1915 demonstrating that infant mortality among the wealthiest families who fed their infants cow's milk was higher than infant mortality among the poorest families who breastfed their infants. Thus, the study concludes, reducing microbial pathogens in the milk supply played "a far more important role [in the decline of infant mortality] than rises in income, other sanitary measures, or any medical interventions."

This is the first of many evaluations of food safety efforts featured in this book. These assessments tend to be based on limited data that, at best, support only general conclusions regarding public health impacts. As the author of the 2007 study admits, a strong correlation between efforts to reduce microbial pathogens in milk and the decline in infant mortality, "would require concurrent longitudinal population data on the quality of market milk, the prevalence of infantile diarrhea, and diarrheal mortality, as well as concomitant information on socioeconomic and environmental factors associated with infant mortality." Such data do not exist. Instead, the author assembled "various fragmentary . . . data on different populations in different time periods" from a variety of local, regional, and national studies, from both the United States and other countries. These data support inferences concerning the aggregate impact of efforts to reduce microbial pathogens in the milk supply in the late nineteenth and early twentieth centuries, but they do not offer insight into the impact of any particular initiative or combination of initiatives. Although it is valuable to know that efforts to solve the milk problem appear to have improved public health, the relevant question in policy evaluation is normally not whether there are benefits from food safety efforts in general, as compared to doing nothing, but whether a particular food safety precaution is likely to be effective and, on balance, worth the cost—a question that typically remains unanswerable with available data. Subsequent chapters elaborate on this and other challenges facing the evaluation of food safety.

For now, it is enough to note that efforts to solve the milk problem evolved despite uncertainty about their efficacy and cost-effectiveness. At first, this evolution proceeded slowly, as reforms were blocked by opposition from powerful distillery dairy owners who influenced local politicians and farmers who lobbied state legislatures against regulation. Eventually, however, the pace of reform accelerated, as large dairy companies joined social activists, public health experts, and government officials in supporting reforms such as pasteurization, tuberculosis testing, and milk grading. Like many aspects of the struggle to reduce milk-borne illness, these shifting dynamics became typical of the evolution of food safety in other sectors of the food industry. The next two chapters take a closer look at these dynamics in the canned food and beef sectors, and they analyze the changing alignment of interests that sometimes resulted in resistance to change and, at other times, generated opportunities for reform.

Canned Foods under Pressure:
HACCP and the Dynamics of Food Safety Reform

Throughout the 1960s, the US space program produced a remarkable array of technological innovations that, by the end of the decade, landed a man on the moon. The National Aeronautics and Space Administration (NASA) developed solar panels, memory foam, and cordless vacuum cleaners. It also launched a revolution in food safety.

In 1963, NASA recruited Paul Lachance, a young air force officer at the Aerospace Medical Research Laboratories with a PhD in biology, to serve as the chief food technologist for the space program. His first task was to design food that would pose no risk of illness, because the effects of vomiting or diarrhea in an enclosed space capsule at zero gravity or within a sealed space suit would be catastrophic. For technical support, he turned to the US Army's Natick Labs, whose staff of specialists in food preservation and packaging conducted research and development for feeding soldiers. Lachance contracted with the Pillsbury Company to produce the food. Pillsbury had been working with the US Army's Natick Labs since 1959 under a NASA contract on cube-sized food for space flight that would not crumble, for fear that crumbs, at zero gravity, might interfere with a space capsule's instruments or contaminate its atmosphere. This new project, producing food with zero pathogens, was a tall order. Although the medical community had experimented with sterilizing foods, Lachance recalls that "they cooked the hell out of it, and it wasn't too damn palatable stuff."[1]

No suitable techniques existed to satisfy NASA's need for pathogen-free food. Standard industrial quality-control techniques at the time typically relied on end-product testing. However, end-product testing for space food was impractical. The level of risk reduction demanded by NASA would require that most of each batch of food produced be utilized for testing, leaving only a small portion for the space flights and resulting in very high production costs. Within the food industry, the most advanced quality-assurance programs at the time used spot testing at various points in the production process. This approach was based more on intuition than on science, and it allowed for a much higher level of risk than NASA would tolerate. Moreover, spot-testing programs varied widely, and there were no industry standards by which to evaluate them. Indeed, in many cases, companies did not even test for microbial contamination until they received consumer complaints or notification of an outbreak from public health authorities.[2]

Lachance's team developed a new approach. They adapted a system of risk analysis called Modes of Failure, which Natick Labs used to anticipate places in the production process for medical supplies where contamination or other product defects might occur. They also borrowed from NASA's Zero Defects Program, a system of risk monitoring that tested spacecraft components at critical stages in the production process. Together, these two components made up a system for identifying hazards throughout the production process and controlling risk at critical points, with the aim of preventing contamination before it occurred rather than simply detecting it in finished products. Howard Bauman, a microbiologist who served as Pillsbury's lead scientist on the project, named the system Hazard Analysis Critical Control Points, or HACCP (pronounced "hassip"). "We concluded after extensive evaluation that the only way we could succeed would be to have control over the raw materials, the process, the environment, personnel, storage and distribution beginning as early in the system as we possibly could," Bauman later recalled. "We felt certain that if we could establish this type of control, along with appropriate record keeping, we should be able to produce a product that we could say was safe with a high degree of assurance. For all practical purposes, if it was done right, it should not require any testing of the finished packaged material other than for monitoring purposes."[3]

Today, NASA considers HACCP "one of the most far-reaching space spin-offs." A 2003 National Academy of Sciences report considers it the "foundation of the food safety assurance system in the modern world." *Food Safety News* dubbed it "the Mount Rushmore of food regulation."[4]

This chapter and the next tell the story of HACCP. This chapter examines HACCP's early application to canned food production, and the next chapter its subsequent introduction into the beef and poultry industries. The chapters delve deeper into the dynamics of the US food safety system. The story of HACCP illustrates that, sometimes, political interests, economic incentives, and administrative concerns converge to foster cooperation that results in policy reform, and at other times, they diverge to produce adversarial relations that thwart change. As will become clear, not everyone agrees about the desirability of cooperation and change. Some praise cooperation between government and industry as the key to successful regulation; others condemn it as a sign of collusion. Some view policy change as necessary for progress; others perceive it as enabling overregulation. These competing views have practical implications, and they play a significant role in the dynamics of regulatory reform.

An Introduction to HACCP

HACCP introduced careful design, rigorous standards, and precise measurement into the largely intuitive, loosely organized, hit-or-miss world of industrial food safety prior to the 1970s. HACCP is a structured management system for food safety. It provides managers with the same types of tools—benchmarks, metrics, and routines—for managing food safety that they use in managing other aspects of manufacturing, such as productivity, workplace safety, and quality control. When it comes to these other aspects of manufacturing, "managers can provide detailed quantitative data in pounds produced per man-hour, number and type of accident, and failure rates," according to Dave Theno, who was a leading private consultant on HACCP design and implementation. "But when I ask the same managers, 'How is food safety in your plant?' the answer is 'pretty good,' or 'better than last week.'" According to Theno, HACCP closes this gap by "translating food safety into a management system." HACCP allows managers to measure and track food safety over time. "If people have something to manage, they will manage it."[5]

Although HACCP's two basic ingredients of risk analysis and risk monitoring have remained the same, successive revisions have elaborated seven core components, or "principles." First, conduct a hazard analysis by cataloging the risks of contamination throughout the entire production process of a food item from farm to fork, including growing, harvesting, processing, manufacturing, storage, distribution, marketing, preparation, and consumption. Second, identify critical control points. These are stages in the process at which control can be exercised to prevent, eliminate, or reduce a food safety risk, such as the risk of bacterial growth. Third, establish critical limits for each critical control point. Critical limits are threshold values for measurable biological, chemical, or physical qualities that must be maintained in order to control particular food safety risks. For example, a common type of critical limit is the minimum cooking time and temperature necessary to eliminate harmful bacteria. Fourth, monitor each critical control point using specific procedures and routines, such as designating a particular worker to check oven temperature every hour. Fifth, prescribe corrective actions to be taken when monitoring indicates that a critical limit has been transgressed. HACCP managers must identify the source of the problem and take steps to ensure that it will not occur again. They must also prevent any potentially contaminated food from entering the food chain. Sixth, verify that the HACCP plan is scientifically valid and that it is being implemented as designed. Verification may include inspecting plant operations, reviewing records, and testing products. Seventh, maintain records concerning the design and implementation of the HACCP plan, such as the initial hazard analysis, the scientific basis for determining critical limits, time and temperature logs, and lot numbers. Figure 3.1 lists these principles.[6]

The seven HACCP principles provide a general template—a list of essential steps to analyze and manage food safety risk. Applying HACCP to a particular production process requires specification of hazards, critical control points, critical limits, monitoring methods, corrective actions, verification procedures, and documentation. This translation from theory to practice requires interdisciplinary expertise and a thorough knowledge of each production step. Successful implementation depends on open communication and a shared commitment among everyone involved, from farmworkers to company executives.[7]

HACCP works only in environments that satisfy certain prerequisites. These include standards and routines for pest control, cleaning, sanitation, worker hygiene, equipment maintenance, and ingredient specifications. Rodent infestation or the absence of hand-washing stations for workers will thwart even the most sophisticated HACCP program. These and many other standards and routines—known in the HACCP framework as "prerequisite programs"—are articulated in FDA and USDA regulations and guidance. Various regulations refer to them as Good Manufacturing Practices (GMPs) and Sanitation Standard Operating Procedures (SSOPs). GMPs and SSOPs ensure basic environmental and operating conditions necessary to produce

1. conduct a hazard analysis
2. identify critical control points
3. establish critical limits
4. monitor each critical control point
5. prescribe corrective actions
6. verify that the HACCP plan is scientifically valid and that it is being implemented as designed
7. maintain records

FIGURE 3.1. The seven principles of HACCP.

safe food, but they are not generally included as part of HACCP programs because they do not merit the intense scrutiny that HACCP demands of critical control points. GMPs date back to the mid-1960s. In some instances, GMPs and SSOPs specify particular technologies or processes; in other instances, they recommend outcomes and leave open the means of achieving them. By contrast, HACCP dictates neither particular processes nor performance outcomes. Instead, it prescribes general management principles.[8]

HACCP takes a preventive approach to food safety. The NASA-Natick-Pillsbury team aimed to eliminate harmful pathogens from the production process by monitoring critical control points. The alternative of waiting for pathogens to show up in end-product testing and investigating the problem after contamination occurs is an expensive method of feedback and learning. "It's much easier to keep all the needles out of the barn than to find the one needle in the haystack," explains one food safety expert, who also notes that "an ounce of prevention is worth several million pounds of recalled product." Of course, a preventive approach to food safety was not entirely new. More than half a century before the space program got off the ground, the milk industry had pioneered the use of sanitation standards, dairy inspections, record keeping, pasteurization, refrigeration, and testing to successfully exclude or destroy harmful pathogens in most of the nation's fluid milk supply.[9]

Cooperative Regulatory Reform

Howard Bauman's experience developing HACCP for space food left him eager to apply it to Pillsbury's regular production operations. The perfect opportunity emerged in the spring of 1971 after a consumer discovered pieces of glass in the company's popular farina infant cereal. A glass shield at the company's Springfield, Illinois, plant had shattered, and shards of glass had fallen into a storage bin and been mixed into the cereal. Amid embarrassing national press coverage and a product recall, Pillsbury CEO Robert Keith called Bauman into his office and asked him to devise a system to ensure that such a problem would never happen again. Bauman assembled an interdisciplinary team of engineers, microbiologists, product-development scientists, and quality-assurance managers to oversee the design and implementation of a companywide HACCP plan.[10]

Bauman also advocated the use of HACCP throughout the food industry. As he was laying the groundwork for a HACCP system within Pillsbury, Bauman promoted HACCP at the National Conference on Food Protection convened by the American Public Health Association "to develop a comprehensive, integrated attack on the problem of microbial contamination of foods."

HACCP was initially only one of many ideas presented at the conference, but it would soon rise to prominence.[11]

That summer, on July 1, a man in Westchester County, New York, died, and his wife suffered critical illness after eating Bon Vivant canned vichyssoise soup contaminated with *C. botulinum* bacteria. On July 2, the FDA published a warning to consumers and the company commenced a nationwide recall of all 6,444 cans of vichyssoise bearing the same lot number. Government inspectors visited the company's Newark, New Jersey, plant and examined Bon Vivant products on store shelves around the country. The inspectors recovered four additional cans of Bon Vivant vichyssoise from the shelf of a Bronx store that tested positive for *C. botulinum*, and they found cans of vichyssoise and other items that were swollen, leaking, and had defective seams. On July 6, the FDA pressed the company to recall its entire stock of products—1.4 million cans containing ninety varieties of soups, sauces, and other items—valued at $600,000. FDA investigators reported that the company regularly undercooked its products, improperly maintained equipment, and kept incomplete records. On July 26, the 108-year-old company, unable to finance the recall or meet its other financial obligations, filed for bankruptcy, and the FDA initiated a nationwide seizure of its products.[12]

Concern about contamination of the nation's canned food supply grew when, on August 22, the Campbell Soup Company—the country's largest soup manufacturer, which produced 80 percent of liquid soup sold in the United States—announced a recall of more than fifty thousand cans of chicken soup after detecting *C. botulinum* in cans tested at a plant in Paris, Texas. Following an FDA inspection, the agency requested on August 27 that Campbell recall an additional fifty thousand cans of vegetable soup produced in the same plant for fear that they, too, might be contaminated. And then, on October 29, the FDA published a warning that Stokely–Van Camp canned green beans might be contaminated with *C. botulinum* when an eight-year-old boy in Pensacola, Florida, fell ill after he and his father ate a few beans from a swollen can and noticed that they tasted off. In response to a request from the FDA, the company promptly recalled fifteen thousand cans of beans.[13]

The Bon Vivant case unleashed a firestorm of criticism against the FDA. Newspaper accounts reported that agency inspectors had not visited Bon Vivant's plant for four years. Congressional hearings revealed that, on average, the agency inspected food plants only once every seven years. The director of the FDA's regional office with jurisdiction over New York and New Jersey told the *New York Times* that some plants had not been inspected for periods as long as ten years. Consumer advocates complained that the agency was heavily influenced by powerful food industry executives and lobbyists who opposed government regulation. The previous FDA commissioner, Herbert Ley, declared openly that the agency lacked the motivation, resources, and support from the administration to adequately regulate food safety. A Government Accountability Office report the following spring charged that FDA oversight of food manufacturing plants was ineffective and that sanitary conditions in many plants were declining.[14]

In response, FDA commissioner Charles Edwards announced plans to develop a comprehensive licensing scheme for the canning industry that would subject the industry to closer scrutiny. Authority to issue and suspend operating licenses would have significantly enlarged the agency's power. The agency already possessed authority under the Federal Food, Drug, and Cosmetic Act (FDCA) of 1938 to impose fines and seize any food product that it could show had been prepared in unsanitary conditions that might render it injurious to health. However, the power to impose fines and seize products was purely responsive. The agency could act only after a problem occurred. Moreover, existing regulations were very vague. In the late 1960s, when the agency had developed GMP regulations defining unsanitary conditions, industry groups had successfully advocated flexible norms that could be tailored to different sectors of the food industry and that would not impose what they considered excessive costs. As a result, the final regulations included general standards rather than specific rules. For example, the regulations required plants to maintain "adequate" lighting and ventilation, employ "effective" screening or other protection against animal and insect intrusion, provide "sufficient" space for equipment and materials storage, and keep production facilities in "good repair."[15]

The agency did possess very limited authority—which it had never invoked—to issue and suspend permits in emergency situations. If the agency discovered that a class of food had been contaminated in a particular locality and that the contaminated food posed a health risk to consumers, the FDCA authorized the agency to issue regulations establishing a temporary permit system to prohibit the sale of any food within the class that was manufactured, processed, or packed by any company within the locality that did not possess an FDA-issued permit. This emergency power allowed the agency to mandate specific safety rules as conditions for obtaining a permit and to respond quickly to any violation of those rules by suspending a company's permit immediately upon notice of the violation.[16]

In contrast to these existing powers to punish regulatory violations and issue permits in the midst of an emergency, the agency's plans for a comprehensive licensing scheme for the canning industry would have enabled it take an industrywide preventive approach to food safety based on specific rules and backed by powerful sanctions. Such an expansion of the agency's permitting power would almost certainly have required new legislation.[17]

While the FDA was contemplating its response in the fall of 1971, the National Canners Association (NCA)—whose six hundred members packed 90 percent of the canned food produced in the United States—submitted a proposal to the agency that contained detailed GMP standards for processing low-acid canned foods drawn from guidelines developed by NCA laboratories and food industry scientists.[18] Under the proposal, individual processors who failed to comply with the standards would be subject to the FDA's emergency permitting powers. The proposal also recommended registration of all processors of low-acid canned foods with the FDA, training and certification of thermal processing equipment operators, making documentation of processing times and temperatures available for review by agency officials, coding of all containers to improve traceability, and maintaining production records.[19]

The NCA feared that contamination of a few leading brands would taint the reputation of the entire industry and undermine consumer confidence in canned foods. It believed that new government regulations would reassure the public and keep wayward members of the industry in line. The NCA proposal—based on guidelines developed by the industry and enforcement methods already available to government regulators—was also designed to preempt any attempt by the FDA to seek more extensive powers from Congress through new legislation. "The industry had no interest in . . . providing Congress with an opportunity to fashion new and extensive regulatory authority," recalls Edward Dunkelberger, a legal adviser to the NCA in the early 1970s. Moreover, the canners believed that a formal licensing scheme would have been unnecessarily burdensome. In addition, explains Dunkelberger, legislation would have been slower than administrative rule making in addressing the problem and would have kept the issue of canned food contamination in the news.[20]

The FDA welcomed the NCA's proposal. Industry experts "knew infinitely more about canning than the FDA did," explains Peter Barton Hutt, the agency's chief counsel at the time. "Before the vichyssoise outbreak, they had developed low-acid food Good Manufacturing Practices; they had done all of the technical groundwork. For FDA to duplicate that would have taken years and hiring of people—but I don't know if we ever could have duplicated it." The NCA's work on food safety standards for canning dated back to botulism outbreaks in 1919 and 1920 that were linked to commercially canned ripe olives. In response, a number of industry associations, including the NCA, had funded research that advanced understanding of *C. botulinum* in canned goods and produced time-temperature recommendations for processing that greatly reduced the risk of contamination.[21]

Upon receiving the NCA's proposal, the FDA published it in the *Federal Register* for public comment. By 1974, the agency issued final regulations governing low-acid canned food production that adopted the NCA's approach. The regulations incorporated the NCA's proposed industry-specific GMPs and relied on the agency's existing emergency permitting powers for enforcement.[22]

The low-acid canned food regulations incorporated HACCP principles. They required plant managers to develop, implement, and document regular monitoring of critical control points within the production process using specified time and temperature limits, metrics, and recording equipment. The FDA turned to Pillsbury—where Bauman was instituting the first companywide HACCP program—to train agency inspectors in how to oversee the implementation of HACCP principles in food plants. Pillsbury provided a three-week course that included lectures and fieldwork evaluating canning plant operations. Overseeing HACCP required inspectors not only to examine production lines, which provided merely a snapshot at the time of the visit, but also to review production records to get a broader view of plant operations and food safety performance over time.[23]

The implementation of HACCP at Pillsbury and among low-acid canned food producers is generally considered successful. Looking back on his experience at Pillsbury, Bauman boasted that "from 1971 when we first implemented HACCP totally in the Corporation until I left in 1988, Pillsbury . . . did not have a serious recall." Joseph P. Hile, executive director of regional operations at the FDA in the early 1970s, asserted that the agency's low-acid canned food HACCP regulations motivated companies to improve their food safety systems. "Some firms had no real quality control program until after FDA made its HACCP inspection and identified the crucial needs." The FDA reported steadily increasing rates of regulatory compliance among low-acid canned food plants from 1973 to 1979. A 2003 Institute of Medicine report on the low-acid canned food regulations proclaimed, "Botulism from commercially canned food has been virtually eliminated since the implementation of these regulations, although occasional outbreaks do occur." A 2012 history of food safety regulation in a volume published by the Food and Drug Law Institute declared triumphantly that the regulations "probably enhanced food safety in the United States more than any other single past FDA action."[24]

One should be careful, however, not to overstate the impact of the low-acid canned food regulations. The industry's response to the earlier outbreaks of botulism in caned ripe olives had laid much of the groundwork. The 1974

regulations derived from NCA processing standards and equipment specifications first published in 1930 that were, by 1966, already in their tenth edition. Moreover, in the fifty years following the olive outbreaks and prior to
the 1974 regulations, the nation had experienced only four botulism-related
deaths linked to commercially canned foods. "These fatalities occurred over a
period during which consumers ate the contents of more than 775 billion containers of canned foods," according to NCA data. The historical significance
of the 1974 regulations lies not in their processing standards and equipment
specifications or in any reduction in historically low rates of foodborne illness but rather in their systematic approach to managing food safety through
monitoring, documentation, error reporting, and record review.[25]

The regulatory response to the Bon Vivant vichyssoise contamination
entailed a high degree of industry-government cooperation. The FDA's final
regulations differed in only minor respects from the NCA's initial proposal.
As the FDA's chief counsel Hutt explained, the agency depended heavily on
the industry's superior scientific and technical expertise and more extensive
practical experience. According to Hutt, by putting forward a well-developed
proposal, the industry "had done the hard work"—"we at the FDA were
deeply grateful."[26]

Collaboration between the NCA and the FDA was facilitated by the relationship between the NCA's chief counsel, Thomas Austern, and Hutt. Austern was a senior partner at the Washington, DC, law firm of Covington &
Burling and had represented the NCA since joining the firm in 1931, assum-
ing the position of chief counsel in 1942. Hutt had entered law practice at
Covington in 1960 and, except for his term as FDA chief counsel from 1971
to 1975, has remained at the firm. In a published tribute to Austern following
his death in 1984, Hutt recalled, "It was he who offered me a job at Covington & Burling, and who trained me in food and drug law." Dunkelberger,
also a partner at Covington, who assisted Austern in representing the NCA,
recalls "a lot of informal discussions back and forth between the agency and
the industry trying to work out how we could achieve something that would
really work." According to Dunkelberger, collaboration between the NCA
and the FDA on the low-acid canned food regulations came easily because
the Covington colleagues shared "the same background understanding of
administrative law."[27]

Adversarial Regulatory Enforcement

Despite the extensive collaboration between the FDA and the NCA in crafting
the low-acid canned food regulations, the FDA's handling of the Bon Vivant

case exacerbated long-standing industry mistrust of the agency. In a state-ment to Congress, Bon Vivant owner Andrew Paretti complained that the FDA was overzealous, heavy handed, and unfair in its enforcement efforts. He asserted that the agency's "unduly harsh and punitive actions" unneces-sarily destroyed a 108-year-old family business. Paretti described how, upon receiving a call from the FDA on July 1 about a death linked to its vichyssoise soup, the company immediately initiated a recall of all 6,444 cans bearing the same lot number, V-141. Using its shipping records, "calls to distributors and consignees enlisting their aid in the recall of the product from retail chan-nels were underway even before the FDA inspectors arrived at the company's plant." By the next day, following nationwide media coverage of the case, the company received a number of additional reports of illness allegedly caused by Bon Vivant vichyssoise, in response to which the company, without wait-ing to validate the reports, instituted a recall of all vichyssoise produced by the company. "This second recall covered all fifty states and approximately twelve countries and included twenty-three private label brands which Bon Vivant packed, even though no foreign account or private label ever received Code V-141." Subsequent investigation by the company determined that the contamination was limited to a single crate of 460 cans within the V-141 lot and that the additional reports of illness that led to the expanded recall were false in every case.[28]

On July 5, Bon Vivant turned over seventy-one improperly sealed cans— referred to in the industry as "leakers" and "swells"—that it had collected during the course of production since January to the NCA for testing to see whether any of them were contaminated with *C. botulinum*, with the aim of determining whether the problem extended beyond lot V-141. Seventy-one defective cans out of a total production of 1.5 million cans of soup repre-sented a defect rate of .005% (one out of twenty thousand), which was well below the good manufacturing practices industry standard of .5% (one out of two hundred). On the advice of NCA's legal counsel, the company authorized the NCA to turn over a representative sample of the cans to the FDA for test-ing. NCA laboratory results established that the leakers were free from any kind of contamination and did not constitute a health hazard.

On July 6, the FDA demanded a total recall of all Bon Vivant products. The agency asserted that it had discovered a "high incidence" of defective Bon Vivant cans, raising "serious question" as to the safety of all Bon Vivant products. Despite repeated requests, the FDA did not give Bon Vivant evi-dence or statistics upon which this allegation was based, according to Paretti's account. "We assume that FDA had reference to the 71 'leakers' voluntarily turned over by Bon Vivant on July 5 and to other leakers or swells picked up at random by FDA employees in outlets around the country. But NCA's laboratory analyses verified that the 71 'leakers' presented no health hazard; and no determinative conclusion can be drawn from any leakers or swells picked up at random in the field," because, as pointed out by a USDA official in congressional hearings on the issue, "leakers and swellers often develop in anyone's product during the distribution process." The FDA insisted that if Bon Vivant did not agree to a "voluntary" recall, the agency would "move at once to institute nationwide multiple seizures of all Bon Vivant–packed products, to enlist the aid of local and state officials to embargo the sale of Bon Vivant products, and to issue an immediate press release stating that the company had refused to cooperate with the FDA."

"From this moment we were the target of unremitting press and media coverage—much of it initiated by the FDA or its regional representatives—unprecedented in its intensity, generally biased against our company, and often, it seemed to me, gratuitously cruel," lamented Paretti. He denounced the "repeated, highly partisan, and often ugly charges made by FDA against us: that our recall was a failure; that Bon Vivant obstructed FDA's investigation; that our manufacturing procedures had deteriorated, resulting in widespread sanitary violations; that our records were worthless; and that our entire product line was unfit for consumption. These charges appeared almost daily in the press, sometimes attributed to official FDA sources, sometimes to unidentified agency spokesmen." As a preface to his detailed response to these allegations, Paretti noted: "On several occasions, [FDA commissioner] Dr. Edwards and FDA's public information officer apologized to us for these stories and on at least two occasions stated that the quoted FDA official had not been authorized to make the statement. Yet no such statement was publicly disavowed by FDA." Paretti protested that the company's recall efforts had promptly removed all cans from the V-141 lot; that the company had opened up its plant and all of its records to extensive FDA investigation; that missing company records were, at least in part, due to the haphazard, uncoordinated, and frenzied manner in which FDA inspectors rifled through and seized files; that the company had no history of undercooking, contamination problems, or sanitary violations; and that neither the FDA nor anyone else had produced any evidence that the contamination problem extended beyond one crate within the V-141 lot.

Having agreed to recall all its products, Bon Vivant notified thousands of retail outlets to remove its products from store shelves and return them to the company or hold them in warehouses and storage areas. By July 13, the company's resources were exhausted. The FDA demanded that the company consolidate the recalled products in central warehouses around the country.

When Paretti "pleaded" the company's "physical inability to do so without assistance and implored the FDA for aid," the agency's associate commissioner for compliance responded simply, "FDA's responsibility is to see to it that Bon Vivant carries out its responsibility." Throughout the entire ordeal, recalls Paretti, "Bon Vivant's total workforce never exceeded 40 persons. Executive management of the company consisted solely of my wife and myself. We all had been working without relief and virtually without sleep since July 1. The company's cash flow had evaporated with the first public announcement of the recall and the recall itself had consumed our entire fund of cash on hand." On July 27, Bon Vivant filed for bankruptcy. After three years of subsequent litigation, the company's efforts to regain possession of its seized products failed, and $600,000 worth of canned food in 1.4 million containers was crushed by bulldozers and buried in a New Jersey dump.[29]

The FDA's handling of the Bon Vivant case frightened food manufacturers. "Responsible businessmen will recognize a threat to their own reputations by the manner in which the Bon Vivant situation was so badly handled," wrote John Lewis, executive vice president of the National Small Business Association, in a letter sent to eighteen thousand people to launch an effort to raise half a million dollars to "Bring Back Bon Vivant." An anonymous industry source was quoted in the *Washington Post* denouncing the FDA's insistence on a total recall of all Bon Vivant products as "the god-damnedest case of overkill I have ever seen in my life." When Commissioner Edwards indicated that the agency was considering criminal prosecution, the NCA dropped its legal representation of Paretti, according to one press account because "criminal suits were not its cup of tea."[30]

In addition to criticism of its handling of the Bon Vivant case, the FDA was accused of jumping the gun when its warning about Stokely–Van Camp beans turned out to be a false alarm. The FDA had issued the warning and requested that the company conduct a recall on the basis of "presumptive evidence." But additional testing revealed that antibiotics in the bloodstream of the eight-year-old Florida boy who fell ill after eating the beans were misinterpreted as evidence that botulin toxin was present. David McVey, senior vice president of Stokely–Van Camp, the nation's third-largest canner, complained that the FDA's overzealousness had cost the company millions of dollars and damaged the company's reputation. "When you defame a product label to 200 million people watching television and reading newspapers it takes a long time to rebuild it."[31]

The FDA's aggressive response to the Bon Vivant and Stokely–Van Camp cases was almost certainly a reaction to sustained criticism from consumer advocates that the agency was afraid of powerful food and drug companies and their trade associations. In a scathing 1970 critique of the agency, a Ralph Nader Study Group report alleged that "the FDA moves cautiously against major components of the food industry because it is much smaller and weaker than they are." The report charged that FDA officials lived in constant (and unfounded) fear that industry would retaliate against enforcement actions by prevailing upon the agency's Congressional overseers to cut its budget. Beyond political cowardice, the report charged that "the FDA relies on industry science, believes in industry honesty, and does not consult consumers in making its decisions. The FDA and industry officials build strong personal friendships. Naturally, the FDA has become a defender of industry power rather than a counterbalance to it. As the ineffectiveness of the FDA becomes more widely known, consumer confidence in the food supply dwindles. It would be in the interest of the consumer, the agency, the industry, and the nation if the FDA stopped apologizing for its industry friends and began to enforce the law."[32]

The Nader report specifically challenged newly appointed FDA commissioner Charles Edwards to get tough on the food industry. The report quoted the industry press's praise of Edwards as "a management-oriented former surgeon who will try to turn the FDA into a more efficient agency that handles its business more rapidly. His regime is expected to de-emphasize the 'cop' aspect and stress a businesslike organizational approach to handling regulatory and product clearance problems." The Nader report countered that "if the FDA is going to conduct an effective enforcement program, its officials, beginning with the Commissioner, must eliminate the notion that police activities cannot be done with speed and efficiency. It must earn a reputation as a businesslike, rapidly moving 'cop.'" Thus prodded into taking a more aggressive approach to enforcement by consumer advocates and their congressional allies, when public fears of widespread *C. botulinum* contamination in canned foods arose in the summer of 1971, the agency moved decisively against Bon Vivant and Stokely–Van Camp.[33]

The swiftness and comprehensiveness of the FDA's response to the Bon Vivant case was also driven by the agency's desire to calm public fear. In the days following the FDA's initial warning, physicians and health authorities received hysterical calls from people who had recently consumed Bon Vivant products in what local newspapers characterized as an atmosphere of "shock" and "panic." The *Washington Post* reported that "a family of four entered a Philadelphia hospital for observation and a Greenwich man checked into St. Vincent's hospital in New York, complaining of food poisoning.... A couple on Coney Island was rushed to the hospital with the telltale symptoms, but it turned out they had become ill from eating home canned antipasto."

Subsequent FDA analysis of Bon Vivant canned products in late July found nontoxic bacteria in additional lots of vichyssoise and one lot of black beans, which indicated undercooking during production. Although the FDA only found *C. botulinum* contamination in five cans from lot V-141, the agency explained that it considered these additional lots "as suspect as V-141," because "where these bacteria survive . . . botulinum spores can also live."[34]

Competing Narratives

The theory of regulatory capture claims that powerful industries exert overwhelming influence on regulators to the detriment of the public interest. According to the theory, industry promotes regulations that provide benefits such as tax advantages and limits on competition. Alternatively, industry may engage in "corrosive capture" by restricting the scope or weakening enforcement of regulations. Capture theory suggests that industry exerts influence through rewards (e.g., promising government officials lucrative jobs in industry) or punishments (e.g., lobbying members of Congress to reduce agency budgets). Industry also influences regulators through "information capture" by communicating with officials outside of the formal rule-making process and submitting large numbers of comments by industry-funded experts during the formal rule-making process. Mounting well-financed legal challenges to agency rules after the rule-making process is another means of capture. Sometimes, industry exerts its influence using subtler methods, such as inducing regulators to identify with industry members and their interests, thereby shaping regulators' conception of the public interest to favor industry-friendly policies, a process called "cultural capture." Capture theorists posit that regulators are especially vulnerable to cultural capture when they share a group identity—especially a profession—with industry representatives or participate in the same social networks, or when they believe that industry representatives have a superior status. Capture theorists also assert that regulators are more vulnerable to capture when a high level of complexity in the activity being regulated renders regulators dependent on industry expertise.[35]

The regulatory response to the Bon Vivant case confirmed consumer advocates' belief that the food industry had captured the FDA. An earlier 1970 Nader report had complained that "the FDA demonstrates its deference toward industry by basing important regulatory decisions on the discussions held at agency meetings with private industry. . . . So little serious and original scientific activity is undertaken by the FDA that it is virtually dependent on the research work of industry." In developing regulations for low-acid canned foods, the agency adopted the NCA's proposal recommending industry-developed standards and existing enforcement powers, which the NCA promoted in order to preempt the more ambitious comprehensive licensing scheme originally contemplated by the FDA.[36]

The Nader report had criticized the close ties between industry representatives and agency officials and the revolving door between industry jobs and government positions. NCA chief counsel Thomas Austern had served as a professional mentor and personal friend of FDA chief counsel Peter Barton Hutt at Covington & Burling, where Hutt had represented food companies and trade associations before working at the FDA, and where he returned after four years at the agency. FDA director of the Bureau of Foods Virgil Wodicka, who held a PhD in food science and technology, provided in-house agency expertise on food processing in developing the low-acid canned food regulations. Before joining the FDA in 1970, he had worked at a series of major canned food companies, and he returned to industry after leaving the agency in 1974.[37]

The Nader report had also charged that the agency's enforcement practices favored big companies and picked on small, easy targets to portray itself as defending consumers. "The FDA combines an implicit belief in the honesty of big food interests and a caution about engaging in big fights with a vigorous and unrelenting pursuit of relatively minor hazards which use up large portions of its resources." FDA officials praised industry leader Campbell Soup for its "responsible action" in carrying out a limited recall of specific lots of its chicken and vegetable soups as it was seizing the much smaller Bon Vivant's entire product line. Nader himself stated in congressional testimony: "I wonder what the Food and Drug Administration would have done if Bon Vivant were the subsidiary of General Foods or General Mills. Would it have behaved in the same way?" In light of the relatively small risk to public health from commercially canned foods—only four deaths in fifty years—the magnitude of the agency's response appeared disproportionate to many, and it taxed agency inspection resources. In congressional hearings, FDA commissioner Edwards admitted that "in the Bon Vivant case, the 125 man-years consumed by this emergency effort to date could have been used to inspect 2,300 food plants. This means that in the fiscal year, FDA will probably not inspect 2,300 plants which might otherwise have been investigated and their products sampled and analyzed."[38]

The FDA's enforcement strategy in the Bon Vivant case simultaneously confirmed industry executives' fear of big government. Industry executives, along with conservative, libertarian, and neoliberal critics of the modern administrative state, assert that agency officials are prone to exercise their power in ways that needlessly undermine the profitability of socially valuable business enterprises. Some critics attribute a tendency towards excessively aggressive regulation to agency officials' ill-informed conceptions of the public interest, inclinations to advance the agency's interests, and desires for career advancement. In contrast to capture theory, according to this perspective, industry expertise enhances the quality of agency policy making by providing technical knowledge and real-world experience, and industry lawyers are necessary to limit the excesses of agency enforcement through consultation, negotiation, lobbying, and litigation.[39]

Concerns about big government had fueled criticism of the FDA in the decade before the Bon Vivant case. For example, in 1965, the Senate Subcommittee on Administrative Practice and Procedure held extensive hearings airing allegations that the FDA regularly employed illegal tactics to enforce food-labeling laws to stop what the agency considered phony health claims. Business owners and their attorneys told stories of entrapment, undercover sting operations, hidden recording devices, wiretapping, mail tampering, and intimidating interrogation tactics. Former Georgia governor Ellis Arnall, who in private practice represented food companies, denounced FDA officials as "self-righteous, overzealous crusaders going around entrapping and trying to snoop on the conversations of American citizens," and he compared the agency's "illegal, unconstitutional police state tactics" to those of the Gestapo, the Ku Klux Klan, and Big Brother. Against this backdrop, the FDA's pressure on Bon Vivant to conduct a nationwide recall of its entire product line following a single, isolated incident, thereby driving the company into bankruptcy, garnered sympathy for Bon Vivant and made industry members very wary of any expansion of the FDA's enforcement power.[40]

When it came to the agency's low-acid canned food regulations, it seemed entirely appropriate to those concerned about big government that the FDA should adopt food safety standards developed by industry experts. Fear of big government accounts for disagreement between the NCA and the FDA concerning enforcement of the regulations. Austern argued that the existing GMP regulations for canned foods were merely interpretive guidelines that provided factors that the agency and courts could weigh in making determinations of adulteration under the FDCA. However, the agency insisted that the GMPs were binding requirements, the violation of which constituted a punishable offense. Austern and other industry representatives lobbied for a number of procedural protections that would limit the FDA's application of its emergency permitting power, and the agency eventually adopted some of them.[41]

For agency officials, the Bon Vivant case was an example of how Congress frequently imposes ambitious mandates on regulatory agencies but fails to provide sufficient resources to fulfill them. Agency administrators must deploy limited financial and human resources strategically, find ways to reduce friction with and enlist the cooperation of regulated entities, and settle for only partial achievement of their goals. From this point of view, criticism that the agency is not meeting its statutory obligations can seem unrealistic and unfair. Moreover, agencies must often act on the basis of incomplete information. Consequently, their responses to potential threats are frequently subject, after the fact, to second-guessing.[42]

The FDA had long suffered attacks on its performance based on what it perceived to be unrealistic expectations. According to a 1965 agency staff report to the commissioner, "the FDA has been under continuous investigation by the Congress for almost a decade, and this continuous and contemporaneous surveillance, this Congressional 'oversight' of the FDA goes on, by and large, with little pretense to legislative purpose." According to another account, "between 1955 and 1970, fourteen major studies of the FDA were conducted by citizens' committees, department task forces, and commissioner-appointed FDA evaluation groups. Between 1963 and 1968, the food and drug commissioner or his selected representative was required to appear on the average of once every three weeks before one of sixteen different congressional committees (excluding appropriations committees) investigating the FDA's involvement in thirty-seven different problem areas. All of the major studies and nearly all of the Congressional investigations focused on one or more of the FDA's failures or weaknesses."[43]

The FDA's many critics made a great deal of the fact that the agency had not inspected the Bon Vivant plant for four years before the vichyssoise botulism incident, but they never mentioned the agency's resource constraints. At that time, the agency counted on a force of only 250 food inspectors to cover sixty thousand food establishments under its jurisdiction. Moreover, allegations that the FDA's reliance on industry's scientific expertise is evidence of capture rang hollow to agency officials seeking to regulate complex industrial activity with limited in-house expertise. Nor did it seem fair to take the agency to task for overreacting in its efforts to protect the public health in the face of growing public concern, potentially widespread harm, and incomplete information. Had there been more widespread contamination in Bon Vivant soups that caused additional illnesses, there would surely have followed accusations of falling down on the job. Hindsight is 20/20, and erring on the side of caution in the interest of the public's health seemed preferable to erring on the side of food industry profits. As FDA commissioner Edwards explained, "In dealing with life or death problems like botulism, there are times when the public interest demands action before the scientific case is complete. The decision always must be made in favor of consumer protection. Such decisions are always difficult, both for government and for the industry."[44]

FDA officials bridle at accusations that the agency is simultaneously captured by industry and overzealous in enforcing regulations. According to Hutt, adaptation of the NCA's proposal for regulating canned food firms was a "solution that would reduce our workload at FDA and adopt industry standards, which, after all, they say they had been living with during that time period. . . . I viewed that as a win-win situation." He points out that, as FDA chief counsel, he rejected Austern's insistence on behalf of the NCA that the existing GMPs were merely nonbinding guidance, and he defended a broad interpretation of the agency's emergency permitting powers to enforce them. "The enforcement changes that Austern requested were reasonable and did not change the regulations stating that the GMPs have the force and effect of law and are therefore fully enforceable in the courts." In his role as chief counsel, Hutt insists that he "was representing the FDA. This idea of industry capture is the biggest bunch of nonsense I've ever heard in my life." Hutt also rejects allegations of heavy-handedness. According his account, he favored targeted use of the agency's emergency permitting powers precisely to avoid repeating the type of nationwide seizure in the Bon Vivant case. "I wanted to set up something under which we would never do that again," he recalls.[45]

Consumer advocates, industry executives, and FDA officials each relied on distinct narratives in making sense of the Bon Vivant case. Consumer advocates relied on a capture narrative; industry executives relied on a big government narrative, and FDA officials relied on an inadequate resources narrative. Each of these narratives predated the Bon Vivant case. Each group emphasized aspects of its experience that fit its particular narrative, and each group's resulting interpretation of events reinforced that narrative. It is likely that each group's narrative was further reinforced by interactions among colleagues who shared the narrative—social activists worked together on investigations, industry executives met at trade association gatherings, and FDA officials participated in agency meetings. Each group could point to sufficient facts to support competing plausible narratives.[46]

These competing narratives fueled disagreement throughout the 1970s over extending HACCP regulations beyond low-acid canned foods. Consumer advocates and their allies in the Senate repeatedly introduced "food surveillance" bills that would have obligated all food processors to develop and implement HACCP plans, referred to as "safety assurance procedures." The bills instructed the FDA to conduct and publish an annual "safety assurance assessment" that would analyze all existing and potential risks of food adulteration, including bacterial contamination, known to the agency. If the agency determined that any food was being processed in a way that presented an unreasonable risk of adulteration and that the existing safety assurance procedures were not adequate to protect against the risk, the bills required the agency to promulgate mandatory safety assurance standards for processors of that food. The bills also mandated registration of all food processors and annual FDA inspection of all processing facilities, and they included new FDA powers to inspect company records, detain product shipments, and institute a uniform coding system on packaged foods that would facilitate tracing and product recalls. In addition to existing criminal penalties, seizures, and injunctions, the bills authorized civil fines of up to $10,000 per day for failure to follow safety assurance procedures. At Senate hearings in 1975, representatives from the Consumers Union and Ralph Nader's Health Research Group enthusiastically endorsed these proposals.[47]

FDA commissioner Alexander Schmidt, who also testified, voiced qualified support. Although he welcomed the prospect of new enforcement powers, he opposed requirements that the FDA publish annual safety assurance assessments and conduct annual inspections of all food processors. Schmidt argued that these obligations would place too great a burden on agency resources. He also requested that the registration mandate be postponed, citing budgetary constraints.[48]

Industry representatives backed a competing bill that proposed voluntary adoption of company-designed safety assurance procedures. They argued that agency access to company records should be limited to investigations involving violations that posed significant health risks. They feared that broad agency authority would be used to conduct fishing expeditions for minor infractions that affected only the aesthetic quality of products. (They may well have had in mind the FDA's use of defective cans that did not contain harmful toxins as evidence in the case against Bon Vivant.) They also voiced concern that agency officials who later took positions in industry might reveal secret ingredients and recipes to competitors. Industry representatives advocated for a requirement that the agency show good cause to obtain access to company records or to administratively detain product shipments. They supported product coding but opposed the imposition of a uniform system to replace existing company or industry specific systems.[49]

Two food surveillance bills passed the Senate in 1974 and 1976, but both died in the House of Representatives, where they were assigned to a subcommittee on health and the environment chaired by Paul Rogers, a pro-business Democrat from Florida who considered the proposed regulations too costly. "The standard tactic in those days was to let things go through the far more liberal Senate knowing that nothing would happen in the House," recalls Hutt. "So the fact that the Senate passed it was meaningless, and everybody knew it at the time. The industry didn't even waste their time opposing it in the Senate because they knew it was dead on arrival in the House."[50]

Despite the sustained efforts of consumer advocates, industry resistance and agency hesitance to expanding HACCP regulations persisted for two decades after Congress's rejection of food surveillance bills. It would take a devastating foodborne illness outbreak and subsequent civil litigation to extend HACCP to the beef and poultry industries. And all along, variations of the narratives of capture, big government, and inadequate resources helped to shape the shifting alliances and rivalries that determined the direction and pace of food safety reform.

Building a Better Burger:
How Media Coverage and Civil Litigation
Facilitate Policy Change

The defeat of food surveillance legislation in the 1970s did not discourage a growing number of experts in industry, government, and academia from advocating HACCP in the 1980s and 1990s as a means of modernizing what they viewed as an outmoded, inefficient, and overtaxed food safety system. Many sectors of the food industry relied on infrequent visual inspections by government officials to verify compliance with loosely defined qualitative sanitary standards. These inspections, although they revealed the presence of filth, could not detect microbial pathogens, which might be abundant in foods and production facilities that appeared to be perfectly clean.

By contrast, HACCP aims to directly control the risk of microbial contamination at key points throughout the entire chain of production using quantitative critical limits, ongoing monitoring, detailed documentation, and specific plans for corrective action. Advocates of HACCP argued that it offers a rigorous, scientific approach to food safety that makes both industry and government more accountable. Advocates also promoted HACCP as a way for government agencies to stretch their limited resources in the face of expanding legislative mandates and increasing industrial production. HACCP shifts primary responsibility for monitoring food safety risks to companies and enables government inspectors to perform the less burdensome task of verifying implementation, which entails reviewing plant records and conducting cursory inspections. Finally, advocates of HACCP asserted that it offers companies greater flexibility and efficiency in managing food safety. HACCP replaces uniform government regulations that are difficult to change with company plans that managers can tailor to their operations and easily revise in light of frequent feedback. HACCP advocates played an especially prominent role in efforts to reform meat and poultry inspection.

This chapter tells the story of how a dramatic foodborne illness outbreak and subsequent pressure from media coverage and civil litigation shook up the alignment of political interests, economic incentives, and administrative constraints that, for two decades, had thwarted attempts to expand HACCP regulations. It explains how the combination of media coverage and civil litigation influenced cultural assumptions about food safety in ways that promoted cooperation between consumer advocates, industry executives, and government officials and, thereby, enabled policy reform. The evolution of HACCP depicted in this and the previous chapter reveals a pattern of long periods of policy stability punctuated by moments of policy reform.

A Brief History of Beef and Poultry Inspection

Concern about the inadequacy of visual inspection to control microbial contamination dates back to the inception of the federal meat inspection system. Government meat inspection, beginning in the 1880s, relied on organoleptic (sensory) inspection of animals and slaughtered carcasses to detect diseased animals or decayed meat—a method popularly referred to as "poke and sniff." In 1891, as a result of concerns among European nations about the wholesomeness of American beef and pork, Congress mandated USDA pre-slaughter inspection of animals whose meat was intended for interstate commerce or export. In 1906, Congress passed the landmark Federal Meat Inspection Act, which required USDA inspection and approval of slaughtered carcasses, slaughterhouses, and meat-processing plants as a condition of interstate sale of meat. Under these laws, USDA inspectors organoleptically examined live animals and carcasses for signs of illness and verified compliance with sanitary guidelines regarding facility design, equipment cleaning, employee health, and hand washing.[1]

The USDA's chief meat inspector, A. D. Melvin, boasted at the time that "meat-inspection has more or less kept abreast of increasing knowledge, and . . . the present law is as advanced a measure as the medical profession and sanitarians demand, and is, perhaps, the most stringent and far-reaching of existing laws on the subject." However, not everyone shared this rosy assessment. Harvard Medical School professor Milton J. Rosenau, who also served for many years as a US health service officer, observed in the 1913 edition of his book *Preventive Medicine and Hygiene*—for decades a leading text on infectious disease and public health—that "the most serious infections and poisons in meat . . . do not, as a rule, affect its appearance, odor, or taste, or do so so slightly as to readily pass unnoticed" by meat inspectors. The presence of harmful microorganisms, he advised, "may only be detected by bacteriological examination," and he concluded that "meat inspection affords but little safeguard against the meat poisoning group of bacteria" such as *Salmonella* and *C. botulinum*.[2]

In the following decades, knowledge concerning the microbiology of food safety increased steadily. Studies in the 1940s expressed concern about the presence of *E. coli* in food as an indication of fecal contamination that posed a threat to human health. The development in the 1930s of laboratory techniques for identifying different strains of bacteria allowed scientists by 1960 to isolate 179 different *Salmonella* bacteria types from clinical patients suffering from foodborne illness and to trace them back to a variety of sources. In meat and poultry production, these included contaminated feed, infected animal herds and flocks, holding pens, slaughterhouses, fecal contamination of meat and poultry during processing, and workers.[3]

In 1957, Congress passed the Poultry Products Inspection Act, which extended USDA organoleptic carcass inspection and sanitary standards to poultry production. At the time of the Meat Inspection Act of 1906, most poultry were slaughtered on private farms for personal use or in butcher shops for local sale, so poultry production was not included in the act, which covered only meat sold in interstate commerce. By the 1950s, industrial production of ready-to-cook poultry for a national market led to USDA regulation of poultry slaughter and processing.[4]

Government oversight bodies, consumer advocacy groups, and academic researchers criticized the USDA's inspection system throughout the 1960s and early 1970s for failing to address high rates of bacterial contamination in meat and poultry. Government and academic studies during this period consistently found high rates of *Salmonella* contamination among USDA-inspected and USDA-approved poultry, ranging from 17 percent to 50 percent of samples taken from retail markets. Multiple reports by the General Accounting Office and the Office of the Inspector General found unsanitary conditions in many plants operating under USDA inspection, and the reports chronicled the agency's ineffectiveness in making companies correct deficiencies. A 1969 report by the National Academy of Sciences found that "many slaughtering procedures provide very effective means of spreading contamination from infected to clean carcasses." A 1971 report by a Ralph Nader study group described how high-speed evisceration often spilled fecal matter onto chicken carcasses that were then soaked with thousands of other carcasses in a large tub of cold water known as a chiller—a recipe for what a 1987 *60 Minutes* exposé later referred to as "fecal soup." The Nader report told of a poultry inspector who witnessed plant employees washing their hands at a water trough into which regularly fell diseased and contaminated chicken parts. Similar contamination occurred in beef plants during slaughter, evisceration, and processing. The report echoed Rosenau's doubts fifty years earlier about the efficacy of a federal meat inspection system that relied heavily on organoleptic inspection of carcasses: "The plant inspector is primarily concerned with bruises, tumors, fecal contamination, enlarged livers, stray feathers—defects which he can see, touch, or smell. But of far greater potential danger to the consumer's health are the hidden contaminants: bacteria like salmonella."[5]

The inadequacy of USDA inspection was exacerbated by a radical expansion of the agency's legislative mandate. In 1967, Congress passed the Wholesome Meat Act and in 1968 the Wholesome Poultry Act, which expanded USDA inspection beyond meat and poultry sold in interstate commerce to include the substantial production of meat and poultry produced and sold within the same state, which had previously fallen under the jurisdiction of state governments and was, in some places, entirely unregulated. These two acts required states to implement inspection regimes at least as rigorous as the USDA's or turn over inspection to the USDA, which many states did. The acts also extended USDA authority over associated industries, including renderers, animal feed manufacturers, freezer storage companies, transporters, and retail sellers. In 1966, the USDA inspected 1,896 plants. By 1976, that number rose to 7,093.[6]

Agency resources were further stretched by changes in meat and poultry production. Beef and poultry production increased in the 1950s, 1960s, and early 1970s. In addition, a growing percentage of production was processed into convenience foods like frozen dinners and ready-to-eat products like sliced meats. Whereas cutting and boning carcasses and producing sausages, ham, and bacon were typically an extension of slaughtering operations and could be inspected by the same personnel, these newer, more complex forms of processing were generally carried out in separate facilities, often by different companies. Processing inspection increasingly required individuals with training in food technology and microbiology, in contrast to carcass inspection, which required expertise in veterinary medicine. Moreover, the need for carcass inspection decreased as improvements in the delivery of health care to farm animals virtually eradicated many animal diseases, and better border controls prevented the importation of diseased animals. Nevertheless, the agency was bound by statute to provide carcass-by-carcass inspection, which required maintaining a large staff of veterinarians. This allocation of resources precluded hiring more food technologists and microbiologists to oversee processing and to conduct laboratory testing of samples for harmful pathogens.[7]

In the 1970s and 1980s, the USDA initiated two types of reforms. First, to address high rates of microbial contamination in meat and poultry, the agency developed new food safety standards. It specified process controls to reduce cross contamination and set microbiological criteria for testing food samples to detect contamination when it occurred. Second, to allocate its limited resources more efficiently and effectively, the agency experimented with different inspection regimes. The agency initially interpreted its mandate under the Meat Inspection Act of 1906 to require the continuous presence of a government inspector in slaughter and processing plants during all hours of operation. In the early 1970s, the agency instituted a "patrol" system by which one inspector visited multiple processing plants in a day, and plants satisfied the requirement of continuous inspection so long as an inspector visited each day. Beginning in the late 1970s, the agency piloted voluntary programs that shifted many inspection tasks to company quality control systems approved by the agency and used government inspectors to verify implementation through daily review of production records and plant observations. In 1986, Congress temporarily eliminated the long-standing daily inspection requirement and granted the agency discretion over the frequency of inspection. Pursuant to this new authority, the agency experimented with inspecting companies with reliable quality control programs and good compliance records less often. The idea behind these so-called streamlined inspection systems programs was to encourage companies to shoulder more front-line food safety responsibility in exchange for a reduced regulatory burden.[8]

Advocating HACCP in Beef and Poultry Production

Beginning in the mid-1980s, a chorus of experts began to promote HACCP as essential to successful implementation of these reforms. In 1983, the USDA's Food Safety Inspection Service (FSIS) asked the National Academy of Sciences to review the federal meat and poultry inspection system and offer recommendations for improvement. The resulting report, *Meat and Poultry Inspection: The Scientific Basis of the Nation's Program*, published in 1985, urged the FSIS "to move as vigorously as possible in the application of the HACCP concept to each and every step in plant operations, in all types of enterprises involved in the production, processing, and storage of meat and poultry products." According to the report, HACCP could reduce the drain of daily plant inspection on the agency's resources: "Continuous inspection is not needed to ensure food safety in meat and poultry processing plants in which hazards and critical control points have been identified and monitored by qualified staff." Subsequent reports by the National Academy of Sciences on poultry inspection in 1987 and cattle inspection in 1990, as well as six General Accounting Office reports between 1992 and 1994, echoed and further elaborated this advice to employ HACCP to implement more rigorous food safety standards, develop microbiological criteria for testing, and shift more responsibility for day-to-day food safety oversight to plant managers.[9]

The expertise behind these reports developed out of experience within industry during the 1970s and 1980s applying HACCP to various aspects of food production. A notable pioneer was Dave Theno. After graduating from the University of Illinois in 1977 with advanced degrees in animal sciences and food microbiology, Theno worked for a variety of leading meat and poultry processors—including Eckrich, Armour Foods, and Foster Farms—where he was tasked with improving quality assurance and food safety systems. "I worked as a field guy moving technologies and applications out of the bench world into plants," he recalled. "I've always been a process control guy—I try to prevent things and try to figure out what to do with them when they show up at your door." He decided to adapt Bauman's HACCP system to raw meat production at Armour in the late 1970s and early 1980s and then to raw poultry production at Foster Farms in the mid-1980s, around the same time *60 Minutes* aired its "fecal soup" exposé of cross contamination in chillers and high rates of *Salmonella* in USDA-inspected poultry. Initially, he encountered skepticism from other food safety experts who argued that HACCP could not be applied to raw meat and poultry production, because, unlike canned food processing, they lacked a "kill step," such as cooking, which would eliminate pathogens. Undeterred, Theno insisted that "process control is valid for anything. And so, we applied HACCP-based principles. . . . Although we couldn't eliminate pathogens in raw chicken, we found we could get *Salmonella* down to where it was running one or two percent coming out of the chiller," compared to the industry average of 35 percent. Theno explained that he adapted HACCP by "redefining the end game" from "zero pathogens" to achieving significant risk reduction, keeping in mind that "unless you cook fresh meat, it is going to carry some level of risk." In the late 1980s, Theno started his own consulting business, specializing in the design and implementation of HACCP systems. His work caught the attention of USDA officials, and they invited him in 1988 to join the newly formed National Advisory Committee on Microbiological Criteria for Foods (NACMCF), which was established to provide scientific advice and recommendations to the FSIS and the FDA regarding microbiological hazards in foods. Theno brought valuable practical experience to the NACMCF—composed of agency officials, industry experts, and academics—and he further developed his thinking about HACCP through interactions with fellow committee members.[10]

Government officials also developed expertise as they analyzed industry initiatives and academic studies. After completing a PhD in food science at the

University of Illinois in 1986, Catherine Adams went to work for the USDA. Within a short time, she was appointed special assistant to FSIS administrator Lester Crawford, and subsequently rose to the position of assistant administrator, the number-three position in the agency. Adams was a strong proponent of HACCP within the agency. She represented the agency at the Codex Alimentarius Commission (CAC), an international membership organization established by the United Nations in 1961 to set standards for food production and food safety, and she served on the NACMCF. In her work with the CAC, she participated in a committee that elaborated and formalized HACCP into a standard of seven core principles, which the NACMCF endorsed in a 1989 report and the CAC formally adopted in 1993. (The initial NASA-Natick-Pillsbury system had articulated three principles that Bauman subsequently expanded to five.) Adams viewed HACCP as a means of replacing an outmoded daily "floors, walls, and ceilings" routine of visual plant inspection with a more scientifically rigorous system.[11]

HACCP advocates encountered significant opposition from consumer advocates and FSIS inspectors, who viewed HACCP as one of a number of industry-backed efforts to replace daily plant inspection by government employees with a system of self-regulation that would leave foxes in charge of the chicken coop, the slaughterhouse, and the processing plant. The 1906 Meat Inspection Act mandate of carcass-by-carcass inspection meant that the majority of inspectors were trained in veterinary science. Adams remembers that, when she arrived at the agency, "there were very few food scientists or food technologists there." The inspectors viewed Adams, a food scientist, with great suspicion. "They had just gone to war over discretionary inspection," recalls Adams, "and then here, on the heels of that, we bring in HACCP. So it was adding insult to injury. They thought that this could mean a reduction-in-force initiative and that it would require a change in technical skills." Although Adams eventually succeeded in convincing a number of inspectors to join an agency working group on HACCP, many continued to believe that the solution to high rates of meat and poultry contamination was more, not less, organoleptic inspection by government employees.[12]

HACCP advocates also faced resistance from within the meat and poultry industries. Many company executives feared that the FSIS would use HACCP to impose unrealistic microbiological standards for meat and poultry production. Industry representatives voiced the widely held view that pathogens such as *Salmonella* were endemic to raw meat and poultry and that the current system of production relied on the only practicable kill step—adequate cooking by consumers. This view had been validated by a federal court opinion in *American Public Health Association v. Butz*. In 1971, the APHA sued the USDA, claiming that agency stamps on meat and poultry stating "US Passed and Inspected" or "US Inspected for Wholesomeness" were misleading, because the agency's organoleptic inspection methods could not verify that such products were free of harmful microbial pathogens. The association sought an injunction compelling the agency to affix labels on meat and poultry products warning consumers about the risk of microbial contamination and providing safe handling and cooking instructions. The court rejected the association's claim, citing the agency's contention that "the American consumer knows that raw meat and poultry are not sterile and, if handled improperly, perhaps could cause illness." "In other words," the court continued, "American housewives and cooks normally are not ignorant or stupid and their methods of preparing and cooking of food do not ordinarily result in salmonellosis."[13]

The FSIS held hearings around the country to provide information about HACCP and respond to industry concerns, but HACCP advocates made only moderate gains. Adams chalks up much of the opposition to resistance to change. Some firms already had what they considered adequate food safety controls, and others did not do much to control for microbial pathogens. Neither group welcomed the additional costs of compliance with a new government program.[14]

Even within the USDA, many officials shared the view that *Salmonella* contamination of raw meat and poultry was practically unavoidable, and the agency's strategy for addressing the problem placed a great deal of responsibility on safe handling and cooking by consumers. In the 1987 *60 Minutes* exposé, journalist Diane Sawyer confronted FSIS administrator Donald Houston with the results of an investigation finding that 58 percent of the chicken sampled from a retail supermarket tested positive for *Salmonella* contamination. The following exchange ensued:

SAWYER: . . . That surprise you?

DR. HOUSTON: No.

SAWYER: Why not?

DR. HOUSTON: Well, the average in the industry is 35%.

SAWYER: Is 58% dismissible?

DR. HOUSTON: No, it's not dismissible. But I'm saying that, when you look at an industry average of 35%, you're going to—that would not be surprising to me.

SAWYER: Can people die from it?

DR. HOUSTON: Some do. We have a very extensive public education program, consumer information program, on how to deal with food preparation.[15]

The efforts of experts to translate their advocacy of HACCP into industry reforms and government regulations would require a more widely shared sense
of urgency regarding routine contamination of raw meat and poultry.

Overcoming Resistance to HACCP Regulations

The 1993 outbreak caused by Jack in the Box hamburgers contaminated with
E. coli O157:H7 has been described as "the meat industry's 9/11." Like the vichyssoise incident twenty years earlier, the Jack in the Box outbreak shook up
the politics of food safety in ways that facilitated the widespread adoption of
HACCP within a major sector of the food industry. Awareness of the danger
of E. coli O157 in ground beef predated the Jack in the Box outbreak by ten
years.[16]

In 1982, McDonald's hamburgers contaminated with E. coli O157 had sickened forty-seven consumers in Oregon and Michigan. The nation's leading
fast-food chain played down the seriousness of the problem, and the outbreak generated little press coverage. The company's stock briefly lost value
and then quickly recovered. CDC researchers subsequently discovered that
E. coli O157 was causing sporadic cases of hemorrhagic colitis—characterized
by severe abdominal pain and bloody diarrhea—around the country. They
reported these results in the agency's Morbidity and Mortality Weekly Report.
Although E. coli O157 in ground beef worried a small group of food safety scientists and public health officials, it attracted little attention from the media
and, consequently, did not concern the general public or policy makers.[17]

The Jack in the Box outbreak a decade later had a much greater impact.
It struck more than five hundred victims, most of whom were children. In
the most serious cases, the infection's progression was especially gruesome:
bloody diarrhea, organ failure, strokes, and severe disability. Four children
died. The outbreak made headlines across the country and remained in the
news for years. It became a symbol for the US food safety system's shortcomings, and to this day, more than twenty-five years later, it still receives
mention in news stories on foodborne illness outbreaks. Congress convened
hearings. President Clinton called the parents of the children who had died
to express his sympathies and pledge that he would do whatever was in his
power to prevent a similar tragedy in the future. Food safety reform rose to
the top of the national domestic policy agenda. Jack in the Box—at the time
the fifth-largest hamburger chain in the nation—suffered a dramatic drop in
business, its parent company's stock plummeted, and supermarket sales of
hamburger meat in some stores declined by as much as 50 percent.[18]

The Jack in the Box outbreak weakened resistance to HACCP within the meat and poultry industries. Before the outbreak, leading industry executives and many government officials regularly insisted that bacterial contamination was an unavoidable risk of raw meat and poultry production and that proper handling and cooking by consumers was the most effective protection against illness. They argued that attempts to improve industry risk management and government oversight would be impractical, ineffective, or inefficient, and they favored a regulatory approach that placed primary responsibility for food safety on safe handling and cooking by consumers. FSIS administrator Russell Cross explained in a memorandum to Mike Espy, secretary of agriculture at the time of the outbreak, that "the presence of bacteria in raw meat, including *E. coli* O157:H7, although undesirable, is unavoidable, and not cause for condemnation of the product. Because warm-blooded animals naturally carry bacteria in their intestines, it is not uncommon to find bacteria in raw meat." President of the American Meat Institute Patrick Boyle explained in a television interview that "as long as we can't get to perfection in terms of *E. coli* in raw uncooked product, raw uncooked hamburger . . . [it is] reasonable to ask the consumer to bear some responsibility for using the product in a reasonable and safe way. And that means cooking it properly." The vice president for product safety at a leading meatpacking company voiced industry concerns at a congressional hearing that implementing HACCP might increase the risk of foodborne illness by giving consumers a false sense of security that would lead them to be less vigilant in food preparation.[19]

The Jack in the Box outbreak undermined the case against HACCP. It weakened the assertion that microbial contamination was a normal feature of raw meat and poultry, and it shifted attention from consumer responsibility to consumer protection. The death of four victims suggested to many that there was something terribly wrong with the meat itself, something unnatural. Moreover, the Jack in the Box victims were unsuspecting restaurant patrons—innocent children—who could hardly be considered responsible for improper handling and cooking of the contaminated ground beef that poisoned them. In response to the outbreak, Michael Taylor, who succeeded Cross as FSIS administrator in 1994, declared *E. coli* O157 an adulterant in raw meat and poultry that rendered it unfit for sale—repudiating the previous agency position that *E. coli* O157 was natural and unavoidable, and placing responsibility for controlling it squarely on industry.[20]

The Jack in the Box outbreak was more a tipping point than a revolution in the reframing of food safety in the meat and poultry industries. Making industry responsible for protecting consumers from the risk of microbial contamination was hardly a new idea. Inspection of live animals and carcasses for visible signs of illness and sanitary standards for slaughtering and processing date back to the late nineteenth century. Since the 1960s, experts in government, industry, and academia had been working to develop process controls to prevent cross contamination and microbiological criteria to detect it when it occurred. In the 1980s and early 1990s, a growing number of these experts advocated widespread adoption of HACCP in meat and poultry production. Moreover, following the Jack in the Box outbreak, industry executives and government officials did not stop insisting that consumers bore responsibility for safe handling and cooking of raw meat and poultry.

What changed after the Jack in the Box outbreak was that industry executives and government officials increasingly conceded that companies bore responsibility for preventing microbial contamination of raw meat and poultry before it reached consumers. In testimony before Congress in the aftermath of the outbreak, Cross admitted that the agency needed to pursue reforms that would "provide comprehensive farm-to-table protection that the American consumer deserves," and a senior executive from the American Meat Institute emphasized "the importance of approaching this problem holistically, looking at the entire food production, processing, distribution and handling system." Theno recalled that "there was a change in everybody's attitudes because now there was this new understanding that somehow things that used to be natural to the meat are contaminants in the meat—and that has regulatory implications. That shift in consciousness about what the relationship is between bacteria and fresh meat changes the way everybody thinks about meat production."[21]

Media coverage contributed to the reframing of bacterial contamination in raw meat and poultry from a natural hazard to the product of human error. News organizations depend on advertising revenue, and advertising rates are determined by circulation. Thus, reporters and their editors, in selecting and shaping news stories, are highly sensitive to what readers want: dramatic narratives involving events of exceptional magnitude with clear moral lessons. Readers also like stories with culturally familiar contexts in which unusual events occur, and they are attracted to stories involving well-known characters. The Jack in the Box outbreak offered all of these elements. Five hundred victims made it one of the largest foodborne illness outbreaks in US history. The tragic stories of small children suffering organ failure, permanent disability, and, in four cases, death, as a result of eating a hamburger at a popular fast-food chain made for an especially haunting account involving the most common of experiences and every parent's worst nightmare.[22]

Civil litigation also contributed to this reframing of bacterial contamination in raw meat and poultry. Convincing judges and juries requires plaintiffs' attorneys to tell compelling stories with clear moral implications about how their clients' injuries were caused by the misconduct of defendants. For plaintiffs' attorneys, accidents do not just happen. Rather, defendants' failures make them happen. Attorneys representing victims of the Jack in the Box outbreak filed lawsuits that articulated morality tales of small children stricken by devastating injuries caused by the carelessness of corporate officials.[23]

Media coverage and litigation have a symbiotic relationship nicely illustrated by the Jack in the Box outbreak. Plaintiffs' attorneys first learned of the outbreak from early news accounts. In turn, the lawsuits that they filed generated additional coverage. The initial filing of a lawsuit is frequently news, and subsequent stages in the litigation process—preliminary motions, revelations during discovery, testimony at trial, jury verdicts, appeals, and settlements—attract ongoing episodic coverage that can last years. In newsroom jargon, such a story has "legs." The 1982 McDonald's *E. coli* outbreak did not give rise to litigation, and news coverage was sparse and short lived. By contrast, the Jack in the Box outbreak was still making headlines nationwide more than two years after initial press reports when Bill Marler, who represented one hundred victims, obtained a $15.6 million settlement from the company for nine-year-old Brianne Kiner in 1995. The litigation, and attendant press coverage, continued until the company finally settled the last of the claims against it in late 1997. Marler, like many high-profile plaintiffs' attorneys, used media coverage—holding press conferences and accepting press interviews—to increase his bargaining power with Jack in the Box. Media coverage of the litigation, especially the large settlements, brought Marler additional clients as Jack in the Box victims read about him in the newspaper or saw him on television or were referred by other attorneys. In turn, the resulting litigation generated more news.[24]

Public health surveillance and tracing provided the essential ingredient of both media coverage and litigation: a chain of causation linking company practice, contaminated food, and human illness. The capacity to establish such causal connections had been developing for a decade before the Jack in the Box outbreak. Shortly after the McDonald's outbreak in 1982 in Oregon and Michigan, public health authorities in Washington State investigated an outbreak of gastrointestinal illness among nursing home residents in Walla Walla, and they identified ground beef contaminated with *E. coli* O157 as the cause. They subsequently issued regulations requiring physicians to report cases of *E. coli* O157 poisoning to the state health department. When, in 1993, a pediatric gastroenterologist at Children's Hospital in Seattle learned of a number of patients admitted with bloody diarrhea, several of whom were in the intensive care unit with kidney function complications associated with

E. coli O157, he promptly notified the state health department, which immediately launched an investigation. An epidemiological case-control study revealed that most of the patients had eaten hamburgers at Jack in the Box. By interviewing company executives, state officials learned that company policy specified cooking hamburgers to an internal temperature of 140 degrees—fifteen degrees below the state requirement of 155 degrees, which had been set specifically to kill *E. coli* O157. State inspectors who visited local Jack in the Box restaurants found that hamburger patties cooked according to company time-temperature guidelines had internal temperatures below the 155 degrees necessary to kill the pathogen. Laboratory testing identified the same strain of *E. coli* O157 in patient stool samples and hamburger-patty samples from Jack in the Box. Together, these findings supported media stories and tort claims that blamed company policy and practice for bacterial contamination that caused human illness.[25]

This common frame propagated by the media and plaintiffs' attorneys—that industry failures were responsible for the outbreak—was instrumental in mobilizing support for policy change. Press coverage enabled victims' families to identify one another, which resulted in their organizing Safe Tables Our Priority (STOP) to provide emotional support and to lobby for food safety reform. Like litigation, STOP's advocacy efforts had a symbiotic relationship with media coverage. "Thanks to media attention and the publication of victims' names, families and individuals were able to come together," explains STOP's website. In turn, the organization provided information to journalists about foodborne illness and food safety policy as part of its advocacy efforts. STOP recounted the personal stories of its members as compelling evidence of policy failure and as a justification for reform. In the fall of 1993, STOP organized a symposium on Capitol Hill attended by House members, senators, and administration officials, and the organization became a leading member of an emerging coalition of organizations seeking food safety reforms.[26]

The combination of media coverage, litigation, and mobilization expanded public concern over food safety, which captured the attention of industry executives, elected officials, and agency regulators. Rosemary Mucklow, executive director of the National Meat Association, a leading industry group, recalls that the Jack in the Box outbreak was "terrifying." "Children dying—everybody can relate to that. This industry is made up of many family businesses. They feed beef to their own families, their children, and that meat was blamed for making people sick was very frightening." Industry executives feared not only for public safety but also for the future of their industry. "We were suddenly in the limelight. We were suddenly the top story every

morning. That was very frightening to people," recounts Mucklow. The outbreak presented the newly elected President Clinton with his administration's
first crisis. In response, he promised at a town-hall-style meeting "to find
ways to do more inspections and to try to do them in a more effective way,"
and he ordered the hiring of additional USDA meat and poultry inspectors as
a first step toward broader reforms. The Senate Committee on Agriculture,
Nutrition, and Forestry held hearings in February 1993 at which industry,
USDA, and FDA officials presented proposals for reform. Developing new
regulations to improve meat inspection became a top priority at the USDA.[27]

The Jack in the Box outbreak opened up what political scientist John Kingdon calls a "policy window"—an occasion "during which a problem becomes
pressing, creating an opportunity for advocates of proposals to attach their solutions to it." The outbreak created a window of opportunity for policy change
by framing bacterial contamination of raw meat and poultry as the product of
human error, for which industry bore responsibility, raising nationwide concern about the problem, and placing it high on the policy agendas of industry
executives and government officials. However, new policies do not typically
originate with the opening of a policy window. Rather, those seeking change
push steadily for consideration of their ideas among policy makers and stakeholders. Over time, change advocates increase the salience of their proposals
so that when a policy window does open, conditions are ripe for adopting the
proposals. Thus, when Jack in the Box executives sought someone to help
them clean up their operations and USDA officials set out to develop new
meat inspection regulations, reformers like Theno and Adams were ready with
a "new" approach to regulating raw meat and poultry production, one that
they and other HACCP advocates had been developing for years.[28]

Implementing HACCP through Supply Chain Management

As the outbreak unfolded, Jack in the Box hired Dave Theno to design and
implement a HACCP program for the company. Theno had developed a
HACCP program at a leading poultry processor that reduced *Salmonella*
counts on raw chicken and turkey, and the National Cattlemen's Beef Association had hired him to implement interventions in beef slaughter plants
to address *E. coli* O157 contamination. At Jack in the Box, Theno instituted
an ambitious program that implemented HACCP controls throughout the
production chain, from slaughter to serving. Theno's program imposed new
requirements on the company's beef suppliers—specific skinning, evisceration, and washing techniques to reduce the risk of fecal contamination;
protocols for cutting, storing, and processing meat into hamburger patties;

methods of cleaning, sanitizing, and sterilizing facilities and equipment; hygienic practices for employees; assignment of lot numbers to facilitate tracking; and independent third-party audits to verify compliance. The company also insisted on routine testing for a range of pathogens, which revealed a much higher level of generic *E. coli* contamination in beef than anyone in the beef industry had expected. Whereas industry estimates suggested that the rate of *E. coli* contamination in beef was .01 or .02 percent, Theno found that the rate was really .5 percent. Routine testing enabled Jack in the Box to verify which suppliers were successfully implementing its HACCP requirements and to purchase beef only from them.[29]

Some suppliers embraced Jack in the Box's program. In May 1993, five months after the outbreak, Jack in the Box signed a contract with Texas American Foodservice Corporation, a leading beef processor, to implement a rigorous pathogen testing program using a new DNA testing technology—called polymerase chain reaction (PCR) technology—that provided quicker and better-defined results than the traditional method of growing bacterial cultures in petri dishes. Texas American's in-house microbiologists worked with DuPont, which had successfully applied PCR technology to diagnose human diseases, to apply it to testing for pathogens in raw beef. The National Cattlemen's Beef Association provided funding to pay Silliker Laboratories, the largest independent commercial testing lab in the United States, to validate Texas American's new testing protocols. The FSIS Office of Public Health and Science also validated the new protocols. Jack in the Box's HACCP program became a model for the fast-food industry, and it was eventually adopted by many competitors.[30]

To support the proliferation of HACCP within the meat and poultry industries, Russell Cross, upon resigning his post as FSIS administrator, joined forces with Rosemary Mucklow, executive director of the National Meat Association, to found the International Meat and Poultry HACCP Alliance in March 1994 (later expanded and renamed the International HACCP Alliance). The alliance is a membership organization of industry associations, professional organizations, consulting firms, universities, and government agencies. It establishes HACCP training standards, approves HACCP training curricula, and educates and accredits HACCP trainers.[31]

Not everyone in industry shared this enthusiasm for HACCP. Beef suppliers complained about the cost of the new requirements. Product development specialists argued that bactericidal washing would adversely affect flavor. Food safety experts asserted that HACCP would give consumers a false sense of security and impede efforts to promote safer consumer handling and cooking. Company executives worried that Theno's findings would scare con-

sumers away from eating beef. However, despite pressure from the National
Council of Chain Restaurants, the fast-food industry's trade association—
whose director called Theno personally to warn him that "some of our members are pretty unhappy about what you are doing"—Theno forged ahead.[32]

New Government Regulations

The USDA's response to the Jack in the Box outbreak was to develop mandatory HACCP regulations for the meat and poultry industries. Following publication of a proposed rule in February 1995, the agency received more than
6,800 comments. It held seven informational briefings around the country,
convened six meetings focused on specific issues, sponsored three scientific
and technical conferences, conducted a two-day public hearing, and hosted a
meeting with state regulators. The final rule, published in July 1996, occupied
184 pages in the *Federal Register*. Officially titled Pathogen Reduction; Hazard
Analysis and Critical Control Points (PR/HACCP) Systems, proponents and
critics alike nicknamed it the "Mega-Reg."[33]

The new regulations take a two-pronged approach to reducing the risk of
bacterial contamination in beef and poultry processing. First, the regulations
mandate process controls by requiring companies to design and implement
HACCP programs in their production facilities. The regulations require each
company to develop written standard operating procedures for sanitation as
a prerequisite for operating a successful HACCP program and to test for generic *E. coli*—which resides in the intestinal tract of animals—to verify that
the company's HACCP program is preventing fecal contamination. Second,
the regulations set performance standards in the form of maximum allow-
able levels of *Salmonella* in meat and poultry. The agency tests specifically for
Salmonella for several reasons: it is the most common bacterial cause of foodborne illness, the test for it is relatively easy to perform, *Salmonella* occurs at
sufficiently high frequencies that changes can be detected, and techniques
for reducing *Salmonella* contamination are likely to be effective against
other pathogens. *Salmonella* testing, in addition to *E. coli* testing, helps to
verify the effectiveness of a company's HACCP program. The two tests are
complementary. Whereas generic *E. coli* levels indicate a HACCP system's
success in preventing fecal contamination (generic *E. coli*, though not necessarily harmful, is typically a sign of fecal contamination), *Salmonella* levels
indicate the system's effectiveness in reducing harmful pathogens from other
sources (*Salmonella*, though typically harmful, is not necessarily caused by
fecal contamination). The regulations authorize a progressive reduction in
the *Salmonella* performance standards over time to weed out companies that

lag behind industry standards, to encourage innovation, and to reduce the overall level of bacterial contamination in meat and poultry. The regulations called for large plants, those with five hundred or more employees, to have HACCP programs in place by January 1998, small plants, those with ten or more employees, by January 1999, and very small plants by January 2000.[34]

The USDA's PR/HACCP program signaled several significant changes in meat and poultry regulation. First, the new regulations placed greater responsibility for food safety onto companies. Before the program, meat and poultry companies had focused on maintaining quality and containing costs, and they relied on USDA inspectors to identify any food safety problems. The new regulations placed primary responsibility for food safety on companies and cast USDA inspectors in the secondary role of overseeing their efforts. Second, the regulations provided companies greater flexibility. They replaced command-and-control regulation—in which agency officials dictated specific technologies or production methods to address safety problems—with oversight of company-designed process controls and verification of performance standards that left companies free to decide how to meet them. A primary aim of greater flexibility was to facilitate innovation. Third, the regulations introduced greater scientific rigor into food safety inspection. Whereas USDA oversight traditionally relied primarily on organoleptic methods—"poke and sniff" inspection of carcasses and "floors, walls, and ceilings" inspection of facilities—the new regulations instituted routine microbiological testing. Fourth, the regulations shifted emphasis from detecting contamination to preventing it. Traditional carcass inspection aims to detect contamination, whereas HACCP aims to prevent it by identifying the sources of contamination and implementing verifiable controls. These controls included specific processing techniques: antimicrobial treatment of carcasses and specific time-temperature chilling requirements.[35]

One should be careful not to overstate the novelty of the USDA's PR/HACCP program. Even under the old regime, companies bore some responsibility for food safety, the general nature of GMPs left room for variation and innovation in implementation, the USDA employed occasional microbiological testing for *Salmonella*, and measures like pre-slaughter animal inspection and sanitary regulations were designed to prevent contamination during slaughter and processing. Moreover, the new regulations did not alter the legislative mandates that required the USDA to inspect every carcass and to maintain daily inspection at each plant.

Although an increasing number of industry leaders were promoting HACCP in meat and poultry production, companies and trade associations vigorously resisted the government's efforts to impose HACCP through enforceable regulations. In August 1994, President Clinton appointed Michael Taylor, an attorney who was deputy commissioner for policy at the FDA, to succeed Russell Cross as FSIS administrator. At the FDA, Taylor had worked on developing HACCP regulations for seafood processors, and he was moved to the USDA to lead the agency's efforts to design and implement HACCP regulations for the meat and poultry industries. In his first public speech as FSIS administrator, he urged industry executives at the annual convention of the American Meat Institute "to be driven as much by public health goals as by productivity concerns," and he announced that the agency was planning to develop mandatory HACCP regulations for the meat and poultry industries. As a first step toward that goal, he declared that thenceforth the agency would consider ground beef contaminated with *E. coli* O157 to be adulterated under the Federal Meat Inspection Act. "We are prepared to use the Act's enforcement tools, as necessary, to exclude adulterated product from commerce," he threatened. "We plan to conduct targeted sampling and testing of raw ground beef at plants and in the marketplace for possible contamination with *E. coli* O157:H7." Taylor warned the executives that the agency would enforce a zero-tolerance policy for the pathogen responsible for the Jack in the Box outbreak and would require the destruction or reprocessing of ground beef that tested positive.[36]

Although food safety advocates cheered Taylor's speech, industry executives perceived it as heavy handed. "Mike Taylor was a lawyer who didn't have the benefit of having walked through many meat plants," recalls Rosemary Mucklow. "He sat at his desk in Washington—he didn't know how this industry operated. He thought he could do it all with a top-down approach." In the winter of 1994, the industry filed a lawsuit challenging the new FSIS policy on *E. coli* O157, arguing that, under the precedent set by *APHA v. Butz*, a pathogen in food (*Salmonella* in poultry in that case, *E. coli* O157 in beef in this case) did not qualify as an adulterant if ordinary methods of cooking and preparation kill the pathogen. The court upheld the agency's new *E. coli* O157 policy, reasoning that "many Americans consider ground beef to be properly cooked rare, medium rare, or medium," and that "*E. coli* contaminated ground beef cooked in such a manner may cause serious physical problems, including death."[37]

When the USDA published its proposed PR/HACCP rule, industry reaction was mixed. Leading industry executives supported mandatory standard operating procedures for sanitation, adoption of company-designed HACCP plans, and the use of generic *E. coli* testing as a proxy for fecal contamination to verify process controls. Their objections to the proposed rule fell into three categories. First, they opposed specific mandates in the proposed regulations

regarding processing techniques, which they viewed as excessively controlling and inconsistent with the goal of flexibility that distinguished process
controls and performance standards from traditional command-and-control
regulation. Second, industry executives wanted clearer guidance from the
agency about how it would evaluate the acceptability of company-designed
HACCP plans. In particular, the proposed regulations provided for agency
approval of HACCP plans only after companies implemented them. Industry
executives wanted approval before implementation to help companies avoid
enforcement action in the event that the agency did not approve a company's
plan. Third, the industry objected to the use of *Salmonella* performance standards. They argued that *Salmonella* was neither an adulterant nor a reliable
proxy for unsanitary conditions in a processing plant, the two statutory criteria that defined the agency's authority to withdraw its inspectors and, with
them, a company's ability to sell its products.[38]

In response to the first industry objection, the USDA dropped from the
final rule mandatory antimicrobial treatment of carcasses and specific time-
temperature chilling requirements. However, the agency stood firm on post-
implementation approval of HACCP plans and *Salmonella* performance
standards. Industry attempts to lobby Congress during the rule-making
process to restrict funding for HACCP implementation and eliminate proposed pathogen testing rules ultimately failed. The industry went to court
to fight the regulations in 1999, when the agency attempted to withdraw its
inspectors from a Texas beef-processing plant that failed three consecutive
Salmonella tests. In *Supreme Beef Processors v. USDA*, the court rejected the
agency's reliance on positive *Salmonella* test results as a basis for withdraw-
ing its inspectors. Following *APHA v. Butz*, the court held that *Salmonella*
was not an adulterant in raw meat. Furthermore, it declared that high levels
of *Salmonella* in a company's product did not provide a reliable proxy for
insanitary conditions in its plant, since beef might have been contaminated
by a supplier before it entered the plant—for which the USDA could not
hold the processor responsible—and the agency did not test incoming meat
to establish a baseline that might support a finding of cross contamination in
the plant. In addition, the court found that the presence of *Salmonella* does
not indicate the presence of other harmful pathogens that might qualify as
adulterants. In the wake of this defeat, the agency did not abandon *Salmonella* testing. It used bad results as a basis for further scrutiny of a plant to
encourage improvement or directly detect insanitary conditions that would
support the withdrawal of inspectors.[39]

Opposition to the USDA's HACCP regulations came also from some consumer advocacy groups and inspectors inside the agency who worried that

HACCP replaced traditional hands-on inspection of animals, meat, equipment, and facilities with paperwork review. Concerned that the new regime left food safety in the hands of processors, these critics insisted that HACCP stood for "Have a Cup of Coffee and Pray." In 1999, a group of FSIS inspectors, their union, and the Community Nutrition Institute filed a lawsuit to block implementation of an agency initiative—the HACCP-Based Inspection Models Project (HIMP)—that would have delegated carcass inspections and responsibility for trimming defects to plant personnel, freeing inspectors to verify the plants' compliance with performance standards and process controls under the new PR/HACCP regulations. The court enjoined the USDA from implementing HIMP, accepting the challengers' argument that the Federal Meat Inspection Act and the Poultry Products Inspection Act required government inspectors to perform post-slaughter inspection. "Delegating the task of inspecting carcasses to plant employees violated the clear mandates of the FMIA and the PPIA," the court concluded. In response, the agency modified its initiative and, after additional litigation, the court permitted the agency to pilot its revised version of HIMP at twenty-five poultry plants and five pork plants.[40]

The USDA has continued to develop its PR/HACCP regulations since introducing them in the late 1990s, although their basic structure remains the same. In 2011, FSIS declared that it would treat six additional strains of *E. coli* as adulterants because, like *E. coli* O157, they are similarly virulent, cause illness at low doses, and have been linked to foodborne illness outbreaks. The agency also considers *Listeria monocytogenes* and *Salmonella* to be adulterants in ready-to-eat products such as deli meats. In accordance with the *APHA v. Butz* decision, the agency has rejected 2011 and 2014 petitions by the Center for Science in the Public Interest to classify antibiotic-resistant strains of *Salmonella* as adulterants, although the agency considers *Salmonella*-contaminated products linked to an outbreak adulterated and will take enforcement action to prevent their sale. The agency has also expanded its sampling programs to test for seven types of *E. coli*, *Salmonella*, *Listeria*, and *Campylobacter*, and it has extended its HIMP pilot to more chicken and turkey slaughter operations.[41]

Criticism of the USDA's PR/HACCP Regulations

Numerous reports by government oversight bodies, industry executives, and consumer organizations have criticized the USDA's implementation of its PR/HACCP regulations. Critics allege that the agency fails to ensure the adequacy of companies' HACCP plans. The regulations mandate that each company design, validate, and implement its own HACCP plan. Although the USDA has published extensive guidance offering practical advice about how to do this, the agency does not preapprove a company's HACCP plan. On principle, the agency insists that preapproval would go against the "philosophy of HACCP." In practice, the agency lacks a sufficient number of trained personnel to review thousands of HACCP plans. The agency typically discovers problems in a company's HACCP plan and requires changes only after discovery of a significant food safety failure through routine inspection, pathogen testing, or an outbreak traced to the company's products. In the wake of outbreaks, investigations by the USDA and government oversight bodies have repeatedly found that companies failed to include common pathogens in their HACCP plans. For example, a 2014 investigation of Foster Farms following a nationwide outbreak of salmonellosis traced to its poultry products found that the company had not included *Salmonella* in its HACCP plan despite USDA test results before the outbreak reflecting a high prevalence of *Salmonella* in its products. To provide better oversight, the agency has built up a staff of Enforcement Investigations and Analysis Officers, who have the technical expertise to carefully review HACCP plans as part of investigations. The agency's persistent refusal to preapprove HACCP plans—despite repeated recommendations of government oversight bodies and consumer groups that it do so—reflects a commitment to placing more responsibility for food safety on companies and encouraging experimentation, but it undermines the claim that the agency has shifted its regulatory approach from detecting contamination to preventing it.[42]

In addition, critics assert that the agency fails to take sufficiently strict enforcement action to address repeated violations. Reports by the Government Accountability Office (GAO) fault the agency for failing to ensure that actions taken by companies to eliminate repeated violations are effective. The GAO also complains that the regulations do not specify the number or types of noncompliance notices necessary to find that a plant's HACCP program has failed and that the agency should take enforcement action to prevent the plant from shipping potentially contaminated products. Other reports allege that the FSIS regularly delays enforcement action and rarely follows through on threats to shut down plants with a history of noncompliance. According to one report, the agency's own investigation of the 2014 Foster Farms outbreak revealed "multiple and recurring noncompliances for insanitary conditions, including fecal material on carcasses, insanitary food contact surfaces, and direct product contamination."[43]

Industry critics complain that the USDA's hands-off approach to HACCP design and lack of consistent enforcement standards have produced a regulatory regime that provides little helpful guidance and leaves companies at the mercy of unpredictable agency officials. John Munsell operated a small family-owned beef slaughter and processing plant in Miles City, Montana. In 2002, several ground beef samples from his plant tested positive for *E. coli* O157. The USDA shut down his grinding operation by withholding its mark of inspection and demanded that he revise his HACCP plan. He alleges that the agency's district office rejected fourteen proposed revisions—including two designed by a professional consultant with input from the district office manager—"with no specific reasons for rejection, nor solutions provided as to what would be required by the agency." Agency review of company HACCP plans, as Munsell describes it, is Kafkaesque: "[The FSIS says to small plant owners:] 'Your HACCP Plan has a failure, and is inadequate. We can't tell you what is inadequate, or where the failure is, because it's your Plan.' After small plant owners don't know how to proceed, FSIS concludes: 'You should consider implementing the following steps.' This is allegedly merely a 'suggestion,' mind you. Then, after the plant implements the agency's suggestions, the agency frequently concludes: 'Your actions are inadequate.'" One longtime food safety expert called HACCP regulations "clear as mud."[44]

District office officials finally suggested three specific changes to Munsell's HACCP plan, but they insisted that he submit a letter representing them as his own proposals. Munsell submitted the letter, made the changes, and recommenced grinding operations. Munsell asserted throughout the process that the *E. coli* O157–contaminated beef samples taken from his grinding operations had not originated from his own slaughtering operations but were purchased from industry giant Conagra to supplement his supply and boost ground beef output to meet demand. He insists that the USDA refused to consider evidence that Conagra was the source of the problem. "Small plants lack clout, are much easier prey, and are the agency's primary target for enforcement actions," Munsell concludes.[45]

Other accounts concur with Munsell's claim that the USDA's HACCP regulations privilege large companies over small businesses. According to a USDA report, a large number of plants subject to the regulations have fewer than ten employees and produce numerous products in small batches. Separate HACCP plans must be written, implemented, and documented for each product, imposing significant extra costs, which are spread across relatively small production runs. Moreover, formal HACCP programs are less necessary in small plants, where top management is more likely to be present on the production line and able to monitor food safety first hand. The report concludes that "the perverse result is that costs of developing and implementing HACCP plans are higher in small plants; yet, these plants have the most direct control over production by top management." One study found that exit from the industry increased dramatically among small plants following PR/HACCP implementation.[46]

Assessing the Impact of HACCP in Meat and Poultry Production

Evaluating the impact of HACCP on the risk of foodborne illness from meat and poultry products is complicated. On the level of individual firms, some companies credit HACCP with reducing *E. coli* O157 contamination in ground beef. For example, Dave Theno recalled that before implementing HACCP at Jack in the Box, approximately .5 percent of ground beef samples tested positive for *E. coli* O157. Introducing HACCP reduced the prevalence of *E. coli* O157–positive samples so dramatically that Theno "did not find any *E. coli* O157 for the next two-and-a-half years." Today, the company's HACCP program, like that of others in the fast food industry, entails regular testing of ground beef samples and removal of any lots that test positive for *E. coli* O157. More specific data on the experience of individual companies are generally considered proprietary and are not publicly available.[47]

A 2005 USDA study claims that the agency's PR/HACCP regulations reduced *E. coli* O157 contamination in ground beef production nationally and lowered rates of foodborne illness. The authors estimated a 50 percent decrease in the percentage of raw ground beef samples that tested positive for *E. coli* O157 from 2002 to 2003, which they attributed to "specific regulatory changes by FSIS and actions by industry"—namely, that "FSIS required industry reassessments of HACCP plans with respect to *E. coli* O157:H7 (October 2002) and eliminated criteria in effect since 1998 that permitted exclusions from the *E. coli* O157:H7 testing program (April 2003). Simultaneously, an industry summit in January 2003 created a unified, comprehensive platform with the goal of defining and documenting industry practices in order to 'reduce, and ultimately eliminate, the risk of *E. coli* O157:H7 in the beef supply.'" Citing CDC data on a "significant reduction" in the incidence of human illnesses caused by *E. coli* O157 between 2002 and 2003, the USDA study authors concluded that "the simultaneous reduction in human illnesses resulting from *E. coli* O157:H7 infection suggests that the recent decrease in the rate of *E. coli* O157:H7–positive raw ground beef samples reflects a real change resulting in measurable public health improvements." In a 2006 addendum, the authors presented additional data from 2004 reflecting a further decline in the percentage of ground beef samples testing positive for *E. coli* O157, from which they concluded that their original findings represented "the beginning of a sustained trend, rather than simply reflecting annual variation." A subsequent 2015 CDC study relied on these findings to assert that a decrease in the incidence of reported cases of *E. coli* O157 infections in 2014 compared to the period of 2006–2008 was attributable to "substantial changes in beef industry practices and government policy," which "led to a decrease in ground beef contamination."[48]

The data supporting these claims concerning the impact of the PR/HACCP regulations on *E. coli* O157 contamination in ground beef production have several important limitations that the USDA study authors were careful to acknowledge. They disclosed that they observed no decrease in *E. coli* O157–positive test samples between 2000 and 2002, during which the PR/HACCP regulations applied to all ground beef processors. They also explained that USDA testing "does not provide an ideal estimate of the prevalence of *E. coli* O157:H7 in raw ground beef in the United States" because the selection of processing facilities and retail outlets from which samples were tested was not weighted according to production volume. In addition, the authors cautioned that the increasingly popular practice among processors to conduct their own testing before USDA sampling and to divert "contaminated product away from raw ground beef manufacture to cooking or rendering," probably accounted for some of the decrease in the percentage of USDA samples that tested positive for *E. coli* O157. Moreover, the authors admitted that attributing any of the decrease to specific regulatory changes by the FSIS or resolutions by industry is complicated by the lack of information regarding when processing plants implemented them.[49]

Inferences that reductions in the number of ground beef samples testing positive for *E. coli* O157 resulted in lower rates of illness are also subject to important qualifications. The CDC study authors point out that the decrease in reported cases of *E. coli* O157 infections that they observed is probably attributable, in some measure, to improvements in outbreak investigation that enabled public health officials to more quickly identify contaminated foods and prevent the spread of infection by warning consumers and encouraging companies to implement product recalls. The CDC authors also point out that increasing use of rapid diagnostic tests for microbial pathogens, which help clinicians more quickly diagnose and treat bacterial infections but do not identify the particular pathogen responsible, also likely contributed to the decrease in reported cases of *E. coli* O157 infection.[50]

The impact of the PR/HACCP regulations in poultry production is similarly difficult to assess. USDA sampling data reflect a sustained decline from 2006 to 2013 in the percentage of broiler chickens testing positive for *Salmonella*. However, sampling data between 2002 and 2005, coinciding with early implementation of PR/HACCP, reflect a steady increase in the percentage of broiler chickens testing positive for *Salmonella*. Moreover, skeptics have challenged the link between test results and health outcomes, pointing out that declines in contamination rates have not corresponded with fewer reported cases of salmonellosis attributable to chicken. The USDA has countered with an analysis that reveals a correlation between the estimated actual prevalence of particular strains of *Salmonella* in specific poultry products and the relative rate of salmonellosis due to those products, concluding that the "weight of the evidence" supports the agency's position that efforts to reduce the prevalence of *Salmonella* in poultry have "a significant impact on reducing or averting illness." However, the agency concedes that, although this limited evidence provides a reasonable basis for agency regulations, it is not conclusive.[51]

Additionally, in assessing the impact of HACCP, one should take costs as well as benefits into account. A 2004 study by USDA economists claimed that the benefits of the PR/HACCP regulations outweighed the costs of compliance. The authors estimated the annual benefits in terms of illness reduction at somewhere between $1.9 billion and $171.8 billion, depending on the level of pathogen reduction, and the annual costs to industry of compliance with the regulations at $380 million, with additional fixed costs of $570 million. These cost estimates are based on a 2002 survey of 996 meat and poultry slaughtering and processing plant operators regarding their food safety investments between 1996 and 2000. However, the estimates of annual benefits of the PR/HACCP regulations in terms of illness reduction are 1997 projections prior to implementation, and they rely on two significant assumptions: that implementing HACCP will reduce pathogen levels for all pathogens for all products in cattle, poultry, and pork production by at least 20 percent and as much as 90 percent and that any percentage reduction of pathogen levels will result in the same percentage reduction in the rate of foodborne illness, across all pathogens.[52]

The same USDA study found that voluntary investments in food safety motivated by market incentives had a much greater impact than investments prompted by the PR/HACCP regulations. The authors found that during the same 1996 to 2000 period, meat and poultry industries "spent an additional $360 million on food-safety investments that were not required by the PR/HACCP rule." These additional investments included added workers, personnel training, processing techniques, production-line changes, plant modifications, new technologies, and product specifications, many of which were driven by supplier contracts. The authors estimated that these management-initiated investments accounted for two-thirds of the reduction in the number of samples testing positive for *Salmonella* in meat and poultry production. They concluded that government regulation "is a floor that some plants use as their only means of food safety process control, while the majority of plants use it as a basis for building a more sophisticated food safety process control system," and that "management-determined actions make a substantially greater contribution to meat and poultry food safety process control than [government-mandated] process regulation for most plants." The authors further concluded that market incentives were the primary driver for food safety investments. They found "little evidence" that USDA pathogen performance standards motivated management decisions regarding the adoption of food safety process controls beyond those required by the HACCP regulations. Instead, they asserted, concern that a food safety failure could adversely affect a supplier's relations with major buyers or a brand leader's reputation among consumers exerted a "strong influence" on management decisions to invest more in food safety.[53]

It is difficult to sort out the extent to which impacts such as pathogen reduction and lower rates of illness should be attributed to HACCP programs rather than to adoption of particular sanitary practices or process controls. Skeptics argue that instituting regular hand washing or adding an antimicrobial agent to poultry chill water does not require a HACCP plan, which merely adds needless paperwork to the process of operating a processing plant. HACCP proponents counter that such allegations miss the point: HACCP lends rigor and discipline to food safety risk management, which facilitates implementation, verification, and improvement of pathogen controls, whether they are simple commonsense measures or sophisticated technological processes. Theno explains that, although "everyone knows that employees should wash their hands while working on a food production line," it takes "systematic management"—planning, implementation, and accountability—to make it happen. The debate is partly a matter of interpretation. According to the skeptics, all the formal requirements make HACCP a less efficient means of advancing food safety in plant operations than simply requiring specific sanitary practices and process controls. According to proponents, these processes and controls are not more cost-effective alternatives to HACCP—they are constituent parts of HACCP.[54]

Many HACCP proponents distinguish the impact of the USDA's mandatory HACCP regulations from industry-driven HACCP programs. Theno distinguished "regulatory" HACCP, which focuses on legal compliance, from "real" HACCP, which aims for comprehensive risk management. Industry experts assert that government-mandated HACCP focuses companies on regulatory compliance rather than risk management and replaces creative thinking with checklists. According to Theno, many companies implement "cookie cutter" HACCP programs that comply with USDA guidelines but that do not address all of the food safety hazards in their plants. Speaking on a panel of industry experts at the 2014 annual conference of the International Association for Food Protection, Sara Mortimore of Land O'Lakes, described HACCP as "a set of flexible principles that develops over time," and she lamented that "regulatory HACCP has codified and rigidified it." "HACCP is more than just a food safety program—it is a new mindset of risk-based, preventive, control thinking," said fellow panelist David Acheson, a leading food safety consultant and former associate commissioner for foods at the FDA. Mortimore and Acheson and the other panelists all agreed that successful HACCP implementation requires more than merely "technical expertise." It requires a companywide "culture of food safety." Formal training is just a start and must be followed by "coaching and mentoring," Mortimore explained. Beyond training, applying HACCP effectively requires practical experience, critical reflection, constant revision, and ongoing innovation. "You have to live it; it has to become a way of life," asserted Gillian Kelleher, of Wegmans supermarket chain.[55]

The loss of dynamism in translating HACCP from a constantly evolving set of principles into a government regulation is, perhaps, inevitable. "That's what happens any time you get a regulatory agency involved with something—you get rules and laws," said Theno. "In order to install HACCP into regulations, it had to become much more prescriptive, less open, than it was ever intended to be," explains Catherine Adams, the leading HACCP advocate in FSIS from 1986 to 1991, whose efforts laid the groundwork for the 1996 PR/HACCP regulations.[56]

Industry experts also suggest that lax oversight diminishes the impact of the USDA's HACCP regulations. William Sperber, who worked with Bauman on the development of HACCP at Pillsbury and went on to implement it in food industry giants like Best Foods and Cargill, has been critical of the USDA for failing to "follow the principles of HACCP." For example, he complains that when the USDA discovers samples exceeding its *Salmonella* performance standards the agency typically conducts multiple rounds of testing—a process that can take up to two years—while the plant under investigation continues to ship its products. Very rarely does the agency close a plant. By contrast, two "hallmarks of a valid HACCP plan are that monitoring procedures and corrective actions, insofar as possible, should be taken in real time, and should be as continuous as possible."[57]

In sum, the studies presented in this section provide the strongest available evidence that HACCP has been a cost-effective way to reduce the risk of foodborne illness. However, a fair assessment of them must acknowledge several important limitations. No aggregate data is available to evaluate the impact of voluntary HACCP programs, and data from individual companies is unavailable. The studies claiming that the USDA's PR/HACCP regulations have reduced pathogen levels and prevented foodborne illness rely on narrow data sets selected to best illustrate a positive impact (e.g., *E. coli* O157–positive ground beef samples between 2002 and 2004, and *Salmonella*-positive broiler chicken samples between 2006 and 2013). These studies lack a way to separate out the impact of the regulations from that of other factors that are likely to have contributed to pathogen reduction and lower rates of reported illness (e.g., diversion of *E. coli* O157–positive beef out of ground beef production prior to USDA testing, and improvements in outbreak investigations). The studies claiming that the benefits of the PR/HACCP regulations outweigh the costs rely on 1997 projections using unverified assumptions about the aggregate impact of HACCP on pathogen reduction and human illness, across all pathogens and illnesses. The bottom line is that any claims regarding the impact of HACCP in meat and poultry production in terms of pathogen contamination rates or public health outcomes should be carefully qualified and very tentative.

Punctuated Equilibrium

The evolution of regulatory policy typically alternates between periods of equilibrium, where policy changes little or only incrementally, and moments of rapid change, precipitated by an external shock that shakes things up. These external shocks—which often take the form of focusing events like natural disasters or economic crises—can realign political interests, shift economic incentives, disrupt administrative routines, and alter the competing narratives that feed ongoing disagreement. The evolution of HACCP conforms to this pattern, which political scientists call "punctuated equilibrium."[58]

The HACCP story features long periods of relative stability punctuated by widely publicized outbreaks, followed by changes in industry practice and government policy. The Bon Vivant vichyssoise botulism outbreak in 1971 prompted the low-acid canned food industry to expand systematic time-temperature controls and the FDA to issue new regulations. Following twenty years of unsuccessful efforts to expand HACCP to other sectors of the food industry, the Jack in the Box *E. coli* O157 outbreak in 1993 spurred the meat and poultry industries to adopt HACCP and the USDA to publish its PR/HACCP regulations.

Before proceeding further, several caveats are in order. Emphasizing the role of outbreaks risks oversimplifying the evolutionary dynamics of food safety reform. The years between outbreaks were not periods of dormancy. Food safety merely advanced more quietly and incrementally. For example, during the fifty years between the canned olive outbreaks of 1919 and 1920 and the Bon Vivant vichyssoise outbreak in 1971, the National Canners Association supported three laboratories conducting ongoing research on time-temperature controls and, by 1971, had published ten editions of its food safety guidelines. Nor were government regulators inactive in the decades before the outbreak, during which the USDA expanded its inspection activities and the FDA developed increasingly detailed GMP regulations. Similarly, in the two decades between the Bon Vivant vichyssoise outbreak and the Jack in the Box outbreak, industry experts like Bauman and Theno experimented with HACCP and shared their expertise with each other and government officials through groups like the American Public Health Association and the National Advisory Committee on Microbiological Criteria for Foods. During this time, the USDA sponsored studies on microbiological controls in meat and poultry production and conducted pilot "streamlined inspection systems" that shifted greater front-line responsibility for food safety to industry and rewarded companies with reliable risk management programs and good regulatory compliance records with reduced regulatory burdens.[59]

Moreover, aside from the sudden jolt of focusing events, political ideology exerted steady pressure on government agencies to implement reforms. During the 1960s and 1970s, calls for regulatory reform fueled by consumer advocates like Ralph Nader demanded that federal government agencies impose more stringent and detailed rules, extend their jurisdiction to promote greater national uniformity in health and safety standards, and use formal legal procedures to aggressively enforce the law. The Wholesome Meat Act of 1967, the Wholesome Poultry Act of 1968, the development of GMPs, and the FDA's low-acid canned food regulations of 1971 all reflect the influence of this legalistic ideology of regulatory reform. During the 1980s and 1990s, calls for regulatory reform voiced by pro-business constituencies that backed neo-conservatives like Ronald Reagan and influenced neoliberals like Bill Clinton demanded reducing the cost of government regulation on taxpayers and businesses through increased reliance on industry standards rather than on government mandates, greater flexibility through performance goals instead of detailed rules, and a preference for compliance incentives over enforcement actions. This ideology, initially expressed in calls for "deregulation" and later developed in proposals for "responsive" or "smart" regulation, explains the USDA's interest in shifting from continuous inspection to periodic oversight of company-designed HACCP plans, replacing detailed uniform procedures for carcass-by-carcass inspection with reliance on microbial performance standards, and varying inspection intensity based on a company's regulatory compliance record.[60]

Finally, the advances spurred by outbreaks were less revolutionary and had less impact than some accounts have suggested. They typically involved new or broader applications of existing process controls rather than any fundamental paradigm shift. In the case of the low-acid canned food industry, the rarity of documented food safety failures—only four botulism-related deaths linked to commercially canned foods in the fifty years prior to the Bon Vivant vichyssoise outbreak—makes it difficult to support any claims of major improvement as a result of reforms following the outbreak. In the case of the beef and poultry industries, although there is some evidence that the PR/HACCP regulations have reduced the prevalence of contamination and prevented human illness, the tentativeness of most study conclusions suggests a modest rather than a dramatic impact.[61]

With these qualifications in mind, it is fair to say that outbreaks broke down resistance to change and thereby accelerated the proliferation of HACCP through industry initiatives and government regulations. Reduced resistance to change also allowed for greater experimentation with HACCP and, presumably, more rapid development of new management techniques and technologies to implement it. To understand how outbreaks changed the attitudes of HACCP opponents, it is necessary to examine the influence of media coverage and civil litigation on consumers and outbreak victims, and their influence, in turn, on industry executives and government officials.

Journalists and plaintiffs' attorneys are highly responsive to outbreaks. Journalists aim to reach the widest media audience possible, and the best way to do that is to write about events that can be framed in terms of dramatic narratives involving events of exceptional magnitude with clear moral lessons. Plaintiffs' attorneys are always on the lookout for grave injuries that can be attributed to the egregious misconduct of a large institutional wrongdoer. Consequently, media coverage of the Jack in the Box outbreak brought national attention to the deaths of four small children and the illnesses of hundreds of additional victims and framed them as failures of company executives and government regulators. Plaintiffs' attorneys filed claims that similarly alleged that the wrongdoing of managers caused grievous injury to innocent victims. In a feedback loop, media coverage informed litigation, which attracted media coverage, which encouraged more victims to file lawsuits.

The media coverage and litigation prompted by the Jack in the Box outbreak restructured the beef industry's economic incentives and influenced its food safety narrative. The dramatic story of corporate wrongdoing and catastrophic illness frightened consumers, resulting in a decrease in sales for

Jack in the Box and the industry as a whole. Civil litigation also imposed legal costs and the costs of settlements on Jack in the Box. The prospect of similar reputational damage and liability exposure from future outbreaks motivated company executives, first at Jack in the Box and later at other companies, to initiate HACCP programs. In addition, the compelling story projected by media coverage and litigation led beef industry executives to revise their assumptions about whether *E. coli* O157 was natural to beef and whether responsibility for eliminating it rested entirely with the person cooking the meat. Company executives became less resistant to HACCP, and industry association representatives like Mucklow expressed support for some form of government-supervised HACCP regulation.

Media coverage and civil litigation also realigned the balance of political interests influencing the USDA and changed the dominant narrative about HACCP regulations within the agency. Media coverage and civil litigation mobilized outbreak victims and raised public concern, creating political pressure that motivated President Clinton to stage town-hall meetings and Congress to hold hearings scrutinizing the shortcomings of the USDA's performance and demanding reform of the meat inspection system. In the process, President Clinton and congressional leaders endorsed a narrative that portrayed HACCP regulations as a progressive response to the problem of limited agency resources that would improve food safety. In doing so, they rejected the narrative popular among HACCP opponents within the USDA and some consumer advocates that portrayed HACCP as part of an ongoing attempt by industry to capture the regulatory process with the aim of reducing the agency's already-limited capacity to oversee beef and poultry production.

Debates over responsibility for microbial contamination of food occur in a variety of different institutional settings, or "venues." These include legislatures, administrative agencies, trade associations, professional organizations, media outlets, and civil litigation. Dramatic events may push the center of debate from one venue to another. Different venues may favor different political interests, create different economic incentives, impose different administrative constraints, and increase the salience of different narratives. The balance of power between defenders of the status quo and proponents of policy reform may shift from one venue to another, and victories in one venue may influence dynamics in other venues.[62]

When the Jack in the Box outbreak gave rise to legal claims by victims, debate over responsibility for food safety moved into the venue of civil litigation. In this venue, plaintiffs crafted new economic incentives that pressured companies to manage the risk of reputational damage and liability exposure from future outbreaks. Plaintiffs' claims in this venue also increased

the salience of a narrative that favored making industry responsible for preventing microbial contamination in beef production. The success of reform
advocates in this venue influenced coverage in media outlets, discussions in
corporate board rooms and industry associations, and debates among policy
makers in Congress and government agencies, tipping the balance of power
in favor of HACCP reforms.

The story of HACCP in the beef and poultry industries illustrates that the
dynamics of food safety policy reform take place in multiple interconnected
institutional settings. Policy formation and implementation occurs not
within a single government agency or trade association but within a complex
network of personal and institutional interactions. The next chapter examines more closely the structure of this network.

Making Salad Safe Again:
GAPs and the Complex Network Structure of
Food Safety Governance

Everyone in the leafy greens industry remembers where they were on Friday, September 15, 2006 — the day that news headlines announced an FDA warning to consumers not to eat bagged spinach. Drew McDonald, who managed food safety at Taylor Farms, a leading producer of fresh-cut fruits and vegetables, was at the baggage claim of an airport in Hawaii, where he, his wife, and their baby girl had arrived for a weeklong vacation. When he turned on his phone to activate an out-of-the-office voice mail notification, he discovered dozens of messages from company customers and members of his team concerned about a major foodborne illness outbreak. "As I was listening to the messages," he recalls, "I looked up at the TV monitors, and there, scrolling across the bottom of a CNN news broadcast, was 'spinach outbreak . . . people sick. . . .' So I started calling around to find out what was going on." The FDA was blaming bagged spinach for an emerging nationwide outbreak of *E. coli* O157:H7 responsible for fifty reported cases of illness, including eight involving kidney failure and one death. Later in the day, the FDA expanded the warning to cover all fresh spinach. Agency officials had learned that bagged spinach was sometimes sold out of the package in salad bars and retail stores, and the number of reported cases had risen to ninety-four, with fourteen victims suffering kidney failure. McDonald monitored the situation by phone for a day and a half "as the industry descended into mayhem." Aborting his vacation, he and his family boarded a plane back to California on Sunday. They were upgraded to first class, and as they settled into their seats, the stewardess apologized that she would not be serving the lunch appetizer listed on the menu: spinach salad.[1]

"When FDA said 'Don't eat spinach,' it pretty much shut down the bagged leafy greens industry," recalls David Gombas, a microbiologist who, for more than a decade, directed food safety efforts at the United Fresh Produce Association, a leading trade group. Frightened consumers stopped eating not only spinach but all bagged produce. Consequently, leafy greens production halted for two weeks at the height of the California growing season. "You had an entire crop of spinach that was past due sitting in the ground, so companies were losing hundreds of thousands of dollars a day because everything was essentially on hold," explains McDonald. Every leafy green grower and packer suffered fallout from the FDA's broad warning not to eat spinach. "Our products were not part of this at all," recalls Bob Whitaker, chief science and technology officer at the Produce Marketing Association, who worked at the time for NewStar Fresh Foods, a leading grower and shipper of fresh produce in California's Salinas Valley. "We were not growing in the areas that had a problem, but nobody wanted our products." According to one estimate, California leafy greens producers suffered nearly $100 million in losses following the outbreak.[2]

The magnitude of the 2006 spinach outbreak far surpassed that of previous outbreaks linked to leafy greens in another respect as well. Public health officials eventually attributed more than two hundred reported illnesses in twenty-six states to the outbreak. One hundred and three victims required hospitalization, thirty-one suffered kidney failure, and three died.[3]

Investigators never conclusively identified the precise cause of the contamination. Thirteen bags of Dole baby spinach, recovered from victims, tested positive for the outbreak strain of *E. coli* O157. All the bags were packed by Natural Selection Foods, a company that bagged spinach for a number of leading brands. Eleven of the bags were stamped with the same lot number, and investigators traced the spinach in that lot to four fields. A mile from one of the fields, they found the outbreak strain of *E. coli* O157 in samples that they collected from cattle feces, wild pig feces, and river water. Paicines Ranch, a grass-fed beef operation, owned the field and leased it for crop production. None of the samples collected from the field itself tested positive for *E. coli* O157. Investigators speculated that the contamination could have been caused by the incursion of wild pigs into the spinach rows or the infiltration of contaminated river water into irrigation wells. They also noted that samples taken from the areas surrounding the other three fields in question yielded nonoutbreak strains of *E. coli* O157, which, along with the results of previous outbreak investigations, indicated "systematic contamination" of waterways throughout the Salinas Valley.[4]

In the years preceding the 2006 spinach outbreak, food safety had become a growing concern in the leafy greens industry, although, according to Gombas, it was not yet a top priority. He recalls that, in 2005, when he started working in the fresh produce sector as a microbiology expert at United Fresh, "food safety was a minor part of what the industry was looking at. Most of the questions I received from industry members at the time were about shelf life, varieties, packing—issues related to product quality. I remember a meeting with CDC officials who said that, of the last 130 foodborne illness outbreaks, 35 percent were linked to fresh produce. Around this time, things were starting to shift; food safety was really becoming visible in the fresh produce world."[5]

Companies that instituted more rigorous food safety programs were frustrated when foodborne illnesses were traced back to their products despite their efforts. As an example, Gombas cites Dole, which, after a number of outbreaks traced back to the company's lettuce, "had a good food safety team in place. They were doing everything they could think of to preserve the safety of the leafy greens they were growing. They were trying their best. And yet, the outbreaks were occurring anyway. Everybody at the time was struggling to figure out 'What's going on? How do we stop it?'" The 2006 outbreak spread the pain, explains Gombas. "It was devastating to the industry, and it served as a real wakeup call, a watershed event for food safety in fresh produce."[6]

The 2006 Dole baby spinach outbreak prompted a reassessment of efforts to prevent microbial contamination in fresh produce production, and it motivated a number of food safety reforms. Experts in the fresh produce industry designed and launched a program that relies on government inspectors to verify compliance with industry standards aimed at reducing the risk of microbial contamination in growing fields. Leading retail stores, restaurants, and food service companies intensified the stringency of food safety requirements in their product specifications and increasingly required their fresh produce suppliers to obtain certification of compliance from a private third-party auditor. Outbreak victims filed lawsuits against growers, processors, and retailers, which created an additional source of pressure to improve food safety practices. Consumer advocates successfully pushed for new government regulations, which Congress finally authorized in the Food Safety Modernization Act of 2011.

This chapter traces the evolution of these food safety efforts in the leafy greens industry. It reveals that supply chain management, civil litigation, and government regulation are highly interdependent, linked together by a complex network of relationships among individuals and institutions. By highlighting the interdependence of food safety efforts, this chapter offers a more detailed account of how food safety governance operates as a system.

Produce Industry Guidelines and FDA Guidance

Fresh produce presents a number of unique food safety challenges. "Fresh produce is grown out in the field. It's grown under the sky. It's grown in the dirt. It's grown in the presence of animals," explains David Gombas. "It's exposed to all sorts of risks, and really there's nothing in the farming process that will prevent those risks from coming in contact with the produce. So you can't eliminate the risks; the best you can do is control them." Risk management in the field is especially important because fresh produce is frequently consumed raw, which forecloses the use of cooking to kill harmful pathogens during processing or home preparation. Washing fresh produce with chlorinated water reduces pathogen levels but is not 100% effective. Indeed, if not properly monitored, wash water can be a vehicle for cross contamination. Moreover, recent research suggests that washing fresh produce in chlorine may make remaining pathogens undetectable. Irradiation also reduces pathogen levels. However, it has not been widely adopted because the necessary equipment is expensive and companies fear that many consumers will not purchase irradiated food. In addition, consumer demand for a wide variety of fresh produce available throughout the year has given rise to lengthy global distribution chains in which items are handled by many people, from the field to the checkout counter, who harvest, sort, process, pack, transport, receive, display, and sell exposed items.[7]

Leafy greens that have been cut and processed carry additional risks. Cutting breaks the protective exterior skin of the plant and allows pathogens to infiltrate the leaves where they are harder to remove. Cutting also releases cellular fluids that provide a nutritive medium that can foster pathogen growth. The cutting, washing, and mixing of packaged salad greens exposes them to additional handling, thereby multiplying opportunities for contamination. The aggregation of greens from different sources during processing increases the risk of cross contamination and can disperse a single contaminated spinach plant or head of lettuce into multiple finished products.[8]

Food safety concerns about fresh produce are relatively recent compared to other sectors, such as dairy and meat. "Up until the 1990s, nobody ever thought about fresh produce as being a risk," explains Gombas. A 1985 National Academies report asserted that "raw fruits and vegetables are not common causes of foodborne illness in the United States," and that "there is little use for microbiological criteria for fresh fruits and vegetables at the present time." Although the FDA had broad legal authority under the Federal Food, Drug, and Cosmetic Act to prevent adulteration of any type of food sold in interstate commerce, it had never developed implementing regulations for fresh produce as it had for processed foods. The agency's Good Manufacturing Practices (GMPs) governing food processors expressly excluded "establishments engaged solely in the harvesting, storage, or distribution of one or more 'raw agricultural commodities'"—that is, farms and produce packing operations.[9]

Neither federal nor state authorities inspected farms or packing operations except when investigating outbreaks. Fresh produce "was under the radar for most federal and state officials," recalls Whitaker. "During the first four or five years I was in the industry in the late 1990s, I was never visited by an FDA or State of California official. I never saw them." According to Michelle Smith, a longtime FDA official, "We didn't tend to go on farms unless we had a reason to be there."[10]

Outbreaks associated with fresh produce starting in the mid-1990s raised new food safety concerns. Increased consumption of raw produce as part of changing dietary patterns that favored fresh salads over cooked vegetables likely contributed to a rise in outbreaks. In addition, growing demand for the convenience of precut, ready-to-eat (known as "fresh cut") produce in packages bearing brand names made it easier for public health officials to trace outbreaks caused by bagged salad mixes back to particular companies. Improvements in foodborne illness surveillance and tracing further enhanced the ability of public health officials to connect outbreaks to particular products and companies.[11]

In response to growing concern about the safety of fresh produce, experts in industry, government, and academia began to formulate what became known as good agricultural practices, commonly referred to as GAPs, to reduce the risk of microbial contamination during growing and harvesting. The term GAPs is sometimes used to include good handling practices (GHPs) for post-harvest sorting, packing, storage, and shipping. The International Fresh-Cut Produce Association and the Western Growers Association organized a Food Safety Initiative to coordinate these efforts. They assembled a Steering Committee consisting of representatives from five trade associations, six grower-processors, two cooling companies, a shipper, a private food safety laboratory, and a county agricultural commissioner. In addition, they assembled a nineteen-member scientific task force composed mostly of academics and industry experts with PhDs in food science, crop science, microbiology, virology, and toxicology. Also engaged in the effort were government officials from the FDA and USDA, the California and Arizona departments of agriculture, and the California department of health.[12]

In the summer of 1997, the International Fresh-Cut Produce Association and the Western Growers Association published a thirty-five-page booklet,

Voluntary Food Safety Guidelines for Fresh Produce. Reflecting the limits of science regarding pathogen control on farms, the booklet dedicates only three pages to the risk of contamination in fields from soil, fertilizers, irrigation water, animal intrusion, workers, and harvesting equipment. The remainder deals with risk management in precooling facilities, transportation, packinghouses, and processing plants. That same year, the United Fresh Fruit and Vegetable Association published a similar twenty-eight-page booklet, *Industrywide Guidance to Minimize Microbiological Food Safety Risk for Produce*, and academics at Cornell University published a tri-fold pamphlet, *Prevention of Foodborne Illness Begins on the Farm*.[13]

For the most part, these early GAPs merely direct attention to potential problems without providing specific procedures or metrics for reducing risk. For example, with regard to fertilizers, the *Voluntary Food Safety Guidelines for Fresh Produce* suggest that "fertilizers such as manure and compost should be monitored for possible microbial pathogens," and they advise growers to "consider a minimum application-to-harvest interval to assure that manure or compost has fully broken down in the soil before the crop is harvested." The guidelines on irrigation water encourage growers "to identify and review the source of water used on the ranch" and suggest that "the water may be tested for contaminants on a periodic basis. The frequency of testing may be determined by the water source. Testing may be considered for *E. coli* and total coliforms."[14]

In some areas, the guidelines offer slightly more direction: "portable toilets should not be cleaned in the field," "rubber gloves, leak-proof band aids or other corrective measures are encouraged for minor cuts" on workers' hands during harvesting, and "growers are encouraged to clean and sanitize or disinfect tables, baskets and mechanical harvesters on a daily basis." The guidelines in a few instances refer growers to government regulations. For example, with regard to field sanitation, they state that "the number, condition and positioning of toilets must meet all local, state and federal guidelines."[15]

The authors of the guidelines lament the lack of science to support more specific instructions to growers, and they openly acknowledge the need for further development. They write in the introduction: "There are data gaps in understanding the sources and significance of microbial hazards as well as practices to minimize them. Consequently, it is not well understood what specific impact water, manure or employees may have in contributing to foodborne disease." They caution that "the guidelines are not 'final,' as they will be revised periodically as experience, new research and new technology may suggest."[16]

In October 1997, President Clinton announced a Food Safety Initiative that promised new federal guidance on good agricultural practices for fresh produce. The FDA and USDA officials charged with developing the new federal GAPs guidance for fresh produce relied heavily on the previous efforts of industry associations and academics. "This is probably a really good example of leveraging the work of other people," recalls FDA official Michelle Smith, who played a leading role in developing the guidance. "We quickly found guidance that had been jointly developed by the Western Growers Association and the International Fresh-Cut Produce Association, another guidance by United Fresh, and a third guidance put out by Cornell University. And so our first step was to take the best bits of each, weave them together, and present that as our working draft to stakeholder groups." The draft went through "various rounds of input and modification from industry and academia," recalls Trevor Suslow, one of the nation's leading academic experts on food safety in fresh produce, who advised both industry groups and government agencies in the development of GAPs standards. In October 1998, the FDA published a *Guide to Minimize Microbial Food Safety Hazards for Fresh Fruits and Vegetables*.[17]

Like its industry and academic predecessors, the federal government's 1998 guidance highlights areas of concern but lacks specific instructions. For example, the guidance states that irrigation "water quality should be adequate for its intended use" and defines *adequate* as "that which is needed to accomplish the intended purpose in keeping with good practice"—a definition likely to leave growers wondering how to assess water quality. The guidance advises that "where water quality is unknown or cannot be controlled, growers should use other good agricultural practices to minimize the risk of contamination," such as "protecting surface waters, wells, and pump areas from uncontrolled livestock or wildlife access to limit the extent of fecal contamination" and employing "soil and water conservation practices such as grass/sod waterways, diversion beams, runoff control structures, and vegetative buffer areas" to "help prevent polluted runoff water from contaminating agricultural water sources and produce crops." The guidance offers no details on how to protect water sources from animal intrusion or specifications for earthworks to divert runoff water. Similarly, the guidance states that "growers may elect to test their water supply for microbial contamination" but, as one commentator points out, does not specify "what to test for, what type of test to utilize, where to test, what the frequency of tests should be or any parameters upon which to evaluate the results of the tests."[18]

Also like its industry and academic predecessors, the federal government's 1998 guidance highlights the inadequacy of scientific knowledge at the time and the need for additional research. The guidance explains that "the scientific basis for reducing or eliminating pathogens in an agricultural setting is evolving and not yet complete." For example, the guidance cautions that "there are a number of gaps in the science upon which to base a microbial testing program for agricultural water[,] and microbial testing of agricultural water may be of limited usefulness." Moreover, like the industry and academic guidelines on which it was based, the government's guidance is nonbinding. It merely "represents the current thinking" of its authors, and compliance with its suggestions is entirely voluntary.[19]

Continuing outbreaks associated with fresh lettuce and tomatoes led the FDA to issue a warning letter to these two industries in February 2004 urging companies to "review their current operations in light of the agency's guidance for minimizing microbial food safety hazards." In October, the FDA published a produce safety action plan for fresh produce, pledging to "develop, and assist in the development of . . . commodity-specific and practice-specific guidance." In a subsequent November 2005 warning letter to the California leafy greens industry, the agency urged industry members "to begin or intensify immediately efforts" to "expedite completion of the industry-led lettuce and leafy green-specific supply chain guidance." Smith remembers that agency officials saw the warning letters as a way "to push our expectations for more action than we had been seeing up to that point."[20]

Hank Giclas, of the Western Growers Association, recalls a series of meetings between industry representatives and FDA officials during this time. "We were in a long series of iterative discussions with regulatory agencies at that point in time, both at the state and federal level," says Giclas. "We would tell them, 'we have industry best practices,' and they would respond, 'How do you know they're being implemented?' Well, we didn't, because we weren't tracking that. I mean, we'd talked to people; we had anecdotal information, but we didn't know how far and wide guidelines had penetrated the industry, because they were all voluntary." During the discussions, the FDA focused on "the fact that there were a few commodities where we were continuing to see outbreaks—tomatoes, cantaloupes, leafy greens, green onions, and culinary herbs—which the agency called 'high-risk' crops." The agency insisted that "there must be something unique about those commodities, because general ag practices, if they were being deployed, weren't having the effect of reducing the potential for outbreaks. . . . They said, and we agreed with them: 'You in industry need to go back and look at what is unique about these crops, and decide if there are additional good ag practices that need to be created and put out there to try to reduce the frequency of these outbreaks.' And that was the genesis of the industry's work on commodity-specific guidance."[21]

In April 2006, shortly before the Dole baby spinach outbreak, the International Fresh-Cut Produce Association, the Western Growers Association, the United Fresh Fruit and Vegetable Association, and the Produce Marketing Association published *Commodity Specific Food Safety Guidelines for the Lettuce and Leafy Greens Supply Chain* with input from fifty leading food safety experts from industry, government, and academia. The foreword emphasizes that the guidelines are voluntary and intended to merely "raise awareness" of "potential" food safety issues and to offer general suggestions for addressing them. Consequently, "it is the responsibility of individuals and companies . . . to determine what actions are appropriate in their individual operations. . . . This guidance document, as presented, is not sufficient to serve as an action plan for any specific operation but should be viewed as a starting point."[22]

The industry's commodity-specific GAPs did little to advance food safety in field operations beyond previous attempts. For example, the 2006 commodity-specific guidelines advise growers to reduce human pathogen contamination of soil without providing any further guidance. They suggest that "water may be tested on a regular basis, treated or drawn from an appropriate source as a means of assuring it is appropriate for its intended purpose" without any specification of metrics, methods, or frequency of testing. "We stayed away from numbers because we wanted to remain flexible," recalls Gombas. Moreover, "we were running into some opposition from growers who complained 'How *dare* you propose specific guidelines for fresh leafy greens! We've been growing these crops all our lives, and we know what to do.' So at the time, there was still some resistance to changing food safety practices, especially without the science to indicate 'this is exactly what you should be doing.'"[23]

Although the 2006 industry guidelines placed no specific demands on growers, the authors hoped that the guidelines would encourage growers to pay more attention to food safety. Industry leaders, believing that the new guidelines would be taken more seriously if they came from federal regulators, asked FDA officials to coauthor the guidelines or to publish them as agency guidance. However, FDA officials, despite having participated extensively in the process of formulating the guidelines, were unwilling at that time to adopt them as their own without subjecting them to additional review within the agency. Instead, in August 2006, the agency launched the Leafy Greens Safety Initiative in collaboration with the State of California. This initiative sent officials to farms to assess current practices with the aim of further refining existing agency guidance on microbial contamination in what Smith characterizes as a "two-way educational" process between regulators and growers.[24]

Retail Buyer Specifications, Branded Audits, and Food Safety Schemes

While produce industry committees published voluntary guidelines and government agencies issued guidance, retail buyers of fresh produce (business entities, not consumers)—supermarkets, restaurants, and food service companies—also engaged in the development of GAPs. Fearful of the damage that an outbreak could cause to their brands, buyers increasingly included food safety standards in their product specifications. They ensured compliance with these specifications by requiring that their suppliers undergo periodic food safety audits of their operations. The resulting system of private food safety auditing has developed into a global network that governs growers around the world.[25]

Initially, retail buyers considered food safety as part of quality assurance and regulatory compliance. For example, Gale Prince, corporate director of regulatory affairs from 1979 to 2007 at Kroger, one of the nation's largest supermarket chains, supervised a staff of field buyers who visited growers to determine whether their produce met government quality-grading standards and pesticide regulations and, eventually, whether their operations followed government and industry GAPs. Over time, Kroger developed "additional specifications for various products that went beyond the government standards" based on the recommendations of in-house experts and outside consultants, recalls Prince. Other major buyers—including retailers such as Walmart and Costco and restaurant chains such as McDonalds and Taco Bell—employed similar systems.[26]

In implementing these systems, retail buyers—especially supermarkets—increasingly relied on third-party auditors to oversee their produce suppliers. (For a brief account of the origin of third-party food safety auditing in the United States, see appendix C.) One explanation for this turn to third-party auditors is that retail buyers lacked sufficient in-house capacity to conduct all the necessary audits themselves. A typical supermarket carries more than seven hundred fresh produce items, each of which may have as many as a dozen or more suppliers. "There are just too many suppliers; we couldn't possibly audit every single one," explains John Hansen, former vice president in charge of food safety for Sprouts Farmers Market, a national supermarket chain.[27]

A second explanation for increasing buyer reliance on third-party auditors is the nature of the supply chain for fresh produce. To ensure consistent availability of fresh produce throughout the year, supermarkets purchase many items in an auction system, meaning that their suppliers may change frequently. Thus, retailers do not know who many of their suppliers are until they purchase items at auction, too late to inspect the suppliers' cultivation and harvest practices. Similarly, retail supermarkets sometimes buy produce from distributors, so the retailers have no direct relationship with growers. To ensure oversight of growers in these situations, retail buyers include in their product specifications that they will purchase items only from growers and processors who have obtained a third-party food safety audit.[28]

A third, related, explanation for the turn to third-party auditors is cost-effectiveness. A third-party auditor can spread the cost of travel and other expenses by conducting multiple audits in a single trip to a growing region, resulting in a lower cost per audit compared to the cost per audit by in-house staff whom a retail buyer sends out to audit its one or two suppliers in the region. Similarly, a third-party auditor can generate enough audits in a particular type of operation to develop specialized expertise beyond that of in-house staff tasked with auditing a variety of different types of suppliers. Consequently, retail supermarkets outsource auditing services to reduce costs and obtain a higher level of expertise. On the supplier side, the cost to a producer of shepherding around a different auditor from each of its retail buyers is higher than obtaining a smaller number of third-party audits, each of which typically satisfies multiple buyers.[29]

A fourth explanation is that retail buyers believe that third-party auditors enhance the reliability of audits. Third-party auditors provide "another set of eyes," according to Craig Wilson, vice president for quality assurance and food safety at Costco, who first retained third-party auditors to complement the company's in-house auditing program in 1998. Art Davis, a leading food safety consultant, argues that third-party auditors may be less biased than in-house staff, who may also have responsibilities to obtain aesthetically appealing or low-cost produce that influence their judgments regarding food safety.[30]

However, the behavior of many retail buyers reflects a belief that third-party auditors are less reliable than in-house auditors. Companies that sell their own branded products tend to rely more heavily on in-house auditors to oversee suppliers for those products to protect them from food safety failures that could damage their brand. For example, retail supermarkets are more likely to rely on in-house auditors to oversee suppliers of ingredients for their store-brand items. Cynical observers suggest that retail supermarkets use third-party auditors, which they consider less reliable than in-house staff, for their non-store-brand products because third-party auditors are cheaper and provide sufficient reputational protection when food safety failures are traced back to non-store-brand products, for which supermarkets suffer little reputational damage.[31]

The scale and scope of private food safety auditing in all sectors of the food industry exploded between 2000 and 2010. In 2011, the FDA inspected 19,073 domestic food facilities and 995 foreign food facilities. The USDA maintained inspectors in six thousand domestic facilities that produce meat, poultry, and processed egg products. State governments also conducted thousands of food facility inspections each year.[32] By comparison, an industry association representing nine leading private food safety audit firms, asserted in 2011 that its members, alone, conduct more than two hundred thousand audits and inspections in over one hundred countries each year. Beyond these nine industry leaders, the FDA estimated that there were 568 firms conducting private food safety audits. From these figures, it appears that, by 2011, the scale of private food safety auditing activity far exceeded that of all federal and state efforts combined. Reliance on private food safety audits was even greater on farms, where federal and state officials rarely showed up unless they were investigating an outbreak. Primus Labs, a leading third-party auditing firm in the fresh produce sector was conducting "approximately 15,000 audits . . . per year for over 3,000 clients worldwide" by 2012.[33]

Growing demand among retail buyers of fresh produce for third-party audits fueled the growth of an increasing variety of audit standards. FDA guidance and industry guidelines provided the basis for audit criteria. Private third-party auditing firms competing for accounts developed their own branded audits, which typically appealed to retail buyers by offering an array of options ranging from minimal FDA GAPs compliance to more detailed and stringent audit criteria. In addition, individual retail buyers frequently retained their own particular food safety–related product specifications that audit firms included as addenda to their branded audits.[34]

To consolidate the growing number of audit standards, retail trade associations developed food safety schemes designed to provide a single set of audit criteria for all their members. The schemes consist of standards for food safety, auditor conduct, and audit firm management. For example, in 2003, the Food Marketing Institute (FMI), the leading trade association for US food retailers, acquired the Safe Quality Food (SQF) scheme, a food safety auditing system developed in Australia beginning in 1994. The scheme includes a multivolume SQF Code, which contains general standards for implementing a HACCP-based SQF food safety program and for obtaining certification of compliance through periodic external audits, as well as specific standards for fresh produce, grains and pulses, food processing, fishing and aquaculture, pet food and animal feed production, food packaging, and transportation. The scheme also includes a twelve-page guidance document of standards for auditors, whom the FMI licenses to issue certificates of compliance with the scheme. European retailers developed a similar scheme for fresh produce in 1997 that included criteria also for conservation, labor rights, and animal welfare, called EUREPGAP, later renamed GLOBALG.A.P. Canadian retailers followed suit with a fresh produce food safety scheme called CanadaGAP in 2008.[35]

Benchmarking and Harmonization

Notwithstanding these attempts to consolidate and standardize GAPs audits, retailers continued to insist on adding additional, company specific, food safety requirements in their product specifications. For example, a retailer would require its suppliers to obtain audits using the SQF or GlobalG.A.P. scheme with that retailer's particular addendum. Consequently, suppliers were forced to obtain multiple audits to satisfy the diverse demands of different retail buyers. Some growers were forced to undergo as many as two dozen audits a year. Art Davis recalls one grower in 2004 who was subjected to six audits in two weeks.[36]

In response to growers' concerns about the burden of multiple audits, and seeking to "improve cost efficiency throughout the food supply chain," major retailers launched an effort in 2000 to promote convergence among different food safety standards. The International Committee of Food Retail Chains, a trade association, established the Global Food Safety Initiative (GFSI) to define "benchmarks" that set minimum standards for food safety schemes and encourage buyers to accept certification under any scheme that meets these minimum standards. This goal is summed up in the GFSI slogan: "Once certified, accepted everywhere." GFSI officially "recognizes" a number of food safety schemes that meet its benchmarks, which are published in a 170-page guidance document. By the end of the decade, dozens of leading food retailers, manufacturers, and food service providers—including Walmart, Kroger, McDonald's, Coca-Cola, and Sodexo—had agreed to accept certification based on any GFSI-recognized food safety scheme. In the area of fresh produce, GFSI recognized food safety schemes developed by Primus Labs, SQF, GlobalG.A.P., and CanadaGAP.[37]

GFSI's demanding benchmarks and rigorous recognition process have created an echelon of high-quality third-party auditing services, and they have reduced the problem of multiple, redundant third-party audits—but they have not eliminated it. Not all retail buyers want to impose the relatively high cost of obtaining a high-quality GFSI audit on every supplier for each product. Smaller retailers may lack the market power to push large suppliers to pay for more expensive audits. Larger retailers may not wish to overburden suppliers who operate small or local farms. For suppliers, GFSI "is a heavy lift, and there's a perception among retailers that it's too much to ask a supplier to do," according to Hilary Thesmar, vice president for food safety at the FMI, which advocates for gradual efforts to improve the quality of third-party food safety auditing—what she calls "baby steps to get to GFSI." Retailers are also concerned that they will end up paying at least part of the high cost of GFSI audits in the form of higher prices for fresh produce. "Cost is always an issue because margins are so tight for retailers," explains Thesmar. "There are multiple departments in addition to food safety involved in deciding what demands to place on suppliers." In addition, many retailers still insist that audits include an addendum, which may contain particular concerns of the company or more specific standards tailored to a certain type of product. Consequently, audit firms continue to offer a range of audits, only some of which are now GFSI-recognized and many of which continue to include company- or product-specific addenda.[38]

Produce suppliers launched their own effort to address the problem of multiple audits. In 2009, the United Fresh Produce Association (created from the merger of the International Fresh-Cut Produce Association and the United Fresh Fruit and Vegetable Association in 2006) organized the Produce GAPs Harmonization Initiative with the aim of creating a single set of food safety standards that would enable growers to obtain "one audit by any credible third party, acceptable to all buyers." A committee of 150 food safety and fresh produce experts "reviewed 13 commonly accepted fresh produce food safety standards, identified commonalities and selected the words from each that best suited a common standard, without sacrificing any food safety considerations," explains Gombas, who conceived and directed the effort. The committee gathered input from a wide variety of stakeholders— representatives from food companies throughout the supply chain, government agencies, scheme owners, and audit firms—and, in 2011, rolled out a set of standards known as the harmonized standards.[39]

Like retailer-sponsored food safety schemes and benchmarks, the harmonized standards have reduced the burden on suppliers of multiple audits, but they have not eliminated the problem. Although some major buyers accept any audit that uses the harmonized standards, many buyers accept audits only from particular auditors, or they require their own addenda, or they require GFSI-recognized audits. Audits using the harmonized standards are not recognized by GFSI because GFSI recognizes only food safety schemes that include audit process standards—for example, the qualifications, training, conduct, and oversight of auditors—as well as food safety standards. The harmonized standards contain only food safety standards. United Fresh has worked with SQF and GlobalG.A.P. to develop harmonized standards audits so that buyers can obtain a GFSI-recognized harmonized standards audit. These audits are in addition to the other audits that they offer. Consequently, some suppliers have complained that the harmonized standards, rather than creating a universally accepted audit, have merely increased the number of audit options available to their buyers.[40]

The inefficiency of multiple audits is only one of several criticisms of the private auditing system. Audit quality has suffered because the rapidly growing demand for audits exceeds the limited supply of qualified auditors. Many audit firms have resorted to paying independent contractors to perform audits. The more qualified of these are retired food safety managers and government inspectors, who often lack experience in the particular sector in which they are performing audits. Moreover, many older auditors have backgrounds in sanitation but lack training and expertise in microbiology.

Auditors with many years of experience complain that audit quality has also suffered because of an overemphasis on scores and grades at the expense of detailed analysis. Before the 1980s, food processors hired private auditing firms to help them assess and improve their food safety practices, and auditors awarded scores and grades to help companies track the quality of their food safety efforts over time. Beginning in the 1980s, companies increasingly requested scores and grades to satisfy buyer specifications. Companies became more interested in obtaining a passing grade to satisfy their buyers than using the audit process as a means of gaining insight into shortcomings of their own operations and receiving advice about how to address them.[41]

Experienced auditors also complain that a "checklist mentality" has degraded the quality of audits. As the emphasis on scores and grades increased, audit firms and buyers created checklists to provide a consistent basis for scoring and grading. Checklists also provided auditing instructions for newer auditors who lacked the training and experience of older consultants. As audit criteria multiplied over time, the checklists became longer and more detailed. Moreover, audits increasingly focused on reviewing company records rather than visually inspecting plant equipment and workers, on the theory that records provide insight into how a company's food safety program performs over time, whereas walking the plant floor offers only a snapshot on that particular day. The overall result was audits performed by less-well-qualified auditors filling out long detailed checklists based largely on a review of company records.[42]

Even as audit quality declined, audits became more costly. Retail buyers competed with one another to include increasingly onerous food safety requirements—frequently unsupported by any science—in their product specifications. "You've got a lot of companies trying to one up each other," explains Eric Schwartz, former president of Dole Fresh Vegetables. For example, "the buffer zones on the ground—it's not uncommon for a retailer to say 'I need ten feet between the field and the fence,' and another retailer will say, 'Well if that store is at ten feet, I want fifteen.' There's a lot of that going on in the industry, and, unfortunately, it has taken on a life of its own. It's adding a tremendous amount of cost to the industry with no risk reduction." Competition between audit firms also promoted greater stringency and increased costs. According to David Gombas, "It's a lot easier for an auditing firm to market that 'We have tougher standards,' than to say 'Our auditors are better than the other guy's,'" resulting in a continuous "ratcheting up of the stringency of audit standards." Audits also became less consistent. The growing number of audit checklist items typically provided no metrics, requiring auditors to assign scores based on highly subjective qualitative assessments, which made it difficult for audit firms to maintain consistency among audits.[43]

Auditors face considerable pressure to keep audit costs down, and this creates a conflict of interest. Suppliers, who pay for audits—fees range from $1,000 to more than $25,000—seek auditors who are likely to award them a score that will satisfy buyers, and they are unlikely to rehire an auditor whom they perceive to be too tough. "Some suppliers will hunt down the fastest, cheapest, easiest, and least intrusive third-party audit that will provide the certificate," explains David Acheson, former FDA associate commissioner for foods who now directs a leading food safety consulting firm. Consequently, auditors competing for accounts have incentive to reduce the cost and burden of audits by spending less time, downplaying food safety risks, and inflating audit scores. "Some auditing firms are becoming known for their lower cost quotes, and the result is an inadequate audit," asserts Irwin Pronk, a prominent food safety consultant.[44]

Marketing Agreements

The 2006 baby spinach outbreak prompted leafy greens industry leaders to try a new approach to regulating food safety on farms. Desperate to restart production and win back consumer confidence, industry experts began discussing how to improve food safety in leafy greens production. Bob Whitaker hosted informal daily discussions over bagels and coffee in his office at NewStar Fresh Foods with half a dozen food safety managers from leading processors. These discussions quickly expanded to include additional stakeholders—trade association representatives, federal and state regulatory officials, and academic researchers—who formed a working group and developed a draft proposal. Hank Giclas, of the Western Growers Association, organized meetings of leafy greens growers and processors throughout the state at which he presented the draft and obtained feedback, which the working group used to refine the proposal. By the spring of 2007, this process produced the California Leafy Green Products Handler Marketing Agreement (LGMA).[45] (For a more detailed account of the politics behind the California LGMA, see appendix D.)

The LGMA founders began by analyzing the weaknesses within the existing system of GAPs guidance and private audits. To begin with, industry and government GAPs guidance was too vague. GAPs were drafted in general terms to allow for flexibility in implementing them in different types of operations. However, with the increasing scrutiny of audits, many growers wanted more specific instruction. Gombas recalls that "the growers were complaining: 'You tell me I should use water of adequate quality, but what does that mean? How do I know if it's adequate? You tell me I shouldn't harvest produce that has any contamination on it, but how far away from it can I harvest? What's a safe distance?'"[46]

This lack of specificity, coupled with the voluntary nature of GAPs guidance, led to low rates of adoption among farmers. Drew McDonald explains that industry and government guidance "said things like 'You should *consider* testing water. You should *consider* having a supplier approval program. You should *consider* reviewing the fields where your products are grown.'" Consequently, "a vast majority of the industry responded, 'Well, they don't say that I *have to* do all this' or 'They're not specifically telling me what to do.' And so, in the absence of specificity, people just went their merry way, saying, 'We've been doing it this way for a long time. No one's gotten sick, so everything's fine.' There was what I would call a 'packing-shed mentality.'" In the wake of the 2006 baby spinach outbreak, the LGMA founders worried that the failure of even a small segment of growers to take food safety seriously could bring down the entire industry.[47]

In addition to their concerns about GAPs standards, the LGMA founders believed that private third-party audits had failed to deliver sufficient food safety improvements on farms. The quality of audits varied widely depending on the training and experience of the auditors. The decentralized proliferation of food safety specifications by buyers required growers to undergo multiple, largely redundant, audits, which merely increased their costs without improving safety. Buyers' insistence that growers hire and pay the auditors created a conflict of interest that undermined public confidence in the whole system.[48]

The LGMA founders addressed the problem of vague standards by attaching quantitative measures, which they called "metrics," to the GAPs guidance criteria. For example, the LGMA metrics specified testing protocols and thresholds for generic *E. coli* levels in irrigation water, and for fecal coliforms, *Salmonella*, and *E. coli* O157 in compost. Similarly, they defined minimum buffer zones between flooded areas and crops, as well as the radius around animal droppings found in fields within which crops should not be harvested. In food-processing plants, HACCP's use of critical limits had provided measurable, quantitative criteria that could be monitored over time to enhance the management of food safety. The LGMA metrics did the same thing for farms.[49]

The LGMA founders avoided the problems with private third-party audits by relying instead on government inspectors from the California Department of Food and Agriculture (CDFA). They also found a way to make buyers rather than growers pay for the audits and to ensure near-universal adoption of the metrics among growers. The LGMA founders achieved these reforms by creating a marketing agreement.

In the midst of the Great Depression, the federal government had passed the Agricultural Marketing Agreement Act of 1937. Simultaneously, the State of California passed the California Marketing Act of 1937. Both acts authorized the creation of marketing agreements. A marketing agreement is a voluntary commitment among a group of agricultural producers or handlers of a specific commodity that sets common standards for production volume, quality characteristics, or packaging, with the aim of stabilizing prices. Marketing agreements thus allow agricultural producers and handlers to organize in ways that might otherwise violate antitrust laws designed to prevent collusion and price-fixing.[50]

The LGMA founders created a marketing agreement under the California Marketing Act that set food safety standards for leafy greens growers. The agreement, however, is between leafy greens handlers—defined as "any person who handles, processes, ships or distributes leafy green product for market." The agreement distinguishes handlers from growers, who produce greens, and explicitly states that the definition of handler "does not include a retailer." Thus, handlers are the link between growers and retailers. Handlers who sign the marketing agreement commit to purchasing leafy greens exclusively from growers who pass periodic food safety audits of their operations using LGMA standards by CDFA inspectors trained and licensed by the USDA. In exchange, signatory handlers may display an official mark on their products and their promotional materials indicating membership in the LGMA and CDFA certification of their products. Signatory handlers who violate the terms of the agreement lose their certification and their right to use the mark. Moreover, unauthorized use of the mark constitutes an unfair trade practice in violation of state consumer protection law. The LGMA marks the first time that a marketing agreement has been used to promote food safety standards.[51]

Following public hearings, the CDFA approved the LGMA. To assist the CDFA in the administration of the agreement, the LGMA establishes the California Leafy Green Products Handler Advisory Board, consisting of handler signatories from different growing regions of the state and one representative of the general public, who must be unaffiliated with any industry organization. The agreement authorizes the LGMA board to contract with the CDFA to provide agency inspectors to perform on-farm audits that assess growers' compliance with LGMA food safety standards. These third-party government audits are paid for by handlers, who pay an annual assessment that finances the operating costs of the agreement—including government inspections—as a condition of LGMA certification.[52]

Thus, the LGMA board is a public entity empowered to administer a voluntary agreement among private firms. The rules that govern administration of the agreement have been adopted by the secretary of food and agriculture as state regulations. However, the food safety standards by which the firms agree to abide are private industry standards accepted by the state agency responsible for administering the agreement. This acceptance means that the CDFA agrees to provide audits against those standards. It does not, however, give the standards the status of agency regulations.[53]

The LGMA has achieved nearly universal adoption of its standards among California leafy greens growers by making handlers the subjects of the marketing agreement. A small group of handlers has a particularly high stake in preventing outbreaks, and they command a level of market power that gives them considerable influence over growers. Although outbreaks can affect everyone in the leafy greens industry, they pose the greatest threat to handlers who produce leading brands of fresh-cut bagged produce. These companies lack the anonymity among consumers that shields growers and handlers of unmarked whole produce. Packaging bearing a brand name makes it easier to identify a particular company as the source of an outbreak and tends to focus unwanted media attention on the company, even if contamination originates with a grower further upstream in the supply chain. Thus, the 2006 outbreak is popularly known as the Dole baby spinach outbreak, not the Paicines Ranch or Natural Selection Foods baby spinach outbreak. This vulnerability explains why food safety managers at leading brand-name producers of fresh-cut bagged greens—for example, Bob Whitaker at NewStar Fresh

Produce, Drew McDonald at Taylor Farms, and Eric Schwartz at Dole Fresh Vegetables—initiated the LGMA. A few of these large brand name handlers dominate the market. In 2006, Fresh Express (owned by Chiquita) accounted for 41 percent of all bagged, fresh-cut salad sales, and Dole accounted for 31 percent. Along with the next two leading firms, Ready Pac and Earthbound Farm, four companies controlled 86 percent of the market. Thus, a small group of highly brand-sensitive handlers who controlled most of the market had both the motivation and the leverage to encourage widespread adoption of the new standards among growers. Six months after approval of the LGMA, fifty-one handlers, responsible for 90 percent of the leafy greens produced in California, had joined the LGMA. This number rose eventually to seventy-one handlers, responsible for more than 99 percent of California leafy greens. The handlers were encouraged, in part, by Canada's decision in 2007 to limit the importation of leafy greens to those bearing LGMA certification.[54]

The LGMA has not eliminated the problem of multiple audits. A recent survey by USDA economists of seven California grower-shippers certified as LGMA compliant found that each was subject to additional audits using between two and five different audit standards other than the LGMA metrics. The total cost of these audits ranged between $27,150 and $305,430 per firm.[55]

The LGMA founders insisted, from the outset, that metrics be supported by science. "The guiding principle in developing the LGMA was that everything had to be based in science," recalls McDonald. The LGMA founders took a "three-tier approach" to developing metrics. The introduction to the LGMA standards explains that "a comprehensive literature review was conducted to determine if there was a scientifically valid basis for establishing a metric for the identified risk factor or best practice. If the literature research did not identify scientific studies that could support an appropriate metric, standards or metrics from authoritative or regulatory bodies were used to establish a metric. If neither scientific studies nor authoritative bodies had allowed for suitable metrics, consensus among industry representatives and/or other stakeholders was sought to establish metrics."[56]

Given the dearth of scientific studies directly related to microbial contamination in farming operations, the LGMA relies heavily on established standards from other areas of regulation. For example, in developing a four-hundred-foot standard as the minimum buffer between cattle-feeding operations and crops, Trevor Suslow recalls that "there were no scientific studies that specifically addressed the transfer of pathogens from a feeding operation to a lettuce field." There were, however, "studies that dealt with the movement of what's called fugitive dust from these operations, and you have local ordinances that use this data to establish four-hundred-foot setback distances from residential areas. There wasn't a specific data set that specifically addressed produce safety, but we drew on the best available science that gave us some point of reference for a starting point." In developing the metric for irrigation water of "adequate quality for its intended use," Gombas recalls: "There was no science to come up with a number. So the closest thing that we could come up with was, 'Well the EPA is saying that these recreational water standards are safe enough to swim in, and, if it's safe enough to swim in, it must be safe enough to irrigate with.'"[57]

The LGMA founders anticipated that the metrics would develop over time as the relevant science advanced. The LGMA standards guide, created by industry and accepted by the California secretary of food and agriculture, "has been and continues to be an evolving and live document, as new information comes to light through scientific research or from other sources," explains Suslow. The LGMA board established a technical committee, composed of food safety managers and consultants, to review proposed changes to the metrics and make recommendations to the board. To support scientific research related to food safety on farms, the Produce Marketing Association worked with other trade groups, individual companies, state agencies, and the University of California, Davis, to establish the Center for Produce Safety in 2007. The aim of the center was to fund and disseminate "hands on, boots-on-the-ground research to begin filling some of those knowledge gaps so that, where we were just surmising what a best practice should be based on logic, we might be able to get some data to actually give it more direction," explains Whitaker, who estimates that in its first decade of operation, the center funded "about 120 projects to the tune of about $18 million," raised from industry.[58]

The LGMA founders believed that they had created a model that could be applied to the regulation of leafy greens nationwide. In October 2007, having successfully supported the establishment of a similar leafy greens marketing agreement in Arizona, they asked the USDA's Agricultural Marketing Service (AMS) to consider a national leafy greens marketing agreement. In response, the AMS published an advance notice of proposed rule making to obtain feedback from stakeholders, who submitted more than 3,500 public comments. In June 2009, a coalition of industry associations submitted a proposal for a national leafy greens marketing agreement to the AMS and requested public hearings, which the agency held in September and October. During nine days of hearings in seven cities around the country, 120 individuals testified, generating 4,935 pages of testimony. In April 2011, the AMS published the Proposed National Marketing Agreement Regulating Leafy Green Vegetables and invited comments by the end of July.[59]

The proposed national leafy greens marketing agreement (NLGMA) was modeled on the California LGMA. The proposal contemplated reliance on standards developed by industry experts and accepted by the AMS. Handlers that complied would earn the right to display an NLGMA certification mark. Assessments from signatory handlers would fund monitoring by AMS inspectors or others approved by AMS. A board of industry representatives would administer the agreement with advice from a technical review committee. Board decisions would be subject to the USDA secretary's approval.[60]

Small and midsize leafy greens growers opposed the NLGMA. They argued that the NLGMA, like its California predecessor, was designed to serve the interests of fresh-cut processors. David Runsten, director of policy and programs for the Community Alliance with Family Farmers (CAFF), a trade association representing small and midsize California farmers, in testimony at a USDA hearing on the NLGMA, asserted that a small group of processors dominated the California LGMA board and created safety standards designed specifically to reduce the risk of contamination in monoculture growing operations that supplied the fresh-cut industry. Runsten argued that a crop-by-crop approach to regulating food safety on farms—one set of rules for greens, another for tomatoes, and a third for melons—might be suitable for large-scale commodity agribusiness but imposed unnecessary burdens on small and midsize farms that grew a variety of crops, some of which grow as many as one hundred different crops in the course of a year. A separate set of metrics for each type of crop imposed a multitude of regulatory requirements on diversified farms, which, unlike large operations, could not take advantage of economies of scale that made it easier to absorb the costs of compliance.[61]

Runsten insisted that the NLGMA empowered fresh-cut processors to shut out of the wholesale market any farmer who refused to comply with excessively stringent metrics that imposed unnecessary precautions on small and medium growers. "Metrics that might be appropriate to the large commercial operations with entire fields of one crop destined to be processed and to sit in a bag for weeks are inappropriate for smaller, more diversified producers who are supplying a local wholesale market."

Moreover, according to Runsten, LGMA metrics that required buffer zones between crops and noncrop vegetation and animals were "particularly burdensome for small farms that include animal production or that try to integrate farming practices with protective environmental or ecological practices." LGMA imposition of "clean fields" metrics, complained Runsten, "also had a spillover effect in other crops, even those not eaten raw, such as potatoes, artichokes, and Brussels sprouts. After 20 years of planting hedgerows and other conservation measures on farms, CAFF finds itself in direct conflict with food safety auditors who say that 'food safety trumps the environment.'"

Opposition to the NLGMA came also from consumer advocates. They argued that marketing agreements offered a poor substitute for government regulation. "As a voluntary program, members can simply elect not to participate, and there is no penalty for doing so beyond the removal of a marketing seal on their packaging," objected Caroline Smith DeWaal, then director of food safety at the Center for Science in the Public Interest, at a 2009 congressional hearing on leafy greens marketing agreements. "If Good Agricultural Practices . . . are not required on every farm . . . the door remains open for contaminated produce to reach consumers," complained Elisa Odabashian, the West Coast director for Consumers Union, in comments on the AMS's 2007 advanced notice of proposed rule making.[62]

Consumer advocates criticized the legitimacy of marketing agreements, alleging a lack of transparency, stakeholder participation, and public accountability. Odabashian complained that the California LGMA metrics had been developed "behind closed doors and without public comment. The industry appointed itself as the safety oversight board, including some of the very companies, such as Dole, which have been accused of marketing contaminated leafy greens."

Consumer advocates also challenged the effectiveness of marketing agreements, citing outbreaks traced back to California leafy greens following the implementation of the LGMA. "Industry self-regulation seldom protects consumers," declared Odabashian. "Clearly, the use of a voluntary marketing agreement, developed by the very people who brought spinach and bagged salad mix contaminated with a particularly virulent strain of E. coli (O157:H7) to market, is not the best way to restore consumer confidence or ensure that another terrible outbreak does not occur."

Odabashian and DeWaal argued that existing GAPs guidance and marketing agreements had proved ineffective in ensuring the safety of leafy greens. Instead, they advocated mandatory federal regulations. "The very process of rule making offers an opportunity for notice and comment among all stakeholders, with the aim of ensuring . . . the public health. . . . Such notice and comment is of course absent from the boardrooms where today's private contracts are drafted," asserted DeWaal. Responsibility for developing and enforcing such regulations should be assigned to the FDA, whose mission, in contrast to that of AMS, was consumer protection rather than industry marketing. "Congress should act to curtail the trend toward use of marketing orders by providing FDA with the authority and resources it needs to carry out its food safety responsibilities," she concluded.

Congress eventually heeded these calls to charge FDA with the task of developing and implementing mandatory on-farm food safety regulations for fresh produce when it passed the Food Safety Modernization Act (FSMA) in December 2010. As the FDA was developing those rules, the AMS quietly abandoned its efforts to establish a national LGMA. In December 2013, the agency published a brief notice in the *Federal Register* terminating its NLGMA rule-making procedure.[63]

The FSMA Produce Safety Rule

In his March 14, 2009, weekly radio address, two months after his first inauguration, President Obama declared: "There are certain things that only government can do. And one of those things is ensuring that the foods we eat . . . are safe and don't cause us harm." Citing the baby spinach outbreak of 2006, an outbreak traced back to hot peppers in 2008, and a peanut butter outbreak that was unfolding as he took office, Obama announced the creation of the Food Safety Working Group, cochaired by the secretaries of health and human services and the USDA and composed of senior officials from the FDA, FSIS, CDC, and other federal agencies, with instructions "to report back to me with recommendations as soon as possible" about "how we can upgrade our food safety laws for the 21st century."[64]

The president's Food Safety Working Group reported back "key findings" in June. Among the priorities it listed, the working group pledged that "by the end of the month, FDA will issue commodity-specific draft guidance on preventive controls that industry can implement to reduce the risk of microbial contamination in the production and distribution of tomatoes, melons, and leafy greens. These proposals will help the Federal government establish a minimum standard for production across the country. Over the next two years, FDA will seek public comment and work to require adoption of these approaches through regulation." In August 2009, the FDA published a notice in the *Federal Register* requesting comments on draft commodity-specific guidance documents on tomatoes, melons, and leafy greens.[65]

Although it appeared from the outside that these documents grew out of the president's working group, the draft guidance documents were part of the FDA's ongoing efforts to respond to outbreaks involving these fresh produce items dating back to the early 2000s. Following publication of its initial 1998 GAPs guidance for fresh produce, the FDA had pledged in its 2004 produce safety action plan to work with industry to develop commodity-specific guidance, and FDA experts had participated in the development of the industry's 2006 commodity-specific leafy greens guidance, published just before the baby spinach outbreak. Additionally, the FDA had developed guidance on processing fresh-cut produce between 2004 and 2008 and issued a notice in the *Federal Register* in September 2008 soliciting comments on how to improve the agency's GAPs guidance. The FDA's 2009 draft commodity-specific guidance "reflects the evolution of our thinking between our initial GAPs guidance in 1998 and that point in time," recalls the FDA's Michelle Smith, who started at the FDA in 1991 and has been involved in the agency's fresh produce food safety efforts since President Clinton's 1997 Food Safety Initiative.[66]

While the FDA was developing these guidance documents, the Center for Science in the Public Interest petitioned the FDA in November 2006, following the baby spinach outbreak, and again in 2008, to issue mandatory on-farm food safety regulations for fresh produce. DeWaal had complained that the spinach outbreak demonstrated that FDA reliance on guidance was "weak-kneed" and that "no one is really in charge of food safety on the farm," because the agency "can only suggest but not enforce. They need direction from Congress to address standards on the farm."[67]

Starting in 2008, various members of Congress introduced food safety reform legislation in both the House and the Senate. In the final days of December 2010, both chambers passed the Food Safety Modernization Act, which President Obama signed on January 4, 2011. DeWaal and other consumer advocates heralded FSMA (pronounced "fizma") as "a historic victory for consumers . . . the most important food safety advance in 70 years." The new law instructed the FDA to issue food safety regulations for the production of fresh produce—what became known as the FSMA Produce Safety Rule, which the agency published in November 2015.[68]

In some respects, the FDA's FSMA Produce Safety Rule is a continuation of efforts by industry and the agency to develop GAPs guidance. In crafting standards and metrics for the new rule, the agency drew heavily on the "experience over time and the interactions we've had with industry," explains Smith. "Industry folks really put a lot of effort into educating us—for example, different groups provided us opportunities to tour farms." California LGMA founders, in particular, take credit for shaping the Produce Safety Rule. "FDA has, for many years, been involved in the industry," says Drew McDonald, and consequently "FSMA, by and large, got it right. I mean, they were listening. They wrote up what many of us in the industry were already doing, the exact language if you really do a comparison. In the produce rule, they borrowed so much—and I take it as a compliment—from the leafy greens metrics. So they really got it right." According to David Gombas, "When the FDA created the Produce Safety Rule, they looked at all the different standards out there including GlobalG.A.P., Canada GAP, and all the other standards, and the only one that had numbers was leafy greens. So when they were trying to figure out what is water of 'adequate quality,' the only one that had a standard was leafy greens, so they adopted the standard from leafy greens."[69]

Like earlier industry and agency efforts, FSMA calls for "science-based minimum standards" for the production and harvesting of fresh produce, and the agency's Produce Safety Rule focuses on water quality, soil amendments, animal intrusion, worker hygiene, and harvesting equipment. The rule offers a mix of specific quantitative metrics and general guidelines. For example, the water standards prescribe testing methods and threshold values for *E. coli*. By contrast, the animal intrusion standards require growers to "assess the relevant areas" in growing fields "as needed," and, "if significant evidence of potential contamination is found," to "take measures reasonably necessary" to avoid harvesting the contaminated produce. The agency promises to issue future guidance to assist farms in complying with the regulations.[70]

In other respects, however, the FDA's FSMA Produce Safety Rule marks a departure from the past. The Produce Safety Rule abandons the agency's efforts to develop commodity-specific GAPs, driven by repeated outbreaks of what the agency came to consider "high-risk" crops, such as leafy greens, tomatoes, and melons. Instead, the new rule takes an "integrated approach," which prescribes the same standards for all fresh produce. The agency explains that its new rule "provides a whole farm approach rather than commodity-specific measures, which would be challenging for farms that grow multiple crops." Moreover, the agency views its prior focus on outbreaks as reflecting too reactive and too narrow an approach to regulating food safety. Reliance on outbreak data meant that the agency took action only after consumers fell ill, and its efforts addressed only those risks associated with illnesses traced back to a particular food. FDA data collection from farms associated with outbreaks simply reinforced its exclusive attention to known risks. By contrast, FSMA mandates a "prevention-based approach" to food safety capable of protecting consumers not merely from a narrow range of known risks following an outbreak but from a broad range of suspected risks before anyone gets sick. Moreover, although the FDA's integrated approach rejects commodity-specific GAPs, it does not impose a one-size-fits-all set of standards on every grower and every crop. The new regulations allow for various means of compliance in many cases; they provide procedures for obtaining variances, and they exempt certain types of growers and products altogether.[71]

The most radical departure marked by the FSMA Produce Safety Rule was the shift from guidance to mandatory standards. In the face of a congressional mandate to issue binding rules, the FDA's 2009 draft commodity-specific guidance documents for leafy greens, tomatoes, and melons remained unpublished. Smith believes that the shift from voluntary to mandatory standards had roots in both industry and government: "The initial response to regulating the industry was guidance, and that was fine with everyone. Around the time of the spinach outbreak, some folks started shifting toward being supportive of regulation, including some industry groups who, in advance of FSMA, sent letters to Congress saying that they would support produce regulation because, when an outbreak happens, it negatively impacts the entire industry. So, over time, support for regulations dealing with best practices on farms was growing. And it was FSMA that gave us the final push and direction to actually do it."[72]

FSMA's mandate that the FDA issue binding regulations for farming operations raised questions about the agency's capacity to monitor and enforce compliance. Historically, FDA inspectors had visited farms only as part of outbreak investigations. It seemed highly unlikely that Congress would appropriate sufficient funds to enable the agency to routinely inspect the more than 120,000 US farms that grow fresh produce for sale. Peter Barton Hutt, a former FDA chief counsel known as "the dean of the food and drug bar," opined that "the lack of reality in the statute is staggering." Ronald Doering, former administrator of the Canadian Food Inspection Agency, voiced his deep skepticism about FSMA's success, declaring that "the Americans laboured long and hard and delivered a mouse. . . . There are lessons here for Canada. . . . Don't legislate what you can't enforce."[73]

The FDA responded to doubts about its capacity to enforce the Produce Safety Rule by explaining that FSMA created a new approach to industry regulation that would not require comprehensive government inspection or enforcement. "There is no reasonable expectation FDA will have the resources to make routine on-farm inspection a major source of accountability for compliance with produce safety standards," the agency explained in a 2014 publication. From the outset, the agency insisted, "Congress envisioned a different role for FDA on produce farms compared to food facilities." Whereas FSMA mandated specific inspection frequencies for FDA oversight of food processors, the legislation made no mention of inspection frequency for fresh produce growers.[74]

The agency was "reinventing" itself, said the FDA deputy commissioner for foods and veterinary medicine Michael Taylor (who had previously led efforts in the late 1990s as FSIS administrator to develop and implement the USDA's PR/HACCP regulations for the meat and poultry industries). "Historically we've had a tradition of enforcement at facilities, and it's important, but the shift we're undertaking is to understand that the purpose is not enforcement per se, but to get high rates of compliance with the standards," Taylor explained in a 2014 speech to the United Fresh Produce Association. "We're really focusing on outcomes. We're looking at systems and how we can work with the vast majority of operators who want to produce safe food and to get compliance on a voluntary basis, and that's the outcome that matters. That's a fundamental reorientation of our approach to our oversight." In a posting on the FDA's *FDA Voice* blog, Taylor explained that the agency planned to work "in close collaboration with other government agencies (federal, state, local, tribal, and foreign), the food industry and other stakeholders" to supplement its limited inspection and enforcement resources. The agency would reserve its own inspection resources for "high-risk" industry sectors. In addition, the agency would issue new guidance to clarify standards and conduct "outreach and technical assistance to facilitate voluntary compliance." The agency pledged to "educate before we regulate." In explaining its proposed Produce Safety Rule in 2013, the agency wrote that "we anticipate that compliance will be achieved primarily through the conscientious efforts of farmers, complemented by the efforts of State and local governments, extension services, private audits and certifications, and other private sector supply chain management efforts."[75]

The FDA's heavy reliance on risk-based inspection, supply chain management, and voluntary compliance suggests that, in practice, the FSMA Produce Safety Rule may be less of a departure than initially anticipated from the agency's earlier reliance on commodity-specific guidance. In contrast to President Obama's insistence prior to the passage of FSMA that "only government" can ensure "that the foods we eat . . . are safe and don't cause us harm," Taylor told the audience at a 2012 food safety conference that "FSMA recognizes the primary responsibility and capacity of the food industry to make food safe" and "the complementary role of government."[76]

The challenges of inspection and enforcement also reveal that the FSMA Produce Safety Rule shares with the California LGMA a hybrid public-private structure. They are, in this sense, mirror images of each other. The LGMA relies on government inspectors to audit compliance with private industry standards. Limited FDA and state resources for inspections mean that the Produce Safety Rule is likely to rely heavily on private auditors to audit compliance with government standards.[77]

The publication of the Produce Safety Rule has raised questions about whether the FDA's new standards will simply add to the "audit fatigue" suffered by growers already subject to multiple GAPs audits and, in the case of California leafy green growers, LGMA certification. The FDA explains that its Produce Safety Rule sets mandatory minimum standards for growing and harvesting fresh produce, and the agency recognizes that suppliers and marketing agreements may subject farmers to different and, in some cases, more stringent requirements. Although the FDA has insisted on establishing its own standards and oversight system, and it has, for the present, refused to recognize private certification as a substitute for compliance with the Produce Safety Rule standards, the agency believes that private standards are likely to facilitate compliance with government standards. In response to comments, the agency explained that "over time, we expect that certification programs and food safety programs will develop tools to demonstrate the alignment of their provisions with FDA requirements," so that "to the extent that certification schemes or food safety programs are consistent with the produce safety regulation, then compliance with those schemes or programs could be relevant to compliance" with the Produce Safety Rule. The agency did not further specify what, exactly, "relevant" means here. It appears that the agency hopes its new standards will serve as a benchmark for private schemes and a harmonizing influence. Whether it is more successful than GFSI and the harmonized standards remains to be seen.[78]

Optimism among consumer advocates following the passage of FSMA has given way to mounting frustration. When the FDA failed to meet statutory deadlines for publishing the FSMA regulations, the Center for Food Safety, a nonprofit consumer and environmental advocacy organization, sued the FDA in federal court. The delay was due to a mix of factors, including the complexity of the issues involved, the volume of new regulations required, limited agency resources, the slow pace of White House oversight, and industry resistance to various proposed regulations. The court ordered the agency to finalize the regulations by June 30, 2015. The FDA finally published its Produce Safety Rule in November 2015, which included compliance dates of January 2018 for large farms, January 2019 for midsize farms, and January 2020 for smaller farms (the smallest farms, those with annual sales under $25,000, are exempted altogether from FSMA). Then, in September 2017, FDA commissioner Scott Gottlieb announced that the agency would delay inspections to assess compliance until 2019 and focus instead on "training, guidance development, and outreach." He also announced an extension of compliance deadlines for the agricultural water standard for an additional four years, to 2022, 2023, and 2024 respectively. On January 4, 2018, the seventh anniversary of President Obama's signing of FSMA, the FDA published a guidance document announcing an indefinite delay on enforcing several major FSMA regulations applicable to farm operations, including some provisions of the Produce Safety Rule, pending a revision of the regulations. Peter Lurie, exasperated president of the Center for Science and the Public Interest, accused the Trump administration of "undermining" FSMA.[79]

The FDA insists that it is moving ahead at a steady pace with implementation of the Produce Safety Rule. The agency has partnered with state agriculture departments, academic institutions, and industry associations to develop and provide training programs for farmers and state inspectors. The FDA expects that most on-farm inspections will be performed by state agencies with financial and technical support from the FDA. Whether this arrangement will produce sufficient resources to implement widespread routine government inspection of farms remains to be seen.[80]

Liability and Product Contamination Insurance

Bill Marler, the nation's best-known foodborne illness plaintiffs' attorney, knew about the Dole baby spinach outbreak almost two weeks before the FDA issued its warning to consumers to avoid fresh spinach. "It was Labor Day weekend and I was on the Oregon coast with my two daughters learning how to surf," recalls Marler. "Earlier that week, my office had received calls from a mom in Wisconsin with two children who both had hemolytic uremic syndrome and were in the hospital. She called because she was convinced that it was Dole baby spinach, still in her refrigerator, that caused her kids to get sick, and she felt that the Health Department wasn't paying attention to her. That was not an unusual call for us to get, and we sent her a typical packet for prospective clients. Then, later in the week, before I went down to the Oregon coast, we received another call from a family in Utah with two kids sick from *E. coli*. At that point, I had not yet connected that case to the one in Wisconsin. But then, on the weekend, while I was in Oregon, I got an email on my Blackberry that the office had received another call, this one from a woman in Salem, who said that she had been infected with *E. coli*, she had just gotten out of the hospital, and she had eaten Dole baby spinach. I was like, 'Damn. There's a nationwide outbreak.'"[81]

"Over that weekend, I emailed a few people in public health saying, 'Hey, I've just gotten three phone calls—two of them ID'ing Dole baby spinach— all in the same time frame. Are you seeing anything?' but I got no response. So on Tuesday, after the Labor Day holiday, I started emailing reporters, saying, 'I think there's a nationwide outbreak going on. You need to start poking health departments.' Then I got a call towards the end of that week from an epidemiologist in a state that had cases. He told me that there was a nationwide *E. coli* outbreak, but he did not tell me the product name."[82]

Unable to confirm his suspicions about the source of the outbreak, Marler

nevertheless filed a lawsuit on behalf of the Salem victim against Dole on September 14, the same day that the FDA issued its initial warning to consumers
not to eat bagged spinach and a day before the outbreak made national headlines. "I was thinking to myself, I'm pretty sure I'm right, but if it's not really
Dole, I'm going to look pretty stupid," Marler recalls. Six days later, Marler's
suspicion was confirmed. On September 20, the FDA announced that lab
results from New Mexico found the outbreak strain of *E. coli* O157 in a package of Dole baby spinach. Marler eventually filed seventy-six lawsuits against
Dole and its suppliers on behalf of victims of the 2006 baby spinach outbreak.
He settled all of them for undisclosed amounts. Marler negotiated the settlements with the insurance carriers for Dole, Natural Selection Foods, the company that processed and packed the contaminated baby spinach for Dole, and
Mission Organics, the grower that supplied Natural Selection with spinach
from a number of fields, including the one leased from the Paicines Ranch,
where the contaminated lot of spinach was grown and where investigators
suspected the contamination originated.[83] (For a more detailed description of
the litigation dynamics in foodborne illness cases, see appendix B.)

Plaintiffs' attorneys and liability insurers have a symbiotic relationship.
On the one hand, lawsuits filed by plaintiffs' attorneys expose companies to
liability, which creates demand for liability insurance. On the other hand,
liability insurance provides funds for paying judgments and settlements that
motivate plaintiffs' attorneys to file lawsuits. Liability insurance is key to the
"collectability" of a tort claim—that is, "the defendant's ability to pay and the
facility with which the defendant can be made to pay," according to leading
insurance law scholar Tom Baker. For most plaintiffs' attorneys contemplating litigation, "liability insurance is the only asset that plaintiffs can count on
collecting."[84]

In addition to liability coverage that compensates victims of foodborne
illness, some insurers also sell product contamination insurance, which compensates food companies for losses associated with recalling a product that
the company suspects may be contaminated. Product contamination insurance, also known as recall coverage, covers the costs of pulling a product
from store shelves, collecting it, and destroying it. Some policies also cover
associated business losses when buyers reduce or cancel purchases, or when
damage to a company's brand reduces its sales, as well as the costs of reha-
bilitating a product. At least one insurer offers such coverage even when a
contaminated product of another company causes the policyholder to lose
business income. As public health authorities become increasingly proficient
at tracing outbreaks back to specific products, product contamination insur-

ance with related business interruption coverage has become increasingly common in the food industry.[85]

Insurance companies not only play an essential role in compensating foodborne illness victims and food companies; they also play an emerging role in reducing the risk of contamination. As Baker explains, "Once insurers accept the financial responsibility for civil liability, they not only have an incentive to manage the defense and settlement of liability claims, but they also have an incentive to reduce the likelihood that those claims arise in the first place." A number of insurance industry practices have the potential to reduce the risk of accidents that give rise to liability.[86]

By means of risk selection and risk pricing, insurers create incentives for companies seeking insurance to reduce the risk of accidents. When a company seeks to obtain insurance, it will typically contact an insurance broker to help it find appropriate coverage, or the company may approach an agent representing a particular insurer. When the company applies for insurance, an employee of the insurer known as an underwriter assesses the magnitude of the risks for which the company seeks coverage to determine whether it would be profitable for the insurer to sell the company an insurance policy and, if so, how much to charge in premiums.[87]

In deciding whether to insure food companies and how to price policies, underwriters seek information about the quality of applicants' food safety management systems. Underwriters obtain initial information from brokers and agents, who generate risk profiles of applicants as part of helping them obtain suitable coverage. For example, "in California's Central Valley area, there are a number of brokers and agents who are known to specialize within the farm community," explains Jack Hipp, a longtime senior executive at Fireman's Fund, now part of Allianz Global, which insured Dole, Natural Selection, and Mission Organics during the 2006 baby spinach outbreak. Typically, a broker or agent "will gather information on the risk . . . so that they can then look for carrier matches and make recommendations about the types of coverage." The brokers "are familiar with the food industry, so they know what the issues are within the industry," says Mike Johnson, an executive at Nationwide, another insurer of Mission Organics in the 2006 baby spinach outbreak.[88]

In addition to reviewing broker and agent risk profiles, the underwriter investigates the company's reputation, whether it has been associated with any prior outbreaks, its internal records, and its history of prior insurance claims. "If a company has a poor loss record because of frequent or severe contamination events, then they will need to pay higher premiums, or the insurer may decide not to insure them," says Ed Mitchell, the principal underwriter for product recall insurance at MS Amlin. Underwriters also review the company's third-party food safety audits and send the insurer's own in-house risk experts, or hired consultants, to inspect the company's operations. "We have food safety experts who give us an idea as to the quality of the account," explains Johnson.[89]

Risk selection and pricing are ongoing. According to Doug Becker, director of risk management at Nationwide, his office periodically sends risk management consultants to review clients' operations. "After a policy is issued, if the risk management consultant goes out and identifies that there is risky behavior going on, he will make recommendations to reduce that exposure and then report back to the underwriter about whether those recommendations were followed. If the client doesn't follow the recommendations, that may affect their premium upon renewal or their actual renewal."[90]

Insurers have developed underwriting guidelines to standardize their underwriting practices, and they subject their underwriters to one or more layers of management oversight. "The underwriter works within a set of underwriting guidelines," explains James Derr, a risk management expert at XL Insurance. Underwriters' risk assessments are typically subjected to "a quality assurance review that takes place at the next level of underwriting, just to make sure that we have carefully evaluated the liability potential."[91]

Food companies seeking insurance want to qualify for that insurance, and they want the best price they can get. Risk selection and risk pricing by insurers give those companies incentives to practice a level of food safety that conforms to the insurers' underwriting guidelines. Conformity with these guidelines requires compliance with government and industry GAPs standards. According to Hipp, assessing an application for insurance involves "surveying the actual operation to determine how well they comply with the various industry, proprietary, and state safety controls."[92]

Insurance companies gain experience and build expertise in understanding food safety risks through claims management. When a policyholder files an insurance claim, an employee of the insurer called a claims adjuster investigates the claimed loss, determines the amount owed, and negotiates any payments. "Risk knowledge comes from experience," says Mitchell. "Insurers have paid hundreds of claims and been involved with hundreds of incidents since the insurance market started offering this coverage. One consequence of this is that we are able to gather an ongoing stream of data that enables us to identify and track trends. . . . When a company applies to us for insurance, they have to provide us with detailed information, and that will allow us to make an assessment of the risk against the various metrics that we use to price the risk." Claims management provides feedback that helps make underwriting more sophisticated, explains Hipp. "Our underwriters were able to learn immensely from the Dole case through our claims people, and the legal, medical, and scientific experts that the claims people work with in litigation. You can't duplicate that; you can't buy it elsewhere. The underwriter learns from a claim why the loss occurred and how best to avoid it in the future. You can apply model data all you want, but without the unique insights you get from real world experience, that's only part of the equation, and you're probably missing some very unique aspects of underwriting a risk."[93]

In addition to risk selection and risk pricing, another means that insurers have to reduce the risk of accidents is contract design. Insurance contracts include a variety of terms and conditions that provide policyholders with incentives to take precautions. For example, insurers may limit coverage using deductibles or exclusions, leaving policyholders responsible for up to a certain amount of money or for certain types of conduct not covered by the policy. Deductibles and exclusions counteract any tendency that a policyholder might have to relax its level of care in reliance on insurance coverage, a problem known as "moral hazard."[94]

With the benefit of experience and increasing expertise, insurance companies have begun to tailor the terms and conditions of their policies to reduce the risk of contamination in food production. According to Hipp, some companies use warranty terms, under which a claim is covered only if the company meets the terms of the warranty. For example, "you [the food company] warrant that you are getting third-party inspections on a quarterly basis and, if you are not, then there is either no coverage or reduced coverage."[95]

An additional means that insurers have to reduce the risk of accidents is loss prevention in the form of providing risk management advice to companies on how to avoid losses. "We set aside a portion of the premium that our clients pay us for what we call 'risk engineering work,'" explains Mitchell. This involves hiring an outside consultant to "audit overall food safety systems, looking for gaps or areas of improvement, and then spending the money that we've set aside working with [the client] to improve their food safety." Jane McCarthy, a recently retired senior underwriter at Liberty International Underwriters with more than three decades of experience, explains that such "preincident services" provided by the consultants can run into the tens of thousands of dollars. Offering risk-management consulting services makes an insurer more attractive to clients as they compete against other insurers, and it helps insurers reduce the risk of claims.[96]

Insurers have become increasingly sophisticated in their understanding of food safety standards, which has improved their capacity to select and price risks, craft safety-enhancing contract terms, and provide practical advice to clients about risk reduction. "After the Dole spinach outbreak, I led an intensive ramp-up of farm and agricultural-related expertise around food-borne illness, and ran a number of internal seminars for our underwriting, loss control, and claims personnel around everything from microbiology to safety controls and engineering to claims management that would ensure the increased expertise that we needed to really successfully underwrite in that arena," recalls Hipp. Among the staff members in the seminars organized by Hipp were "actuaries, who need to understand risk as part of their pricing" of insurance policies. Hipp "brought people in from the outside to teach these seminars—lawyers, scientists, government personnel"—the same constellation of experts from industry, government, and academia working on food safety standards for GAPs audits, marketing agreements, and government regulatory programs.[97]

A Systems Theory Analysis

Donella Meadows, a pioneering scholar of systems theory, defines a system as "an interconnected set of elements that is coherently organized in a way that achieves something." A system achieves its purpose through feedback. For example, the air-conditioning system of a house is composed of an interconnected set of elements—air-conditioning unit, ducts, thermostat—that is organized in such a way as to maintain a constant temperature in the house. The thermostat measures the current temperature of the house and provides feedback to the air-conditioning unit, which causes the unit to continue or cease producing cool air.[98]

A system may itself be composed of subsystems. The air-conditioning unit—composed of a compressor, coils, and a fan—is a subsystem of the air-conditioning system of the house. So, too, are the ducts and the thermostat, which can similarly be broken down into the interconnected elements that constitute them. If one zooms in, each of these subsystems can be further analyzed into subsystems of subsystems, such as the electrical, coil, and air-circulation systems within the air conditioner. If one zooms out, the air-conditioning system of the house can be viewed as a subsystem within the larger electrical system of the region, which is a subsystem of the national electrical grid, which is a subsystem of the global energy system. Systems theory refers to this nested structure of systems and subsystems as "hierarchical" organization. In analyzing such a system, one can zoom in or zoom out to examine the workings of the system at different "levels" of organization.[99]

Systems theory provides a useful vocabulary for describing the structure of food safety governance. For example, a private third-party food safety audit is a system involving relationships among a buyer, a supplier, and an auditor. The auditor provides feedback to the buyer and the supplier concerning the food safety practices of the supplier. Based on this feedback, the buyer will decide whether to purchase goods from the supplier. The feedback may also encourage the supplier to change its food safety practices. At the same time, the buyer and the supplier provide feedback to the auditor concerning their satisfaction with the audit, which may lead the auditor to modify its auditing practices in ways that balance rigor and cost.

Moreover, food safety governance consists of multiple levels of hierarchically organized systems and subsystems. For example, when one zooms in, each element within the system of a private third-party food safety audit itself can be viewed as a subsystem. Thus, the auditor is typically a firm made up of multiple elements—including individual auditors, audit quality managers, and sales personnel to obtain new accounts—which are interconnected by a variety of feedback loops that influence their actions. Similarly, the supplier is also typically a firm that contains multiple elements—including production workers, food safety managers, and marketing personnel—which are also interconnected by a variety of feedback loops. The same is true of the buyer. When one zooms out, private third-party food safety audits are often one element within the system of a food safety scheme, the elements of which include standard setting, auditing, and accreditation. Food safety schemes, in turn, are one element in food safety benchmarking systems such as GFSI. "Zooming out" even more, one can analyze these industry supply chain systems as one element within the food safety system as a whole, which also includes the elements of government regulation and civil liability, each of which is a system containing many layers and varieties of subsystems.[100]

The analysis is further complicated by the many interconnections among these various systems created by networks of food safety professionals who communicate with one another to create systems of information sharing and collaboration. Each profession—veterinarians, microbiologists, food technologists, and so on—is itself a system (including elements such as training programs, client services, oversight procedures), and together they make up a larger system of professions as they interact with and develop in reaction to one another. The scale of this complex system is magnified by the replication of these systems and subsystems in the many different sectors—for example, dairy, meat, and fresh produce—that constitute the food industry.[101]

Contemplating the people, institutions, and interconnections that make up the food safety system can be overwhelming. "Once you start listing the elements of a system, there is almost no end to the process," warns Meadows.

"You can divide elements into sub-elements and then sub-sub-elements. Pretty soon you lose sight of the system. As the saying goes, you can't see the forest for the trees." Beyond the multitude of elements, the evolving web of interactions and multifarious and multidirectional paths of influence at different levels of organization makes it difficult to describe complex systems or analyze how they function. Complexity theory, a branch of systems theory, seeks out recurring structural and behavioral patterns within complex systems that provide insights into how they work and how one might "steer" them to work more effectively. Identifying such patterns allows one to keep in mind the structure and dynamics of the food safety system as a whole while analyzing particular parts of it—to have a map of the forest as one examines the trees.[102]

STRUCTURAL FEATURES

A prominent structural feature of the food safety system is its network structure. Individuals and institutions at every level of organization in the system are typically connected to multiple other individuals and institutions. Thus, food safety auditors interact with suppliers, buyers, food safety schemes, accreditors, and other auditors, and the feedback they generate flows to multiple entities. A visual depiction of such interactions would resemble a web rather than a line or a circle or a pyramid.[103]

Redundancy is a second structural feature of the food safety system. Multiple actors frequently subject regulated entities to overlapping oversight using versions of the same rules. For example, buyers, marketing agreements, and insurance underwriters require growers to obtain multiple audits based on similar, if not identical, GAPs standards articulated in product specifications, audit schemes, government guidance, and underwriting guidelines. Redundancy has both potential costs and benefits. On the one hand, it can inefficiently duplicate efforts. On the other hand, redundancy can give a system greater resilience—the ability of a system to continue to function despite a breakdown or failure in one part of the system. Redundancy can also enable multiple regulators to provide mutual oversight.[104]

A third structural feature of the food safety system is network density—the extent of interconnection among participants in the network, defined by the proportion of links between individuals to the total number of possible links within the network. Network density has a number of implications for food safety governance. For example, higher network density in part of the system may improve the quality or pace of feedback and learning, making that part of the system more responsive and thereby perhaps more effective and legitimate. Higher network density may also increase transparency, enhance oversight, and facilitate the diffusion of shared values. This last implication of network density is of particular importance. In a landmark study of government bureaucracy, political scientist James Q. Wilson demonstrated that a strong sense of mission was key to successful regulation by administrative agencies. Legal scholars Joseph Rees and Neil Gunningham have similarly argued that a shared industrial morality, what food safety experts refer to as a "culture of food safety," is essential to industry efforts to protect health and safety. A strong sense of mission and a shared industrial morality can also be sources of resistance to change. Examples include the resistance of USDA inspectors to HACCP reforms that would have replaced continuous inspection, and the shared cultural assumptions of industry executives before the Jack in the Box outbreak that consumers bore the primary responsibility for killing pathogens in raw beef and poultry. When those cultural assumptions shifted, as they did in the wake of the Jack in the Box outbreak, the rapidity of the shift may have been due to network density in the meat industry.[105]

A fourth structural feature of the food safety system is heterogeneity. Individuals and institutions in different parts of the network possess different information, have different political interests, face different economic incentives, operate under different administrative constraints, and adopt different narratives. In conjunction with the dispersion of power and initiative throughout the system—which is a fifth structural feature called polycentricity—heterogeneity fosters experimentation and innovation. For example, the early embrace of HACCP in the canned food industry during the 1970s was the result of information and incentives particular to that sector of the food industry. Heterogeneity and polycentricity can also produce disagreement and deadlock. The subsequent disagreement for twenty years over expanding HACCP to other sectors of the food industry arose out of the heterogeneity of interests and narratives in an ongoing standoff between industry executives, government officials, and consumer advocates.[106]

New ideas germinate within the relatively dense networks that define subsystems, and they spread to other subsystems because of a sixth structural feature of the foods safety system—what sociologist Mark Granovetter refers to as the strength of weak ties. Relationships in close-knit social or professional networks tend to be characterized by a common pool of information, shared priorities, and a common outlook. Relationships with acquaintances outside of these dense networks expose the individuals in the relationships to new information and ideas that they then can introduce into their close-knit networks. These "weak" ties are "much more likely than strong ones to play the role of transmitting unique and nonredundant information across otherwise largely disconnected segments of social networks." The strength of weak ties influences the diffusion of feedback and learning in the food safety system. At the same time, weak ties between regulators and regulated entities may also increase opportunities for capture and corruption.[107]

Weak ties are forged throughout the food safety system at different levels of organization and by many different means. Industry associations facilitate weak ties between food safety managers within different companies. Interagency task forces forge weak ties between officials in different government agencies. Academic conferences allow the diffusion of research findings among researchers working in different universities. Professional societies link food safety professionals working in government, industry, academia, and insurance. Other examples include government and industry funding for academic research, reliance by food companies and insurance underwriters on outside consultants from industry and academia, study groups convened by industry and government to issue reports on specific issues, and the movement of professionals between jobs in industry, government, and academia.

SYSTEM BEHAVIORS

In addition to these structural features, systems theory provides a vocabulary to describe repeated behavioral patterns within the food safety system. The first of these is interdependence. The 2006 Dole baby spinach outbreak illustrates the reputational interdependence of members of the same industry. The contamination of spinach plants in the field and the spread of that contamination during processing damaged the reputation of the entire spinach industry. Even producers with rigorous food safety practices suffered dramatic losses as the market for spinach collapsed. At a higher level of organization in the system, one sees a similar reputational interdependence between an entire food industry sector and the government agency responsible for regulating it. As the spinach industry collapsed in the fall of 2006, the FDA faced allegations by consumer advocacy groups that its food safety efforts were ineffective and failed to protect the public, and agency officials faced probing questions about the agency's competence in Senate hearings.[108]

Interdependence is a powerful motivator. When the failure of one agent can damage the reputation of others, they frequently band together to repair damage that has already occurred and prevent additional damage in the future. Rivals become collaborators; competition gives way to cooperation. Industry insiders credit the industrywide shock of the 2006 baby spinach outbreak as the impetus for the LGMA. The leading role of the Western Growers

Association in developing and sustaining the LGMA illustrates how trade associations institutionalize cooperation among industry competitors to protect the collective reputation of an industry. Similarly, government agencies like the California Department of Food and Agriculture and the FDA have been heavily involved in and highly supportive of leafy green industry initiatives such as the LGMA, in no small measure because the agencies' reputations are intertwined with the industry's.[109]

A second repeated pattern of behavior in the food safety system is non-linearity. This refers to the occurrence of large, systemwide effects caused by small changes in the system's configuration. The most prominent example of this behavior is the dramatic manner in which outbreaks create a ripple effect throughout the food safety system and precipitate major reforms, such as the implementation of HACCP in the beef and poultry industries following the Jack in the Box outbreak or the launch of the LGMA among leafy greens handlers in the wake of the Dole baby spinach outbreak.[110]

A third repeated pattern of behavior is path dependence, whereby actions are constrained by the sequence of earlier events. For example, the requirement of continuous organoleptic inspection of beef and poultry carcasses by USDA personnel established by the Meat Inspection Act of 1906 created legal precedents, professional commitments, and a powerful narrative that constrained efforts starting in the 1980s to reallocate agency resources toward greater reliance on HACCP plans and pathogen testing. Similarly, approaches to GAPs developed in the late 1990s by industry associations shaped the subsequent development of GAPs in later revisions of industry guidelines, FDA guidance, buyers' product specifications, the LGMA, and the FSMA Produce Safety Rule.[111]

A fourth recurring behavior within the food safety system is intermediation. Regulatory scholars Kenneth Abbott, David Levi-Faur, and Duncan Snidal observe that "regulators" seeking to influence the behavior of "targets of regulation" often rely on what they call "regulatory intermediaries." According to Abbott and his coauthors, "the principal reason for regulators to incorporate intermediaries into the regulatory process is that intermediaries possess capacities relevant to regulation that regulators themselves lack, or that intermediaries can provide more effectively or at lower cost." Regulatory intermediaries add "operational capacity" to regulatory efforts by, for example, gathering information, facilitating implementation, monitoring the behavior of targets, enforcing standards, and channeling feedback that leads to learning and improvement over time. Regulatory intermediaries also provide expertise to regulators, and their independence may boost the legitimacy of the regulatory process.[112]

Relationships throughout the food safety system exhibit this regulator-intermediary-target structure. For example, in the subsystem of government regulation, administrative agencies serve as intermediaries between legislatures and food companies when the agencies create, implement, and enforce regulations pursuant to general statutory mandates to regulate industry. As an intermediary between Congress and industry, the FDA provides operational capacity through administrative rule making, inspection, implementation, monitoring, enforcement, and reporting; lends expertise in areas such as microbiology, epidemiology, and forensics; and enhances the legitimacy of regulation by distancing it from legislative politics. In the subsystem of industry supply chain management, retail stores set food safety specifications for their suppliers and rely on private food safety auditors as intermediaries to verify compliance. In the subsystem of civil litigation, underwriters serve as intermediaries to translate the threat of litigation by plaintiffs' attorneys into insurance incentives—using risk selection, pricing, contract design, and loss prevention—that encourage food companies to improve their food safety practices. Note that this third example does not involve a conscious decision by the regulator (the plaintiffs' attorney) to rely on the intermediary (the underwriter), nor does the regulator instruct, direct, or oversee the intermediary. Moreover, the attorney's role as a regulator is a by-product of efforts to obtain compensation for his or her client. Nevertheless, underwriters enhance the regulatory impact of private lawsuits in ways that conform to the pattern of reliance on regulatory intermediaries.[113]

Intermediation crosses the boundaries between the three subsystems of government regulation, industry supply chain management, and civil liability. For example, industry supply chain managers may rely on government inspectors to audit their suppliers, as illustrated by LGMA audits. Conversely, government agencies may rely on private auditors to assess regulatory compliance, as contemplated in FSMA.

Moreover, intermediation occurs at different levels of organization. For example, zooming in to the level of firms, one finds that insurance underwriters rely on in-house loss control experts and outside food safety consultants as intermediaries to select and price risks, design contract terms, and advise food company clients about reducing risk. Zooming out to the level of sectors, one sees that the liability insurance system as a whole serves as an intermediary that enhances food industry compliance with government regulation. These examples illustrate that intermediaries can be individuals, institutions, or entire sectors of activity.[114]

Relationships between regulators and the intermediaries on whom they rely are subject to agency problems. For example, buyers worry that auditors may reduce the rigor of audits because suppliers are paying the auditors. To address such agency problems, regulators rely on additional intermediaries. Thus, buyers rely on food safety schemes to impose licensing standards on auditors that will counteract any incentive to reduce the rigor of audits. Buyers also typically rely on accreditors as intermediaries to oversee auditors. Note that the initial intermediary (the auditor) becomes a target of regulation. The additional regulator-intermediary relationship created between the buyer and the scheme to oversee the auditor is itself subject to agency problems, which may be addressed by reliance on additional intermediaries. Thus, buyers rely on GFSI to provide benchmarks and certify the reliability of schemes. Similarly, buyers address concerns about agency problems with accreditors by requiring that accreditors be accredited by the International Accreditation Forum (IAF), which accredits accreditors through a system of peer review. Figure 5.1 illustrates these arrangements.

There are several reasons to believe that additional intermediaries (e.g., food safety schemes, accreditors) reduce agency problems between regulators (buyers) and the initial intermediaries (auditors) on whom they rely. First, it is marginally easier for regulators to monitor the performance and reputation of a relatively small number of additional intermediaries. The capacity of an intermediary to oversee multiple targets gives intermediary oversight a pyramidal structure, in which additional intermediaries (food safety schemes and accreditors) are fewer in number than the relatively larger number of intermediaries (auditors) they oversee. Second, regulators can employ multiple additional intermediaries to provide simultaneous oversight of the same intermediary, as buyers sometimes do by relying on both food safety scheme owners to license auditors and accreditors to accredit them. The assumption here is that multiple sources of oversight are more reliable than a single source. Moreover, if the additional intermediaries operate independently, as do food safety schemes and accreditors in overseeing auditors, regulators are

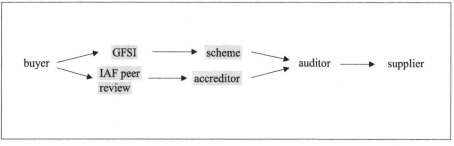

FIGURE 5.1. Additional intermediaries to address agency problems with initial intermediaries.

less vulnerable to an oversight failure by one additional intermediary. Third, additional intermediaries can oversee one another, creating a web of oversight, as is the case with IAF peer review. Such a web may be less vulnerable to failures by a single overseer than a strictly sequential chain of oversight.[115]

The advantages that intermediaries offer to regulators and the need to employ additional intermediaries to address agency problems lead to the proliferation of intermediation at various levels of organization throughout the complex system of food safety governance. Complexity theory calls such spontaneous adaptation "self-organization" and systems that display this pattern of behavior "complex adaptive systems."[116]

A fifth recurring pattern of behavior in the food safety system is rule emergence. In the food safety system, some rules are not issued by an identifiable individual or institution. Instead, they emerge out of the interactions of many actors and institutions linked by multiple networks within and between subsystems. GAPs provide a good example. GAPs originated as collections of recommendations formulated by panels of experts assembled by industry associations and a group of academics at Cornell University. They then developed through iterative cycles of feedback and learning, which occurred through conversations among food safety experts working in a variety of different institutional settings. Eventually, they evolved into a complex system of standards embedded in industry association guidelines, government agency guidance, buyer specifications, audit criteria, best practices among growers, academic and university extension publications, marketing agreement metrics, government regulations, standards of care in tort litigation, and liability and recall insurance underwriting guidelines. These GAPs standards have become interdependent insofar as they draw heavily on one another for their content. For example, insurance underwriting guidelines are drawn directly—sometimes verbatim—from government regulations and guidance, standards of care in tort litigation, food safety schemes, expert recommendations, and industry practices. The same is true for these other rules vis-à-vis one another. As GAPs continue to develop in this system, rule making has no beginning or end. Rule making in the food safety system does not reside in rule makers insofar as that term denotes a discrete individual or institutional agent from which rules issue. Instead, it appears that rules emerge from ongoing interactions within a complex adaptive system.[117]

This account of the source of rules has implications for analyzing authority within complex adaptive systems of governance. Within such systems, the authority of some rules cannot be easily anchored to the authority of a discrete rule maker or even an easily identifiable rule of recognition. It may be the case that the authority of rules that emerge within such systems does not derive from the source of the rule but instead accretes over time with growing acceptance of the rules by participants in the system.[118]

The idea of rule emergence also challenges the assumption among many advocates of industry regulation that government rule making is the best option and a benchmark in terms of participation, transparency, and accountability against which to evaluate the legitimacy of private alternatives. This systems theory analysis of food safety governance does not privilege government regulation in these ways. Instead, it views government regulation as a component of a complex adaptive system, the legitimacy of which is difficult to assess in isolation from the other parts of the system. Within a complex adaptive system of governance, the legitimacy of one rule depends on that of another. For example, the incorporation by government regulations and guidance of industry standards may give government rules greater legitimacy in the eyes of regulated entities. Similarly, the validation that government regulations and guidance may bring to private industry standards by incorporating them may make private standards more legitimate to consumers.

All this complexity exacerbates the difficulty of evaluating the impact of food safety efforts. The previous chapter introduced the challenges of limited available data and the difficulty of attributing reduced pathogen levels and lower illness rates to specific food safety initiatives. The interdependence of government regulation, industry supply chain management, and civil liability makes such attributions even harder. The next chapter more closely examines these challenges by surveying attempts to assess the efficacy and cost-effectiveness of GAPs.

Bean Counting:
The Challenges of Assessing Food Safety Efforts

In food safety, as in many other aspects of life, there is no such thing as a free lunch. Reducing the risk of foodborne illness increases the cost of food production, resulting in higher food prices for consumers. Beyond food prices, more stringent food safety measures may involve other types of trade-offs as well. For example, wider margins of clear-cut land around fresh produce fields to limit animal intrusion may have detrimental environmental effects, such as increased soil erosion. More expensive food safety requirements, such as frequent audits or pathogen testing, may favor large growing operations, which can take advantage of economies of scale, increasing industry consolidation and reducing consumer choice, especially options to buy locally sourced products from small farms. Higher prices for fresh produce may lead some consumers to substitute cheaper, less healthy foods. Limiting supply chains to more easily inspected domestic producers may make it impossible to offer seasonal products, such as avocadoes, all year round.[1]

At some point, the extra costs of increased food safety outweigh the additional benefits. Stepping up food safety in fresh produce production becomes less desirable when it means that melons are no longer affordable, leafy greens cultivation drastically exacerbates soil erosion, local family farms can no longer afford to compete with agribusiness, trends toward eating more fresh fruit and vegetables are reversed, and the only items in the produce section of the supermarket in winter are root vegetables. Not all outbreaks are worth eliminating, and not every episode of food poisoning is a signal that reform is needed.

Ideally, food safety reform should strike the right balance between the benefits of risk reduction and the costs in terms of food prices, environmental stewardship, support for family farms, and the availability of healthy dietary options. In practice, however, the information necessary to strike this balance is not available. On the benefits side, incomplete surveillance and reporting make it difficult even to set a baseline from which to begin an evaluation. The most sophisticated estimate of the burden of foodborne illness puts the number of cases at somewhere between 28.6 million and 71.1 million cases each year, most of which are caused by unspecified pathogens. (See appendix A for details.) Measuring changes in illness over time is complicated by improvements in surveillance and reporting, which make the burden of illness appear to increase by an unknown amount even if there are no more actual cases of illness. Moreover, only a small fraction of reported cases is ever associated with a specific food, a link that is necessary to credit any particular food safety reform with a change in the burden of illness. On the cost side, calculating the dollar value of environmental damages, fewer family farms, or reduced availability of healthy foods not only requires a great deal of information that may be costly to obtain but also rests on a host of subjective judgments about how to value environmental conservation, family ownership, and year-round variety in the produce section, leaving a great deal of room for disagreement even among experts.[2]

This chapter reviews attempts to assess the impact of food safety efforts in the fresh produce sector. Available data suggest that efforts to improve on-farm food safety have increased the adoption of Good Agricultural Practices (GAPs). However, it remains unclear whether this increase in the adoption of GAPs has reduced foodborne illness. Moreover, the data do not isolate the influence of any particular effort on the adoption of GAPs. All this uncertainty makes it difficult to determine whether the resources already spent on food safety have been put to good use and where to allocate future investments.

Assessing Regulatory Compliance

A number of surveys assess the prevalence of on-farm food safety measures. Unfortunately, most of these are local or regional and provide data for only a single point in time. One source of longitudinal data is California Leafy Green Products Handler Marketing Agreement (LGMA) annual reports, which document increasing rates of compliance with LGMA standards each year since 2008. The USDA collected national data in a 1999 USDA survey of fruit and vegetable growers in fourteen states to assess the use of GAPs in the cultivation of thirty fresh produce items. The USDA conducted follow-up national surveys of fruit and vegetable growers in 2015 and 2016.[3]

A second group of surveys provides data on the costs of compliance with food safety standards. For example, one survey of forty-nine California leafy greens growers measured an increase in compliance costs between 2006 and 2007, finding that respondents' seasonal food safety costs more than doubled following implementation of the LGMA. A more recent survey of seven California leafy greens growers in 2012 noted that "food safety costs are very difficult to measure; not every firm could provide complete responses. Only costs for some food safety practices could be measured."[4]

Taken together, these data provide some evidence regarding the effectiveness of efforts to promote the adoption of GAPs. The most recent USDA national surveys indicate that the number of growers implementing GAPs has increased since 1999. Increasing rates of compliance and increasing compliance costs among California leafy greens growers subject to LGMA metrics suggest that an increasing number of these growers are implementing GAPs or that they are implementing with greater rigor GAPs that they used prior to the LGMA.

However, given the concurrence of pressure to adopt GAPs from different sources—buyers, the LGMA, trade association guidelines, FDA guidance, and insurers—existing studies cannot attribute this increase in adoption or rigor to any particular approach. For example, the study finding a more than doubling of food safety costs following implementation of the LGMA acknowledges "the varying degrees to which [growers] were already in compliance with the LGMA best practices" and cautioned that "some of the costs reported by the respondents as LGMA modification costs could relate to expenses incurred to comply with other food safety programs, such as those of private third-party food safety auditors and [retailer associations]." The 2012 survey of seven California leafy greens growers reported that "all firms incorporated additional food safety practices into their food safety plans beyond LGMA requirements, for their own convenience, risk management needs, and/or to satisfy buyer requests." Two agricultural economists at the University of Maryland conducted a national survey in 2015 of 394 fruit and vegetable growers and found that a majority of respondents already employed most of the food safety practices prescribed by the FSMA Produce Safety Rule before its publication.[5]

Moreover, even granting that some of the data provide evidence that one or more of the efforts to improve on-farm food safety increased the adoption or rigor of GAPs, this does not amount to evidence that these efforts have reduced the risk of foodborne illness. Experts have suggested that GAPs reduce the risk of contamination or reduce microbial counts on contaminated produce, although even this is difficult to prove. According to a review of the effectiveness of the LGMA commissioned by the LGMA board and the Western Growers Association, a distinguished panel of four leading food safety experts "expressed confidence that the [LGMA] Guidelines have likely contributed to reducing the human pathogen contamination risk in leafy greens," but they "struggled with finding supportive data to prove their general positive sense of a decreased risk." However, even specific data proving that increased GAPs adoption or rigor has reduced the risk of contamination would not be sufficient to show that GAPs have reduced the rate of illness.[6]

Some observers claim that GAPs have reduced or eliminated the recurrent large outbreaks associated with leafy greens. California LGMA CEO Scott Horsfall asserts that "there are fewer *E. coli* outbreaks and illnesses, and regulators and folks who track these things have been very quick to say that the steps taken by the industry, including the LGMA, have led to these kinds of improvements." Bill Marler similarly opines that "if success is measured by a lack of spinach outbreaks of the size that we've previously seen, I would say that looks like success." However, a 2018 nationwide outbreak caused by romaine lettuce grown in Arizona contaminated with *E. coli* O157—which sickened 210 reported victims, 96 of whom were hospitalized, 27 of whom suffered kidney failure, and 5 of whom died—gave even the most ardent LGMA supporters pause. Marler expressed the concern shared by many that perhaps not enough had changed since the Dole baby spinach outbreak by publishing a blog post titled "12 Years Later: Seems Like the Same *E. coli* Nightmare."[7]

Generalizations about food safety progress in the fresh produce sector are complicated by the rise and fall in the number of outbreaks traced back to many commodities subject to GAPs. For example, the number of reported US outbreaks attributed to contaminated spinach has fluctuated since 1998, as illustrated in figure 6.1.

Consumer advocate Caroline Smith DeWaal seized on this point in 2009 congressional testimony, asserting that the California LGMA "has not proven effective, as indicated by several recent outbreaks. In May 2008, bagged Romaine lettuce sickened 10 people in Washington state with *E. coli* O157. The lettuce was traced to Salinas Valley, California. In September that same year, California-produced lettuce was implicated in an *E. coli* outbreak that sickened 40 people in five states." However, LGMA critics should be no less cautious than proponents in making bold claims about the effectiveness of the LGMA or other food safety programs on the basis of aggregate data regarding reported outbreaks. Just as the assertions of LGMA success based on broad generalizations are complicated by aggregate data regarding outbreaks that show no clear trend, so too assertions of failure based on the continuation of outbreaks following LGMA implementation are also complicated, as even

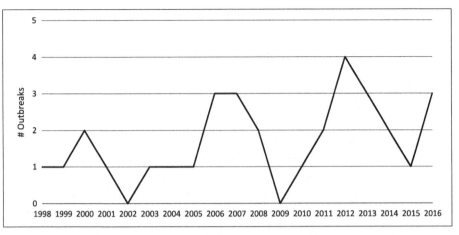

FIGURE 6.1. US reported spinach outbreaks, 1998–2016.
Data from CDC, online database NORS Dashboard, https://wwwn.cdc.gov/norsdashboard/. Results archived at https://perma.cc/VD8M-7YZE.

optimal safety programs tolerate residual risk and do not reduce the rate of illness to zero.[8]

Predicting Regulatory Impact

The FDA has attempted to link the use of GAPs to health outcomes in a regulatory impact analysis of its Produce Safety Rule, a centerpiece of the Food Safety Modernization Act (FSMA). The agency asserts that the rule will avert between 331,964 and 362,059 illnesses per year. In calculating the influence of the Produce Safety Rule on the rate of foodborne illness, the agency first estimated the rule's impact on the risk of contamination. To obtain that estimate, the agency relied on a method called "expert elicitation." A consulting firm under contract with the FDA asked a panel of six recognized food safety experts to indicate, using a series of scenarios, whether the risk of contamination in a scenario using a particular agricultural practice was less than, equal to, or greater than a baseline scenario without it. The experts were asked to quantify the magnitude of the difference using a scale of zero to one hundred, placing the baseline scenario at fifty as a benchmark. For example, the particular agricultural practice might be the use of treated flowing surface water for irrigation, and an expert might assign a relative risk value to this practice of twenty-five relative to a baseline scenario of using untreated flowing surface water set at fifty. The consulting firm conducted two such studies, one estimating the effect of interventions on *E. coli* O157 contamination of leafy greens and the other estimating their effect on *Salmonella* contamination in tomatoes. Using the relative risk values generated by the six experts for each set of scenarios, the agency calculated a risk ratio for implementing particular food safety interventions, which it expressed as the reduction in the risk of contamination that would be achieved by means of that intervention. In the example just given, if the average relative risk value for all six experts for treated flowing surface water was twenty-five, the agency would infer that the use of treated flowing surface water for irrigation would mitigate 50 percent of the risk of produce contamination from using untreated flowing surface water. The agency then similarly calculated the reduction from other interventions aimed at risks from other sources, such as animal intervention, soil amendments, and worker hygiene. By aggregating these estimates for each intervention, the agency calculated that "taken together, this adds up to about a 56.43 percent reduction in risk of contamination."[9]

Having estimated the rule's impact on the risk of contamination, the agency then estimated its impact on the risk of foodborne illness. "To translate this percentage reduction in farm contamination to human health outcomes, we estimated that a reduced possibility of contamination will result in a corresponding reduction in the expected number of illnesses." By this, the agency meant that a 56.43 percent reduction in the risk of contamination would mean a 56.43 percent reduction in the rate of foodborne illness.[10]

The agency's assertion that the Produce Safety Rule will prevent a quantifiable number of foodborne illnesses rests on educated guesses and an unsupported assumption. Expert elicitation produces quantitative risk reduction estimates based on an aggregation of educated ballpark guesses. The precision of the resulting risk reduction percentages obscures the fundamentally impressionistic nature of these estimates and their lack of the kind of scientific rigor characteristic of the life sciences. Moreover, although the agency claims that it "estimated that a reduced possibility of contamination will result in a corresponding reduction in the expected number of illnesses," it appears— from the lack of any additional explanation—that the agency merely assumed this relationship. Of course, it is not at all counterintuitive to think that reducing the risk of contamination will result in a lower rate of illness, but the agency offers no basis for its assertion of a linear one-to-one relationship between reduction in the risk of contamination and the rate of illness.[11]

One should be careful not to infer from this scrutiny of the FDA's regulatory impact analysis any suggestion of agency incompetence or bad faith. The agency operates under a number of competing pressures that explain its reliance on expert elicitation and unexplained assumptions. First, Congress mandated that the FDA publish produce safety regulations within two years of the passage of FSMA regardless of any limitations in the scientific knowledge necessary to support them. When the agency missed the statutory deadline for publishing proposed produce safety regulations along with other rules required by FSMA, it was sued by a consumer advocacy organization and ordered by a federal court to publish final produce safety regulations by the end of June 2015. Second, a series of executive orders dating back to the Reagan administration require federal agencies proposing a new rule to provide a regulatory impact analysis that includes a detailed quantitative estimate demonstrating that the expected economic benefits of the rule outweigh its costs. Third, a federal agency faces the prospect of legal challenges that will subject its regulatory analysis to judicial review that may result in the overturning of a published regulation if the agency fails to provide sufficient scientific evidence to support the regulation. Thus, although FDA officials undoubtedly appreciate the limits of scientific knowledge regarding the effectiveness of GAPs in reducing foodborne illness, the agency was legally mandated by Congress to publish produce safety regulations, obligated by the president to provide a detailed cost-benefit projection, and under pressure to create an impression of sufficient scientific certainty to satisfy judicial review.[12]

In the end, administrative necessity provides some justification for the claims asserted in the FDA's regulatory impact analysis. Moreover, one might even believe that, given the limits of current science, the agency provided a reasonable justification for its Produce Safety Rule. Nevertheless, the agency's projections do little to advance knowledge of how effective GAPs have been in reducing foodborne illness. Frustrated by the dearth of quantitative evidence necessary to evaluate the effectiveness of GAPs, one leading food safety expert in the USDA's Economic Research Service exaggerated only slightly when she concluded that "produce is a world without data." Jim Prevor, president and editor in chief of *Produce Business* magazine and author of the widely read online trade publication *Perishable Pundit*, cautions that there is no data to show that fresh produce subject to one food safety approach is safer than produce subject to any other approach. Indeed, he concludes, "We have no real data proving that any of these standards make for safer produce."[13]

The FDA's regulatory impact analysis also estimates the costs to industry of compliance with the Produce Safety Rule and compares them to an estimate of the rule's economic benefits, based on its estimate of the number of deaths that the rule will prevent multiplied by a figure for the value of a life. Of course, the agency's estimate of the rule's economic benefits suffers from the same weaknesses as the underlying estimate of the number of deaths that will be prevented. Moreover, it is interesting to note that the regulatory impact analysis does not include an estimate of the administrative costs to government, industry, and advocacy groups of enacting FSMA and developing the rule, which have occupied hundreds of highly skilled professionals for many years. Despite these limitations, the FDA's regulatory impact analysis confidently asserts that the benefits of the Produce Safety Rule will outweigh the costs by two to one.[14]

A 2010 case study by a group of economists took a retrospective approach to cost-benefit analysis. This study estimated the cost-effectiveness of implementing more efficient product tracking systems throughout the leafy greens industry. The study based its cost estimates on the costs incurred by California growers in complying with new traceability rules under the LGMA in the aftermath of the 2006 Dole spinach outbreak. It compared those costs to the benefits that such systems would generate in terms of more quickly identifying the source of contaminated spinach and thereby limiting the extent of an outbreak similar to that of the 2006 outbreak. There is a heavy dose of speculation even in this type of hindsight analysis. The study's cost estimates are based on data regarding company investments in traceability improvements following the outbreak, and its benefit estimates are based on data regarding the health costs and business losses associated with the outbreak. The analysis concludes that, had the improved tracking systems been in place at the time, the losses averted would have outweighed the cost of the systems. However, whether such investments are cost-effective going forward requires an estimate of the likelihood of such an outbreak occurring in the future. How likely that is, not even the authors of the study ventured to guess.[15]

Evaluating the Influence of Civil Liability

When it comes to civil litigation and insurance, some studies have suggested that civil liability has had little or no effect on encouraging food companies to improve their food safety practices. After reviewing jury verdicts and settlements in foodborne illness tort claims reported in legal databases between 1988 and 1997, USDA economists Jean Buzby and Paul Frenzen concluded that tort litigation provides companies "weak" incentives to improve their food safety practices. Buzby and Frenzen estimated that fewer than 0.01 percent of all foodborne illness cases during this period gave rise to litigation and found that only a fraction of lawsuits resulted in companies paying any compensation. Buzby and Frenzen explained that most victims never recognize food as the source of their illness, fail to obtain medical tests that identify the responsible pathogen, or do not save samples of the contaminated food—all of which are necessary to link the victim's illness to a particular company that sold the contaminated food. Moreover, Buzby and Frenzen found that companies paid compensation in 56 percent of the lawsuits in their sample, and that "the median compensation was only $2,000 before legal fees." They explained that "most foodborne illnesses are mild and short-lived and do not incur medical and other costs high enough to make litigation worthwhile for plaintiffs," and that the amount of compensation paid, even in more serious cases, provided little incentive to plaintiffs' attorneys to pursue litigation.[16]

Buzby and Frenzen's analysis has several important limitations. Denis Stearns, an attorney who works with Bill Marler, has suggested that Buzby and Frenzen's sample of reported jury verdicts and settlements between 1988 and 1997 may not be representative of litigation in more recent years. In 2009, Stearns wrote that "the vast majority of legitimate food-injury claims never go to trial and are privately settled. In the 10-year history of Marler Clark, only one of the firm's cases ever went through trial to verdict; all others settled." Marler adds that companies with well-known brands typically settle claims before they are even filed to stay out of the news.[17]

Buzby and Frenzen themselves note that the influence of litigation on food companies is "slightly stronger in outbreak situations and markets where foodborne illness can be more easily traced to individual firms." They also suggest that "indirect incentives for firms may be important and deserve more research. For example, firms may be influenced by costly settlements and decisions against other firms in the same industry." However, the impact of tort claims arising out of outbreaks extends beyond what Buzby and Frenzen suggest in these qualifications of their analysis.[18]

Buzby and Frenzen's focus on the economic costs of litigation outcomes (jury verdicts and settlements) overlooks the framing effects of the litigation process (filing, pleading, discovery, and negotiation), which has, at crucial junctures in the evolution of food safety, generated and sustained media coverage that recast the issue of bacterial contamination from a natural hazard to a product of human error, and thereby focused attention on industry food safety practices. The impact of litigation following the Jack in the Box beef outbreak in 1993 or the Dole baby spinach outbreak in 2006 cannot be accurately assessed merely in terms of the economic costs of the final settlements. In both instances, litigation and the news coverage that accompanied it heightened the reputational concerns of company executives throughout an entire food industry sector, focused the attention of government regulators on those sectors, stoked consumer demands for advances in food safety, and mobilized consumer advocates to lobby for policy reforms.[19]

According to one study, the reputational concerns stirred up by litigation influence food company behavior more than the economic impact of a jury verdict or settlement: "Word-of-mouth notoriety is far more devastating in

its cumulative effect than the fleeting shadow of a single publicized judgment awarded to an unknown plaintiff." Buzby and Frenzen note that "it is
primarily the business disruption and negative publicity of the catastrophic
foodborne illness or outbreaks that cost firms money[,] so it is these extraordinary, nonrecurrent illnesses or outbreaks that have the potential to sub-
stantively shape corporate behavior. In the rare instances where foodborne
disease outbreaks are linked to particular firms, the impact on those firms
can be large. For example, . . . Jack in the Box Inc. lost an estimated $160 mil-
lion in the first 18 months after the 1993 *E. coli* O157:H7 outbreak." Here again,
Buzby and Frenzen understate the impact of the Jack in the Box litigation—
which not only influenced Jack in the Box but also generated pressure for
reform throughout the entire beef industry.[20]

Marler concedes that the volume of litigation compared to the rate of
foodborne illness is very small. Agreeing with Buzby and Frenzen, he observes that "the vast majority of outbreaks are never identified. People have
no idea what poisoned them, and so they don't see anybody to hold accountable." Civil liability does not provide a straightforward check on the food
industry, according to Marler. Instead, the litigation process serves as "a cata-
lyst to professionals in industry, health officials, and consumer advocates."
Of course, framing, reputational, agenda setting, and mobilization impacts
are not subject to measurement in the way that economic costs are—but any
comprehensive analysis of civil litigation's impact on food safety must somehow take them into account.[21]

Modeling the Effects of Insurance

John Cogan, a law professor at the University of Connecticut, relies on Buzby
and Frenzen's findings regarding the low rate of litigation to raise doubts
about the effectiveness of liability insurance as a means of regulating food
safety risk within food companies. Cogan explains that insurance premiums
send a "signal" about the magnitude of a risk that influences the amount of
money that companies are willing to invest in safety precautions to reduce
the risk. Lower premiums suggest that a risk is relatively small, which leads
companies to spend less on precautions. Higher premiums suggest that a risk
is relatively large, which leads companies to spend more on precautions. Low
foodborne illness litigation rates result in liability insurance premiums that
reflect the relatively small risk of getting sued rather than the relatively larger
risk of contamination within a company's operations that causes foodborne
illness. This signal leads companies to spend less on precautions than they
would if they were taking into account the true level of risk that their oper-

ations pose to consumers. Cogan further explains that low litigation rates undermine the capacity of insurers to use risk selection, risk pricing, contract design, and loss prevention to incentivize food companies to adopt food safety practices to reduce the risk of contamination. Low foodborne illness litigation rates generate relatively few insurance claims, which deprives insurers of information regarding the nature and sources of food safety risk that they need to structure incentives. Moreover, low premiums do not allow for discounts sufficiently large to motivate food companies to adopt additional precautions. Cogan concludes that "liability insurance has a limited capacity to improve food safety."[22]

Cogan's account may overstate the weakness of the risk signals provided by liability insurance premiums because insurance underwriters may price premiums higher than his model suggests. In adopting Buzby and Frenzen's focus on litigation rates and the economic cost of litigation outcomes, Cogan overlooks the influence of the litigation process on the perception of liability risk. In the relatively new field of food safety risk underwriting, pricing is influenced not only by litigation data but also by underwriters' intuitions. According to James Derr of XL insurance, "A lot of times the perception of risk may be even more important than the actual liability involved." Doug Becker of Nationwide explains that Bill Marler's growing reputation was a significant influence on food safety liability coverage in California. "We know Bill very, very well," he says with a hint of trepidation. Marler's frequent appearances speaking to food company executives and insurers, as well as his expansive web presence and larger-than-life media profile, have increased his influence beyond the more than $600 million in compensation that he has extracted from food companies and their liability insurers. Thus, underwriters set premiums based not only on quantitative analysis of litigation data but also on their qualitative perceptions about the risk of litigation—a risk that Bill Marler and other plaintiffs' attorneys have made increasingly salient through media coverage and personal appearances.[23]

Cogan's account may also exaggerate the extent of insurers' ignorance about the nature and sources of food safety risk. Underwriters rely on a wide array of types and sources of information, including industry and government guidance documents; academic, professional, and trade publications; food safety conferences and webinars; in-house and external consultants with a variety of technical expertise and practical experience; and extensive investigations of claims. These sources of expertise inform risk selection, risk pricing, contract design, and loss prevention.[24]

Cogan is probably right that the inability of most foodborne illness victims to identify the seller of the contaminated food that sickened them results in liability insurance pricing that is too low to realize the full potential of insurance to reduce food safety risk. However, his analysis may exaggerate the magnitude of the problem. Cogan is also right to point out that, in the absence of a large volume of claims that could provide detailed information about losses, insurers lack the capacity to price risk with the type of precision typical of more mature insurance markets, such as auto or premises or fire, and they must rely heavily on qualitative analysis and intuition. However, this does not mean that liability insurance involves more guesswork than other approaches to reducing the risk of foodborne illness. Cogan's analysis offers no baselines or metrics by which to compare the performance of liability insurance to the alternatives of industry supply chain management or government regulation—which also suffer from problems that make them fall short of their potential to reduce the risk of foodborne illness, and also rely heavily on professional judgment in the absence of hard data.

Cogan suggests that product recall insurance might have a greater impact on reducing foodborne illness than liability insurance. He asserts that the discovery of product contamination requiring a recall is a more common event with more predictable consequences than a legal claim of injury from foodborne illness. This makes it easier for insurers to price premiums to reflect the risk of contamination and to design loss prevention services to reduce it. Moreover, explains Cogan, recall insurance may encourage companies to more quickly withdraw contaminated products from the market, which can prevent or mitigate the size of an outbreak. Food companies have an incentive to forgo or delay expensive recalls of contaminated products, because the companies are unlikely to be sued for any resulting illness. However, by covering the cost of recalls, argues Cogan, recall insurance can reduce companies' resistance to taking prompt action.[25]

Insurance industry insiders are divided on whether liability and product recall insurance have reduced the risk of foodborne illness. Some insiders suggest that liability insurance plays no role in food companies' decisions regarding how much to invest in food safety. According to this view, company executives make decisions about how much to spend on food safety by balancing reputational concerns about damage to the company's brand value if an outbreak occurs; ethical commitments to protecting consumers; suppliers' specifications; and economic considerations about production costs, profit margins, and competitiveness. After determining how much to spend on food safety, any remaining risk is viewed as simply another cost, and purchasing liability insurance is "just a business decision to get this risk off of the books," according to Charles Stauber, a senior claims executive with more than two decades of experience at several leading insurance companies.[26]

By contrast, other insurance industry insiders believe that insurance plays a role in encouraging companies to reduce the risk of foodborne illness. Although insurance coverage may not be as significant a driver of company decisions regarding food safety as are reputation, ethics, suppliers, or cost, it reinforces these other incentives. According to Jack Hipp, an insurance executive with thirty-years of experience, "insurance doesn't necessarily force a company to take a food safety measure that they wouldn't otherwise take, but if the cost of insurance goes up significantly, it would have an influence on a company's practices." Hipp asserts that insurers' consulting services influence company food safety practices. For example, following the 2006 baby spinach outbreak, he recalls that Fireman's Fund helped leafy greens growers whom it insured set up better field sanitation practices and testing protocols. Similar consulting services provided by insurers are a growing resource for companies seeking advice about how to comply with the new FSMA regulations.[27]

Anecdotes and general impressions are no substitute for rigorous, quantitative assessment of how effective insurance is as a means of reducing foodborne illness compared to other approaches. Over time, advances in public health surveillance and tracing technologies will link more illnesses to specific causes of contamination. The consequent increase in accountability is likely to increase demand for liability and product recall insurance and generate more extensive loss data, which may help provide a clearer picture of the role of insurance in advancing food safety. In the meantime, it might be wisest to reserve judgment.

Comparing Different Approaches on the Basis of Process Values

Attempts to assess different approaches to food safety sometimes focus on process rather than outcomes. This type of assessment—which scholars refer to as "comparative institutional analysis"—compares the relative strengths and weaknesses of different approaches in terms of process values such as, for example, stakeholder participation. From a process point of view, one might favor an approach to food safety characterized by broader and more meaningful stakeholder participation over an approach characterized by relatively narrower and less meaningful stakeholder participation, on the theory that any resulting standards will be the product of a wider spectrum of expertise and experience, and that they will engender greater respect among the stakeholders to whom they apply. Thus, consumer advocates have argued that government regulations are preferable to industry guidelines because the government's notice-and-comment process is characterized by more robust stakeholder participation than the processes used by industry to make private standards. In addition to stakeholder participation, other process values that may be used to assess different food safety approaches include impartiality, transparency, accountability, compliance, administrative efficiency, and the capacity to generate feedback and learning.[28]

Comparative institutional analysis is complicated by a number of factors. To begin with, in the absence of quantitative baselines and metrics, comparisons between different regulatory approaches made on the basis of process values is an impressionistic exercise. For example, comparisons between the robustness of stakeholder participation in notice-and-comment rule making and in standard setting by industry association technical committees are matters of interpretation not subject to well-defined standards of proof.[29]

In addition, pursuit of one process value may come at the expense of another. For example, more robust stakeholder participation may reduce administrative efficiency and the agility of regulatory institutions to revise standards on the basis of feedback and learning. Ensuring that decisions rely on impartial expertise may require insulating decision makers from the influence of stakeholders, thereby making them less publicly accountable. Comparative institutional analysis provides no basis for weighing competing process values when tension between them requires unavoidable trade-offs.

Moreover, different regulatory approaches are not necessarily exclusive. They frequently coexist and may, in some instances, be complementary. For example, as detailed in the previous chapter, private food safety audits and marketing agreements may promote compliance with government regulations. According to the FDA, "To the extent that certification schemes or food safety programs are consistent with the produce safety regulation, then compliance with those schemes or programs could be relevant to compliance with the requirements of [the regulation]." This type of complementarity suggests that comparative institutional analysis should not analyze the process advantages and disadvantages of any one approach in isolation but rather evaluate different combinations of approaches.[30]

To complicate matters further, some aspects of food safety regulation involve collaboration between more than one institution. For example, the development of GAPs standards has been characterized by the extensive involvement of government agency officials in private standard-setting groups and heavy reliance on private standards as the basis for government guidance and regulation. As previous chapters have demonstrated, food safety norms are the product of ongoing conversation among experts in industry, government, and academia that takes place in a variety of institutional settings. Implementation is similarly characterized by collaboration between institutions. For example, the California LGMA relies on government auditors to certify compliance with private industry standards. FSMA mandates government standards for private accreditors to accredit private auditors to certify compliance with government regulations. Hybridization blurs standard institutional taxonomies—such as the distinction between public regulation and private ordering—that simplify comparative institutional analysis.[31]

Finally, beyond complementarity and collaboration, different institutions involved in food safety regulation exhibit what sociologists Paul DiMaggio and Walter Powell have called "institutional isomorphism"—a process in which organizations copy principles, practices, and structural features of other organizations with which they are in competition for political power and institutional legitimacy. One example of institutional isomorphism is the evolution of private standard-setting processes that increasingly seek to emulate government notice-and-comment rule making. Having endured criticism that the original LGMA leafy greens metrics were developed in unannounced, private meetings by a small, self-selected group of executives from large processing companies, the Western Growers Association has established a process for developing new and revised standards that provides public notice at every stage of the process, encourages broad stakeholder input, responds to comments, provides written justification for decisions, subjects final proposals to open public hearings with a written record before the LGMA's Technical Committee, and includes two post-hearing reviews by the LGMA board and the California secretary of agriculture before a change is approved. The Western Growers Association and its member companies have sought to bolster the legitimacy and influence of the LGMA metrics by copying these elements of government agency rule making associated with transparency, participation, and accountability.[32]

In another example of isomorphism, government agencies have increasingly adopted elements of industry supply chain management, such as reliance on voluntary guidance and outsourcing inspection. Since the late 1990s, the FDA has relied heavily on voluntary guidance modeled on guidelines issued by trade associations like the International Fresh-Cut Produce Association, the Western Growers Association, and the United Fresh Fruit and Vegetable Association. Reliance on voluntary guidance rather than enforcement actions helped the FDA to boost its legitimacy among growers and handlers by building an image as a flexible partner in food safety rather than a government police officer. More recently, FSMA contemplates that the FDA will rely extensively on private auditors paid for by importers and growers who are subject to new import and produce safety regulations. Outsourcing monitoring in this fashion is associated with greater efficiency than trying to maintain a sufficiently large in-house inspection force. Outsourcing thus helps the agency avoid the common criticism that government regulation is inefficient compared to private alternatives.

Institutional isomorphism makes it harder for comparative institutional analysis to rely on broad categorical generalizations about the process advantages and disadvantages of different types of institutions—for example, that government agencies tend to be more transparent, impartial, participatory, and publicly accountable than industry organizations, and that industry organizations are typically more efficient and quicker to incorporate feedback and learning. Differences between alternative approaches to food safety regulation do remain, but capturing them requires leaving aside increasingly inaccurate generalizations in favor of more detailed analysis.[33]

In the end, comparative institutional analysis helps clarify process values and highlights their role in regulation. Process concerns have driven the evolution of the different approaches to food safety in ways that their proponents believe make them more effective in reducing the risk of foodborne illness. However, one should keep in mind that—because of lack of baselines and metrics, incommensurability among various trade-offs between process values, complementarity among different approaches, collaborations that cross institutional boundaries, and institutional isomorphism—comparative institutional analysis yields limited insight into the preferability of one approach over another.

At this point, a great deal remains uncertain. It is difficult to say with any confidence that efforts to reduce microbial contamination of fresh produce using GAPs have reduced the risk of foodborne illness, much less that these efforts have been cost effective. It is even hard to say which approaches to addressing the problem are most promising.

Improving our ability to assess the efficacy and cost-effectiveness of food safety efforts depends on developing a better understanding of how particular food production practices cause or prevent foodborne illness. Much of what we already know about this connection comes from outbreak investigations. The next chapter traces the history of outbreak investigations and illuminates their central role in the evolution of the food safety system.

From Fork to Farm:
Honing the Tools of Outbreak Investigation

"There is a law written somewhere that all crises come to a head at 4:30 on Friday afternoon of a three-day holiday weekend," says Jack Guzewich, a former senior FDA official. He recalls that, on the Thursday before Memorial Day weekend in 2008, the New Mexico Department of Health notified the CDC about nineteen cases of *Salmonella* infection reported during the month of May—an unusually high number. Laboratory tests had revealed that at least seven cases involved a strain of *Salmonella* bacteria called *Salmonella* Saintpaul. Additional tests had established that *Salmonella* bacteria from four of the seven shared identical DNA fingerprints, meaning that they derived from a common source. The next day, Friday, CDC staff received reports of three additional cases of illness in Colorado and Texas that had been caused by bacteria sharing the same DNA fingerprint.[1]

Officials at the departments of health in New Mexico and Texas, as well as the CDC, immediately launched an investigation to determine the cause of the outbreak. They interviewed two groups of individuals—those who fell ill and a control group—inquiring about what they had eaten in the days prior to the onset of illness. The interviews revealed that outbreak victims were six times more likely to have eaten raw tomatoes than those in the control group.[2]

With the number of reported cases rapidly mounting, the FDA issued a warning on June 3 "alerting consumers in New Mexico and Texas that a salmonellosis outbreak appears to be linked to the consumption of certain types of raw red tomatoes and products containing raw red tomatoes." Over the next few days, the number of reported illnesses more than doubled. By June 7, the CDC counted 145 cases from an increasing number of states,

including California, Connecticut, Oklahoma, Oregon, Virginia, Washington, and Wisconsin. Feeling pressure to warn consumers but worried about
implicating companies that had not sold tomatoes in the affected states, the
FDA released a statement "expanding its warning to consumers nationwide"
to avoid eating the suspected varieties of tomatoes unless the tomatoes were
from a list of states and countries that would be updated on the agency's website "as more information becomes available."[3]

The FDA warning set off a panic. "When we told people to stop eating
tomatoes, they stopped eating tomatoes," recalls Guzewich. "Fresh tomato
sales tanked." McDonald's, Burger King, and Wendy's stopped serving sliced
tomatoes on burgers and chicken sandwiches. Subway eliminated tomatoes
from its fixings. Chipotle Mexican Grill sold burritos without salsa. Leading
supermarket chains, including Walmart, Kroger, and Whole Foods pulled
from their shelves the varieties of tomatoes named in the FDA warning, regardless of where they came from. "The movement of tomatoes in this country has come to a halt," declared Reggie Brown, executive vice president of
the Florida Tomato Growers Exchange.

Eager to control both the outbreak and the collateral damage to the tomato industry, an FDA spokesperson assured the public on June 10 that "we
are getting closer to identifying the source or sources" of contamination.
However, three weeks later, with more than 850 confirmed cases, including 170 hospitalizations, spanning thirty-six states, the agency had still not
identified the source. Epidemiologists interviewed the growing number of
victims. Investigators scoured supply chain records. Laboratory personnel
tested 1,700 samples from fields, warehouses, retail stores, restaurants, and
households, looking for the outbreak strain of *Salmonella* to confirm that
tomatoes were, in fact, the vehicle of infection.[4]

As the weeks wore on, and none of the agency's samples from tomatoes,
tomato fields, or tomato-handling facilities tested positive for *Salmonella*
Saintpaul, an increasing number of people questioned whether tomatoes
were to blame. "The tomato investigators are stumped," declared the *Washington Post* on July 2. "Over the past four weeks, they have pored over records, collected hundreds of samples and interviewed dozens of patients to
find the cause of a salmonella outbreak. So far, their efforts haven't produced
an answer, and they have begun to question whether their prime suspect—
raw tomatoes—has been wrongly accused." In the face of such skepticism,
the FDA's associate commissioner for foods Dr. David Acheson insisted that
"the tomato trail is still hot."[5]

The next day, the investigation took a surprising turn when the Minnesota Department of Health informed federal investigators about a cluster of outbreak victims who had all eaten at the same Mexican restaurant. None of the victims had eaten tomatoes, but all of them had eaten jalapeño peppers—which Minnesota health officials traced back to a distributor in McAllen, Texas, and from there to three farms in Mexico. Two weeks later, FDA investigators visited the distributor and found jalapeño peppers that tested positive for the outbreak strain of *Salmonella* Saintpaul. They then visited the distributor's Mexican suppliers and obtained samples from one farm of irrigation water and serrano peppers that tested positive for the outbreak strain. The farm also grew jalapeño peppers. It did not grow tomatoes.[6]

A barrage of criticism accused the FDA of incompetence. An NBC News headline ridiculed the agency: "Pepper Provided Hot Lead in Hunt for Salmonella: Minnesota Pinpointed Jalapeños While Feds Fruitlessly Chased Tomatoes." Representative Dennis Cardoza of California lectured FDA officials at a congressional hearing: "Poor handling of this outbreak has confused consumers, damaged producers and led to just mass confusion in the public. You could describe our current food safety system as outbreak roulette: one spin of the outbreak wheel and your industry may be bankrupt, your love ones sickened."

Tomato industry experts estimated the business losses in Florida and Georgia alone at more than $100 million, and estimates of the total losses nationwide ranged from $300 million to $500 million. In their defense, CDC and FDA officials argued that initial interviews had suggested a strong association between outbreak victims and consumption of raw tomatoes. These officials knew from the very outset that tomatoes might not be the source of contamination but might have merely accompanied it or been mixed with it—for example, in salsa or guacamole—especially because, as the investigation proceeded, they also found a strong association with eating in Mexican-style restaurants. However, with the number of reported cases rapidly mounting, the agency felt enormous pressure to take any action that might halt the outbreak. In the days before its June 7 tomato warning, the agency received more than twenty reports each day of new cases, and by mid-June, more than forty such reports poured in daily. Had agency officials not issued a consumer warning, they would likely have been blamed for inaction in the face of what turned out to be the largest foodborne illness outbreak in a decade, ultimately involving 1,500 reported cases, including 315 hospitalizations and two deaths, spanning forty-three states and Canada.[7]

Investigators never definitively identified the source of the 2008 *Salmonella* Saintpaul outbreak. The evidence did not implicate the McAllen distribution facility where investigators found contaminated jalapeño peppers, and the Mexican growing fields where they might have originated yielded contaminated water samples and serrano peppers, but no contaminated jalapeño peppers. Moreover, some public health officials refused to rule out tomatoes, which, they argued, could have been one of multiple sources in what might have been two or more simultaneous outbreaks caused by the same strain of bacteria.[8]

Though inconclusive, the investigation provided valuable information. It linked illnesses around the country to reveal the emergence of a nationwide outbreak involving 1,500 reported cases of illness. The investigation made visible a major outbreak that would otherwise have remained under the radar.[9]

The investigation also provided useful feedback to industry and government concerning weaknesses in the food safety system. For example, the FDA's frustration in attempting to trace tomatoes from consumers back to growers revealed a need to improve supply chain record keeping. Following the investigation, a broad coalition of industry associations launched an initiative to promote uniform standards and practices for recording the movement of products through distribution networks using barcode technology. The FDA funded a major study that produced recommendations for improving product traceability within the food industry. The issue became a major component of the Food Safety Modernization Act, in which Congress mandated further research and new rules to improve the traceability of high-risk products.[10]

Outbreak investigations, when they quickly and accurately identify the food vehicle responsible for causing illness, can stem the spread of infection. When they successfully identify the initial cause of contamination, they can inform food safety advances that prevent future outbreaks. And as the 2008 *Salmonella* Saintpaul outbreak investigation illustrates, even when they take wrong turns or are inconclusive, they can still generate valuable public health information and useful feedback.

This chapter examines the tools that make up what investigators call the "three-legged stool" of outbreak investigations: epidemiology, pathogen testing, and product tracing. Robert Tauxe, a senior official at the CDC who has spent more than thirty years investigating foodborne illness outbreaks, describes the evolution of these tools as part of a "cycle of public health prevention" in which outbreaks offer opportunities for feedback and learning that gradually improve the capacity of the food safety system to identify, respond to, and ultimately prevent foodborne illness. This chapter catalogs some of the ways in which outbreak investigations produce information and promote collaboration that is essential to advancing food safety.[11]

Epidemiology

Epidemiology is a branch of medicine that deals with the spread of infectious disease. Epidemiologists use information about groups that suffer from a disease to formulate hypotheses concerning the cause of the disease. In foodborne illness outbreak investigations, this begins with identifying a food that may have served as a vehicle for spreading a bacterial or viral infection. Investigators then trace the suspected food's path of production and test samples from different points on that path to further refine and verify their hypotheses. Epidemiology provides a focus for tracing and testing.

The epidemiological leg of an outbreak investigation can itself be divided into three components: public health surveillance, food history interviews, and data analysis. Public health surveillance dates back in the United States to colonial times, when laws required doctors, innkeepers, and family members to report cases of specific communicable diseases to local officials. Of particular interest were smallpox, yellow fever, and cholera. Systematic statewide data collection began in 1874, when the Massachusetts State Board of Health initiated a voluntary program for physicians to provide weekly reports of specific diseases using a standard form. In 1893, Michigan mandated reporting of certain infectious diseases, and other states quickly followed with similar laws. The federal government began publishing weekly reports of infectious disease outbreaks in 1878.[12]

Surveillance of foodborne illness started in the early twentieth century with data collection on typhoid fever, caused by *Salmonella* bacteria. Following outbreaks caused by contaminated canned ripe olives in 1919 and 1920, California instituted systematic statewide surveillance for botulism and published reports in *Public Health Reports*, a weekly journal that disseminated the US Public Health Service's data on infectious disease. In 1922, the Public Health Service established a field station "for the investigation and study of all outbreaks of food poisoning occurring in the United States," which collected and reported national data.[13]

The evolution of foodborne illness surveillance has been closely connected to advances in microbiology. In the late 1800s, scientists learned how to distinguish different species of bacteria by growing colonies of bacteria in culture media using a petri dish. This advance enabled public health officials in the 1920s to classify foodborne illness by bacterial species—for example, *Salmonella* or *B. botulinum*—and to verify that particular foods served as vehicles for infection based on analysis of matching bacterial isolates grown from samples taken from illness victims and contaminated foods.[14]

In the 1920s, scientists developed laboratory techniques to distinguish variations within species of bacteria by identifying different forms of a type of protein or carbohydrate, called an antigen, on the surface of bacteria. A subspecies of bacteria is called a serotype, because the laboratory techniques use serum made from blood to identify different types of antigens. In the 1930s and 1940s, laboratories adopted a standard classification system for bacterial serotypes that assigns a numerical identifier to the type of antigen on the body of the bacteria (referred to as the O antigen) and on the tail of the bacteria (referred to as the H antigen). For example, *E. coli* O157:H7 refers to a serotype of *E. coli* bacteria with the 157th type of O antigen discovered on *E. coli* and the 7th type of H antigen discovered on *E. coli*. In the case of *Salmonella*, serotyping led to the discovery of more than 2,500 serotypes.[15]

Serotyping enabled improvements in surveillance. Before serotyping, outbreaks discovered by public health officials typically occurred among patrons of the same venue or event. Public health officials today refer to these as "church supper" outbreaks. Concern about foodborne salmonellosis outbreaks in the 1950s and early 1960s gave rise to the National Salmonella Surveillance Program (NSSP) in 1962. Under the program, state health departments voluntarily submitted reports to the CDC each week with data concerning *Salmonella* isolates from illness victims, which the CDC aggregated and shared with the states. The NSSP's aggregation of state data that specified serotypes made it possible for the first time to link geographically dispersed cases of illness in different states that were associated with the same *Salmonella* serotype. Subsequent epidemiological interviews with victims, product tracing, and laboratory testing of samples allowed public health authorities to identify multistate outbreaks with a common source that would otherwise have occurred undetected. The advent of the NSSP marks the origin of the current model of foodborne illness outbreak investigation.[16]

Further advances in bacterial typing techniques in the 1980s led to additional improvements in surveillance in the 1990s. Public health surveillance frequently detects single sporadic cases of foodborne illness of unknown origin that, when aggregated over time, constitute a baseline, or "endemic" level, of illness. Sometimes surveillance programs observe a number of cases of illness associated with a particular bacterial serotype that exceeds the endemic level. This indicates that an outbreak has occurred. However, some of these cases are outbreak cases from a common source, and some are endemic sporadic cases from different sources. Although serotyping reveals the occurrence of an outbreak, it cannot distinguish between outbreak cases and endemic sporadic cases associated with the same serotype. The inclusion of endemic sporadic cases in an outbreak investigation can confound efforts to identify the common source of the outbreak cases and distort estimates of the size of the outbreak.[17]

In the aftermath of the 1993 Jack in the Box outbreak, state public health officials around the country wanted to determine whether E. coli O157:H7 isolates obtained in their states were part of the outbreak or merely single cases of endemic sporadic disease. These state officials sent the isolates to the CDC, where scientists applied a laboratory technique developed in the 1980s called pulsed-field gel electrophoresis (PFGE), which enables scientists to discern a DNA "fingerprint" of each isolate to determine whether it matches the DNA of outbreak isolates. PFGE thus allowed public health officials to distinguish outbreak from endemic sporadic cases by discerning different DNA patterns among bacteria of the same serotype.[18]

Over the following few years, CDC officials harnessed PFGE technology to establish a national surveillance system called PulseNet, consisting of a network of laboratories throughout the United States that perform molecular subtyping of bacterial isolates obtained from patients and upload the results to a centralized database. PulseNet tracks a number of common pathogens, including Salmonella, E. coli, Shigella, and Listeria. National surveillance using molecular subtyping enables public health officials to quickly exclude endemic sporadic cases from multistate outbreak investigations. The PulseNet system shares this surveillance data with state and local health departments.[19]

After public health surveillance identifies an outbreak, the next step in the epidemiological leg of an investigation is to interview victims to determine which foods they ate. Within the CDC, the Outbreak Response and Prevention Branch (ORPB) analyzes PulseNet data to identify and prioritize investigation of outbreaks. ORPB also manages a network of public health officials at the federal, state, and local level—known as OutbreakNet—participating in the investigation. Officials in this network conduct food history interviews with outbreak victims. Most interviews are conducted by local public health workers, often with guidance from state or CDC officials, some of whom may be members of the agency's Epidemic Intelligence Service, a corps of doctors, scientists, veterinarians, and health professionals specially trained in disease investigation and posted in federal, local, and state offices.[20]

Food history interviews face a number of challenges. The incubation period for a foodborne illness—the time between eating contaminated food and the onset of symptoms—varies from a few hours to several weeks, depending on the pathogen. Several additional days may pass between the onset of illness and a victim's decision to seek medical care, and several more days may pass as a stool sample is obtained, analyzed, reported, and identified as part of an outbreak. This means that interviewers must ask victims about foods they ate days or weeks earlier, about which most individuals have incomplete memories. Moreover, victims are typically ill at the time of the interview, which may impair both their memories and their patience for lengthy interviews.[21]

The CDC and state health departments have developed standard pathogen-specific questionnaires for interviews, which have evolved over time with experience. "Once a food is identified in an outbreak as a potential vehicle, then it shows up on questionnaires in the future," explains longtime FDA official Michelle Smith. The questionnaires in the 2008 *Salmonella* Saintpaul outbreak included tomatoes because tomatoes had been associated with previous *Salmonella* outbreaks. The CDC coordinates the National Outbreak Reporting System (NORS), which collects and reports nationwide data on the pathogens, foods, handling practices, and establishment characteristics associated with outbreaks. NORS data provide feedback from outbreak investigations that helps refine food history questionnaires. To supplement interviews, investigators may rely on food purchasing records, such as store receipts. Customer loyalty cards create electronic records linking customer identification information with specific food purchases and checkout times, which investigators can retrieve from supermarkets.[22]

The third step in the epidemiological leg of an investigation is to analyze the data from interviews using one of two methods to identify which food eaten by victims might have served as the vehicle for infection. The first method is known as a retrospective cohort study, in which investigators begin with a well-defined population—for example, patrons of a particular restaurant on a particular day—and compare the rate of illness among those who ate a suspected food to the rate of illness among those who did not. This type of study calculates what epidemiologists call a risk ratio: those who ate food X were Y times more likely to get sick than those who did not. The second method is known as a case-control study, in which investigators begin with a group of outbreak victims and compare the foods that they report having consumed at the time of infection to the foods typically consumed by a control group of similar individuals not associated with the outbreak. This type of study calculates what epidemiologists call an odds ratio: those who got sick were X times more likely to have eaten food Y. Case-control studies are common in multistate outbreak investigations that do not include large clusters of victims who all ate in the same venue, which is a necessary condition for a retrospective cohort study. One observer characterizes case-control studies as the "gold-standard procedure" for testing hypotheses in outbreak investigations.[23]

Public health officials used the case-control method in 1924 to identify raw oysters sold by a company in New York as the source of a nationwide typhoid fever outbreak consisting of 1,500 reported cases of illness, including 150 deaths, in twelve cities from New York to San Francisco. In 1996, the same year that the CDC launched PulseNet, it also initiated FoodNet, an active surveillance program, in collaboration with the FDA, USDA, and ten state health departments to collect data on food consumption and foodborne illnesses and to track changes over time. FoodNet conducted a series of surveys between 1996 and 2007 asking respondents about their consumption of selected foods as well as experiences with diarrheal illness, many of which were never reported. FoodNet survey data regarding food consumption provides ready-made control groups for case-control studies in outbreak investigations. In addition, researchers have used FoodNet survey data to estimate the total burden of foodborne illness in the United States and to conduct case-control studies among survey respondents to determine the risk factors for sporadic cases of disease. The Interagency Foodborne Outbreak Response Collaboration—composed of officials in the CDC, FDA, and FSIS—meets monthly to improve coordination of multistate outbreak investigations. The collaborative group develops best practices for detecting outbreaks, testing causation hypotheses, identifying food vehicles, enhancing data sharing and analysis, and communicating risk information.[24]

Pathogen Testing

Outbreak investigations require close collaboration between epidemiologists and microbiologists. Epidemiologists conduct surveillance, interviews, and data analysis to develop hypotheses about the food vehicle of an outbreak. Microbiologists help epidemiologists verify these hypotheses by analyzing bacterial isolates obtained from illness victims and food samples. Epidemiology generates statistical correlations based on the study of populations. Pathogen testing provides specific evidence of causation by finding matching microbes.[25]

By incorporating pathogen-testing results into surveillance networks, public health officials have greatly enhanced their capacity to identify outbreaks. The combination of serotyping and the National Salmonella Surveillance Program in the 1960s enabled officials to connect geographically dispersed cases of illness and identify multistate outbreaks that would previously have remained undetected. The uploading of PFGE data into PulseNet in the 1990s enabled officials to identify multistate outbreaks involving a wider array of pathogens, and to do so faster and with greater accuracy. During the twenty-five years before launching PulseNet, the CDC identified an average of five hundred outbreaks per year. During the decade following the launch of PulseNet, that figure more than doubled to an average of 1,200 outbreaks per year.[26]

Today, a new laboratory technique called whole genome sequencing (WGS) increases the granularity and accuracy of bacterial DNA analysis. Whereas PFGE creates a DNA fingerprint by sorting segments of genetic material from a bacterial sample according to size, WGS provides a much more detailed inventory of that genetic material. Thus, WGS provides a more robust basis for comparison of bacterial samples—as the CDC explains, "like comparing all of the words in a book (WGS), instead of just the number of chapters (PFGE), to see if the books are the same or different." According to Robert Tauxe, WGS represents "the biggest revolution in microbiology since Petri invented his dish."[27]

The CDC is currently in the process of expanding the use of WGS for an increasing number of pathogens in a growing number of states. The agency is updating its PulseNet surveillance system to collect WGS data. Together, WGS and PulseNet allow public health officials to identify a multistate outbreak on the basis of as few as two matching fingerprints. Tauxe describes the infusion of WGS into the PulseNet system—with its capacity to identify links between what would otherwise appear to be isolated cases of illness—as the "Hubble Telescope" of food safety surveillance, "revealing a much more complex universe with enormous numbers of star clusters, even in the darkest parts of the sky." Because WGS data enable public health officials to identify outbreaks on the basis of very few cases, they can more quickly intervene to contain the spread of illness.[28]

In addition to PulseNet, the FDA has created a new data network called GenomeTrakr, which collects WGS fingerprints of bacterial samples from food and production facilities. By identifying matching WGS fingerprints in PulseNet and GenomeTrakr, investigators can link illness victims to contaminated foods and production facilities. Evolving computer technology is fueling the rapid pace of the WGS revolution in outbreak investigations. Increasingly powerful and affordable computers have accelerated the analysis of bacterial samples and made WGS equipment accessible to a growing number of labs. In 2013, GenomeTrakr's first year of operation, a handful of US laboratories uploaded an average of 169 sequences per month. By 2017, an expanding network of US laboratories, as well as labs in Canada, the United Kingdom, Italy, Austria, Germany, Denmark, Argentina, and Australia, uploaded an average of 5,826 sequences per month, and the total number of sequences in the database exceeded 160,000.[29]

Just as epidemiology relies on pathogen testing to verify hypotheses based on statistical correlations, pathogen testing, in turn, relies on epidemiology to verify whether similar bacterial isolates are close enough to indicate an outbreak. Because PFGE does not provide a full inventory of molecular material, isolates that are PFGE matches may not, in fact, have the same DNA fingerprint (like books that have the same number of chapters but contain different words). This is the problem of false positives—the classification of unrelated cases of illness as an outbreak or the inclusion of one unrelated case within a cluster of outbreak cases under investigation. Epidemiology can test for false positives by determining whether the patients from which PFGE-matching isolates were obtained consumed the same food. The increased granularity of WGS generates a related problem. Isolates that are not exact WGS matches may, in fact, be slight genetic mutations of a bacteria from the same source (like copies of the same book with a few insignificant word changes). This is the problem of false negatives—the failure to classify related cases of illness as an outbreak or the exclusion of an outbreak case from a cluster of outbreak cases under investigation. Epidemiology can help investigators determine whether two bacterial genetic sequences are sufficiently similar by determining whether the patients from which the isolates were obtained consumed the same food.[30]

The spread of a recent scientific advance threatens the PulseNet system. An increasing number of clinical labs are using a new technology that enables them to test patient samples for illness-causing bacterial species and obtain results within hours without having to grow a bacterial isolate in a culture, a much slower process that takes days. This new technology, known as culture-independent diagnostic testing (CIDT), reduces the cost and time necessary to obtain a patient diagnosis. However, having obtained a quick result regarding the species of bacteria, labs using CIDT forgo the more time-consuming and expensive process of obtaining an isolate necessary to produce a PFGE or WGS DNA fingerprint, on which PulseNet depends for the identification and investigation of multistate outbreaks. The CDC is working with the Association of Public Health Laboratories to encourage clinical labs, when they obtain positive CIDT results, to produce isolates and submit them to public health laboratories for PFGE or WGS analysis. The CDC is also exploring new technologies that would allow for rapid, low-cost genome sequencing directly from patient samples by clinical or public health labs, without the need to produce an isolate.[31]

Supply Chain Tracing

Once epidemiology and pathogen testing have identified the food vehicle for an outbreak, investigators must determine where illness victims obtained the food and trace its path back along the supply chain to find out where and how it was originally contaminated. Additional pathogen testing of environmental samples obtained from production and distribution facilities can reveal the root cause of contamination. Moreover, after investigators have traced the food vehicle of an outbreak back to its source, company and public health officials then attempt to track the distribution of that food from its source forward through the supply chain to recall any potentially contaminated products from store shelves and warn consumers who purchased them.[32]

Supply chain tracing is especially difficult in outbreak investigations involving fresh foods sold in bulk, such as produce and fish, which lack packaging bearing information such as brand name, manufacturer and distributor contact information, lot number, and production dates. The 2008 *Salmonella* Saintpaul outbreak illustrates the challenges faced by investigators in attempting to trace fresh produce back through the supply chain. Early in the investigation, recounts Guzewich, "we went to our contacts in the produce industry, and we asked, 'Where do tomatoes come from this time of year?' We were told, 'Mostly they come from Mexico or Florida.'" However, "the Florida industry said, 'A lot of the cases are out west. They're in New Mexico, they're in Texas, so it can't be Florida tomatoes since our tomatoes don't go that far. It's too expensive to haul them that far, so it *has* to be Mexican tomatoes.' Then we had a cluster of cases in Idaho linked to Florida tomatoes because Walmart was shipping them all the way from Florida to Idaho!"[33]

The agency's efforts were complicated when investigators learned that tomatoes from Florida and Mexico are sometimes commingled and shipped together. "The Floridians swore that there wouldn't be any Mexican tomatoes in with the Floridian tomatoes," recalls Guzewich. "Then we discovered that there were tomatoes coming from Mexico, going to Florida, being labeled as Florida tomatoes, and shipped out to distributors. Some Florida growers owned Mexican farms and, if they couldn't meet the demand with Florida tomatoes, they would bring in Mexican tomatoes." Investigators also learned that growers typically sell tomatoes to distributors, who take the tomatoes out of their original boxes, resort them by grade, color, shape, and shade, and put them back in the same boxes. That way the distributor can deliver a more uniform box of tomatoes that meets a retail buyer's specifications. To complicate matters further, tomatoes are often renamed as they move through the distribution chain. "One guy might call them Beefsteaks, and the next guy calls them Red Rounds. Then, when they are getting later in their shelf life, the next guy calls them Cookers." All of this resorting and renaming made it nearly impossible for FDA investigators to trace a tomato consumed by an outbreak victim from the retail store or restaurant from which he or she purchased the tomato back through a distributor to a grower, since both the number on the box in which it was shipped and the name by which it was sold to the retail store or restaurant might not appear in the growers' records. Moreover, retail stores and restaurants typically have no information about the origin of the tomatoes that they sell, because distributors frequently conceal the identities of growers who supply them to prevent their retail customers from trying to deal directly with growers. For FDA investigators, it was "a nightmare," recalls Guzewich. "The tracebacks really weren't getting us anywhere."[34]

Investigation of the 1924 raw oyster outbreak in New York City is an early example of successful supply chain tracing in a multistate outbreak investigation involving fresh foods sold in bulk. The first federal tracing law is the 1930 Perishable Agricultural Commodities Act (PACA), which requires large-scale fresh produce shippers selling on behalf of growers to assign a lot number to each shipment and record the identity of the grower and the buyer, thereby creating a paper trail that can be used later to resolve any disputes about quality and payment. These ninety-year-old PACA record-keeping requirements—still on the books today—facilitate traceability in the initial link of the fresh produce supply chain.[35]

The Bioterrorism Act of 2002, passed in the wake of the 9/11 attacks, authorized the FDA to establish regulations requiring all persons "who manufacture, process, pack, transport, distribute, receive, hold, or import" food products regulated by the agency to maintain records that identify the immediate previous supplier of the food and the immediate subsequent buyer—an approach known as "one-up/one-down" supply chain traceability. These records must also include the date of receipt or release of the food; a description of the brand name, specific variety of the food, quantity, and how the food is packaged (e.g., six-count bunches, twelve-ounce bottle); and lot number ("to the extent that this information exists"). However, the act exempts farms, some packing operations, and restaurants. Perhaps even more significant, the act does not require record keeping for food transfers within a company, which may stymie traceback efforts in an outbreak investigation involving lots that are re-sorted or comingled during distribution or processing. The FDA's final regulations under the Bioterrorism Act went into effect in 2005 and 2006.[36]

The Food and Drug Amendments Act of 2007 instructed the FDA to establish regulations requiring food facility operators subject to the Bioterror-ism Act to submit an electronic report to the Reportable Food Registry of any food that they have reason to believe may "cause serious adverse health consequences or death to humans or animals." Under the act, the agency may require the facility to notify the immediate supplier and buyer of the food, based on its one-up/one-down traceability records. The FDA launched the registry in 2009.[37]

Within industry, traceability has developed as part of supply chain man-agement. For example, although PACA does not require recording lot in-formation on boxes, most fresh produce shippers have long marked boxes with lot numbers as part of their quality-assurance program, enabling them to identify the source of products that buyers especially like or that generate complaints. Distributors place tags on pallets to facilitate inventory manage-ment. Public health officials have traditionally relied on these supply chain management records in traceback investigations.[38]

Food safety concerns have also motivated industry efforts to improve traceability. In response to outbreaks involving fresh produce items, the Pro-duce Marketing Association (PMA) and the Canadian Produce Marketing Association (CPMA) joined forces in 2002 to form a Traceability Task Force of representatives from leading growers, packers, shippers, distributors, re-tailers, food service providers, and trade associations. The task force identi-fied two primary obstacles to more efficient whole-chain traceability: lack of universal record keeping standards and reliance on paper files. In tracing the path of a product through the supply chain, investigators conducting a trace-back and producers implementing a recall had to correlate different product identifiers at each stage of distribution. Packers, wholesalers, shippers, dis-tributors, and supermarkets each assigned different internally generated item numbers in their records for the same product. Moreover, the re-sorting and repacking of produce items by distributors further complicated the task of tracing a product's path. Paper files frequently produced records that were inaccurate or incomplete, hard to locate, or missing altogether.[39]

The task force published a guidance document, *Traceability Best Prac-tices*, in 2004, which addressed both of these obstacles. The guidance docu-ment endorses the use of Global Trade Item Numbers (GTINs) to identify products throughout the supply chain. Global Standards One (GS1), a private standard-setting organization for product coding, sells applicants a unique company prefix that, when combined with an item number assigned by the company, results in a GTIN, represented in both a string of numbers and an electronically readable barcode. The best practices recommend that packers mark each case with a GTIN and lot number in both human-readable form and in a barcode. Using the same GTINs and lot numbers, each company along the supply chain records information concerning the previous supplier and the subsequent buyer. The best practices aimed to refine, rather than replace, the government's preexisting one-up/one-down supply chain traceability regulations, and to create interoperability between companies' existing internal inventory management systems. If distributors re-sort and repack items, then the best practices consider them packers, responsible for keeping a record of the GTIN and lot number from each of the original commingled items in the repacked case, which receives a new GTIN and lot number with the distributor's company prefix and a distinct item number. The best practices encourage companies to adopt electronic record keeping to expedite tracing requests.[40]

A primary motivation for the produce industry's focus on traceability was to minimize the economic impact of outbreaks. Rapid identification of contaminated lots would allow companies responsible for an outbreak to limit the scope of a recall. It would also enable other companies to exonerate their products. "Without traceability," the task force's guidance document explains, "the scope of a product recall may encompass an entire commodity group, source of supply, or product brand. A negative ripple effect could also cross over to other companies with similar products or geographic regions. The cost of a massive recall, in addition to potential future litigation could be a fatal blow to even the largest of organizations."[41]

When the 2006 Dole baby spinach outbreak devastated the entire spinach industry—because the FDA took two weeks to identify the source of *E. coli* O157 contamination—fresh produce companies called upon their trade associations to devise a traceability system that would expedite tracebacks and thereby limit collateral damage to innocent companies in future outbreak investigations. In response, the United Fresh Produce Association teamed up in 2007 with the PMA, the CPMA, and GS1 to launch the Produce Traceability Initiative. In April 2008, a steering committee representing thirty-seven leading fresh produce growers, packers, shippers, distributors, retail stores, and food service companies endorsed a plan based on the *Traceability Best Practices*, with the aim of reducing the time necessary to trace the path of a contaminated product back and forward through the supply chain to between twenty-four and forty-eight hours.[42]

The *Salmonella* Saintpaul outbreak in the summer of 2008—which devastated the tomato industry—increased the sense of urgency among fresh produce industry leaders to implement their plan for electronic whole-chain traceability. In October, the Produce Traceability Initiative steering commit-

tee published an action plan proposing full implementation of its best practices throughout the fresh produce industry by 2012. The plan called on brand
owners to obtain company prefixes, assign GTINs to each product that they
pack, and label each case with a GTIN and lot number in human-readable
and barcode formats. The plan instructed handlers to scan and store those
data on inbound and outbound cases.[43]

Although many companies made efforts to adopt the Produce Traceability Initiative's best practices, the timeline for full implementation proved
too ambitious. In May 2012, the initiative announced the results of a survey
completed by 228 companies situated throughout the supply chain. Of brand
owners, 77 percent reported assigning GTINs to some or all of their produce
cases, and 84 percent of suppliers reported that they were communicating
GTINs to their buyers. However, only 43 percent reported that they were
"totally or partially equipped for reading" label data, and 40 percent that they
kept records on "all or some" label data. These survey data likely overstate
the level of adoption, because they do not include companies that declined to
complete the survey.[44]

A study by the Institute of Food Technologists (IFT) found that some
companies failed to implement the Produce Traceability Initiative best practices because of costs associated with setting up new computer systems, purchasing label printers and scanners, building internet infrastructure in old
facilities, slowing down production speeds to label and scan products (or,
in some cases, enter data manually), and training workers with limited formal education to use computer technology. Companies in the supply chain
worried that if they implemented costly traceability practices, less scrupulous
competitors would offer the same products for less. The IFT study also suggested that some companies feared that improved traceability would increase
their exposure to reputational damage and liability. Finally, the study found
that some companies put off changing their record-keeping systems out of
concern that the Produce Traceability Initiative best practices were subject
to frequent revision. These companies preferred to wait until the FDA imposed a binding regulation, although, noted the study, they did not welcome
a government-imposed system.[45]

In addition, the IFT study found that the lack of universal implementation frustrated supply chain participants who were otherwise willing to adopt
the best practices. In some cases, their suppliers failed to provide sufficient
information or provided information in an idiosyncratic format, making it
difficult for them to create standardized records. In other cases, their buyers required product information different from that specified by the best

practices, forcing them to maintain multiple record-keeping schemes. Companies reasoned that if their trading partners along the supply chain did not conform to the best practices, there was no point in adopting them.

As the Produce Traceability Initiative was rolling out its best practices, consumer advocates called for more stringent government traceability regulations. Following the 2006 Dole baby spinach outbreak, the Center for Science in the Public Interest (CSPI) filed a citizen petition urging the FDA to issue new labeling regulations "to ensure easy traceback when fruits and vegetables are implicated in an outbreak." In the midst of the 2008 *Salmonella* Saintpaul outbreak, the CSPI and the Consumer Federation of America called for "emergency regulations" mandating standard labels for all fresh produce and record-keeping requirements to ensure traceability from "farm to table."[46]

A 2009 report by the Office of Inspector General in the Department of Health and Human Services on compliance within industry with FDA tracing regulations found that 70 out of 118 food facilities in a traceback simulation using forty products "did not provide all of the required contact information about their sources, recipients, and transporters," and that managers in twenty-six of the facilities "were not aware of FDA's records requirements." The OIG report recommended that the FDA "strengthen existing records requirements" by mandating that "every facility that handles a food product . . . maintain records about every facility or farm that handled the product" using interoperable electronic record-keeping systems.[47]

Not everyone agreed that the *Salmonella* Saintpaul outbreak proved the need for new government mandates regarding traceability. In testimony before Congress, PMA president Bryan Silbermann and United Fresh president Thomas Stenzel credited reliable traceback systems in the produce industry for exonerating tomatoes and enabling investigators to quickly locate the source of the contaminated peppers. "In fact," stated Stenzel, "this would be my exhibit for traceability working. . . . Once they started looking for jalapeños, they got there very, very quickly." They blamed the initial confusion on missteps in the CDC's epidemiological analysis and the slow reporting of pathogen test results from state labs. Robert Brackett, who had directed the FDA response to the 2006 Dole baby spinach outbreak and who then served as the senior vice president and chief science and regulatory affairs officer at the Grocery Manufacturers Association, agreed that "traceability was not the real issue in the *Salmonella* Saintpaul outbreak." Jim Prevor commented, "Whatever the problems may be with traceback, this outbreak indicates a problem with our public health system's epidemiological efforts—not a problem with traceback."[48]

In any event, the FDA contracted with the IFT to conduct research and draft a report on existing traceability systems throughout the food industry and to provide the agency with a list of recommendations for reform. The IFT published a final report in 2010 containing recommendations that are substantially similar to the Bioterrorism Act requirements and Produce Traceability Initiative best practices—maintenance of one-up/one-down records for each case of a product using standard labels to identify the packer, item, and lot number, all stored in interoperable electronic databases. The report further recommends that compliance with traceability standards be incorporated into private third-party food safety audits, and that the agency develop guidance and training programs to assist companies with implementation.[49]

When Congress passed the Food Safety Modernization Act in 2010, it included a section titled "Enhancing Tracking and Tracing of Food and Recordkeeping," which requires the secretary of health and human services (the Department of Health and Human Services is the parent agency of the FDA) to "establish pilot projects in coordination with the food industry" to "explore and evaluate" methods for improving traceability and report its findings to Congress within eighteen months along with "recommendations." The FDA again turned to the IFT, which conducted the pilot projects mandated by FSMA with input from industry groups, federal and state officials, and consumer advocates, resulting in a report recommending that the FDA issue rules under FSMA to establish uniform record-keeping requirements for companies at each stage of the supply chain and develop standardized electronic formats for reporting this information to the FDA during investigations. The IFT report recognizes the symbiosis of government and industry traceability efforts. It recommends that the FDA "encourage current industry-led initiatives" and actively seek "stakeholder input" in developing traceability regulations. In 2016, the FDA submitted a report to Congress with findings and recommendations that closely tracked those of the IFT report. With a few reservations, industry groups have embraced the findings and recommendations of the FDA report.[50]

A Leverage Point in the System

Dramatic advances in epidemiology, pathogen testing, and product tracing since the 1990s have enhanced the capacity of public health officials to more quickly identify the sources of foodborne illness outbreaks and limit the spread of illness. The faster investigators can detect an outbreak, identify a food vehicle, trace it back to the source of contamination, and track it forward through the distribution chain, the sooner contaminated products can be removed from store shelves and consumers warned to refrain from eating them. According to the CDC's Robert Tauxe, advances mean that "more out-breaks are detected and controlled at an earlier stage, and that fewer continue to a large size." Bob Whitaker, chief science and technology officer at the PMA, agrees. "It used to be hundreds of people sick" in a major outbreak, he explains. The new tools of outbreak investigation "allow you to identify these outbreaks much sooner than we have in the past and to limit their scope." In addition to containing outbreaks after they occur, these advances also sup-port efforts to prevent outbreaks from happening in the first place. They pro-duce and disseminate feedback that results in better-informed government regulation, more rigorous industry supply chain management, and stronger liability incentives to reduce food safety risks.[51]

The interconnections within a system often produce what systems theory calls "leverage points." These are "places in the system where a small change could lead to a large shift in behavior." Within the food safety system, there is perhaps no leverage point more significant than the technologies and tech-niques for identifying foodborne illness outbreaks and tracing them back to specific food safety failures. Advances in outbreak investigation have espe-cially broad ramifications for several reasons.[52]

First, advances in outbreak investigation make additional outbreaks vis-ible. For example, before the 1990s, food safety experts paid little attention to fresh produce. "Raw fruits and vegetables are not common causes of food-borne illness in the United States," asserted a 1985 National Academies re-port. A little more than a decade later, public health officials considered fresh produce a leading source of foodborne illness, responsible for 46 percent of all foodborne illness outbreaks and 23 percent of foodborne illness related deaths between 1998 and 2008, according to a 2013 CDC study. During this period fresh produce caused an estimated 4.4 million illnesses—as many as those caused by dairy, eggs, meat, poultry, and seafood, combined.[53]

Although experts attribute a rise in multistate outbreaks tied to fresh pro-duce to a variety of factors—including increased consumption of raw fruits and vegetables, additional processing in products like fresh-cut bagged salad mixes, global supply chains that expose products to many people from har-vest to sale, and a growing number of elderly consumers with immune sys-tems less able to fight off pathogens—most agree that advances in outbreak investigation explain the sudden appearance of contaminated fresh produce as the leading cause of foodborne illness. "All of a sudden, in the 1990s, we started to see foodborne illness outbreaks because the epidemiology had got-ten better, the surveillance had gotten better, and they were better able to associate produce with foodborne illness outbreaks," explains James Gorny, a prominent food safety expert in the fresh produce sector with experience in academia, government, and industry. The CDC's Tauxe points out that the purported rise in outbreaks caused by contaminated produce may not reflect an actual increase in outbreaks and illness at all but merely be the result of better detection. As Whitaker of the PMA put it, "There probably were outbreaks going back decades that simply didn't get picked up or associated with a food product."[54]

The efforts of public health authorities, industry managers, standard-setting bodies, auditors, plaintiff's attorneys, and insurance underwriters all depend on the detection of outbreaks. HACCP advocates often cite the old management adage that "you can't manage what you can't measure." The reforms prompted by advances in outbreak investigation demonstrate a corollary, that "you can't regulate, audit, or insure what you can't see."[55]

Second, advances in outbreak investigation increase reputational pressure by increasing the frequency with which public health officials can identify the source of foodborne illness. Reputational pressure arising out of outbreak investigations has been a consistent driver of food safety reform. Brand sensitivity and a fear of damaging media attention have motivated companies and their trade associations to invest in research, standardization, and implementation of new food safety practices. Prominent examples include Jack in the Box's leading role in pioneering HACCP controls in ground beef production following its exposure by public health authorities as the source of a multistate *E. coli* O157 outbreak in 1993, the leafy green industry's development of LGMA metrics following the Dole baby spinach outbreak in 2006, and the fresh produce industry's traceability initiatives following the *Salmonella* Saintpaul outbreak in 2008.

Third, advances in outbreak investigation also expand liability exposure. Investigations that identify a food vehicle, isolate a pathogen, and trace them back to a particular company provide plaintiffs' attorneys with evidence of contamination and causation—the essential elements of a viable legal claim. "Because much of the necessary information is in the public domain," government investigations frequently provide much of what, in other kinds of litigation, plaintiffs' attorneys would have to ferret out for themselves in discovery, explains leading food safety litigator Bill Marler: "Public health agencies, by dint of what they do, do the causation piece quite well on these outbreaks."[56]

By expanding liability exposure, advances in outbreak investigation increase the demand for insurance coverage, which provides economic incentives and consulting services that encourage food companies to comply with government regulations and conform to industry standards. "The history of foodborne illness liability exposure and insurance coverage mirrors the pace at which the technology developed to trace it back," explains senior insurance executive Jack Hipp. "The exposure is always reflected in the pace of investigative developments, because without that, you can't create liability." Similarly, by creating pressure to implement recalls, advances in outbreak investigation also increase the demand for product contamination insurance.[57]

Fourth, advances in outbreak investigation improve the quality of feedback and learning, throughout the system. Outbreak investigation is an essential element of what Tauxe calls "the cycle of public health prevention," in which surveillance prompts investigations, which motivate public health research, leading to new prevention efforts, the efficacy of which are verified by surveillance (figure 7.1). Improvements in surveillance trigger the cycle with greater frequency.[58]

"We detect problems through our surveillance systems; we investigate them, identifying both immediate control measures and long-term research needs to improve prevention. Then industry implements what it can and regulators slowly move their agendas forward. Then our surveillance shows whether the immediate control worked, and that the long term trend either is or is not headed in the right direction. Then surveillance picks up the next problem, and around we go again." Outbreak investigation is also an essential element in a similar liability-driven cycle of risk reduction. Outbreak investigations provide causal information which equips plaintiffs' attorneys to file civil claims, increasing the demand for liability insurance and fueling industry research into traceability that allows companies to quickly shift blame for outbreaks to the companies responsible for them which, in turn, facilitates future outbreak investigations (figure 7.2).[59]

Fifth, advances in outbreak investigation stimulate professional collaboration and institutional coordination. For example, in 2005, the FDA and the California Department of Public Health established the California Food Emergency Response Team to integrate the efforts of epidemiologists, laboratory scientists, and regulatory enforcement officials working in a variety of

FIGURE 7.1. The cycle of public health prevention.

FIGURE 7.2. The cycle of liability-driven risk reduction.

agencies on outbreak investigations. In 2008 the FDA expanded this model to other states through its district offices to create interdisciplinary interagency rapid response teams. In 2011, the FDA launched the Coordinated Outbreak Response and Evaluation Network, which established permanent interdisciplinary teams within the FDA to coordinate all stages of multistate outbreak investigations, from detection to post-response evaluations. The teams collaborate with officials working in various offices within the FDA, other federal agencies, and state and local authorities.[60]

The CDC's Foodborne Diseases Centers for Outbreak Response Enhancement (FoodCORE) program, established in 2009, funds centers around the country to help state and local public health authorities develop model outbreak investigation practices and performance standards for epidemiology, pathogen testing, and environmental health assessments. FoodCORE has speeded up the pace and improved the reliability of local and state outbreak investigations, and it has led to better coordination among local, state, and federal agencies collaborating in multistate outbreak investigations. Federal funding and support is provided by the CDC for Integrated Food Safety Centers of Excellence in six states in different regions of the country to equip state health departments to assist other state and local health departments through training programs, guidance documents, and consulting services.[61]

Other initiatives to promote greater collaboration and coordination include the Partnership for Food Protection, created in 2008 by the FDA in cooperation with representatives from federal, state, and local agencies with expertise in epidemiology, laboratory science, and regulatory enforcement to integrate federal, state, and local efforts in outbreak investigations; the Interagency Food Safety Analytics Collaboration, created in 2011 by the CDC, the FDA, and the Food Safety Inspection Service of the USDA, to improve coordination of federal food safety data collection, analysis and use; the Interagency Risk Assessment Consortium, created by a 1998 executive order to improve and oversee food safety risk assessments by federal agencies; and the Food Safety Working Group Information Technology Task Force, established to promote uniform data collection standards and database interoperability between federal, state, and local agencies. The Council to Improve Foodborne Outbreak Response (CIFOR) is a multidisciplinary working group that produces standards and training materials aimed at increasing collaboration between different professional groups working in different levels of government. The organizations that collaborate within CIFOR include the Association of Food and Drug Officials, the Association of Public Health Laboratories, the Association of State and Territorial Health Officials, the Council of State and Territorial Epidemiologists, the National Association of County and City Health Officials, the National Association of State Departments of Agriculture, the National Association of State Public Health Veterinarians, the National Environmental Health Association, and the FDA, CDC, and the USDA.[62]

Advances in outbreak investigation have also fostered greater collaboration between government and industry. For example, the FDA's desire to improve traceability in the aftermath of its 2008 *Salmonella* Saintpaul outbreak investigation prompted it to collaborate closely with the IFT, a professional organization with membership drawn from industry, academia, and government. In the FDA's 2016 Report to Congress on Enhancing Tracking and Tracing of Food and Recordkeeping, mandated by FSMA, the agency recommends that "industry, FDA, USDA, and CDC should explore ways to formalize the use of industry subject matter experts in the preliminary phase of product tracing investigations."[63]

Advances in outbreak investigations function as a leverage point in the food safety system by making additional outbreaks visible, increasing reputational pressure, expanding liability exposure, improving the quality of feedback and learning, and stimulating professional collaboration and institutional coordination—all of which have broad ramifications for government regulation, industry supply chain management, and civil liability. Further investment in the infrastructure of outbreak investigation should feature prominently in thinking about food safety reform, which is the focus of the next chapter.

Recipes for Reform:
Supporting Evidence-Based Food Safety Governance and Improving Private Oversight

On April 11, 2014, the nonemergency, 3-1-1 municipal hotline in Baltimore received three reports from callers complaining that they had contracted food poisoning after eating at an event held in the city's convention center. Following a fourth report four days later, the city and state health departments launched an investigation, which eventually identified 216 victims, all of whom had eaten from the same buffet at the Food Safety Summit—an annual meeting of more than a thousand food safety professionals and government officials from forty-two states, Canada, Costa Rica, and Mauritius.[1]

Headline writers had a field day. "This Is Exactly What Is *Not* Supposed to Happen at the National Food Safety Summit," declared the *Inquisitr*, a popular news blog. "The Plot Sickens: More Than 100 Food Safety Summit Attendees Fall Ill," chortled *Food Quality News*, an industry publication. "Side of Irony? Meal Sickens People at Food Safety Summit," mocked NBC News.[2]

On the basis of epidemiological questionnaires filled out by about half of the conference attendees, investigators found that respondents reporting illness were three times more likely to have eaten chicken Marsala at a lunch buffet on the second day of the conference than those who did not report illness. Laboratory tests of clinical specimens from two dozen outbreak victims found four specimens clearly positive for the bacteria *Clostridium perfringens*, another ten suspected positive, and three positive for *Norovirus*. However, by the time of the investigation, the conference caterer had discarded all the leftovers, and laboratory tests of the ingredients used to cook the chicken yielded no positive results for the presence of either pathogen.[3]

In a presentation at the Food Safety Summit the following year, Alvina Chu, an official at the Maryland Department of Health, summarized the investigation's conclusions: "An outbreak happened. The likely etiology for most cases was *C. perfringens*. There were other illnesses that did not appear to be related to the majority of cases. One vehicle for infection was likely the Chicken Marsala dish served at the April 9 lunch. We don't know exactly what happened."[4]

The 2014 Food Safety Summit outbreak illustrates two persistent challenges in the evolution of the food safety system. First, despite steady advances in understanding the pathogens that cause foodborne illness and the food vehicles that spread it, a great deal of uncertainty remains about the root causes of contamination. Second, the proliferation of increasingly sophisticated approaches to food safety has not always been accompanied by reliable oversight to ensure uniformly rigorous implementation.

Better understanding of the root causes of contamination and more reliable oversight are essential to advancing food safety. For example, pinpointing the root causes of contamination is the key to accurately identifying critical control points in HACCP programs and to specifying GAPs in ways that reduce exposure to pathogens. Reliable oversight of implementation is necessary to putting HACCP programs and GAPs into practice.

This chapter endorses a division of labor between government and industry to address these challenges. On the one hand, it advocates focusing government investment in food safety primarily on improving the infrastructure of outbreak investigations rather than on hiring and training more agency inspectors to oversee farms and processing facilities. Government resources are limited, and government is uniquely equipped to conduct outbreak investigations, which are essential to expanding knowledge about the root causes of contamination. On the other hand, the chapter advocates relying primarily on industry rather than government to fund oversight of food safety program implementation in farming and processing operations. This can take the form of making companies pay for government inspections or private food safety audits. The chapter examines two different models for industry funding of government inspections, and it surveys a number of efforts to improve the reliability of private food safety audits.

This is hardly the first time anyone has advocated more funding for outbreak investigation, making industry pay for government inspections, or improving the reliability of private food safety audits. Leading experts, as well as numerous advocacy groups, have publicly supported one or more of these ideas. Moreover, previous chapters have emphasized how little is known about the impact of existing food safety efforts—which might make readers wonder what the basis is for supporting these particular proposals.[5]

I have singled out these reforms from the many ideas about how to advance food safety because they will generate information necessary to improving feedback and learning. Food safety governance is highly experimental. Government and industry have made significant investments in implementing ambitious reforms—such as HACCP in food processing (see chapters 3 and 4) and GAPs in fresh produce cultivation (see chapters 5 and 6)—on the basis of limited data and considerable speculation about whether, by how much, and at what cost they reduce the risk of foodborne illness. Investing more of the government's limited resources in the infrastructure of outbreak investigation is one way to expand available data and replace speculation with more reliable statistical inferences. This infrastructure (see chapter 7) generates information about the root causes of contamination, the ways it spreads, how people get infected, and data over time that make it possible to track trends regarding rates of infection from various food sources, pathogens, and particular food production practices. All this information is essential to evidence-based evaluation of food safety efforts. In addition, one cannot accurately evaluate the impact of particular food safety efforts unless they are properly implemented, which requires monitoring compliance with prescribed standards and practices. Industry funding of public inspections and private audits, along with safeguards to ensure the quality of private audits, are means of enhancing the reach and reliability of oversight. Another reason for singling out the reforms highlighted in this chapter is that they are examples of leverage points within the system, places where relatively minor adjustments can effect large changes.

The chapter also briefly considers two additional reforms that have attracted widespread attention: creation of a single federal food safety agency and criminal prosecution of food company executives in the wake of outbreaks. Finally, the chapter notes two promising trends: technological advances in digitizing supply chain management information and the maturation of product contamination and food safety liability insurance.

Focusing Government Investment on Outbreak Investigation

The Food Safety Modernization Act of 2011 (FSMA) contains an ambitious agenda of reforms built on decades of feedback and learning in food safety regulation. Its organizes these reforms into four categories: preventing outbreaks, detecting and responding to outbreaks, regulating imported food, and authorizing spending and protecting whistle-blowers. Table 8.1 provides a summary of the statute's provisions. Congress has appropriated hundreds of millions of dollars for FSMA implementation, and the FDA has produced more than a dozen assessments, studies, and reports required by the statute, as well many new regulations and guidance documents.[6]

TABLE 8.1. Summary of FSMA provisions

Title I: Preventing outbreaks	• extends registration requirements for food facilities • enhances agency authority to inspect company production records • mandates that food processors implement HACCP-type programs • calls for updating guidance and regulations related to manufacturing practices, produce safety, food allergies, and intentional adulteration • encourages closer cooperation among federal, state, and local authorities
Title II: Detecting and responding to outbreaks	• prioritizes inspection of high-risk food facilities • recommends using only accredited laboratories for pathogen testing • promotes information sharing among laboratories • mandates pilot projects and record-keeping requirements to improve traceability • supports additional investment in and coordination of public health surveillance, incident reporting, and outbreak investigations at all levels of government • arms the FDA with enhanced enforcement powers, including mandatory recall authority • invests in training programs for state and local food safety officials and educational programming for food producers • authorizes five regional centers to serve as models and coordinate capacity building necessary to carry out reforms
Title III: Regulating imported food	• requires importers to verify that their foreign suppliers satisfy US food safety standards • approves reliance on third-party regulatory compliance audits for food production facilities abroad • mandates the opening of FDA offices in other countries
Title IV: Funding and whistle-blowers	• authorizes spending to hire additional FDA personnel • provides legal protections for corporate whistle-blowers

Government resources to carry out these reforms are limited, and both Congress and the FDA are mindful of this constraint, especially when it comes to the agency's inspection capacity. FSMA mandates FDA inspection of high-risk domestic food facilities merely once every three years and non-high-risk facilities only once every five years. FSMA requires FDA inspection of only six hundred foreign food facilities in the year following enactment and a doubling of that number for the five years following—a goal of less than 4 percent of the more than 250,000 such facilities. The statute contemplates heavy reliance on private third-party auditors to certify that imported foods comply with agency regulations. In the area of produce safety, where the FDA provides no routine inspection services, the FDA announced that it plans to achieve compliance with the Produce Safety Rule mandated by FSMA "primarily through the conscientious efforts of farmers, complemented by the efforts of State and local governments, extension services, private audits and

certifications, and other private sector supply chain management efforts."
Michael Taylor, FDA associate commissioner for foods during the Obama
administration, told the audience at a 2012 food safety conference that "FSMA
recognizes the primary responsibility and capacity of the food industry to
make food safe" and "the complementary role of government."[7]

However, unlike inspection, outbreak investigation is an area of reform
in which government must play the primary role. Only government has the
legal authority to mandate disease reporting, which is essential to detecting
outbreaks. Moreover, government agencies at the state and federal levels have
developed extensive networks, unrivaled by private efforts, to collect and
share pathogen-typing data from patient, food, and environmental samples
and to coordinate epidemiological interviews, analysis, and tracebacks in
multistate outbreaks.

This is not to suggest that industry has no role to play in advancing outbreak investigation. Many in industry favor faster and more accurate tracebacks capable of pinpointing responsible parties quickly to avoid the kind of
reputational damage to an entire industry sector that occurred in the 2006
Dole baby spinach outbreak. To this end, industry has demonstrated considerable leadership in improving traceability throughout the supply chain,
as detailed in chapter 7. However, industry has no incentive to identify outbreaks in the first place or to link them to particular food vehicles. Thus,
funding for public health surveillance and investigative teams of epidemiologists must come from government.

Outbreak investigations rely on a combination of federal and state resources.
As improving surveillance reveals a growing number of outbreaks, inadequate
government resources leave many investigations unresolved. A 2015 study by
the Center for Science in the Public Interest found that more than 60 percent
of outbreaks reported to the CDC remain unsolved largely because of inadequate resources. "Many health departments are underfunded, understaffed,
and overwhelmed by the volume of illness reports," the study states. Another
CSPI study found wide variation among states in their capacity to conduct
surveillance and investigate outbreaks. State investments in equipment and
trained technicians to conduct PFGE analysis and WGS for uploading into the
PulseNet system also vary widely. In addition, FoodNet population surveys of
eating habits and foodborne illness, which provide control group data for outbreaks and the basis for estimating the total burden of foodborne illness, need
to be regularly updated. After a decade-long hiatus, the agency finally started
collecting data in December 2017 for a new FoodNet population survey.[8]

Many reasons justify prioritizing improvements in outbreak investigation
as government allocates its limited resources for FSMA reforms. First, more

extensive surveillance that collects whole genome sequencing data from patient, food, and environmental samples, coupled with more expeditious and
better-coordinated epidemiological interviews, analysis, and tracebacks, will
enable public health authorities to identify additional outbreaks that would
otherwise occur undetected. Second, these advances in outbreak investigation will enable public health authorities to more frequently, quickly, and
accurately identify the food vehicle responsible for an outbreak in order to
halt the spread of infection. Third, more successful outbreak investigations
will expose a greater number of companies throughout the supply chain to
potential reputational damage and civil liability, which gives them financial
incentives to invest in food safety. Fourth, advances in outbreak investigation
will increase the capacity of public health authorities and industry to identify the root causes of outbreaks, which provides feedback to government
agencies, industry experts, and insurance companies in their efforts to refine regulations, guidance, HACCP plans, GAPs, audit criteria, underwriting
guidelines, and loss control advice. Fifth, public health surveillance furnishes
a baseline against which to measure later changes in disease rates that may
offer insight into the efficacy and cost-effectiveness of food safety efforts. The
impact of additional investment in outbreak investigation will reverberate
throughout the food safety system.[9]

Relying on Private Resources for Oversight

With the exception of meat and poultry production, government has never
had sufficient resources to provide routine food safety inspection of more
than a fraction of the food processing facilities in the United States—not to
mention the foreign operations that supply imports. A 2017 report by the Department of Health and Human Services Office of Inspector General found
that the number of food facilities inspected by the FDA declined from 19,369
(25 percent of total) in 2011 to 16,135 (19 percent of total) in 2015, and that,
during this period, the agency failed to conduct follow-up inspections within
a year of half of the facilities where it found significant violations. Moreover,
neither the federal nor state governments have ever funded routine inspections of farms. FSMA contemplates government inspections of farms, and in
2018 the FDA began working with state departments of agriculture to train
state inspectors to inspect farms for compliance with the agency's new Produce
Safety Rule. The FDA says that its own inspectors will conduct inspections in
states unwilling to do so. However, the availability of new and extensive state
resources to conduct routine farm inspections remains to be seen, and many
commentators doubt the FDA's capacity to inspect farms. "The fact is that the

FDA doesn't have the resources or the people to be able to adequately inspect produce farms in any way," asserts David Acheson, former FDA associate commissioner for foods, who now directs a leading food safety consulting firm. "They don't have the people and they don't have the funding to hire them."[10]

Consequently, monitoring compliance with food safety regulations and guidance will continue to fall primarily on food safety audits paid for by industry, most of them conducted by private third-party auditors. As explained in chapter 5, the reliability of these private audits varies widely, due to the limited supply of qualified auditors, an overemphasis on scores and grades at the expense of detailed analysis, pressure throughout the supply chain to keep audit costs low, and the conflict of interest that arises when auditors are paid by the entity being audited.

The private food safety auditing system has been the target of sharp criticism in the aftermath of outbreaks. Doug Powell, a former professor of food safety at Kansas State University, observes that "almost all outbreaks involve firms that received glowing endorsements from food safety auditors." Mansour Samadpour, president of IEH Laboratories & Consulting Group, which specializes in food contamination, asserts, "I have not seen a single company that has had an outbreak or recall that didn't have a series of audits with really high scores." Following a 2008 *Salmonella* outbreak that FDA investigators traced back to a peanut factory where they found dead rodents, open holes in the roof with bird feces washing in, and stagnant pools of water, which, six months earlier, had received a "superior" rating from a private food safety auditing firm, one congressman quipped, "How many dead mice do you have to find in your food before you get an 'Excellent' rating?" Bill Marler believes that "the whole audit system is just a fig-leaf so that everyone in the chain of distribution can say, 'We've checked and everything is okay,' but everybody in the system knows that the whole system is a scam."[11]

One way to improve the reliability of audits is for buyers to train and pay their own auditors. For example, manufacturers and retail stores sourcing ingredients for branded products typically rely on their own in-house auditors, whom they consider more reliable than private third-party auditors. However, when it comes to commodities, such as fresh produce, the number and variety of suppliers makes it impractical and inefficient for distributors and large retail stores to maintain a sufficiently large in-house staff. (For a more detailed analysis of why many buyers in the fresh produce sector rely on third-party auditors rather than their own in-house auditors, see chapter 5.)

Alternatively, buyers could pay for government auditors. For example, under the California Leafy Green Products Handler Marketing Agreement (LGMA), handlers pay an annual assessment that funds state inspectors to audit the growers who supply them. "Our members strongly believe that the government auditors are ideally positioned to conduct effective and independent food safety audits, as neither the buyer nor the seller hires them directly. The auditors report only to their government supervisors. Most importantly, if these auditors identify an imminent health risk during an audit, he or she is required to inform local, federal or state health authorities of the situation," explains the California LGMA CEO Scott Horsfall.[12]

Buyers could also require their suppliers to pay for government auditors. Since 2000, the USDA's Agricultural Marketing Service (AMS) has offered a voluntary fee-for-service food safety auditing program for fresh produce growers and handlers to assist them in complying with federal GAPs guidance. The USDA initiated the program—named the Good Agricultural Practices and Good Handling Practices Audit Verification Program—which relies exclusively on USDA inspectors and state department of agriculture inspectors specifically trained and licensed to perform the USDA's GAP and GHP audits. Since 2011, the USDA has offered fee-for-service GAPs audits using the harmonized standards.[13]

However, despite the option of requiring a government auditor, most buyers in the fresh produce sector still rely on private auditors. There are more than 120,000 farms in the United States that grow fresh produce for sale, yet government inspectors performed only 4,224 audits of farms and handlers in 2016 as part of the USDA's GAP and GHP and Harmonized GAP audit programs. Government inspectors performed an additional 470 audits of leafy greens farms in the 2015–2016 growing season under the California LGMA, and 109 audits under the Arizona LGMA. By contrast, Primus Labs, alone, was performing an estimated fifteen thousand audits per year by 2012.[14] Figure 8.1 illustrates these different options for industry funding of food safety audits.

Curiously, the option that has been subject to the harshest criticism for poor quality and conflict of interest—reliance on private auditors paid by suppliers—is the most widely used in the fresh produce sector. Given the options of using government auditors or having buyers pay for audits, one of the great mysteries of food safety oversight is why so many buyers continue to rely on private auditors paid for by suppliers.

One reason might be that private auditors may charge less for their services. Another explanation might be that private audit firms, unlike government auditors, can customize audits to fit the particular product specifications of any buyer. As retailers analyze feedback and learn from experience, they frequently revise the food safety standards that they incorporate into their product specifications. For example, after requiring GAPs audits in the

Who Pays for the Audit?

		Buyer	Supplier
	Government Inspector	LGMA audits	USDA Harmonized audits
Who Performs the Audit?	Private Auditor	in-house auditors for branded products	private 3rd party audits

FIGURE 8.1. Industry funding of food safety audits.

early 2000s, many buyers, in the aftermath of outbreaks linked to fresh produce, insisted on additional food safety measures in their product specifications. Private auditors, who, unlike government agencies, are free to audit against any standards requested by a buyer, can more easily adapt to buyers' evolving product specifications. By contrast, government auditors can audit only against standards that are incorporated into agency regulations or guidance, or that, at least, undergo a review by multiple layers of agency personnel to obtain agency approval.[15]

Buyers' long-term relationships with specific audit firms may also explain their preference for private auditors. Ken Petersen, chief of the Audit Services Branch of the USDA-AMS Fruit and Vegetable Program, observes that, when it comes time to select approved auditors for suppliers of fresh produce, retail buyers gravitate to private auditing firms that have previously provided auditing or testing services for processing operations in their supply chain. "Retailers already have relationships with [private] audit organizations because they are typically working with their food manufacturers." Because the auditors "already have relationships with these retailers and buyers, they say, 'We can do these farm audits for you now.' They leverage their existing relationships."[16]

Globalization of supply chains and the influence of the Global Food Safety Initiative (GFSI) benchmarking system suggest another possible explanation for why buyers rely on private auditors. GFSI encourages buyers to accept food safety certification under any one of the handful of GFSI-recognized food safety schemes as equivalent to certification under any other. "If you are a big multinational retailer, you are getting product from hundreds of countries in hundreds of different categories. If you can simply say to your suppliers, 'get a GFSI-recognized certification,' that's a kind of one-stop shopping," explains LGMA CEO Scott Horsfall. Food safety programs that require government audits, like the LGMA, are ineligible for GFSI recognition, which requires that a recognized food safety scheme "shall be open, without restriction, to application by any Certification Body [i.e., auditing firm] and, for the purposes of certification, must be operated in a non-discriminatory manner." In addition, GFSI-recognized food safety schemes must ensure that auditors be accredited—which excludes government auditors because, as the USDA's Petersen puts it, "As a government entity, we can't be beholden to a private certification scheme that tells us how to do our job."[17]

Finally, not everyone believes that government auditors are more reliable than private auditors. Dave Theno argued that the amount of pressure on private auditors to skew results may be exaggerated and that auditors working for leading private audit firms generally do a good job. "Do government auditors produce better food safety outcomes than private auditors?" asks Jim Prevor. "The research on this subject is scanty. It is not obvious to us that if the C[alifornia] LGMA, for example, chose to hire Primus auditors that the audits would be worse or that food safety would decline." Moreover, auditors often come from the same communities as the farmers that they audit and may be tempted to relax standards because they "want to be liked," asserts Prevor. He believes that government inspectors are no less subject to this social pressure than private auditors.[18]

One way to improve the reliability of private third-party audits might be to have buyers pay for them. This would avoid the conflict of interest that arises when an auditor is paid by the supplier being audited. However, in many situations, it may not be feasible for buyers to pay auditors. As described in chapter 5, buyers often purchase commodities at auction or through a distributor, so buyers do not know who their suppliers are until after harvest. This makes it impossible for buyers to contract with auditors to inspect their suppliers during cultivation and harvest. Alternatively, buyers might contribute in advance to a collective fund to pay for third-party audits, as is the case with government audits paid for by handlers under the LGMA. However, such an arrangement would generate coordination costs that buyers appear unwilling to pay and raise the same concerns about anti-competitive effects that prompted opposition to a national LGMA.

Several efforts have attempted to promote greater professionalism among private third-party auditors. In 2009, leading audit firms established a trade association, the Food Safety Service Providers, which initiated development of standardized training and best practices for auditors. Professional associations like the International Association for Food Protection and the Institute of Food Technologists regularly offer seminars and trainings for auditors. Universities have also developed new programs of study in microbiology and food safety at the certificate, bachelors, masters, and doctoral levels. The National Environmental Health Association launched a credentialing program for food safety auditors that includes standard training materials, supervised field experience, an exam, and continuing professional education requirements. The association designed the program with input from government agencies, food safety scheme owners, leading auditing firms, industry associations, and major buyers. Professionalization aims to impart technical skills and ethical norms that will improve the reliability of audits.[19]

In addition to professionalization of auditors, there are also efforts to develop better oversight of auditing firms. Retailers increasingly insist that they will accept only audits from audit firms that are accredited. Accreditors verify the reliability of private food safety audit firms through a process of inspection, auditing, and ongoing surveillance, using widely accepted standards jointly developed by the International Organization for Standardization (ISO) and the International Electrotechnical Commission (IEC). In turn, the reliability of accreditors is ensured by a peer-review accreditation system coordinated by the International Accreditation Forum using another set of ISO/IEC standards that apply to accreditors. The ISO/IEC standards for audit firms define ethical norms, institutional structures, and administrative practices that promote auditor impartiality. For example, the standards require an audit firm to have written conflict of interest policies and an oversight committee that includes representation from suppliers, buyers, trade associations, consumer groups, auditing experts, and government agencies. The audit firm must submit periodic reports to the committee identifying risks to its impartiality and demonstrating how it has minimized or eliminated those risks. The firms must empower the committee to conduct independent investigations into alleged violations of the conflict of interest policies and to report serious noncompliance to accreditors, government authorities, and other interested parties. Leading food safety schemes make audit firm accreditation a requirement of obtaining a license to provide certification of scheme compliance. GFSI benchmarks require schemes seeking GFSI recognition to require accreditation of auditors. And as part of FSMA, the FDA has developed standards for accreditors of private food safety auditors who can be accredited to provide regulatory compliance certification under new regulations covering imported foods.[20]

The reliability of private audits could be further improved by exposing private third-party food safety auditors to civil liability for negligence. As a general rule, individuals and companies owe a duty to exercise reasonable care in their operations and are subject to civil liability for any failure to exercise reasonable care when such failure causes foreseeable or direct harm to another. The law distinguishes between misfeasance (affirmative acts of negligence for which an individual or company is subject to liability) and nonfeasance (a failure to act for which an individual or company is not subject to liability in the absence of special circumstances). The law also limits the liability of individuals or companies that provide services when their negligence causes harm to third parties beyond the immediate recipients of those services. In applying these principles to food safety auditors, two legal questions arise: First, should an auditor's lack of rigor be characterized as misfeasance or nonfeasance? Second, is a negligent auditor subject to liability to anyone other than the supplier who paid for the audit, such as an injured consumer?[21]

Several courts addressed these issues following the 2011 listeriosis outbreak caused by contaminated cantaloupes grown and packed by Jensen Farms in lawsuits against Primus Labs, then a leading food safety audit firm in the fresh produce sector. Outbreak victims alleged that Primus was negligent in awarding the Jensen Farms packing operation a passing score of 96 percent and a "superior" rating, in light of food safety problems that it cited in its audit report—most notably, the lack of antimicrobial solution in the wash water to disinfect the melons, which Primus knew was cause for serious concern, as evidenced by its mention of this problem on the first page of the report. Primus moved to dismiss the claims, arguing that its failure to subject Jensen Farms to more rigorous audit standards constituted nonfeasance rather than misfeasance and that, even if it were subject to liability for this failure, its liability was limited to losses suffered by Jensen Farms and did not include injuries to consumers, who were not the immediate recipients of its auditing services. Nine of twelve courts that considered these arguments ruled in favor of the injured consumers and against Primus.[22]

In one notable opinion covering twenty-four lawsuits consolidated in a Colorado court, the trial judge held that a lack of rigor on the part of an auditor constitutes misfeasance for which the auditor could be subject to liability for negligence. The judge further held that a negligent food safety auditor's liability extends beyond the supplier who pays for the audit to include injured consumers. The judge cited a legal standard adopted in many states, Restatement (Second) of Torts §324A Liability to Third Person for Negligent Performance of Undertaking:

> One who undertakes . . . to render services to another which he should recognize as necessary for the protection of a third person . . . is subject to liability to the third person for physical harm resulting from his failure to exercise reasonable care to protect his undertaking, if
>
>> (a) his failure to exercise reasonable care increases the risk of such harm, or
>>
>> (b) he has undertaken to perform a duty owed by the other to the third person, or
>>
>> (c) the harm is suffered because of reliance of the other or the third person upon the undertaking.

The trial judge held that the allegations by consumers, if proven to the satisfaction of a jury, would satisfy this standard. The judge pointed to allegations asserting that one purpose of Primus's audit was to protect consumers from exposure to contaminated food, that Primus's failure to exercise reasonable care in conducting the audit increased the risk of harm to consumers, that Primus undertook Jensen Farms' duty to protect consumers from exposure to contaminated food, and that outbreak victims suffered harm because both Jensen Farms and they themselves reasonably relied on Primus to detect contamination that puts consumers at risk of illness.[23]

The significance of this and the other rulings in favor of the outbreak victims was to signal the willingness of some courts to allow negligence claims against Primus—and, by extension, other auditors—to reach juries, who would ultimately have to render a verdict in each case by deciding, on the basis of the evidence, whether, in fact, the auditor in question failed to exercise reasonable care in conducting the audit and, if so, whether that failure directly or foreseeably caused harm to consumers. Following the denial of its motions to dismiss by nine courts, Primus did not wish to take its chances with juries, so it quickly settled the lawsuits for an undisclosed amount.[24]

Exposing food safety auditors to civil liability for negligence is likely to improve the reliability of private third-party auditors by providing a disincentive to relax standards or inflate audit scores. The standard of reasonable care in negligence cases involving professional services is defined by reference to the formal and informal standards of the profession—in the case of food safety auditors, this would include audit firm policies, audit schemes, auditor accreditation standards, common practice among peers, and, where available, government regulations and guidance. To avoid negligence liability to potentially dozens or hundreds of outbreak victims, auditors must conform to these standards of the profession.[25]

Because employers may be held liable for the negligence of their employees or for their own negligence in hiring, training, and supervising their employees, the rulings against Primus give audit firms an incentive to filter out unqualified applicants, provide training to ensure minimum competence, and furnish management oversight to ensure that audits meet the firm's quality standards. Audit firms' liability insurance carriers also now have an incentive to make sure their insureds institute and maintain these types of hiring, training, and oversight practices. Patricia Wester, a well-known food safety consultant with more than twenty years of experience in food safety auditing who has played a leading role in organizing professional associations and certification programs for auditors, believes that "auditor liability is a potential driver for quality assurance in the industry."[26]

The civil litigation process itself, regardless of outcome, can improve the reliability of audits. In filing claims, plaintiffs will highlight particular inadequacies in the execution of audits or the hiring and supervision of auditors. During discovery, plaintiffs can compel suppliers, auditors, and buyers to disclose information about audit quality that might not otherwise come to light. Each stage of litigation, from filing to final outcome, can generate media coverage that magnifies the reputational pressure on audit firms to ensure the reliability of audits.[27]

Moreover, civil litigation may be more effective than government oversight as a means of improving the reliability of private third-party food safety audits. Plaintiffs' attorneys pursue litigation in exchange for contingency fees—if a claim is successful, the attorney receives a portion of the damages awarded to the plaintiff (typically somewhere between 20 percent and 40 percent), but if the claim is unsuccessful, the attorney charges the client nothing. This method of financing litigation incentivizes plaintiffs' attorneys to file lawsuits whenever an audit falls short of industry standards and the resulting injuries are severe. For plaintiffs' attorneys, searching out and suing unreliable auditors is a business opportunity. By contrast, for government regulators, such efforts are a drain on already-overtaxed agency budgets.

Liability exposure may also have a downside. In their efforts to avoid lawsuits, audit firms and their liability insurers might seek to standardize audits in ways that rely more heavily on checklists that minimize the need for auditor discretion and discourage nuanced professional judgment tailored to each operation under review. An audit by a novice who mechanically follows a company protocol is less likely to generate litigation than an audit by an experienced auditor who makes professional judgments subject to second guessing. This type of defensive auditing would impair the ability of audits to generate creative solutions to food safety problems. Audit firms might also shy away from auditing higher risk sectors, like fresh produce—the very sectors that most need reliable auditing—to avoid liability exposure.[28]

Examples from other professions offer support for the claim that liability exposure can promote improvements and greater consistency in the quality of professional services. Tom Baker, a leading scholar on medical malpractice and insurance, surveyed empirical literature on the influence of litigation on doctors in his 2005 book *The Medical Malpractice Myth*. On the basis of this literature, Baker argues that malpractice lawsuits exposed medical errors and prompted professional associations and hospitals to address the problem by developing new safety practices. He also argues that lawsuits are one of the only ways to get rid of incompetent or unethical doctors. Baker highlights the example of the American Society of Anesthesiologists, which reviewed more than four thousand medical malpractice insurance files and discovered that "adverse respiratory events" were more damaging and more preventable than other anesthesia injuries. Following this discovery, the society "backed the development of better anesthesia equipment and new practice guidelines and then worked hard to get anesthesiologists to use them," resulting in a dramatic decrease in injury and malpractice insurance rates. Joanna Schwartz, a law professor at UCLA, conducted a national survey of health-care professionals and personal interviews with hospital risk managers across the United States and concluded that "lawsuits play a productive role in hospital patient safety efforts by revealing valuable information about weaknesses in hospital policies, practices, providers, and administration."[29]

In addition to the example of medical malpractice litigation, civil lawsuits have also influenced a variety of other professions. Civil lawsuits have had a profound influence on the professional standards of financial accounting. Judicial rulings have shaped Financial Accounting Standards Board financial accounting and reporting standards and Securities and Exchange Commission regulations. Civil lawsuits have also influenced legal practice. Baker and a coauthor have found that liability exposure prompts law firms to obtain advice from their liability insurers about industry best practices for reducing the risk of legal malpractice. In a study of police departments that reviewed litigation files to identify personnel and policy weaknesses, Schwartz found that "lawsuit data has proven valuable to these departments' performance improvement efforts: suits have alerted departments to incidents of misconduct, and the information developed during the course of discovery and trial has been found to be more comprehensive than that generated through internal channels." Similarly, lawsuits on behalf of sexual assault victims against institutions that provide youth services—such as schools, churches, and scouting organizations—has prompted more rigorous oversight of teachers, pastoral workers, and troupe leaders by administrators. For example, Catholic dioceses throughout the United States, under the direction of their liability insurers, have implemented background checks for hiring, training programs to reduce the risk of sexual assault, protocols for investigating allegations, and policies for reporting abuse to public authorities. Additional studies have documented the impact of litigation on the oversight of store personnel and prison guards.[30]

Admittedly, empirical evidence for the beneficial effects of litigation is limited. Excepting the study of anesthesiologists—in which litigation led to the improvement of health outcomes—these examples link litigation to the promulgation of new and more detailed professional standards and practices, but they do not provide any data beyond anecdotal evidence that these new standards and practices improved the quality of financial audits, discouraged legal malpractice, reduced the incidence of police misconduct, or decreased the rate of sexual abuse. Indeed, not everyone shares the view that litigation has improved the quality of all these professional services. In the case of medicine especially, many advocates of medical malpractice reform assert that litigation has degraded medical practice by encouraging expensive and unnecessary tests and procedures designed to preempt legal claims rather than to serve the best interests of patients. Nevertheless, the evidence from these examples suggests that exposing private food safety auditors to civil liability would encourage further professionalization of private auditors, expose auditors who fail to conform to the established standards of the profession, and incentivize audit firms to avoid hiring or to dismiss auditors who lacked the requisite professional skills and diligence to do an average or better job.

Like improving outbreak investigation, enhancing auditing is a lever in the food safety system, because so many parts of the system rely on audits. For example, audit records provide government investigators with information about a company's compliance with food safety standards and can help lead investigators to the root causes of contamination when an outbreak occurs. Audits provide industry supply chain managers a means of overseeing and policing hundreds or thousands of often geographically dispersed suppliers. Insurance underwriters also rely on audit records when selecting risks, pricing premiums, and setting terms and conditions.[31]

Creating a Single Federal Food Safety Agency

In August 1975, Consumers Union, a leading consumer advocacy organization that publishes *Consumer Reports*, having found insect parts and rodent hairs in each of eight brands of frozen chicken pot pies that it tested, petitioned the FDA to set minimum thresholds, or "action levels," for filth in meat and chicken pies. In September, the agency forwarded the request to the USDA, explaining in a letter to Consumers Union that "pot pies are either poultry or meat products, foods which are subject to the jurisdiction of the [USDA]." In October, the USDA bounced the petition back to the FDA, informing Consumers Union that "while it is true that the production of meat and poultry pies is subject to USDA's inspection program, the responsibility for the wholesomeness of spices delivered for use in meat and poultry plants rests with the FDA." A Senate report on the incident explained, "The filth, it seems, was associated not with the meat filling—USDA's exclusive responsibility—but with the pie shells." In November, the FDA acknowledged that it was responsible for regulating the food safety of cereals and grains and, hence, pie crusts. However, a year and a half later, after the exchange of several letters between the FDA and Consumers Union, the agency decided that it would not initiate the process necessary to set action levels for meat and poultry pie crusts.[32]

The arcane jurisdictional divisions of FDA and USDA food safety regulation—as illustrated by the chicken-pot-pie affair—have, for more than sixty years, fueled calls for the establishment of a single federal food safety agency to replace the fifteen federal agencies that currently administer thirty-five different federal laws related to food safety under the oversight of nine congressional committees. Proponents of a single federal food safety agency allege that this multiplicity of agencies causes confusion when it produces inconsistent standards, creates inefficiencies due to duplication and overlapping jurisdiction, leaves gaps in coverage from inadequate coordination, and diffuses political accountability. Some proponents of a single agency recommend consolidating all federal food safety programs in the USDA. Others recommend combining them in the FDA or its parent agency, the Department of Health and Human Services. A third group favors a new, independent agency.[33]

The curious division of labor between the USDA and the FDA dates back to the passage of two laws enacted in 1906. The Federal Meat Inspection Act mandated inspection of all beef carcasses. The Pure Food and Drug Act prohibited the sale of adulterated food in interstate commerce. Initially, both laws were implemented by officials at the USDA. Its Bureau of Animal Industry stationed inspectors trained in veterinary science in every meat plant during all hours of operation. Meanwhile, its Bureau of Chemistry employed laboratory scientists to test foods for adulteration. This division of labor became even more pronounced when Franklin Roosevelt moved the Bureau of Chemistry, renamed the Food and Drug Administration, out of the USDA and into the Federal Security Agency, which was later reorganized into the Department of Health and Human Services (HHS). Today, the FDA is responsible for overseeing the production of most foods other than meat and poultry using expanded powers of inspection and enforcement granted by the Federal Food Drug and Cosmetic Act of 1938. The USDA's Bureau of Animal Industry eventually became the Food Safety Inspection Service (FSIS), which is still responsible for meat and poultry inspection. Concerns about "regulatory fragmentation" grew as Congress assigned new tasks related to food safety to a variety of other agencies. For example, Congress instructed the Federal Trade Commission to regulate food advertising, the Environmental Protection Agency to set pesticide tolerances, and the National Marine Fisheries Service within the Department of Commerce to inspect seafood.[34]

Prominent proposals to consolidate federal food safety regulation within a single department date back to 1949, when the Hoover Commission, an advisory body chaired by former president Herbert Hoover and charged by then president Harry Truman to develop reforms to reorganize executive branch agencies, recommended transferring oversight of all federal food safety efforts to the USDA. Ralph Nader in 1972 advocated relocating federal food safety regulation to a new Consumer Safety Agency. A Senate committee studying federal regulation in 1977 suggested moving the USDA's food safety responsibilities to the FDA. These are just a few of more than twenty such proposals. Seven Government Accounting Office reports dating back to 1970, and as recently as 2017, have decried the problem of fragmentation in food safety regulation and proposed various forms of consolidation. In 2018, the Trump administration proposed consolidating the food safety functions of the FDA and the FSIS within a single federal food safety agency under the USDA.[35]

A number of challenges render consolidation of federal food safety regulation in a single agency unlikely. First, the congressional committees that currently oversee the different agencies engaged in food safety regulation are unlikely to support any reorganization that would reduce their power. Congressional oversight affords lawmakers who serve on committees valuable opportunities to help interest groups and constituents in exchange for political support. Second, industry associations are unlikely to support any reorganization that disrupts their relationships with existing agencies. As previous chapters have described, industry groups work closely with the federal agencies with jurisdiction over their members, and they are resistant to any change that might reduce their access to officials or influence over policy decisions. Third, agencies like the FSIS and the FDA administer food safety policy under different statutory schemes, and merely merging them under the oversight of a single administrator would not eliminate differences in jurisdiction, powers, professional expertise, and agency culture that would likely perpetuate regulatory fragmentation. Meaningful consolidation would require a complete overhaul of federal food safety laws and regulations—a task of extraordinary legal and political complexity. Fourth, consolidating food safety efforts in a single agency might create new forms of fragmentation. For example, moving authority to bring enforcement actions for food safety violations into the FDA would disperse government litigation efforts, which are currently centralized in the Department of Justice. Similarly, transferring the FDA Center for Veterinary Medicine's program for regulating drug residues in beef and poultry to the USDA would separate it from the FDA's veterinary drug approval program. Fifth, reorganization is costly, and it takes years for the constituent parts of a new agency to develop the bonds of trust and depth of cooperation that lead them to share a sense of common mission. These costs must be largely front-loaded long before it is clear whether the gains from consolidation outweigh them.[36]

Proponents of consolidation point to what they consider successful efforts in other countries. A 2005 GAO report described the experiences of seven developed nations in establishing a "single food safety agency to lead food safety management or enforcement of food safety legislation." The report quoted government officials in those countries who believed that "consolidation costs have been or will likely be exceeded by benefits," citing "significant qualitative improvements in the effectiveness or efficiency of their food safety systems," including "less overlap in inspections, greater clarity in responsibilities, and more consistent or timely enforcement of food safety laws and regulations." However, the report conceded that none of the countries could provide data to determine whether reorganization had reduced foodborne illness or to support a cost-benefit analysis.[37]

Consolidation need not be all or nothing. Some proposals recommend more modest consolidation of inspection services, risk communication, or policy planning. Although partial consolidation would avoid some of the complexity and cost of more comprehensive proposals, Congress has shown little interest in considering bureaucratic reorganization of federal food safety regulation.[38]

Better coordination between government agencies offers an alternative to bureaucratic consolidation as a way to address concerns about duplication of effort and gaps in coverage. President Clinton's 1997 Food Safety Initiative directed the Department of HHS and the USDA "to work cooperatively with the agricultural community to develop guidance on good agricultural and manufacturing practices for fruits and vegetables." The initiative launched the Foodborne Outbreak Response Coordinating Group (FORC-G), a joint effort of the USDA, HHS, and EPA, to develop standard operating procedures for outbreak response. In 2009, President Obama created the Federal Food Safety Working Group, composed of representatives from the FDA, FSIS, CDC, EPA, Department of Homeland Security, Department of Commerce, Department of State, and the US Trade Representative, convened by the White House Domestic Policy Council and led by the Department of HHS and the USDA, to serve as "a central coordinating mechanism for the federal government's food safety activities." A 2011 progress report by the working group notes that the "CDC, FDA, and FSIS convened an interagency outbreak response working group to clarify roles and interactions among agencies during outbreak response activities," presumably to replace

FORC-G, which appears to have discontinued its activities in 2001 with the change in administrations. The report also mentions the establishment of the Information Technology Task Force (ITTF), which developed recommendations "for achieving greater interoperability and harmonizing electronic data collection standards between the agencies and State and local authorities," as well as the restructuring of the Interagency Risk Assessment Consortium (IRAC), "to develop and oversee the conduct of joint FDA-FSIS-CDC risk assessments." Following its 2011 report, the working group appears to have disappeared, like the Food Safety Initiative ten years before. Moreover, from the progress report, it is unclear what the working group actually did other than report on various agency initiatives. The report does not describe any role that it played in the creation or operation of the outbreak response working group, the ITTF, or the IRAC. The GAO criticized the working group for not developing a comprehensive government-wide plan for directing the federal government's food safety efforts. Following passage of FSMA, the CDC, FDA, and FSIS established the Interagency Foodborne Outbreak Response Collaboration to improve coordination of multistate outbreak investigations and the Interagency Food Safety Analytics Collaboration to improve coordination of federal food safety data collection, analysis, and use.[39]

Since 1998, the Association of Food and Drug Officials—a membership organization founded in 1896 by state officials that has grown to include federal and local officials, as well as industry representatives and consumer advocates—has worked with the FDA to promote closer coordination of regulatory efforts at the federal, state, and local levels. The FDA and the Association of Food and Drug Officials have convened a series of fifty-state workshops to organize federal, state, and local officials and to generate proposals for integration. In 2008, the FDA launched the Partnership for Food Protection, an administrative structure of working groups "to develop and implement procedures, best practices, and other work products that would advance integration." The partnership has working groups on inspections, compliance and enforcement, surveillance, information technology, outbreak response, laboratory science, and training. One outcome of these efforts has been the signing of cooperative agreements between the FDA and state authorities to fund and develop rapid response teams to better coordinate multijurisdictional outbreak response efforts and to capture best practices and share them. The USDA sponsors a program with similar aims, the National Integrated Food Safety Initiative, which funds "competitive projects that address priority issues in food safety that are best solved using an integrated approach." FSMA mandates that multiple agency heads collaborate to support greater integration of laboratory networks, the training of state and local food safety officials, and outbreak response.[40]

The Council to Improve Foodborne Outbreak Response (CIFOR) is a collaboration to coordinate federal, state, and local efforts that includes the Association of Food and Drug Officials, the Association of Public Health Laboratories, the Association of State and Territorial Health Officials, the Council of State and Territorial Epidemiologists, the National Association of County and City Health Officials, the National Association of State Departments of Agriculture, the National Association of State Public Health Veterinarians, the National Environmental Health Association, and the CDC, the FDA, and the FSIS. CIFOR publishes *Guidelines for Foodborne Disease Outbreak Response*. Although these various coordination efforts do not face the political obstacles that consolidation does, they suffer from a problem that consolidation is designed to address—a dizzying proliferation of decentralized and disparate initiatives and organizational structures.[41]

Criminal Prosecution of Food Company Executives

On September 21, 2015, Stuart Parnell, the sixty-one-year-old former president and CEO of his family business, the Peanut Corporation of America (PCA), was sentenced to twenty-eight years in federal prison. Parnell had founded the company with his father and two younger brothers in 1977. He rose quickly in the peanut business and was twice appointed by the US secretary of agriculture to the USDA's Peanut Standards Board. By 2008, Parnell's successful business had ninety employees operating plants in Virginia, Georgia, and Texas, which supplied peanuts, peanut butter, peanut meal, and peanut paste to manufacturers and food service operations throughout the country. With $25 million in sales, PCA manufactured approximately 2.5 percent of the nation's processed peanuts.[42]

Parnell's downfall began in late 2008 and early 2009, when the CDC traced a nationwide outbreak of *Salmonella* poisoning to products processed in PCA's Georgia and Texas plants. The tainted peanut products caused nine deaths and 714 reported cases of illness in forty-six states. The more than four hundred associated recalls involved more than 360 companies that manufactured 3,913 finished products containing PCA ingredients. The recalls cost companies an estimated $1.5 billion.[43]

FDA investigators at the company's plants in Georgia and Texas found dead rodents, open holes in the roof, and pools of stagnant water. One company employee reported that he saw a rat dry-roasting in peanut processing equipment, and another told of water contaminated with bird feces leaking in from a hole in the roof. A worker told reporters that plant conditions were "filthy and nasty."[44]

In February 2013, Parnell and three associates were charged with seventy-six counts of adulteration, misbranding, fraud, conspiracy, and obstruction of justice in a scheme to sell peanuts and peanut products which they knew to be contaminated with *Salmonella*. Federal prosecutors presented evidence that Parnell and his associates shipped peanut products after they tested positive for *Salmonella*, shipped products before they were tested and failed to inform customers of subsequent positive test results, and shipped products with falsified certificates of analysis citing negative testing results from previously manufactured lots. They also ordered retesting of lots that tested positive to obtain a negative result, then concealed the initial positive test results from customers.[45]

In one email exchange, an employee told Parnell that shipment of a lot would have to be delayed because *Salmonella* testing results were not yet available, to which Parnell replied, "Just ship it. I cannot afford to lose another customer." In another email forwarded to Parnell, a company executive instructed a sales manager to clean up totes of peanut meal using an air hose "because they are covered in dust and rat crap," to which Parnell replied "Clean em all up and ship them." Parnell also sent an email to employees regarding retesting a lot after receiving a positive test, stating: "I go through this about once a week . . . I will hold my breath . . . again." A former PCA plant manager testified at trial that when he complained to Michael Parnell, Stuart Parnell's brother and codefendant, that certificates of analysis being prepared for a shipment to Kellogg's, a major customer, were false, Michael Parnell told him: "I can handle Kellogg's. We've been shipping to them with false COAs since before you got here. I'll handle Kellogg's. Don't worry about it."[46]

A jury found Parnell guilty of sixty-seven felony counts and also returned verdicts against his codefendants. Parnell is currently serving a twenty-eight-year sentence in federal prison. The PCA case marks the first time that a food company executive has been prosecuted for a felony related to a foodborne illness outbreak. Parnell became the poster child for an emerging trend of criminal prosecutions against food company executives tied to foodborne illness outbreaks. Many news stories on the topic feature a photograph of him in a business suit with his right hand raised, as he is sworn in at a congressional hearing on the PCA outbreak and during which he invoked his Fifth Amendment right against self-incrimination to avoid answering questions. The photograph is unmistakably reminiscent of the iconic photograph of tobacco executives being sworn in collectively to a congressional hearing at which they declared that they did not believe that cigarettes were addictive or that there is conclusive evidence that smoking causes cancer.[47]

What frightens food industry executives more than the prospect of jail time for intentional misconduct—rare instances of fraud, conspiracy, or obstruction of justice, as in the PCA case—is the increasing number of criminal prosecutions against company officials for unwittingly selling contaminated food, which is a misdemeanor under the Federal Food, Drug, and Cosmetic Act (FDCA), punishable by a fine up to $250,000 and a year in prison for each violation. The first such prosecution dates back to 1975, when federal prosecutors charged Acme Markets, a national supermarket chain, and its president, John Park, with violating the FDCA by allowing products being shipped in interstate commerce to be exposed to rodent infestation in the company's Baltimore warehouse, thereby rendering them adulterated, which the act defines to include food that contains animal excrement or is "held under insanitary conditions whereby it may have become contaminated with filth" or "rendered injurious to health." The corporation pleaded guilty and paid a fine, but Park contested the charge. He defended himself at trial by arguing that, although he was "responsible for the entire operation of the company," he assigned subordinates to manage sanitary conditions in the company's operations and was not personally involved. The trial court instructed the jury that, under the FDCA, Park could be held accountable for the insanitary conditions in the warehouse even if he were not personally involved, provided he had "authority and responsibility" to deal with them. The jury convicted Park, and the judge ordered him to pay a $250 fine. Park appealed, and the US Supreme Court affirmed the jury instructions and upheld the conviction. The court held that the FDCA "imposes upon persons exercising authority and supervisory responsibility reposed in them by a business organization not only a positive duty to seek out and remedy violations but also, and primarily, a duty to implement measures that will insure that violations will not occur." Thus, under the *Park* doctrine, a CEO can be held criminally liable for a company violation of the FDCA without any knowledge of wrongdoing. However, in the Park case itself, the prosecution did submit evidence that the FDA had notified Park in 1970 of earlier sanitary violations at Acme's Philadelphia warehouse, which suggests that *Park* doctrine prosecutions are more likely in cases involving repeated violations.[48]

Similar prosecutions of company executives in the 1970s and 1980s involving unsanitary conditions at food companies generally ended in convictions with small fines. However, by the end of the 1980s, the Department of Justice stopped prosecuting *Park* doctrine cases, in part because of a sense that the inconsequential sanctions imposed on convicted executives were not worth the effort necessary to pursue the cases. The FDA revived the doctrine in 2009, following a critical report from the GAO and pressure from Congress to step up agency efforts to regulate criminal conduct by pharmaceutical companies.[49]

In February 2011, the FDA issued guidelines for recommending *Park* doctrine prosecutions of company executives to the Department of Justice. Under the guidelines, "knowledge of and actual participation in the violation are not a prerequisite to a misdemeanor prosecution but are factors that may be relevant when deciding whether to recommend charging a misdemeanor violation." Other factors to be considered include whether the violation is part of a "pattern of illegal behavior and/or failure to heed prior warnings." The guidelines favor prosecution in cases involving "actual or potential harm to the public," where the violation was "obvious," "widespread," and "serious." Finally, the guidelines require prosecutors to consider whether "the proposed prosecution is a prudent use of agency resources."[50]

In 2012, the FDA's Office of Criminal Investigation recommended criminal charges against the Eric and Ryan Jensen following the 2011 listeriosis outbreak caused by contaminated cantaloupes. The brothers pleaded guilty and were sentenced to five years of probation, six months of home detention, and payment of $15,000 in restitution to victims. In 2013, Austin "Jack" DeCoster and his son were each sentenced to three months in jail and a $100,000 fine following a 2010 salmonellosis outbreak traced back to contaminated eggs from their Wright County Egg and Hillandale Farms operations. The CDC counted nearly two thousand cases of reported illness from the outbreak, and DeCoster—known as the "Egg King," who, at the height of his power, reigned over thirty-five million hens and controlled more than 10 percent of the US egg market—recalled half a billion eggs.[51]

Criminal fines against companies responsible for outbreaks have also been on the rise. In 1998, Odwalla Inc. paid a $1.5 million criminal fine for FDCA violations after selling apple juice tainted with *E. coli* O157 that killed one victim and sickened seventy. In 2013, the DeCosters' company, Quality Egg, was ordered to pay a $6.8 million criminal fine. In 2015, Conagra pleaded guilty to unknowingly selling *Salmonella*-tainted peanut butter linked to a 2006–2007 outbreak that sickened more than seven hundred victims. The company agreed to pay an $11.2 million criminal fine.[52]

The aim of criminal prosecution is to incentivize company executives to be more vigilant about food safety in their operations. However, advocates of criminal prosecution have offered no evidence that it has encouraged companies to make additional investments in food safety or that any additional efforts would be worth the costs. The comments of Jaydee Hanson, a senior policy analyst for the Center for Food Safety, a consumer advocacy organization, are typical: "It will at least make the boards of these companies pay a

little more attention to their oversight. . . . It does at least send a clear message that the government is watching you." At the same time, Hanson won-
ders whether criminal sanctions are likely to deter company officials who
intentionally violate the law, opining: "Greedy people are greedy people. . . .
They always think they will be the one to get away with it." Similarly, Bill
Marler, commenting on the sentencing of Stuart Parnell and his associates,
told CNN, "This sentence is going to send a stiff, cold wind through board
rooms across the US." However, cautioning that criminal prosecutions were
not an adequate substitute for rigorous routine regulation of the food industry, Marler explained to an interviewer in a documentary on the case: "China
shoots people. That doesn't necessarily make their food safer." In the absence
of even anecdotal evidence that criminal penalties are a cost-effective way
to improve food safety practices, the case for criminal prosecutions remains
entirely impressionistic.[53]

Digitizing Supply Chain Management Information

The typical supermarket carries between thirty thousand and fifty thousand
distinct items from around the world. Retailers normally require manufacturers of branded products to provide a warranty and indemnification, but
they do not require third-party food safety certification. Retailers conduct
their own audits or pay for third-party audits of manufacturers of their store
brand products. The remaining products—including hundreds of fresh produce items, which may each have as many as a dozen or more suppliers—
generate a large volume and variety of food safety audit information for retailers and their upstream distributors. The half dozen in-house food safety
staff employed by a major retailer do not have time to do much more than
review audit scores and grades and, perhaps, a short audit summary, of the
company's thousands of fresh produce suppliers, some of whom may be submitting more than one annual audit. Retailers have created an audit system
that generates more food safety information than they can process.[54]

New products and services that capture, standardize, digitize, and store
audit information aim to improve information management throughout the
supply chain. For example, a team of tech entrepreneurs has developed compliance software called CoInspect, which allows company personnel to fill
out inspection forms on mobile phones or tablets, include notes and pho-
tographs, and upload results to a centralized database. Company managers
can review the results, aggregate data, identify problems, track performance,
and produce reports. CoInspect helps companies oversee the quality and
uniformity of internal compliance inspections; collect, organize, and analyze

inspection data; and use that data to measure performance and implement improvements.[55]

Another tech firm, Azzule, a division of Primus Labs, has developed a digital platform called Dynamic Data that collects audit reports, pathogen test results from product and environmental samples, sanitation program records, and consultant observations and makes them all available online to companies throughout the supply chain. Dynamic Data can help buyers by highlighting areas of concern and tracking performance over time. Azzule also administers Primus Labs' leading food safety scheme for fresh produce, Primus GFS, which allows it to collect audit compliance data from many companies. From this data, Azzule can identify and track industrywide compliance trends and give its clients a sense of how they match up to industry norms.[56]

In addition to these software solutions to data management, a new generation of hardware is generating more and more accurate data. Technology companies have developed electronic temperature and humidity sensors that companies can place permanently in production, transportation, or storage environments, or on products themselves, and that transmit continuous measurements via wireless networks to data storage devices that allow managers to remotely monitor, analyze, and record the information in real time. Technology experts refer to networks of interconnected computing devices as the internet of things, which represents a new frontier for food safety inspection, oversight, and data collection.[57]

Using artificial intelligence to scan audit reports and search databases could enhance the capacity of buyers to identify, or even predict, food safety failures in their supply chain. In the legal profession, artificial intelligence is helping lawyers scan large numbers of documents to identify information relevant to a transaction or litigation and to predict the outcome of potential claims. Food companies and their insurers have already begun to discuss the application of artificial intelligence to managing food safety.[58]

This new generation of information technology in industry supply chain management complements the efforts of public health officials and insurance underwriters. When outbreak investigations identify root causes of contamination, aggregate compliance information can reveal how widespread the same types of food safety failures are throughout the industry and identify specific companies where improvement is needed. This growing industry data offers aggregate compliance information that is more inclusive, detailed, and frequently updated than USDA or academic GAPs compliance surveys discussed in chapter 6. Compliance histories of food companies applying for insurance can help underwriters select risks and price premiums, and industrywide information can inform underwriting guidelines and loss prevention services. The development and proliferation of information technology such as barcoding and radio-frequency identification devices to capture data coupled with data management systems to organize and store the data have increased the speed and reduced the cost of both tracing products back during an investigation and tracing them forward during a recall.[59]

The development of blockchain technology—a single digital record of information stored and updated simultaneously on multiple computers and accessible to many parties—could further reduce the time necessary to trace products back and forward through the supply chain. Blockchain would enable participants in a supply chain to centralize all the one-up/one-down traceability records related to a particular product lot. Following a pilot project, Walmart suggested that blockchain technology would reduce the time necessary to trace a product back through the supply chain from weeks to seconds. Moreover, blockchain records could incorporate information from the internet of things, such as periodic temperature measurements taken by sensors attached to pallets, which could help identify food safety failures, for example, a lapse in refrigeration at a particular time during shipment. Blockchain could make this information available to anyone, including food companies, public health authorities, and consumers. In the short run, the weaknesses in supply chain record keeping detailed in chapter 7 will limit the transformative potential of information technology advances such as blockchain. However, in the long run, as record keeping improves, blockchain technology could dramatically reduce the time from outbreak detection to consumer warnings and product recalls.[60]

The Maturation of Product Contamination
and Food Safety Liability Insurance

Insurance has played a pervasive role in regulating health and safety risks comparable in scope to foodborne illness. Examples include commercial fires, workplace injuries, and automobile accidents. These mature insurance markets—in which underwriting is based on over a century of experience, big data, and extensive research—offer reason for optimism concerning the potential of insurance to play an increasing role in reducing the risk of foodborne illness. Consider briefly the example of fire insurance.

In a period of devastation that became known as the Conflagration Era, fires ravaged American cities throughout the late nineteenth and early twentieth centuries. The Great Chicago Fire of 1871 destroyed more than seventeen thousand buildings and killed 250 people. Total damage was estimated at $196 million ($4 billion in 2017 dollars). Cities from Boston to Seattle endured fires on a similar scale.[61]

In the wake of these disasters, government attempts to improve fire safety were consistently hampered by short public attention spans and active political opposition from powerful developers and ordinary citizens eager to keep building costs down. Resource constraints and limited expertise further frustrated government efforts. Fire risk varied unpredictably from building to building in rapidly changing urban environments, and effective policies required extensive information gathering, sophisticated standards development, and vigilant compliance monitoring—all of which were beyond the government's capacity.

Seeking ways to more accurately price risk and reduce losses, insurance companies organized industry associations to develop expertise in fire safety. They investigated fires to determine what caused them and sponsored laboratory research to analyze building materials and firefighting equipment. Underwriters also devised fire safety standards, conditioned coverage on adherence to them, and conducted routine inspections of buildings covered by their policies.

As part of these efforts to reduce fire losses, insurance companies funded the Underwriters Laboratories (UL) to test and certify the fire safety of electrical equipment, building materials, and fire-prevention devices. They also funded the National Fire Protection Association (NFPA) to develop fire safety standards and lobby for their adoption by state legislatures, local authorities, and industry. Today the UL certifies more than twenty thousand different types of products for sixty-nine thousand manufacturers, and its safety logo appears on twenty-two billion items worldwide. The organization estimates that the average American home contains 125 UL markings. The NFPA's membership has grown to more than fifty thousand individuals worldwide, including underwriters, adjusters, firefighters, public officials, engineers, architects, and a wide array of industry representatives. Eight thousand volunteers work on more than 250 technical committees, which have produced 300 model fire codes and standards. These NFPA recommendations serve as the basis for fire codes, industry specifications, and underwriting guidelines.[62]

In addition to standards development organizations like the UL and the NFPA, firms that provide ancillary services to the fire insurance industry also influence fire safety practices. Insurance brokers who represent companies seeking fire insurance counsel their clients on how to reduce fire risk in order to obtain more favorable insurance rates and terms. The Insurance Services Office (ISO), a company that provides information, advice, and tools for fire insurers, analyzes and rates the effectiveness of local fire codes and the fire suppression services of localities, which insurance companies use to determine their rates. These ISO ratings also provide local fire officials leverage to lobby their political overseers for stricter standards and more resources.[63]

Today, commercial fire insurance is ubiquitous. It is typically included as a component of more general commercial property policies. Insurance underwriters, risk engineers, and adjusters are embedded in a network of institutions that develop and enforce a constantly evolving constellation of fire safety standards.

Product contamination insurance and fire insurance have several common features. Both are first-party insurance—the insured is covered for its own losses incurred as a result of a fire or product recall without having to identify the cause of the fire or the contamination. Both are embedded in complex regulatory systems characterized by networks of interacting professionals working in government, industry, academia, consulting, and insurance institutions. As detailed in chapter 5, product recall underwriters conduct inspections and scrutinize audit reports to determine a company's compliance with government regulations and industry standards when selecting clients, pricing premiums, and setting terms and conditions on coverage. Underwriters also employ outside consultants to coach companies on reducing food safety risk in their operations and to provide training to company personnel to implement risk reduction measures.[64]

The comparison is not, however, perfect. The impact of the insurance industry on fire safety research and regulation cannot be overstated. Fire insurers founded and initially funded the leading fire safety testing and standard-setting organizations—the UL and the NFPA—which have spearheaded efforts to reform fire safety. Organizations that serve insurers, such as ISO, generate data and ratings that feature prominently in government and industry discussions of fire safety policy. By contrast, in food safety, insurers have played no noticeable role in the development of GMPs, HACCP, or GAPs. Insurance companies and their ancillary organizations are, so far, strictly consumers, rather than producers, of food safety risk information.[65]

However, as product contamination coverage proliferates, and the financial stakes of insurance companies increase, they may begin to play a more active role in supporting research, setting standards, and reducing risk. There are signs that product contamination insurance is proliferating. The growing capacity of outbreak investigations to connect foodborne illness to particular companies has heightened the risk to companies of expensive recalls and consequent damage to their brands, for which they increasingly seek insurance. The explosion of social media, which can quickly spread news of a recall, further exacerbates the risk of reputational harm and potential losses. In addition, FSMA grants the FDA new authority to order mandatory recalls, and this has, according to some underwriters, fueled demand for insurance coverage. Trade associations all along the supply chain—from the Western Growers Association to the Food Marketing Institute—are starting to encourage their members to purchase product contamination coverage.[66]

Although data regarding the identities of food companies who carry product contamination coverage and the limits of that coverage are proprietary and not publicly available—and therefore not available in aggregate form—there are some indications of a general trend of expanding coverage. In 2000, one insurance industry insider counted only three insurance carriers that offered product contamination policies that covered recall costs. By 2017, Aon, a leading insurance brokerage firm, published a report counting more than thirty such carriers with policy limits as high as $250 million.[67]

The proliferation of product contamination insurance, originally among retailers and manufactures, and more recently among their suppliers as well, has been a slow process that requires educating food companies. "It takes two or three years to sell a policy to a new buyer," explains Jane McCarthy, a veteran underwriter with more than thirty years of experience, the last twenty specializing in product recall insurance. "The first year a company will look at it and say, 'Holy cow! How much do you want for this?! No way,' and then walk away. And then the second year, they say, 'You know what—we think we really need this, but we just don't have the money in the budget. And the third year they come by and they say, 'We want to buy. We've budgeted for it.' And that's how we sell this coverage. It's a long-term pipeline." Even if insurance is not likely to play a leading role in advancing food safety science, as it has in fire safety, the steady proliferation of product contamination coverage is likely to spread existing best practices throughout different industry sectors as an increasing number of food companies continue to come through the pipeline.[68]

A similar analysis applies to the maturation of food safety liability insurance. The growing capacity of outbreak investigations to connect foodborne illness to particular companies is likely to increase the number of civil lawsuits against food companies for foodborne illness and, consequently, to boost demand for food safety liability insurance. The resulting proliferation of coverage and growing experience will increase the capacity of liability insurance to reduce risk through risk selection, pricing, contract design, and loss prevention.[69]

This book has presented an account of the food safety system as composed of three interacting components: (1) government regulation, (2) industry supply chain management, and (3) civil liability and consumer advocacy. This chapter has identified in each of these components a leverage point—outbreak investigation, private auditing, and product contamination insurance, respectively—at which modest changes can produce significant advances throughout the system. The chapter endorses two reforms: first, focusing government resources on improving and maintaining the infrastructure of outbreak investigation, and second, holding private food safety auditors liable to consumers for professional malpractice. The chapter also applauded two trends: the emergence of new technologies to digitize supply chain information and the proliferation of product contamination and food safety liability insurance. The next, and final, chapter summarizes the findings of the book, offers some additional observations, and suggests that these insights about the food safety system can help change the often misleading and unproductive public political discourse in the United States about regulation more generally.

Food for Thought:
Reflections on Complexity, Uncertainty, and Evolution

If a major food company were to invest a million dollars in a marketing campaign, and after a year, ask the marketing department, "What did we get for our investment?" the manager in charge would likely provide a precise dollar figure for the resulting profits or losses based on sales data. If the same company were to invest a million dollars in a piece of manufacturing equipment, and after a year, ask the same question, the manager in charge would likely provide a precise dollar figure for added efficiency based on production data. If the company were to invest a million dollars to improve its quality control, and a year later, ask the same question, the manager in charge would likely provide a precise dollar figure for reduced waste based on the number of units that failed inspection. However, if the company were to invest a million dollars in a food safety program, and a year later, ask the same question, the manager in charge would be unable to provide even a rough dollar estimate for risk reduction. At best, the manager might be able to provide quantitative data on reduced pathogen levels or improved audit scores, along with vague qualitative claims about building a culture of food safety within the company.

In interviews for this book, senior company managers consistently indicated that they have no way to assess the efficacy or cost-effectiveness of food safety efforts aimed at reducing the risk of foodborne illness. For example, when asked about the effectiveness of two decades of Hazard Analysis Critical Control Points (HACCP) implementation, a senior food safety manager at a large poultry processor explained that HACCP plans in poultry production are designed to reduce pathogen prevalence to target maximum thresholds, or tolerances, and that even when a plant meets the target, there is no clear link between the target and the risk of human illness. "There is no reliable food safety feedback loop in the US poultry industry that connects pathogen levels to human illness." Similarly, when asked how effective she thinks nearly a decade of implementing the California Leafy Greens Marketing Agreement (LGMA) metrics has been, the director of food safety for a leading fresh produce grower in California's Salinas Valley responded: "I think that's a hard one to kind of capture. When it comes to the LGMA, the proof in the program is looking at deviations [i.e., noncompliance with the LGMA metrics]. The focus at this point, after all these years, is training programs and seeing what the impact of the additional training has on those deviations. Our goal is to decrease the deviations. At the end of the day, the success of the program is in those numbers."[1]

Industry managers are not alone in lacking sufficient data to assess the efficacy or cost-effectiveness of investments in food safety. When asked whether the USDA's fee-for-service Good Agricultural Practices (GAPs) audits have improved food safety, the senior official who runs the program responded: "It's an interesting question—How do you evaluate a negative? For the vast majority of producers out there, they're producing the same food, and they're doing what they need to do. If we go out and audit the guys that have been doing things right all along just for verification, and they continue to produce the same food that doesn't cause people to get sick, is that a positive aspect of our program? I'd like to make that claim, but I don't know that that's our program driving that." A former high-ranking FDA official explained that the agency aspires to evaluate the effectiveness of its new Food Safety Modernization Act (FSMA) regulations using public health outcomes, but "no one has figured out how to do that right. That's very hard."[2]

Litigators and insurance underwriters similarly lack evidence regarding the efficacy or cost-effectiveness of their efforts. Bill Marler, the nation's leading litigator in the field, who has dedicated twenty-five years of legal practice to securing compensation for victims of foodborne illness, admits that he is not sure whether suing companies in the wake of outbreaks has had much impact. "I always wanted to change things, make things better. That's why I became a lawyer. After whacking Jack in the Box, after whacking Odwalla, more and more foodborne illness cases were coming over into our office, because we were seen as successful. I thought, 'You know, isn't what I'm doing supposed to *stop* this? I've been whacking these guys with $10 million here, $20 million there, don't you think that people should change their behavior?' And it just didn't seem like it was making a difference at all!" When asked if the problem of foodborne illness is really big enough to merit the additional company investment and government regulation that he passionately advocates in his inexhaustible supply of blog posts and speeches, Marler responded, "You're asking a question that I struggle with all the time."[3]

This uncertainty is also shared by insurance underwriters, whose livelihoods depend on accurate risk assessment. When asked whether risk selection, pricing, contract design, and loss prevention had reduced the risk of foodborne illness, a leading broker responded, "The information necessary to know that is simply not available." A longtime underwriter put it this way: "We are all, in a sense, gamblers. Our expertise is very limited, and the data is not there to support anything more than supposition."[4]

None of this is to suggest that these various efforts have not advanced food safety. As the analysis in previous chapters has shown, there is some evidence that pasteurization in milk production, HACCP programs in beef and poultry processing, and GAPs in fresh produce cultivation have reduced contamination, and there is a widely shared belief that this translates into fewer cases of foodborne illness. There are also a few rare cases in which data support inferences about the impact of food safety efforts on public health, such as the study mentioned in chapter 2 correlating efforts to reduce milk contamination with declining infant mortality and the study in chapter 4 linking HACCP implementation in the beef industry to reduced rates of *E. coli* O157–related illnesses. However, for the most part, no one knows just how much illness food safety efforts prevent or whether these health benefits have been worth the costs. The point is that food safety reform has consistently been implemented despite considerable uncertainty about its efficacy and cost effectiveness.

It is possible to understand how the food safety system works even if no one really knows how well it works. Previous chapters have offered detailed accounts of the evolution of food safety efforts. This chapter summarizes the most important features of the resulting complex system of governance that has emerged and continues to evolve. The chapter then returns to the problem of uncertainty to discuss the role it plays in the evolution of food safety and its implications for regulatory reform more generally.

A Mix of Public and Private Efforts

In all the case studies in this book, food safety regulation involves a variety of professional experts working in multiple public and private institutions employing an array of regulatory tools. Together, these examples illustrate how regulatory authority and activity are dispersed throughout the food safety system. Regulation is more than merely government rule making and enforcement. Indeed, in some efforts to regulate food safety—for example, medical milk commissions, early HACCP programs, and GAPs auditing— government plays a minor role. And when government plays a larger role, it depends heavily on private efforts. Private standards serve as the basis for most government food safety rules, and industry supply chain management is essential to ensuring compliance with them. Within the food safety system, government is not the only source of regulation.[5]

The case studies in previous chapters offer many examples of the contributions of private-sector actors to food safety governance. Trade and professional associations convene stakeholder conversations, sponsor research, develop standards, and disseminate information. Buyers set product specifications that include government and private food safety standards, which they enforce through supply chain management. Plaintiffs' attorneys file lawsuits, which draw attention to the issue of food safety, influence attitudes about it, and prompt reform. Insurance companies sell product liability and product contamination coverage, which provides incentives and assistance to help companies comply with government and industry food safety standards. Highlighting these private contributions to food safety is not meant to undervalue USDA or FDA efforts to produce guidance and regulations, fund research, disseminate information, conduct investigations, and take enforcement actions, but to suggest that government regulation should be understood as part of a great deal of regulatory activity in which private actors often play an essential, and sometimes a leading, role.

Competing Narratives

Within the food safety system, individuals' perceptions about their own and others' political, economic, and administrative motivations are filtered through a set of competing narratives. According to one narrative, successful efforts by industry executives to block or influence legislation and regulation are part of a larger pattern of regulatory capture, in which powerful business lobbies exert overwhelming influence on government officials to the detriment of the public interest. According to a second narrative, aggressive regulatory enforcement actions by government agencies are part of a larger pattern of big government, in which officials needlessly damage or destroy socially valuable business enterprises out of an ill-informed conception of the public interest, concern for an agency's reputation, or a desire for career advancement. According to a third narrative, ambitious legislative mandates unsupported by sufficient funding for their full implementation are part of a larger pattern of inadequate resources, which leaves government agencies vulnerable to harsh criticism and punitive budget cuts in the wake of inevitable regulatory failures. Events provide sufficient evidence to support and sustain each of these competing narratives.

These different narratives have, at times, fueled mutual distrust between government officials, industry executives, and consumer advocates. Such distrust helps explain the unsuccessful efforts of consumer advocates in the 1970s to pass food surveillance legislation in the face of industry opposition and tepid government support. Consumer advocates argued that the legislation was a response to regulatory capture, industry executives denounced it as an egregious example of big government, and government regulators worried that it would overtax agency resources.

At other times, these different narratives can foster cooperation. For example, all three narratives contributed to the successful efforts of consumer advocates, beef industry executives, and USDA meat inspectors in the 1980s to block attempts by reform proponents to replace organoleptic inspection of carcasses with company-designed HACCP plans and routine government pathogen testing. Consumer advocates dismissed the proposal as the product of regulatory capture; the beef industry denounced it as a top-down, highly intrusive, and heavy-handed approach to industry regulation; and the USDA inspectors viewed it as a ploy to cut the agency's budget.

Punctuated Equilibrium

The evolution of food safety efforts is characterized by long periods of relative policy stability punctuated by moments of rapid reform. Major outbreaks precipitate these moments of rapid reform by shaking up the system — realigning political interests, shifting economic incentives, disrupting administrative routines, and altering competing narratives that support the status quo. Civil litigation and the media coverage that accompanies it magnify the impact of outbreaks by framing issues in ways that highlight particular industry failures, mobilizing victims and consumer advocates to lobby for reform, and placing the issue of food safety reform at the top of the national policy agenda. One sees this pattern of punctuated equilibrium and the impact of civil litigation in the implementation of HACCP and pathogen testing in the beef and poultry industries following the Jack in the Box outbreak, and in the adoption of more rigorous GAPs standards for leafy greens production following the Dole baby spinach outbreak.[6]

A Complex Adaptive System

Food safety governance exhibits many characteristics of complex adaptive systems. To begin with, efforts to advance food safety occur through feedback and learning. Importantly, the most valuable feedback often comes from failures. The most dramatic examples are significant advances in the aftermath of major outbreaks. For example, following the Jack in the Box outbreak, the CDC launched its FoodNet and PulseNet surveillance systems. Similarly, fresh produce outbreaks starting in the late 1990s prompted successive industry-led efforts to improve traceability. Feedback and learning may also be more routine and less dramatic. HACCP programs and third-party audits are designed to expose weaknesses in a production facility's food safety efforts and offer an opportunity for managers to take corrective action. Thus, both large-scale public health crises and smaller shortcomings offer opportunities for improvement.[7]

Networks of professionals working in different institutional settings disseminate the lessons of feedback and learning. Food safety experts in government, industry, and academia interact informally, monitor common sources of information, meet at trade and professional association meetings, serve together on advisory committees and working groups, exchange views in government notice-and-comment rule making and industry standard-setting processes, and collaborate on research projects and in investigations. Experts also move between positions in government, industry, and academia during the course of their careers. Food safety reform takes place in ongoing conversations among experts working in and moving between different institutional settings in the public and private sectors. Ideas cross not only institutional boundaries but also industry sector and disciplinary boundaries. Professional networks focused on food safety have played an essential role in the proliferation of concepts, standards, and practices.[8]

Within the food safety system, reputational interdependence provides a powerful motivation for cooperation. For example, rival firms banded together following the 2006 Dole baby spinach outbreak to institute reforms that would rehabilitate their industry's reputation. Similarly, following the 2008 *Salmonella* Saintpaul outbreak, fresh produce trade associations collaborated to develop better traceability practices. When outbreaks occur, outraged congressional committees level harsh public criticism not only at companies but also at the government agencies that regulate them. Consequently, reputational interdependence also motivates closer cooperation between industry and government, as it did between the fresh produce industry and the FDA in the design of agency guidance and the FSMA Produce Safety Rule following repeated high-profile outbreaks involving fresh produce.

Reform within the system is path dependent. Take, for example, the meat and poultry industries. Congress's choice in the Meat Inspection Act of 1906 to address concerns about contamination of beef through organoleptic inspection of carcasses and the agency's decision to place inspectors in plants during all hours of operation have profoundly shaped the subsequent development of food safety in the meat and poultry industries. The USDA's Food Safety and Inspection Service still assigns inspectors to visit every production plant under its jurisdiction daily and to conduct carcass inspections. Proposals to abandon daily plant visits in favor of a more risk-based allocation of personnel resources and to delegate carcass inspection to plant employees to enable agency inspectors to more closely oversee HACCP plans have, for decades, met with stiff and, so far, successful, resistance from inspectors. Sometimes path dependence is the product not of stakeholder attitudes but of existing infrastructure, as new initiatives are layered on top of, and depend on, previous ones. Thus, the CDC's decision to monitor illness associated with specific pathogens in particular states was dictated, in part, by the existing infrastructure for disease reporting at the state level.[9]

As the food safety system grows, it generates increasing demand for specialized expertise and reliable oversight, which are provided by a constantly expanding number and variety of intermediaries. The need to oversee these overseers further fuels the proliferation of intermediaries. Thus, industry supply chain management is now populated by a host of intermediaries—auditors, accreditors, food safety schemes, and benchmarking organizations—all of whom buyers rely on to monitor their suppliers.

Within the system of food safety governance, standards emerge as the product of ongoing, interconnected conversations among experts working in industry, government, and academia. Public and private are also intertwined in the implementation of those standards. It is not uncommon to find private enforcement of public laws and public enforcement of private standards. For example, the system of private third-party audits required by buyers and paid for by growers is largely responsible for enforcement of government GAPs guidance in the fresh produce industry. Conversely, government inspections funded by buyers enforce the industry standards of the California LGMA. The point here is not that it is impossible to distinguish public from private, or that the distinction serves no useful purpose, but rather that the standard dichotomy between public regulation and private ordering obscures the interdependence of government and industry food safety efforts.[10]

Technological Advances

New technologies often accelerate changes in the food safety system. For example, pasteurization added a kill step to fluid milk production. The internet greatly increased the capacity to collect, store, and share disease reporting data. Serotyping, PFGE and WGS, progressively advanced the ability of public health officials to identify outbreaks, determine food vehicles, and pinpoint root causes. Barcodes and radio-frequency identification tags have enhanced traceability throughout the supply chain. Digitizing supply chain management information makes it easier for buyers to monitor their suppliers effectively and could, potentially, be a source of big data concerning industry food safety practices.

The Increasing Formalization of Risk Management

A consistent theme in the evolution of food safety is the increasing formalization of risk management. The development of quantitative measures—baselines, metrics, and thresholds—has been one means of formalization. For example, measurable critical limits in HACCP plans for food processing supplemented the vague qualitative sanitary standards of Good Manufacturing Practices (GMP) regulations. Similarly, LGMA metrics in California leafy greens production added quantitative measures to preexisting GAPs guidance. Food safety inspections and audits transitioned from impressionistic assessments to numerical scoring. The maturation of insurance markets, characterized by increasingly detailed underwriting guidelines, loss control advice, and terms and conditions of coverage, is another example of this trend toward measurability.[11]

Standardization is a second means of formalizing risk management. The Codex Alimentarius Commission standardized HACCP into seven steps. Food safety schemes standardize production practices and management routines and require auditors to use uniform checklists. Underwriting guidelines standardize underwriting practices. The proliferation of standards in some areas has led to efforts to standardize the standards, such as the harmonized standards for GAPs and the GFSI benchmarks for audit schemes.

Professionalization is a third means of formalizing risk management. The process of professionalization entails fulltime dedication to a task, specialized academic knowledge acquired through formal training, a relatively high level of autonomy with regard to workload and working conditions, one or more peer associations to support and discipline members of the profession, credentialing that limits practice of the profession, ethical norms, and a service ideal. In many cases, established professional groups have undertaken new food safety tasks. For example, medical milk commissions employed physicians to inspect dairies, veterinarians to test cows for tuberculosis, and bacteriologists and chemists to analyze milk samples. In other cases, the tasks themselves have given rise to new professions, as illustrated by the recent emergence of new technical training and certification programs for private third-party food safety auditors, whose qualifications in previous generations were typically limited to prior experience as production or supply chain managers. In some cases, professional groups have competed for dominance, for example, microbiologists within USDA pushed for HACCP programs and pathogen testing in an agency traditionally dominated by inspectors trained in veterinary science carrying out organoleptic inspection of animal carcasses. Finally, collaboration between different professional groups at times has produced synergy, as in the cooperation among epidemiologists and lab scientists in conducting outbreak investigations. An important lesson of this book is that professional experts are an important unit of analysis in understanding the evolution of food safety governance.[12]

Uncertainty

When asked whether decades of investing company and government funds into food safety in the fresh produce sector has paid off, food safety managers and government regulators admit that they are motivated by a largely unsubstantiated faith that their efforts are making consumers safer. As one leading expert put it, "There's a sense that the industry has really raised the bar, in part because we do see fewer of these outbreaks and fewer of these illnesses. I just have a hard time pointing to any specific numbers." A widely circulated report praising food safety reforms in the leafy greens industry following the 2006 Dole baby spinach outbreak conceded that a distinguished panel of experts "struggled with finding supportive data to prove their general positive sense of a decreased risk."[13]

Uncertainty—the inability to quantify risk or, in the example above, to quantify risk reduction—is a pervasive and enduring condition faced by decision makers throughout the food safety system. One prominent account of uncertainty defines it as "apprehension without obvious capacity for assessment and action." The history of efforts detailed in previous chapters to advance food safety is characterized by what one might call a logic of uncertainty—they are fueled by apprehension and constrained by a lack of capacity for assessment.[14]

To be sure, there is a no dearth of expert opinion concerning the impact of food safety reforms. The problem is that available data do not demonstrate that food safety reforms have reduced the risk of foodborne illness. For example, the studies reviewed in chapter 4 of pathogen testing and HACCP implementation in the beef and poultry industries provide some evidence that these measures may have reduced the number of ground beef samples testing positive for *E. coli* O157 between 2002 and 2004 and broiler chicken samples testing positive for *Salmonella* between 2006 and 2013, but inferences that these reforms are responsible for declines in foodborne illness rates during these same periods rely on considerable speculation. Surveys reviewed in chapter 6 of GAPs implementation in the fresh produce sector indicate that stricter standards and more rigorous audits have increased investments in food safety and improved compliance with safety standards, but none of the surveys attempts to link these outcomes to lower rates of foodborne illness.[15]

Apprehension, rather than data analysis, has been the primary engine of food safety reform. Stories of death and serious illness from consuming contaminated milk, hamburgers, and lettuce have motivated decision makers in government and industry to support new initiatives involving pasteurization, HACCP, and GAPs. At the same time, the inability to assess the public health impact of these reforms has tempered the pace and extent of reform. Decision makers in government and industry have typically been loath to launch new initiatives or deviate significantly from established practices in the absence of reliable cost-benefit information. Outbreaks break up this inertia by suddenly and dramatically increasing apprehension and, with it, public pressure and political opportunities for change. This logic of uncertainty suggests that decision makers ultimately act on the basis of dramatic narratives about illness victims and anxiety about the limits of empirical analysis.[16]

Learning from Experience

That which does not kill us, makes us stronger, suggested the German philosopher Friedrich Nietzsche. This observation is of little comfort to the victims of foodborne illness outbreaks who died or to their loved ones. It is also not obviously true for those victims left with long-term disabilities, or even those who suffered only temporary illness. However, from a broader perspective, these human tragedies provide the motivation and the learning opportunities that propel the evolution of the food safety system.[17]

We live in a political culture in which abstract debate about the desirability of government intervention in the economy inhibits a deeper understanding of how regulation actually works. Shrill rhetoric about the abuses of unregulated "big business" and the tyranny of "big government" crowds out careful assessment of complex policy choices and candor about limited information. One hope of this book is that closer attention to the details of an area of health and safety regulation that affects everyone and that is, in many ways, typical, will replace some of this rhetoric with an appreciation for the variety of available tools and techniques of governance, the interdependence of public and private efforts to manage risk, and the importance of feedback and learning. Setting aside the sharp dichotomy between public regulation and private ordering, and focusing more on the realities of risk management, one sees that government is frequently less heavy handed and industry more socially responsible than popular political discourse would lead one to believe.

The complexity of food safety reform and uncertainty among even the most sophisticated experts should lead honest advocates to be not necessarily more moderate but certainly more tentative. Food safety reform is, in almost all instances, highly experimental—no one really knows whether it will work before implementing it, and even afterward, policy evaluation typically yields limited information about its efficacy and cost-effectiveness. Proponents of more rigorous standards for food safety should be mindful that policy experimentation carries the potential for significant financial losses, and even economic ruin, for food companies. They should respect the wariness of those in industry who pay the price for regulatory experimentation.[18]

At the same time, skeptics of more rigorous standards for food safety should acknowledge that there are limits to what can be known about the efficacy and cost-effectiveness of food safety efforts, and that food safety only advances through experimentation, feedback, and learning. They should respect the need to act on limited information. The sacrifices of outbreak victims demand it, and the health and safety of the rest of us depend on it.

Appendix A
How Researchers Estimate the Number of Cases and
Economic Costs of Foodborne Illness

In 2011, Elaine Scallan, a professor of public health at the University of Colorado who previously worked at the CDC, and a team of CDC coauthors, published the leading studies to date estimating the annual rate of foodborne illness acquired in the United States. These studies count only cases of acute illness, including gastroenteritis involving three or more loose stools in twenty-four hours or vomiting, that lasts more than one day or results in restricted daily activities. They also count some forms of acute nondiarrheal illness.[1]

The authors began by collecting data from several national surveillance systems that record laboratory confirmed illnesses caused by twenty-five microbial pathogens. They then adjusted the data for each pathogen to correct for underdiagnosis and underreporting to estimate the total number of illnesses from each of these twenty-five pathogens in the United States. Next, they discounted the total number of cases for each pathogen by the estimated proportion of cases acquired domestically, as opposed to abroad, and further discounted that number by the estimated proportion of cases transmitted through food. For six additional pathogens not routinely reported to any surveillance system, they used public health data from various other sources to estimate the total number of pathogen-specific illnesses and then scaled these down to estimate the number of cases acquired domestically that were transferred through food. In addition, they used data from illness reports to estimate the proportion of cases for each pathogen requiring hospitalization or resulting in death. By summing the estimates for each pathogen, Scallan and colleagues estimate that these thirty-one major pathogens cause approximately 9.4 million illnesses, 55,961 hospitalizations, and 1,351 deaths from foodborne illness acquired in the United States each year.[2]

These thirty-one major pathogens account for only a fraction of foodborne illness caused by all microbial pathogens. Additional illnesses are caused by what Scallan and colleagues call "unspecified agents," which include "known agents with insufficient data to estimate agent-specific illness, known agents not yet recognized as causing foodborne illness, substances known to be in food but of unproven pathogenicity, and unknown agents." In a concurrent study, the authors used CDC survey data to estimate the total number of annual episodes of acute gastroenteritis in the US population, subtracted the estimated number of cases caused by twenty-four major known pathogens associated with acute gastroenteritis, and estimated 38.4 million illnesses, 71,878 hospitalizations, and 1,686 deaths from foodborne illness acquired in the United States each year caused by unspecified agents. Although unspecified agents include chemicals, metals, and other inorganic toxins, acute gastroenteritis is typically caused by a microbial pathogen, so these estimates include primarily illnesses caused by microbial pathogens. Combining the estimates from their two studies, Scallan and colleagues estimate 47.8 million illnesses, 127,839 hospitalizations, and 3,037 deaths from foodborne illness acquired in the United States each year.[3]

Scallan and colleagues are careful to qualify their estimates. Multipliers for correcting underdiagnosis and underreporting as well as discount ratios for calculating domestically acquired illness transmitted by food are themselves based on a mix of limited surveillance data and survey results that may be more or less accurate when applied to different pathogens. To indicate the degree of uncertainty in their estimates, Scallan and colleagues provide a range of values such that there is a 90 percent chance that the true value lies within this range—a range known in statistics as a 90 percent credible interval. Thus, the estimate of 47.8 million illnesses lies within a 90 percent credible interval between 28.6 million and 71.1 million. Perhaps most significant, the authors caution that their estimate should not be compared with earlier studies of foodborne illness in the United States or in other countries because of differences in methodology. Thus, although the Scallan and colleagues study provides the most sophisticated estimate of the overall burden of foodborne illness acquired in the United States, it should not be understood as a precise measure, and it does not illuminate any domestic trends over time or support international comparisons of overall burden. Surveillance systems that track reported cases of illnesses do reveal trends for specific pathogens, which are discussed in chapters 4 and 6.[4]

Because the health outcomes of nonfatal foodborne illness vary widely—from temporary discomfort to chronic illness and long-term disability—merely estimating the total number of illnesses does not provide a particularly meaningful measure of foodborne illness's impact on public health. Sandra Hoffmann, an economist at the USDA, and two coauthors estimated the annual economic cost of foodborne illness caused by fourteen pathogens that account for 95 percent of the illnesses and hospitalizations and 98 percent of the deaths caused by the thirty-one known major pathogens in Scallan and colleagues' study. Based on the value of a statistical life—a measure commonly used by economists to calculate the economic impact of a premature death—and estimating health-care costs and the lost wages of employed adults for the estimated incidence of nonfatal illness caused by each pathogen, they estimated an annual cost of $14.1 billion. Taking into account Scallan and colleagues' 90 percent credible interval, the cost of illness from these fourteen pathogens is likely to be somewhere between $4.35 billion and $33 billion. An alternative estimate by Robert Scharff, an economist at Ohio State University, estimated the economic cost of foodborne illness from all major pathogens and unspecified agents at $77 billion. When taking into account the 90 percent credible interval, this means somewhere between $28.6 billion and $144.6 billion. Scharff's estimates also include estimates of quality-of-life reductions beyond health-care costs and lost wages, as well as the lost wages of family members who care for those suffering from foodborne illness. Scharff estimates the cost of health care and lost wages, excluding quality-of-life reductions and family member care, to be $51 billion, based on a credible interval of somewhere between $31.2 billion and $76.1 billion. Hoffmann cautions that, given the wide credible intervals of all these estimates, care is required when making any strong claims about the cost of foodborne illness. At the same time, she points out that both estimates consistently rank the relative impact of different pathogens and can provide useful guidance in setting regulatory priorities.[5]

In twenty-five states, strict liability applies not only to the manufacturer of contaminated food but also to any company downstream in the distribution chain that sells the food. This includes distributors, wholesalers, and retailers. The law in some states, however, departs from the general rule of strict liability to shield subsequent sellers from strict liability. For example, thirteen states hold nonmanufacturing sellers liable only upon proof of negligence unless the manufacturer is insolvent or beyond the reach of a lawsuit.[1]

In cases where more than one entity is liable, states also have different laws governing how to apportion liability among them. The law in some states allows a successful plaintiff to recover the full amount of damages from any liable defendant. In these jurisdictions, plaintiffs seek payment from defendants who can most readily pay—defendants with "deep pockets." Defendants who end up paying more than their fair share of the liability (as determined by a court) may subsequently sue fellow defendants who have paid less than their fair share to recoup the overpayment, in what is known as an action for contribution. By contrast, the law in other states limits the amount that a successful plaintiff can recover from any one defendant to that defendant's share of the liability. In all these scenarios, a defendant held strictly liable may recover from another defendant any amount paid to the plaintiff if the defendant can prove that the other defendant was negligent. This is known as an action for indemnity.[2]

Food safety litigation typically focuses on determining which defendants' liability insurance policies will pay a plaintiff's claim and which portion of that claim each policy will pay. Contracts between buyers and their suppliers include indemnification agreements, in which the supplier assumes any liability incurred by the buyer as a result of an injury to consumers caused by the supplier's product. As part of this indemnification, buyers may also require that suppliers obtain liability insurance that covers the buyer as an additional insured. Further, the agreements may include "hold-harmless" provisions, under which the supplier assumes all costs incurred by the buyer in defending against claims, costs which might not be covered under the buyer's liability insurance. Retailers have such agreements with processors, and processors in turn have them with growers. The effect of these indemnification agreements is to push liability upstream in the supply chain back to growers.[3]

However, growers—especially small and midsize growers—frequently do not carry sufficient liability insurance coverage to satisfy large claims arising out of serious injuries or a large number of claims arising out of an outbreak. Once a grower's capacity to pay a claim is exhausted, liability flows back downstream, and the processor becomes responsible for paying the claim, which triggers the processor's liability insurance coverage. If the processor's capacity to pay the claim is exhausted, liability will then flow further downstream to retail buyers. In some jurisdictions, liability flows back downstream only when the supplier cannot, for some reason, be sued or is bankrupt. In other jurisdictions, liability flows back downstream as soon as the supplier's liability coverage is exhausted.[4]

Some suppliers, even after their insurance coverage is exhausted, choose to pay for liability out-of-pocket rather than pass the liability on to buyers, for fear of damaging a supply chain relationship on which the viability of the supplier's business depends. Processors are especially loath to upset their large retail customers by passing along liability for a contaminated product that they supplied. Thus, processors often find themselves sandwiched between underinsured growers and powerful retailers, leaving them to bear the brunt of liability, which is paid by their liability insurers and, when their coverage runs out, by the processors themselves.[5]

Matters are further complicated by variations in the law. The typical supply chain crosses many different state boundaries, and when a plaintiffs' attorney files multiple claims arising out of the same outbreak, those claims can arise under different state laws. The law in many jurisdictions holds any company that sold a contaminated product strictly liable for the full amount of a plaintiff's damages, regardless of where that company falls in the supply chain. Some states impose liability on downstream sellers of a contaminated product only if the seller with whom the contamination originated is insolvent or beyond the reach of a lawsuit. Other states allow plaintiffs to recover from downstream sellers, but only upon showing that a seller was somehow negligent. In addition, different jurisdictions vary in their willingness to enforce indemnity agreements between buyers and their suppliers.[6]

In the Jensen Farms case, the grower's bankruptcy in May 2012 yielded about $2 million in insurance money for victims, and it enabled Marler to pursue sellers in the distribution chain with deeper pockets. For example, he sued Frontera Produce, a company that purchased Jensen Farms cantaloupes and resold them to retail supermarkets. Before the bankruptcy, Frontera was not subject to strict liability for its sale of contaminated Jensen Farms cantaloupes in states that shielded nonmanufacturing sellers from strict liability unless the manufacturer was insolvent. Once Jensen Farms declared insolvency, that shield disappeared. Because Frontera carried only $11 million in liability coverage, Marler sued other sellers in the chain of distribution as well.[7]

The deepest pockets were those of the supermarket chains that sold Jensen Farms cantaloupes, including retail giants Walmart and Kroger. With victim claims totaling in the tens of millions of dollars, retailers faced the distinct possibility that litigation or settlement would consume the resources of the Jensens and their distributors, leaving retailers liable for the remaining balance. Consequently, Walmart settled all twenty-three claims against it for an undisclosed amount in May 2014. By contrast, Kroger, facing sixty-six claims, refused to settle, hoping that its suppliers would have sufficient insurance to satisfy victims' claims and relying on its indemnification agreements to shield it from liability. It, too, eventually settled in February 2015.[8]

Marler handles a high volume of foodborne illness claims, and he tends to settle them expeditiously. Based on his many years of experience, he has a good sense of how much a jury would award any given claim and, consequently, he is able to make settlement offers that liability insurers find acceptable. When defendants reject his initial offer, he frequently resolves claims through mediation. He is eager to avoid the substantial costs of trying cases in multiple jurisdictions with varying laws regarding the liability of downstream buyers, the enforceability of indemnity agreements, and insurance coverage. The insurance company lawyers who routinely negotiate with Marler share his desire to settle cases quickly.[9]

In the Dole baby spinach litigation, Marler negotiated on behalf of all but a few of the victims, both his own clients and those represented by other attorneys. "There was a group of lawyers led by Bill Marler," recalls Al Maxwell, the attorney who represented Natural Selection in the case and who had faced off against Marler in foodborne illness cases dating back to 1998. "After some preliminary discovery, we put those on what I would call a settlement track, with some initial agreements about how we were going to approach the settlement process—what claims would be earmarked for initial consideration: wrongful death claims first, nonhospitalization cases second, hospitalization cases third, and severe hospitalization cases last." Marler recalls: "We had some preliminary discovery—interrogatories and requests for production—but I never took one deposition. We settled over one hundred cases. The lead counsel in the case was Sarah Brew, who represented Dole. I had just wrapped up cases against Dole from the 2005 lettuce outbreak. Because both Sarah and Al and I had already been around the block together in this type of litigation, we agreed to mediate multiple cases in cities around the country."[10]

Negotiations among the liability insurers of different companies along the supply chain typically complicate settlement of foodborne illness claims. Indemnification agreements and state laws may render buyers liable only if they are negligent. Thus, liability insurers may argue over the comparative fault of the companies involved. They may also argue over causation if the source of contamination is not entirely clear. In the absence of robust discovery and a jury trial, these negotiations involve a great deal of speculation. Insurers sometimes point to the quality of food safety management in the various companies involved as a proxy for direct evidence of fault or causation. Disputes over contract provisions—such as the types of events that trigger coverage or indemnification—often further complicate matters. The market power of large buyers and the desire of suppliers to conduct future business with them are important business considerations added to this thorny set of legal problems.[11]

In the Dole baby spinach litigation, Dole successfully pushed all the liability upstream. "Dole had a draconian contract that required Natural Selection to indemnify Dole for everything except Dole's sole negligence," recalls Marler. Dole's liability insurance carrier, however, was not off the hook. As it turned out, Fireman's Fund not only insured Dole but was also one of several insurers covering Natural Selection and Mission Organics. In settlement negotiations, Marler quickly exhausted Mission Organics' insurance coverage. Because the grower was a relatively small company, Marler did not attempt to force it to pay more out of its corporate assets. "Mission Organics, in the spinach case, had limited insurance resources," recalls Maxwell. "It wasn't Marler's intent to bankrupt them, so he made arrangements with Mission Organics about how their insurance proceeds would be contributed to the settlement and how they would be allocated. Generally, Marler is not one to try to bankrupt companies. . . . He does not typically pursue corporate assets." By contrast, when Marler proceeded to exhaust Natural Selection's insurance coverage, he extracted additional out-of-pocket payments, as the processor was a much larger company and able to shoulder the financial burden. Natural Selection did not even attempt to shift any of the liability onto Dole, on whom it was heavily dependent as a major buyer.[12]

Appendix C
The Origins of Third-Party Food Safety Auditing
in the United States

As detailed in chapter 2, medical milk commissions provided third-party inspections of dairies beginning in 1893. Third-party food safety auditing emerged in the baking industry following World War II. Shortly after the war, an FDA initiative to enforce the 1938 Federal Food, Drug, and Cosmetic Act led the agency to issue citations and impose fines on numerous food processors whose equipment and plants had deteriorated following a decade of depression and war shortages. Companies turned to the American Institute of Baking (AIB) for help with regulatory compliance. AIB launched a nationwide training program for industry managers and hired five former government officials to inspect plants, identify instances of noncompliance, and provide advice about how to correct existing problems and prevent future failures. During the 1950s and 1960s, AIB's Department of Bakery Sanitation grew as a result of increasing demand for its services and published bakery sanitation standards. AIB drafted an inspection manual, including a scoring system that companies requested to measure and manage their food safety efforts. In the 1980s, buyers began requesting their suppliers' AIB inspection scores and hiring AIB to conduct third-party audits of suppliers who had not already been audited. Eventually, AIB expanded its services beyond the baking industry to other sectors, including, by 2001, fresh produce. AIB was not, however, the first firm to provide third-party food safety audits on farms.[1]

Industry insiders credit Primus Labs with conducting the earliest third-party food safety audits on farms. In the 1970s and 1980s, government regulations limiting pesticide residues in fresh produce created a demand among growers for laboratory testing services. In 1987, Robert Stovicek founded Primus Labs in a strip mall in the heart of California's Salinas Valley to test preharvest produce samples for chemical residues. In 1998, following well-publicized outbreaks involving lettuce and tomatoes, Primus agreed to conduct fresh produce food safety audits for the popular restaurant chain Subway and quickly established itself as a leading firm in third-party auditing in the fresh produce sector.[2]

The National Sanitation Foundation (NSF) was founded in 1944 by two professors at the University of Michigan School of Public Health to provide sanitary design standards for food service equipment. Over time, NSF expanded the scope of its standard-setting activities to include water treatment and bottled water. In 2001, NSF acquired the smaller firm of Cook and Thurber, which provided third-party food safety audits to food processors; in 2006, NSF acquired Davis Fresh Technologies, a small third-party food safety auditing firm founded in 1997 specializing in fresh produce farming operations.[3]

Tom and Gary Huge's grandfather ran a pesticide application business for hospitals, which their father expanded to food production facilities when he joined the business. In the 1950s, they hired a sanitation expert from AIB and began to provide sanitation auditing services. Today, the family company, ASI Food Safety offers a variety of food safety certifications to clients around the world.[4]

AIB, Primus, NSF, and ASI are just four examples of the hundreds of firms that today provide third-party food safety audits worldwide. Like these three examples, many third-party auditing firms originated in industry associations, testing laboratories, standard-setting organizations, and sanitation services. Others were founded by individuals who previously served as government inspectors or quality assurance and food safety managers in food companies.[5]

The California Leafy Green Products Handling Marketing Agreement (LGMA) was not the only response to the 2006 Dole baby spinach outbreak. In October, while investigators were still trying to identify the source of contamination, California state senator Dean Florez held committee hearings on the outbreak at which he accused federal and state regulators of being "asleep at the wheel." Florez declared that "the time for industry-sponsored approaches [is] over . . . consumers are looking for stronger measures than the voluntary measures that have produced 20 of these outbreaks." Florez introduced legislation, the California Produce Safety Action Plan, authorizing the California Department of Health Services (DHS) to develop mandatory GAPs for leafy greens growers. Florez's plan would have required all growers to obtain a license from the DHS based on an initial agency audit of their operations, to undergo periodic audits by government inspectors, and to pay an annual fee to fund the inspection program. The plan further empowered the DHS to impose civil penalties for noncompliance and to order a mandatory recall or product quarantine to "prevent, circumscribe, or eliminate any condition where any produce or food processed from produce may carry an illness, infection, pathogen, contagion, toxin, or condition that, without intervention, could transmit an illness that could kill or seriously affect the health of humans."[1]

Fearful of an overreaction by legislators eager to score points with voters, and wary of agency officials with no more insight into the sources of microbial contamination than industry insiders, the LGMA founders lobbied hard against the Florez plan and accelerated their efforts to get a marketing agreement up and running. In their efforts to "thwart adverse legislation," the Western Growers Association asserted that "the California legislature . . .

doesn't understand our industry or its practices." The association also argued that industry could more quickly than government agencies develop and implement rigorous new food safety standards that would protect the public and restore consumer confidence in the industry. In addition, the association contended, there would be an ongoing need to revise the standards in light of experience, new science, and technological advances, and industry standards would be easier to update than government regulations. To its members, the association explained that by completing the LGMA before the passage of any legislation, the industry would "have leverage with the Governor in requesting a veto." Although concerns about avoiding future outbreaks and restoring consumer confidence motivated the LGMA founders, the prospect of aggressive government regulation accelerated their efforts. "We felt pressure in the State of California from legislators that was staring us in the face," recalls Hank Giclas of the Western Growers Association. The LGMA obtained approval from the California Department of Food and Agriculture (CDFA) in February 2007, and by July it was up and running in growing fields. The Florez plan never made it out of the legislature.[2]

The LGMA founders also had to contend with the reaction of buyers to the 2006 baby spinach outbreak. In October, executives from nine leading retail supermarkets and food service companies—including Kroger, Costco, Safeway, SuperValu, Wegmans, and Sysco—formed a working group called the Initiative for Food Safety and sent a letter to the Western Growers Association, the United Fresh Produce Association, and the Produce Marketing Association demanding that the associations formulate "specific, measurable, and verifiable" food safety standards to be enforced through third-party audits, "develop a website or other mechanism whereby buyers can verify whether growers/suppliers have received certification," and "fund and lead robust industry and consumer outreach about the certification program." In an imperious tone, the buyers informed the trade associations that "a small working group will monitor the associations' progress and report on it at least every other week; we expect the associations to update the working group at least every week via e-mail, and further suggest that associations continue to communicate proactively with all stakeholders in North America." Finally, the buyers threatened that "we expect that the major components of this process can and will be accomplished by December 15, 2006. If this is not the case, our options include fast-tracking our own working group to establish a meaningful certification program with objective criteria." By November, ten more large retail supermarket chains had joined the buyers' Initiative for Food Safety. That same month, the powerful National Restaurant Association formed the Produce Safety Working Group to develop new food safety standards for fresh produce suppliers to restaurants. In February 2007, a third group of leading buyers—including Walmart, Publix, McDonald's, and Disney—calling itself the Food Safety Leadership Council, announced that it was developing its own set of on-farm food safety standards that were more stringent than the LGMA metrics.[3]

The LGMA founders persuaded the Initiative for Food Safety and the Produce Safety Working Group to hold off on any new standards and give the LGMA a chance to work. However, in October 2007, Publix, a member of the Food Safety Leadership Council, sent its suppliers a letter along with a new set of "FSLC On-Farm Produce Standards" and a contract. The letter informed suppliers that, henceforth, Publix would "utilize these FSLC On-Farm Produce Standards to evaluate vendor farms that provide produce to Publix" and that, by signing the contract, a supplier agreed "to adhere to the standards" and "conduct and pay for an audit by an FSLC certified auditor at least once per growing season." The results of these audits would "be shared among members of the FSLC as a means to enhance consistent safety standards." Blindsided, the Western Growers Association fired off an angry letter to Publix. Writing to Garry Bergstrom, the Publix produce and floral manager who authored the company's "Dear Produce Supplier" letter, Western Growers president Tom Nassif wrote:

> We are bewildered as to how and why your "Council" concluded that the California Leafy Green GAPs and metrics were insufficient to address the food safety concerns of the public and our members' customers, apparently without the benefit of input from the grower/handler community.
>
> After our review of your On-Farm Produce Standards, we believe that the new standards are unreasonable, excessive and scientifically indefensible and will require produce suppliers to submit to redundant, expensive and unnecessary food safety inspections and audits. Further, they will result in significant loss of available farmland and may cause serious environmental harm.
>
> The FSLC's standards clearly imply without any scientific basis that the GAPs, scientifically developed and peer reviewed by some of the nation's leading food safety scientists and experts, are inadequate. We know that is not the case as federal and state government food safety agencies all agree that the GAP metrics include the latest, cutting edge food safety science.
>
> Your effort marks the beginning of a destructive food safety "arms race," where different groups of produce buyers, in an effort to claim that they have safer produce than the next, will impose on fresh produce suppliers ever more stringent, expensive and scientifically indefensible food safety requirements without even the implication that the additional costs will be reimbursed.

Nassif took aim at a number of particular FSLC standards. For example, he wrote: "The new standards require a one-mile buffer zone between fresh produce fields and concentrated animal feeding lots. What is the scientific basis and justification for such an extensive buffer that will take substantial farm land out of production? What environmental studies have you conducted that evaluate the effect on wildlife habitat, flood control and water quality?"[4]

A week later, United Fresh president Thomas Stenzel wrote a letter on behalf of twenty-three leading produce industry associations from around the country to the director of food safety at Disney, one of the FSLC's founders, in which he stated, "We ask that you step back from this unilateral and unfounded direction to engage in real scientific and professional dialogue with your produce suppliers, technical representatives from our industry's trade associations, academia, and government." He suggested that the FSLC's standards were motivated more by "liability placement than actual sound, scientific and achievable food safety practices." "On a practical level," he wrote, "you must know that some standards such as the water requirements outlined in the FSLC document cannot physically be achieved in many cases, even by world class producers. Perhaps you were thinking of a target for producers to strive for, but without further discussion, our best scientists just don't understand what you have in mind." Stenzel also took aim at the FSLC's standard requiring a quarter-mile buffer between growing fields and animal grazing. "Some of the recommendations in your document are inherently based on opinion and judgment where science is insufficient, such as distance of production from animal grazing. Science today cannot tell us an exact distance, and we would therefore argue that expert consensus among industry, academia and government is the best way to address such unknown scientific questions until research can provide better evidence for risk-based decision-making. Otherwise, we are faced with an escalating, unscientific approach—if a 100-foot buffer is good; a 1,000-foot buffer must be better. Or why not 1,000 yards; or perhaps a mile, or two, or three. This is indeed a slippery slope without real science to guide these judgments."[5]

Notwithstanding the protests of trade associations representing producers, the FSLC standards were part of a more general trend. Many buyers, and some processors—fresh-cut industry leader Fresh Express among them—developed new food safety standards that were more demanding than the LGMA's metrics. Buyers increasingly required supplier audits that included these new standards, which became known as "supermetrics." Some buyers even went so far as to insist, unrealistically, on "zero risk" in growing fields.[6]

Abbreviations

AMS	Agricultural Marketing Service of the USDA
APHA	American Public Health Association
CAFF	Community Alliance with Family Farmers
CDC	Centers for Disease Control and Prevention
CDFA	California Department of Food and Agriculture
CIDT	culture-independent diagnostic testing
CSPI	Center for Science in the Public Interest
EPA	Environmental Protection Agency
FDA	Food and Drug Administration of the Department of HHS
FDCA	Federal Food, Drug, and Cosmetic Act
FMI	Food Marketing Institute
FSIS	Food Safety and Inspection Service of the USDA
FSMA	Food Safety Modernization Act of 2011
GAO	Government Accountability Office (General Accounting Office prior to 2004)
GAPs	good agricultural practices
GFSI	Global Food Safety Initiative
GMPs	good manufacturing practices
GS1	Global Standards One
GTIN	Global Trade Item Number
HACCP	Hazard Analysis Critical Control Points
HHS	Department of Health and Human Services
IFT	Institute of Food Technologists
LGMA	Leafy Green Products Handler Marketing Agreement
NASA	National Aeronautics and Space Administration
NCA	National Canners Association
NLGMA	National Leafy Greens Marketing Agreement

OIG	Office of Inspector General
PACA	Perishable Agricultural Commodities Act of 1930
PCA	Peanut Corporation of America
PFGE	pulsed-field gel electrophoresis test for DNA "fingerprinting" of pathogens
PMA	Produce Marketing Association
PR/HACCP	Pathogen Reduction/Hazard Analysis and Critical Control Point Systems Regulation
SQF	Safe Quality Food scheme
USDA	United States Department of Agriculture
WGA	Western Growers Association
WGS	whole genome sequencing

Timeline of Significant Events

	Outbreaks	Private initiatives	Government actions
1893		Henry Leber Coit establishes the first medical milk commission	
		Nathan Straus opens his first infant milk depot to sell pasteurized milk	
1906			Pure Food and Drug Act
			Federal Meat Inspection Act
1919	Canned olive botulism outbreak		
1924	Raw oyster typhoid fever outbreak		
1930			Perishable Agricultural Commodities Act
1938			Federal Food, Drug, and Cosmetic Act
1957			Poultry Products Inspection Act
1962			National Salmonella Surveillance Program
1963		Paul Lachance and Howard Bauman develop HACCP for the NASA space program	
1967			Wholesome Meat Act
1968			Wholesome Poultry Act
1971	Bon Vivant vichyssoise botulism outbreak		*American Public Health Association v. Butz*
1974			FDA low-acid canned food regulations
1975			*United States v. Park*

	Outbreaks	Private initiatives	Government actions
1993	Jack in the Box ground beef *E. coli* outbreak		
1996			USDA PR/HACCP Regulations (Mega-Reg) final rule published
			PulseNet initiated by the CDC
1997		GAPs guidelines published by produce industry trade associations and academics	
1998			FDA publishes first GAPs guidance
2000		GFSI founded	
2001			*Supreme Beef Processors v. USDA*
2004		*Traceability Best Practices* published by the Traceability Task Force	Bioterrorism Act tracing regulations final rule published by the FDA
2006	Dole baby spinach *E. coli* outbreak	Commodity-specific leafy greens guidance published by industry associations	
2007		California LGMA Produce Traceability Initiative	
2008	Jalapeño pepper *Salmonella* outbreak		
	Peanut Corporation of America peanut *Salmonella* outbreak		
2009			FDA initiates Reportable Food Registry
2010	DeCoster egg *Salmonella* outbreak		
2011	Jensen Farms cantaloupe *Listeria* outbreak		Food Safety Modernization Act
2015			FDA publishes the Produce Safety Rule

Acknowledgments

This book was made possible by the generous support of Georgia State University College of Law and Albany Law School. At Georgia State University, Dean Steven Kaminshine and Dean Wendy Hensel generously funded my research. Associate Dean Kristina Niedringhaus and her extraordinarily talented law library staff provided essential research assistance. Thank you to Meg Butler and Terrance Manion for responding so quickly to queries and requests. I owe special thanks to Pam Brannon, for whom no source was too obscure and no question too arcane. There would be major gaps in the history and analysis of this book were it not for her help and advice. I also received excellent research assistance from Georgia State students Christina S. Scott, Andrea Beltran, and Allison Kim. My colleagues at the Center for Law, Health and Society, under the dynamic leadership of Leslie Wolf, have provided a vibrant scholarly community. My colleague Paul Lombardo offered sage advice about the project.

At Albany Law School, Dean Alicia Ouellette provided financial support for the early stages of my research, and I received research assistance from law librarians Robert Emery, Colleen Ostiguy, Leslie Cunningham, and Rebecca Murphy; student research assistants Stacy Mazzara, Sean Mix, and Kristin Keehan; and my supportive administrative assistant for fifteen years, Theresa Colbert. Thank you also to Wayne Olson and Wayne Thompson, reference librarians at the National Agricultural Library.

I am grateful to many individuals who shared their expertise, answered many questions, offered helpful advice, and commented on drafts: Mitchel Abolafia, David Acheson, Tom Baker, Tim Bartley, Douglas Becker, Betsy Bihn, Marlena Bordson, Angie Boyce, Robert Brackett, Bob Brown, Linda Calvin, Megan Chedwick, Tom Chestnut, Roger Clemens, Charlie Cook,

Roy Costa, John Cogan, Jorge Contreras, Alicia Cronquist, Russell Cross, Art Davis, James Derr, Dusty Dickey, Ron Doering, Michel Doyle, Edward Dunkelberger, Richard Epstein, Henry Falk, Drew Falkenstein, Dan Farber, Tony Farrell, Tom Fenner, Ryan Fothergill, Hank Giclas, David Gombas, James Gorny, Erin Grether, Jack Guzewich, John Haaland, John Hansen, Jack Hipp, Scott Horsfall, Sandy Hoffmann, Gary Huge, Tom Huge, Catherine Adams Hutt, Peter Barton Hutt, Steve Ingham, Michele Jay-Russell, Mike Johnson, Lorraine Lewandowski, Forest Lewis, Carl Liggio, Jim Loseke, Bill Marler, Al Maxwell, Jane McCarthy, Drew McDonald, Anne Marie McNamara, Ed Mitchell, Rosemary Mucklow, Jill Nathan, Marion Nestle, David Nicholas, Mike Ollinger, Chip Peccio, Jaime Peña, Daryl Pippin, Ken Petersen, Rina Pierami, Doug Powell, Jim Prevor, Gale Prince, Bill Pursley, Joe Regenstein, J. B. Ruhl, Andrew Russell, Elaine Scallan, Robert Schmelzer, Keith Schneider, Eric Schwartz, William Schwartz, Michelle Smith, Dan Sosin, Chuck Stauber, Denis Stearns, Tom Stenzel, Bernie Steves, Richard Stier, Brad Sullivan, Manik Suri, Trevor Suslow, Kimberly Tarvis, Robert Tauxe, Dave Theno, Hilary Thesmar, Ed Treacy, Patrick Van Roey, Mike Vandenbergh, Kip Viscusi, Martin Weidmann, Harold Weston, Jim Wagner, Trisha Wester, Bob Whitaker, Craig Wilson, Frank Yiannas, and Devon Zagory. I benefited from workshop presentations at Cornell, University of Georgia, New York University, University of Texas, UC Berkeley, UCLA, and Vanderbilt. Ray Brescia, Jerry Mashaw, and Austin Sarat helped me frame the initial proposal for this book. Dan Ho and Tom McGarity offered detailed comments on the entire manuscript and provided many thoughtful suggestions for improvement. Bob Rabin, Peter Schuck, and Steve Sugarman have mentored me through many projects, and this book would not have been possible without their guidance and friendship.

Chuck Meyers, my editor at University of Chicago Press, provided steady encouragement and wise counsel. Holly Smith and Joel Score shepherded the manuscript through production. Katherine Faydash artfully copyedited the manuscript, which is greatly improved because of her efforts. Antoinette Dauber generously and carefully proofread it.

My father, Bernard Lytton, read the entire manuscript and offered thoughtful advice. Dawn Wood, Liz Anisfeld, Margot Kohorn, Ernest Kohorn, Jenny Lytton-Hirsch, and Eric Lytton-Hirsch provided ongoing encouragement. My children, Medad, Margalit, and Asher, were no help at all, but this seems like a good place to acknowledge that they are a constant source of joy. My wife, Rachel Anisfeld, makes everything possible. She is living proof that angels do exist.

Notes

Chapter One

1. Scott Bronstein and Drew Griffin, "Third-Deadliest US Food Outbreak Was Preventable, Experts Say," CNN.com, May 3, 2012, http://www.cnn.com/2012/05/03/health/listeria-outbreak-investigation/index.html, archived at https://perma.cc/NA5Q-DCKF; Ryan Jaslow, "Feds Charge Jensen Farms over 2011 Listeria-Cantaloupe Outbreak," CBS News, September 27, 2013, https://www.cbsnews.com/news/feds-charge-jensen-farms-over-2011-listeria-cantaloupe-outbreak/, archived at http://perma.cc/M3TF-E39C; Laurent Belsie, "Cantaloupe Recall: Colorado Farm Linked to Listeria," *Christian Science Monitor*, September 15, 2011; Bill Marler, "Publisher's Platform: Three Years since People Died from Cantaloupe," *Food Safety News*, July 22, 2014, http://www.foodsafetynews.com/2014/07/publishers-platform-three-years-since-the-primus-jensen-farms-audit/#.WnHoL6inGUk, archived at https://perma.cc/FS7F-92KK; CDC, "Multistate Outbreak of Listeriosis Linked to Whole Cantaloupes from Jensen Farms, Colorado (final update)," August 27, 2012, https://www.cdc.gov/listeria/outbreaks/cantaloupes-jensen-farms/index.html, archived at https://perma.cc/NG2K-J6NZ.

2. Bill Marler, telephone interview by the author, November 5, 2014; Primus Labs, "The Outbreak: The Untold Story of *Listeria Monocytogenes* at Jensen Farms," unpublished report, 3–4, http://www.foodsafetynews.com/files/2014/07/Attachment-No.-4.pdf, archived at https://perma.cc/B5JS-52HB; Jim Prevor, "Could There Be Common Ground between the Spinach Crisis and the Cantaloupe Catastrophe? Might Both Have Been Sourced from Transitional Acreage?" *Jim Prevor's Perishable Pundit* (blog), February 27, 2012, http://www.perishablepundit.com/index.php?date=02/27/2012&pundit=1, archived at https://perma.cc/EQ62-4D5P; Kevin Simpson, "Cantaloupe Growers in Rocky Ford Reeling from 'Listeria Hysteria,'" *Denver Post*, October 11, 2011, A1. For more on *Listeria* in compost, see M. Oliveira et al., "Transfer of Listeria Innocua from Contaminated Compost and Irrigation Water to Lettuce Leaves," *Food Microbiology* 28, no. 3 (May 2011): 590–96.

3. US House of Representatives, Committee on Energy and Commerce, Committee Staff, "Report on the Investigation of the Outbreak of *Listeria monocytogenes* in Cantaloupe at Jensen Farms," January 10, 2012, 4–5, archived at https://perma.cc/Y79W-A64S.

4. "Results of the FDA-Led Root Cause Investigation of the Multi-State Listeria Outbreak Related to Jensen Farms Cantaloupe," FDA telephone conference transcript, October 19, 2011, https://wayback.archive-it.org/7993/20170406154011/https://www.fda.gov/downloads/

NewsEvents/Newsroom/MediaTranscripts/UCM277070.pdf, 19; Primus Labs, "Outbreak," 19–35; House of Representatives, "Report," 1–8; Primus Labs, audit certificate for Jensen Farms, July 25, 2011, http://www.foodsafetynews.com/files/2014/07/Attachment-No.-2.pdf, archived at https://perma.cc/YSC6-W4FB. On washing cantaloupes, see Jim Prevor, "Cantaloupe Crisis, the Truth Dare Not Speak Its Name: The Priority Can Be Safe or the Priority Can Be Local, but It Cannot Be Both," *Jim Prevor's Perishable Pundit* (blog), October 4, 2011, http://www.perishablepundit .com/index.php?date=10/04/2011&pundit=1, archived at https://perma.cc/GF4T-9PHP.

5. "Exclusive: Jensen Farms React to Lawsuit, Recall," *7 News Denver*, September 16, 2011, https://www.thedenverchannel.com/news/exclusive-jensen-farms-react-to-lawsuit-recall, archived at https://perma.cc/YVT8-RKR2; Jeffrey T. McCollum et al., "Multistate Outbreak of Listeriosis Associated with Cantaloupe," *New England Journal of Medicine* 369 (September 5, 2013): 951; Primus Labs, "Outbreak," 8–9, 28; Michael Booth and Jennifer Brown, *Eating Dangerously* (Lanham, MD: Rowman & Littlefield, 2014), locs. 580, 622, Kindle; Association of Public Health Laboratories, "Success Stories: A Colorado Cantaloupe Saga," *Food Safety News*, February 13, 2012, http://www.foodsafetynews.com/2012/02/a-colorado-cantaloupe -saga/#.WnH8DqinGUl, archived at https://perma.cc/L694-F7HC; CDC, "Multistate Outbreak of Listeriosis"; CDC, "Timeline of Events: Multistate Outbreak of Listeriosis Linked to Whole Cantaloupes from Jensen Farms in Colorado," October 24, 2011, https://www.cdc.gov/ listeria/outbreaks/cantaloupes-jensen-farms/timeline.html, archived at https://perma.cc/ FFA6-SVQS; FDA, "Information on the Recalled Jensen Farms Whole Cantaloupes," January 9, 2012, https://wayback.archive-it.org/7993/20170404202611/https://www.fda.gov/Food/ RecallsOutbreaksEmergencies/Outbreaks/ucm272372.htm; Marler, "Three Years."

6. "Parker Woman's 48-Year-Old Mother Latest Victim of Listeria Outbreak," *CBS Denver*, September 20, 2011, http://denver.cbslocal.com/2011/09/20/parker-womans-48-year-old-mother -latest-victim-of-listeria-outbreak/, archived at https://perma.cc/ZVS3-C7Z3; "Daughter of Listeria Cantaloupe Victim," *9 News*, September 20, 2011, archived at https://perma.cc/J5VV-KQ75.

7. Bill Marler, "2011 Listeria Cantaloupe Outbreak—Four Families," *Marler Blog*, video, http://www.marlerblog.com/legal-cases/2011-listeria-cantaloupe-outbreak-four-families/# .VFOgZIl0x1M, archived at https://perma.cc/5E6E-TCL7; Sonya Colbert, "Mustang Man, 87, among Victims of Listeria Outbreak," *NewsOK*, October 3, 2011, http://newsok.com/mustang -man-87-among-victims-of-listeria-outbreak/article/3609915, archived at https://perma.cc/ E9YC-QXSU.

8. CDC, "Multistate Outbreak of Listeriosis"; Dan Flynn, "Letter from the Editor: Cause(s) of Death," *Food Safety News*, October 27, 2013, archived at https://perma.cc/F8RW-NFRP; "Jensen Farms Cantaloupe Listeria Outbreak Lawsuits—Nationwide (2011)," Marler Clark, https://marlerclark.com/news_events/jensen-farms-rocky-ford-cantaloupe-listeria-outbreak -colorado-new-mexico, archived at https://perma.cc/BYS9-EXD2; Bill Marler, personal communication with the author, February 7, 2018.

9. Elaine Scallan et al., "Foodborne Illness Acquired in the United States—Unspecified Pathogens," *Emerging Infectious Diseases* 17, no. 1 (January 2011): 16–22; "Our Food Safety System Is Broken," *HLN*, June 7, 2013, http://www.hlntv.com/video/2013/05/30/our-food-safety -inspection-system-broken/, archived at https://perma.cc/FFR2-PN5B; "Total Food Recall: Unsafe Food Putting American Lives at Risk," US PIRG, October 24, 2012, https://uspirg.org/ sites/pirg/files/reports/USP%20TotalFoodRecall%20final%2012-12.pdf, archived at https:// perma.cc/ZES6-F3AA. Available data do not provide a basis for determining the proportion of foodborne illness that arises out of contamination during industrial processing, food service preparation, or home handling and cooking.

10. Patricia Wester, personal communication with the author, August 3, 2014; Tom Vilsack, "Secretary's Column: Ensuring a Safe Food Supply for Americans," USDA, December 7, 2012, https://www.usda.gov/media/blog/2012/12/7/secretarys-column-ensuring-safe-food-supply-americans, archived at https://perma.cc/KM4F-6QRC.

11. Hospitalization and illness episode data for typically chronic illnesses attributable to tobacco smoking, obesity, and alcohol use are not available.

12. G. Bergen, L. H. Chen, M. Warner, and L.A. Fingerhut, *Injury in the United States: 2007 Chartbook* (Hyattsville, MD: National Center for Health Statistics, 2008), https://www.cdc.gov/nchs/data/misc/injury2007.pdf.

13. CDC, "Multistate Outbreak of Listeriosis"; CDC, "Incidence and Trends of Foodborne Illness, 2011," January 22, 2013, https://web.archive.org/web/20151004055640/http://www.cdc.gov:80/features/dsfoodnet/.

14. International Food Information Council Foundation, "2012 Food & Health Survey: Consumer Attitudes toward Food Safety, Nutrition & Health," 89, http://www.foodinsight.org/Content/3840/2012%20IFIC%20Food%20and%20Health%20Survey%20Report%20of%20Findings%20(for%20website).pdf, archived at https://perma.cc/YMH4-UPAH; International Food Information Council Foundation, "2014 Food & Health Survey: The Pulse of America's Diet: From Beliefs to Behavior," 72, http://www.foodinsight.org/sites/default/files/FINAL%202014%20Food%20and%20Health%20Survey%20Executive%20Summary_0.pdf, archived at https://perma.cc/MPA9-6532; FDA, "2010 Food Safety Survey," https://www.fda.gov/downloads/Food/FoodScienceResearch/ConsumerBehaviorResearch/UCM407008.pdf, archived at https://perma.cc/QGS9-P3MK. These surveys are consistent with other contemporaneous polls. A 2010 CBS News poll found that 16 percent of respondents were "not too confident or not at all confident in the safety of their food." Brian Montopoli, "Poll: Most Not Fully Confident in Food Safety," CBS News, January 9, 2010, https://www.cbsnews.com/news/poll-most-not-fully-confident-in-food-safety/, archived at http://perma.cc/7TNV-29DJ. A 2014 Harris poll found that 86 percent of survey respondents were "seriously concerned" or "somewhat concerned" about food recalls due to health or safety concerns. Harris Poll, "Nearly Three-Quarters of Americans Looking to Government for More Food Safety Oversight," *PRNewswire*, February 5, 2014, https://www.prnewswire.com/news-releases/nearly-three-quarters-of-americans-looking-to-government-for-more-food-safety-oversight-243648081.html/, archived at https://perma.cc/F79F-RYZA. A 2008 Gallup poll found that 29 percent of respondents asked about how much confidence they had in the federal government to ensure the safety of the food supply in the US said "none" or "not much at all." Gallup, "Nutrition and Food," http://news.gallup.com/poll/6424/nutrition-food.aspx?version=print, archived at https://perma.cc/ZWS8-662P. See also Sara B. Fein et al., "Trends in US Consumers' Safe Handling and Consumption of Food and their Risk Perceptions 1988–2010," *Journal of Food Protection* 74, no. 9 (2011): 1513–23.

15. Marion Nestle, *Safe Food: The Politics of Food Safety* (Berkeley: University of California Press, 2010), loc. 372, Kindle. See also Unni Kjaernes, Arne Dulsrud, and Christian Poppe, "Contestation over Food Safety: The Significance of Consumer Trust," in *What's the Beef? The Contested Governance of European Food Safety*, ed. Christopher Ansell and David Vogel (Cambridge, MA: MIT Press, 2006), 61–79; Lawrence Busch, "Grades and Standards in the Social Construction of Food," in *The Politics of Food*, ed. Marianne Elisabeth Lien and Brigitte Nerlich (Oxford, UK: Berg, 2004), 163–78. For an excellent introduction to the literature on risk perception, see Richard V. Ericson and Aaron Doyle, *Uncertain Business* (Toronto: University of Toronto Press, 2004), 9–15.

16. This and the next four paragraphs rely on Booth and Brown, *Eating Dangerously*, loc. 580;

Association of Public Health Laboratories, "Success Stories"; McCollum, "Multistate Outbreak"; Alicia Cronquist, email message to the author, September 12, 2017.

17. Bronstein and Griffin, "Third-Deadliest US Food Outbreak."

18. FDA, "Environmental Assessment: Factors Potentially Contributing to the Contamination of Fresh Whole Cantaloupe Implicated in a Multi-State Outbreak of Listeriosis," October 19, 2011, https://web.archive.org/web/20150605210147/http://www.fda.gov/Food/RecallsOutbreaksEmergencies/Outbreaks/ucm276247.htm.

19. FDA, "Environmental Assessment"; Kathryn M. Mogen, "Memorandum to the File on the Environmental Assessment," FDA, December 15, 2011, 14, https://www.fda.gov/ucm/groups/fdagov-public/@fdagov-afda-orgs/documents/document/ucm291076.pdf, archived at https://perma.cc/V7Z5-4HCX; House of Representatives, "Report," 3; *U.S. v. Jensen, Rule 11(c)(1)(A) and (B) Plea Agreement and Statement of Facts Relevant to Sentencing*, Crim. No. 13-mj-01138-MEH (Dist. Ct. Colo., filed October 22, 2013), https://www.justice.gov/sites/default/files/usao-co/legacy/2013/10/23/US%20v%20Jensen%20COP.pdf, archived at https://perma.cc/J28C-6J3L; Bronstein and Griffin, "Third-Deadliest US Food Outbreak." David Gombas, a leading expert on food safety in the fresh produce sector, notes that, although precooling to remove field heat has benefits for extending the life of melons by retarding softening and potentially reducing the growth of some pathogens, it does not reduce condensation, which is the result of warm air coming into contact with a cold surface, not cold air coming into contact with a warm surface. David Gombas, personal communication with the author, August 28, 2017.

20. "Results of the FDA-Led Root Cause Investigation," 20; FDA, "Environmental Assessment," 2; Michael Booth, "Listeria Probe Blasts Farm, the FDA Says Unsanitary Handling Conditions at Jensen Were the 'Root Cause' of the Fatal Outbreak," *Denver Post*, October 20, 2011, A1; "Exclusive: Jensen Farms to React to Lawsuit, Recall," *News 7*, September 6, 2011, https://www.thedenverchannel.com/news/exclusive-jensen-farms-react-to-lawsuit-recall, archived at https://perma.cc/YCD7-9YVY; James Andrews, "Jensen Farms Files for Bankruptcy," *Food Safety News*, May 26, 2012, http://www.foodsafetynews.com/2012/05/jensen-farms-files-for-bankruptcy/#.Wng9u6inGUk, archived at https://perma.cc/6MAF-ESXR.

21. CDC, "Deadly Listeria Outbreak Halted in Record Time," November 1, 2011, https://web.archive.org/web/20140919134817/http://www.cdc.gov/24-7/savinglives/listeria/; Jane Allen, "Tainted Cantaloupes behind Deadliest Food-Borne Outbreak," ABC News, November 3, 2011, http://abcnews.go.com/Health/Health/cantaloupes-tied-deadliest-food-outbreak/print?id=14874373, archived at https://perma.cc/SC4R-LBKD; Dan Flynn, "Oyster-Borne Typhoid Fever Killed 150 in Winter of 1924–25," *Food Safety News*, March 28, 2012, http://www.foodsafetynews.com/2012/03/editors-note-in-the-winter/#.Wng_56inGUk, archived at https://perma.cc/GF2X-V59T.

22. James Gorny, telephone interview by the author, August 8, 2016; Forest Lewis, telephone interview by the author, June 10, 2015.

23. Pritzker Law, "Jensen Brothers Face Charges for Selling Cantaloupe Contaminated with Listeria," *Food Poisoning Law Blog*, September 26, 2013, archived at https://perma.cc/6VUK-DHKP; James Andrews, "Farmers in Cantaloupe Outbreak Sentenced to Probation, House Arrest, Fines, *Food Safety News*, http://www.foodsafetynews.com/2014/01/farmers-in-cantaloupe-listeria-outbreak-sentenced-to-probation-house-arrest-fines/#.WniUDKinGUk, archived at https://perma.cc/5JA6-QK7Z; for more details on the *Park* doctrine, see the discussion of criminal prosecution of food company executives in chapter 8.

24. Gorny, interview; Lewis, interview; Marler Clark, "Multistate Outbreak of Salmonella Linked to Cantaloupe," *Foodborne Illness Outbreak Database*, July 12, 2012, http://www.outbreakdatabase.com/search/?vehicle=cantaloupe, archived at https://perma.cc/4UPV-5TYS. Compare FDA, "Guidance for Industry: Guide to Minimize Microbial Food Safety Hazards of Melons; Draft Guidance" (citing only ten outbreaks associated with Cantaloupe melons between 1996 and 2008), https://www.fda.gov/food/guidanceregulation/ucm174171.htm, archived at https://perma.cc/XL4H-5H2K. McCollum, "Multistate Outbreak"; Brown and Booth, *Eating Dangerously*, locs. 121, 1455–56, 2562–64; FDA, "Eric and Ryan Jensen Charged with Introducing Tainted Cantaloupe into Interstate Commerce," September 26, 2013, http://wayback.archive-it.org/7993/20180126095407/https://www.fda.gov/ICECI/CriminalInvestigations/ucm374349.htm; FDA, "Eric and Ryan Jensen Plead Guilty to All Counts of Introducing Tainted Cantaloupe into Interstate Commerce," October 22, 2013, http://wayback.archive-it.org/7993/20180125150727/https://www.fda.gov/iceci/criminalinvestigations/ucm373174.htm. See also *U.S. v. Jensen, Rule Plea Agreement*.

25. Jeff Benedict, *Poisoned: The True Story of the Deadly E. coli Outbreak that Changed the Way Americans Eat* (New York: February Books, 2011) x; Bill Marler, "Brianne Kiner—The 1993 Jack in the Box *E. coli* Outbreak," Marler Clark, https://billmarler.com/key_case/jack-in-the-box-e-coli-outbreak/, archived at https://perma.cc/2CXZ-YWTG.

26. Primus Labs, "Outbreak"; Marler, interview; Marler, "Three Years."

27. Restatement (Second) of Torts, Section 402A (Philadelphia: American Law Institute, 1992); Denis Stearns, "Chain of Distribution Liability: Tag, You're It," Marler Clark, https://marlerclark.com/pdfs/chain-of-distribution-liability.pdf, archived at https://perma.cc/M8KJ-PUXS; Marler, interview; Bill Marler, "Why Retailers in Colorado Are Ultimately Responsible for Selling Listeria-Tainted Cantaloupe That Sickened 40—Killing Nine," *Marler Blog*, April 28, 2013, http://www.marlerblog.com/legal-cases/why-a-retailer-in-colorado-is-ultimately-responsible-for-listeria-tainted-cantaloupe-that-sickened-40-killing-nine/, archived at https://perma.cc/G736-3B2U; Denis Stearns, "Contaminated Fresh Produce and Product Liability: A Law-in-Action Perspective," in Xuetong Fan et al., *Microbial Safety of Fresh Produce* (Ames, IA: Wiley-Blackwell, 2009), 385–98.

28. Marler, interview; Andrews, "Jensen Farms Files for Bankruptcy"; Tim Linden, "Liability Insurance: How Much Is Enough?" *Produce News*, May 31, 2012, http://producenews.com/news-dep-menu/test-featured/7945-liability-insurance-how-much-is-enough, archived at https://perma.cc/7TDX-E5DV; Marler, "Three Years."

29. Marler, interview; Andrews, "Jensen Farms Files for Bankruptcy"; Kurt Niland, "Jensen Farms Cantaloupe Victims Reach Settlement with Walmart," *Righting Injustice*, May 15, 2014, http://www.rightinginjustice.com/news/2014/05/15/jensen-farms-cantaloupe-victims-reach-settlement-with-walmart/, archived at https://perma.cc/K9QW-KXHB; Coral Beach, "Victims Settle with Kroger, Frontera; Dismiss Primus," *The Packer*, February 11, 2015, https://www.thepacker.com/article/updated-victims-settle-kroger-frontera-dismiss-primus, archived at https://perma.cc/SQ6X-QLCE; Steven Paulson, "Denver Judge Settles Most Wrongful-Death Lawsuits in 2011 Listeria Outbreak that Killed 33," Associated Press, March 11, 2015, archived at https://perma.cc/UH88-WK2E; Marler, "Three Years."

30. Marler, interview.

31. Bill Marler, "FSMA: The End of My 20-Year Law Practice? Let's Hope So!" *Marler Blog*, March 9, 2014, http://www.marlerblog.com/case-news/fsma-the-end-of-my-20-year-law-practice-lets-hope-so/, archived at https://perma.cc/66EH-5XQ6.

32. *Contaminated Food: Private Sector Accountability, Hearing before the Subcommittee on Oversight and Investigations of the Committee on Energy and Commerce*, 110th Cong. 74–82 (statement of Bill Marler) (February 26, 2008), 74–82; Bill Marler, "Put Me Out of Business—Please—2007," *Marler Blog*, June 9, 2007, http://www.marlerblog.com/lawyer-oped/put-me-out-of-business-please-2007/, archived at https://perma.cc/HZ9M-JH8Q.

33. Primus Labs, "Outbreak," 62; Bronstein and Griffin, "Third-Deadliest US Food Outbreak"; Elizabeth Weise, "Listeria-Linked Cantaloupe Farm Had Rated High in Audit," *USA Today*, October 21, 2011, https://web.archive.org/web/20111106011014/http://yourlife.usatoday.com/fitness-food/safety/story/2011-10-20/Listeria-linked-farm-had-rated-high-in-third-party-audit/50844856/1, archived at https://perma.cc/Z4FW-WD44

34. Committee on Energy and Commerce to FDA commissioner Margaret Hamburg, 112th Cong., *Marler Blog*, January 10, 2012, http://www.marlerblog.com/uploads/image/forMarler.pdf, archived at https://perma.cc/75PK-N5ZP.

35. Primus Labs, audit certificate for Jensen Farms; Primus Labs, "Outbreak," 31, 33.

36. Primus Labs, "Outbreak" 17, 19, 21, 22, 27, 28, 29, 30, 33; Jim Prevor, "Cantaloupe Crisis Analysis: While 'Blame the Auditor' Frenzy Rages, It Pays to Look at Best Practices vs. Standard Practices," *Jim Prevor's Perishable Pundit* (blog), October 23, 2011, http://www.perishablepundit.com/index.php?article=2677, archived at https://perma.cc/N6X8-VU3L.

37. Primus Labs, "Outbreak," 23, 25, 26, 49,54; Jim Prevor, "Prevor Pundits Mailbag: Food Safety Must Be an Executive Imperative: 24/7/365," *Jim Prevor's Perishable Pundit* (blog), October 27, 2011, http://www.perishablepundit.com/index.php?article=2686, archived at https://perma.cc/B5VS-2D6Z; Jim Prevor, "When a Buyer Is Short of Product . . . Do We Have a Plan to Ensure Food Safety?" *Jim Prevor's Perishable Pundit* (blog), October 23, 2011, http://www.perishablepundit.com/index.php?article=2681, archived at https://perma.cc/C63T-83AU. On food safety culture, see Frank Yiannas, *Food Safety Culture: Creating a Behavior-Based Food Safety Management System* (New York: Springer, 2009); Douglas A. Powell, Casey J. Jacob, and Benjamin J. Chapman, "Enhancing Food Safety Culture to Reduce Rates of Foodborne Illness," *Food Control* 22, no. 6 (June 2011): 817–22.

38. Primus Labs, "Outbreak," 31, 33, 35.

39. Coral Beach, "Walmart Says Primus, Others Should Pay in Listeria Case," *The Packer*, February 20, 2014, archived at https://perma.cc/6X79-KKCS; "Kroger Claims Primus Has Primary Liability for Deadly Listeria Outbreak," *Food Safety News*, June 9, 2014, http://www.foodsafetynews.com/2014/06/kroger-says-primus-has-primary-liability-for-deadly-outbreak/#.WnjGQ6inGUk, archived at https://perma.cc/7TAU-NUR6; Primus Labs, audit certificate for Jensen Farms; Jim Prevor, "When It Comes to Audits . . . Retailers Get What They Specify," *Jim Prevor's Perishable Pundit* (blog), October 23, 2011, http://www.perishablepundit.com/index.php?article=2679, archived at https://perma.cc/R73P-XKBF.

40. According to Primus, in the Jensen Farms case, Walmart appears to have violated its own company policy, which requires all fresh produce suppliers to pass audits that include detailed evaluation of a facility's food safety risk management system, known as a Hazard Analysis Critical Control (HACCP) system, but Walmart accepted a packinghouse audit without HACCP. Primus Labs, "Outbreak," 17–19, 29; Jim Prevor, "Wal-Mart Uses New Food Safety Initiative as a Marketing Tool," *Jim Prevor's Perishable Pundit* (blog), February 8, 2008, http://www.perishablepundit.com/index.php?date=02/08/08&pundit=1 https://perma.cc/HS8T-2ZGM; Kroger, "Kroger Receives the Prestigious Black Pearl Award for Food Safety," *PRNewswire*, May 15, 2012, https://www.prnewswire.com/news-releases/kroger-receives-the-prestigious

-black-pearl-award-for-food-safety-151543385.html, archived at https://perma.cc/9GJ6-5FC9; Jim Prevor, "Wal-Mart Uses New Food Safety Initiative as a Marketing Tool"; Prevor, "When It Comes to Audits."

41. The vice president for food safety at Walmart was reluctant during a January 8, 2015, telephone interview by the author to discuss details of how the company reviews third-party audits and refused the author's requests for a second interview. The director of food safety and regulatory compliance at Kroger refused to respond to the author's requests for an interview.

42. Primus Labs, "Outbreak," 56; Jim Prevor, "Industry Representatives from All Sectors Weigh In on Criminal Prosecution in the Jensen Farms Case, but Trade Associations Remain Silent," *Jim Prevor's Perishable Pundit* (blog), October 28, 2013, http://www.perishablepundit .com/?date=10/28/2013&pundit=5, archived at https://perma.cc/L3AU-RTGF; Jim Prevor, "Pundit's Mailbag—Cantaloupe Leaders Provide Roadmap to Safer Future," *Jim Prevor's Perishable Pundit* (blog), May 2, 2008, http://www.perishablepundit.com/index.php?date=05/02/ 08&pundit=5, archived at https://perma.cc/3JSA-WYBF.

43. Prevor, "Cantaloupe Leaders"; Prevor, "Cantaloupe Crisis Analysis"; Primus, "Outbreak," 14, 18, 39, 49, 54

44. For an introduction to regulatory governance theory, see Graham Burchell, Colin Gordon, and Peter Miller, eds., *The Foucault Effect: Studies in Governmentality* (Chicago: University of Chicago Press, 1991); Ian Ayres and John Braithwaite, *Responsive Regulation: Transcending the Deregulation Debate* (Oxford: Oxford University Press, 1992); Jody Freeman, "The Private Role in Public Governance," *New York University Law Review* 75, no. 3 (2000): 543–675; Julia Black, "Critical Reflections on Regulation," *Australian Journal of Legal Philosophy* 27, no. 1 (2002): 1–36; Jan Kooiman, *Governing as Governance* (London: Sage Publications, 2003); Anne Mette Kjaer, *Governance* (Cambridge, UK: Polity Press, 2004); Kenneth W. Abbott and Duncan Snidal, "The Governance Triangle: Regulatory Standards Institutions and the Shadow of the State," in *The Politics of Global Regulation*, ed. Walter Mattli and Ngaire Woods (Princeton, NJ: Princeton University Press, 2009), 44–88; David Levi-Faur, ed., *The Oxford Handbook of Governance* (Oxford: Oxford University Press, 2011); Harm Schepel, "Rules of Recognition: A Legal Constructivist Approach to Transnational Private Regulation," in *Private International Law and Global Governance*, ed. Horatia Muir Watt and Diego P. Fernandez Arroyo (Oxford: Oxford University Press, 2014), 201–10; Catherine E. Rudder, A. Lee Fritschler, and Yon Jung Choi, *Public Policymaking by Private Organizations* (Washington, DC: Brookings Institution, 2016); and Christopher Ansell and Jacob Torfing, eds., *Handbook on Theories of Governance* (Cheltenham, UK: Edward Elgar, 2016). For an introduction to governance theory applied to food safety, see Klementina Krezieva and Pieternel Luning, "The Influence of Context on Food Safety Governance: Bridging the Gap between Policy and Quality Management," in *Hybridization of Food Governance: Trends, Types and Results*, ed. Paul Verbruggen and Tetty Havinga (Cheltenham, UK: Edward Elgar, 2017), 156–79.

45. Donella H. Meadows, *Thinking in Systems: A Primer* (White River Junction, VT: Chelsea Green, 2008), loc. 327, Kindle. For an elaborate account of food safety governance as a system, see Yasmine Motarjemi, "Modern Approach to Food Safety Management," in *Encyclopedia of Food Safety*, ed. Yasmine Motarjemi, Gerald Moy, and Ewen Todd (Amsterdam: Elsevier, 2013), 4:1–12.

46. For an introduction to network theory in regulatory governance, see Walter W. Powell, "Neither Market nor Hierarchy: Network Forms of Organization," *Research in Organizational Behavior* 12 (1990): 295–36; Jacob Torfing, "Governance Network Theory: Towards a Second

Generation," *European Political Science* 4 (2005): 305–15; Abraham Newman and David Zaring, "Regulatory Networks: Power, Legitimacy, and Compliance," in *Interdisciplinary Perspectives on International Law and International Relations: The State of the Art*, ed. Jeffrey Dunoff and Mark Pollack (Cambridge: Cambridge University Press, 2012), 244–65; Patrick Kenis, "Network," in *Handbook on Theories of Governance*, ed. Christopher Ansell and Jacob Torfing (Cheltenham, UK: Edward Elgar, 2016), 149–57. For a fascinating analysis of the complexity of China's food safety system, see John K. Yasuda, *On Feeding the Masses: An Anatomy of Regulatory Failure in China* (Cambridge: Cambridge University Press, 2018).

47. For an introduction to complex adaptive systems in regulatory governance, see J. B. Ruhl, "Law's Complexity: A Primer," *Georgia State University Law Review* 24, no. 4 (2008): 885–911; Christopher Koliba, Lasse Gerrits, Mary Lee Rhodes, and John W. Meek, "Complexity Theory and Systems Analysis," in *Handbook on Theories of Governance*, ed. Christopher Ansell and Jacob Torfing (Cheltenham, UK: Edward Elgar, 2016), 364–79; Paul Craig, "Global Networks and Shared Administration," in *Research Handbook on Global Administrative Law*, ed. Sabino Cassese (Cheltenham, UK: Edward Elgar, 2016), 153.

Chapter Two

1. Norman Shaftel, "A History of the Purification of Milk in New York, or, 'How Now, Brown Cow,'" in *Sickness and Health in America: Readings in the History of Medicine and Public Health*, ed. Judith Walzer Leavitt and Ronald L. Numbers (Madison: University of Wisconsin Press, 1978), 277–78 (I owe the phrase "pioneer effort" to Shaftel); John J. Dillon, *Seven Decades of Milk: A History of New York's Dairy Industry* (New York: Orange Judd, 1941), 20; John Duffy, *The Sanitarians: A History of American Public Health* (Urbana: University of Illinois Press, 1990), 184; Ralph Selitzer, *The Dairy Industry in America* (New York: Magazines for Industry, 1976), 37; "Hudson-Mohawk Genealogical and Family Memoirs: Hartley," Schenectady Digital History Archive, http://www.schenectadyhistory.org/families/hmgfm/hartley.html, archived at https://perma.cc/YP3Z-9AUP.

2. Duffy, *Sanitarians*, 183–84; John Duffy, *A History of Public Health in New York City 1625–1866* (New York: Russell Sage Foundation, 1968), 427–28; Selitzer, *Dairy Industry*, 34–37, 123; Ron Schmid, *The Untold Story of Milk: The History, Politics and Science of Nature's Perfect Food: Raw Milk from Pasture-Fed Cows* (Washington, DC: New Trends Publishing, 2009), loc. 465, Kindle; E. Melanie Dupuis, *Nature's Perfect Food: How Milk Became America's Drink* (New York: New York University Press, 2002), 67; Robert M. Hartley, *An Historical, Scientific and Practical Essay on Milk as an Article of Human Sustenance* (New York: Jonathan Leavitt, 1842), 234.

3. Dupuis, *Nature's Perfect Food*, loc. 392, James Harvey Young, *Pure Food: Securing the Federal Food and Drugs Act of 1906* (Princeton, NJ: Princeton University Press, 1989), 37; Duffy, *History 1625–1866*, 427–28, 434; Shaftel, "Short History," 278; Selitzer, *Dairy Industry*, 37; Hartley, *Essay on Milk*, 138–43, 148–52; Mitchell Okun, *Fair Play in the Marketplace: The First Battle for Pure Food and Drugs* (DeKalb: Northern Illinois University Press, 1986), 20n37. For a defense of the use of spent grains for cattle feed, see Baylen J. Linnekin, *Biting the Hands That Feed Us: How Fewer, Smarter Laws Would Make Our Food System More Sustainable* (Washington, DC: Island Press, 2016), loc. 690, Kindle.

4. Dupuis, *Nature's Perfect Food*, 451; Hartley, *Essay on Milk*, 247–48; Young, *Pure Food*, 39; Duffy, *History 1625–1866*, 427.

5. Hartley, *Essay on Milk*, 218–37, 239, 244–45, 330–31; Selitzer, *Dairy Industry*, 35. Compare Rowland Godfrey Freeman, "Address of the President," *Proceedings of the Third Annual Confer-*

ence of the American Association of Medical Milk Commissions, Atlantic City, NJ, June 7, 1909, 98 (stating that Hartley lost the child) (hereafter *Third Annual Conference*).

6. Shaftel, "Short History," 278–79; Hartley, *Essay on Milk,* 108; Duffy, *History 1625–1866,* 429. For a recent account of Hartley's campaign against distillery dairies, see Mark Kurlansky, *Milk! A 10,000-Year Food Fracas* (New York: Bloomsbury Publishing, 2018), locs. 2590–2620, Kindle.

7. Okun, *Fair Play,* 9–10, 18; Duffy, *History 1625–1866,* 429–30; Young, *Pure Food,* 36; Shaftel, "Short History," 279–80; Selitzer, *Dairy Industry,* 123; David Fox, "John Mullaly of New York (c. 1835–1915)," History of the Atlantic Cable and Undersea Communications from the First Submarine Cable of 1850 to the Worldwide Fiber Optic Network, archived at https://perma.cc/ Q238-X3XW.

8. Shaftel, "Short History," 280; Dillon, *Seven Decades,* 19; Selitzer, *Dairy Industry,* 124.

9. This paragraph and next draw from Duffy, *History 1625–1866,* 431–33; Okun, *Fair Play,* 18–25; Selitzer, *Dairy Industry,* 124; Young, *Pure Food,* 38; Shaftel, "Short History," 280.

10. Duffy, *History 1625–1866,* 435–36; Shaftel, "Short History," 280–81.

11. Duffy, *History 1625–1866,* 436–37; Shaftel, "Short History," 280–81; Selitzer, *Dairy Industry,* 125–26; Okun, *Fair Play,* 24–25 (see note 47 for legal citations); Dillon, *Seven Decades,* 19–20.

12. Duffy, *History 1625–1866,* 435–36; Shaftel, "Short History," 280–81; Selitzer, *Dairy Industry,* 125–26; Duffy, *History 1625–1866,* 437; Dillon, *Seven Decades,* 19–20; Okun, *Fair Play,* 43.

13. Wikipedia, s.v. "miasma theory," last modified January 28, 2018, https://en.wikipedia .org/wiki/Miasma_theory, archived at https://perma.cc/2594-CJRN; Duffy, *Sanitarians,* 67–68. On the advent of the germ theory of disease, see Alan L. Olmstead and Paul W. Rhode, *Arresting Contagion: Science, Policy, and Conflicts over Animal Disease Control* (Cambridge, MA: Harvard University Press, 2015), loc. 467, Kindle.

14. Manfred J. Waserman, "Henry L. Coit and the Certified Milk Movement in the Development of Modern Pediatrics," *Bulletin of the History of Medicine* 46 (1972): 364–90, 361; Shaftel, "Short History," 284; Mildred V. Naylor, "Henry Leber Coit: A Biographical Sketch," *Bulletin of the History of Medicine* 12 (July 1, 1942): 367–76, 367; Fred Rogers, "Henry Leber Coit: 1854–1917: Pioneer in Public Health," *Journal of the Medical Society of New Jersey* 52 (January 1955): 37; Jacqueline H. Wolf, "Saving Babies and Mothers: Pioneering Efforts to Decrease Infant and Maternal Mortality," in *Silent Victories: The History and Practice of Public Health in Twentieth Century America,* ed. John W. Ward and Christian Warren (Oxford: Oxford University Press, 2006), 140.

15. Henry L. Coit, "The Origin, General Plan, and Scope of the Medical Milk Commission," in *Proceedings of the First Conference of the Medical Milk Commissions in the United States,* Atlantic City, NJ, June 3, 1907, 10–11 (hereafter *First Conference*); Naylor, "Henry Leber Coit," 368; Rogers, "Henry Leber Coit," 37.

16. Milton J. Rosenau, *The Milk Question* (Boston: Houghton Mifflin, 1912), 1; John Spargo, *The Common Sense of the Milk Question* (New York: Macmillan, 1908), vii. See also Charles E. North, "Milk and Its Relation to Public Health," in *A Half Century of Public Health,* ed. Mazyck P. Ravenel (New York: American Public Health Association, 1921), 237–38.

17. Rosenau, *Milk Question,* 1–3. See also Herbert W. Conn, "The Milk Supply of Cities," *Popular Science Monthly* 55 (September 1899): 628; J. Scott MacNutt, *The Modern Milk Problem in Sanitation, Economics, and Agriculture* (New York: Macmillan, 1917), 1–5; W. K. Brainerd and W. L. Mallory, *Milk Standards: A Study in the Bacterial Count and the Dairy Score Card in City Milk Inspections* (Blacksburg, VA: Virginia Polytechnic Institute, 1911): 4–5; North, "Milk and Its Relation," 242, 257; Dupuis, *Nature's Perfect Food,* 73; Kendra Smith-Howard, *Pure and Modern Milk: An Environmental History since 1900* (Oxford: Oxford, 2014), 12.

18. Public Health and Marine Hospital Service of the United States, ed., *Milk and Its Relation*

to the Public Health, 2nd ed. (Washington, DC: Government Printing Office, 1912), chaps. 2–8, 20; Shaftel, "Short History," 277, 283; Rosenau, *Milk Question*, 3, 231–34; North, "Milk and Its Relation," 243–55; Waserman, "Henry L. Coit," 359; Selitzer, *Dairy Industry*, 35; Spargo, *Common Sense*, chap. 2; G. F. McCleary, *The Early History of the Infant Welfare Movement* (London: H. K. Lewis, 1933), 341; Dupuis, *Nature's Perfect Food*, 19–20, 47– 49, 64; Smith-Howard, *Pure and Modern Milk*, 15; Olmstead and Rhode, *Arresting Contagion*, loc. 4403; Bee Wilson, *Swindled: The Dark History of Food Fraud, from Poisoned Candy to Counterfeit Coffee* (Princeton, NJ: Princeton University Press, 2008), 158; Kwang-Sun Lee, "Infant Mortality Decline in the Late 19th and Early 20th Centuries: The Role of Market Milk," *Perspectives in Biology and Medicine* 50, no. 4 (Autumn 2007): 585–602; Jacqueline H. Wolf, "Low Breastfeeding Rates and Public Health in the United States," *American Journal of Public Health* 93, no. 12 (December 2003): 2000–2010.

19. Naylor, "Henry Leber Coit," 16; Rogers, "Henry Leber Coit," 37; Coit, "Origin,"11–12; Waserman, "Henry L. Coit," 362; Horatio N. Parker, *City Milk Supply* (New York: McGraw-Hill, 1917), 403; Schmid, *Untold Story*, loc. 640.

20. Shaftel, "Short History," 284; Waserman, "Henry L. Coit," 362–63 (dating the founding of the Essex County Medical Milk Commission to January 1893); Coit, "Origin," 12–17; Naylor, "Henry Leber Coit," 369 (dates founding to December 5 1892); Rogers, "Henry Leber Coit," 37. See also Archibald R. Ward, *Pure Milk and the Public Health: A Manual of Milk and Dairy Inspection* (Ithaca, NY: Taylor & Carpenter, 1909), 156–73; Schmid, *Untold Story*, loc. 643; John W. Kerr, "Certified Milk and Infants' Milk Depots," in Public Health and Marine-Hospital Service, *Milk and Its Relation to the Public Health*, 613–20. Before the founding of the Essex County Medical Milk Commission, physicians at the Harvard Medical School founded Walker-Gordon Laboratories in Boston in 1891 to supervise milk production and distribution. In 1892, William T. Sedgwick conducted the first bacterial analysis of a city milk supply in Boston. Selitzer, *Dairy Industry*, 132. See also McCleary, *Early History*, 61–67.

21. Coit, "Origin," 13; Waserman, "Henry L. Coit," 363–64; Naylor, "Henry Leber Coit," 369–70; Stephen Francisco, "Relations between Certified Milk and Market Milk," in *Proceedings of the Fifth Annual Conference of the American Association of Medical Milk Commissions*, Philadelphia, May 23–24, 1911, 48 (hereafter *Fifth Annual Conference*); Naylor, "Henry Leber Coit," 370; Waserman, "Henry L. Coit," 356n20; Rogers, "Henry Leber Coit," 38; Floy M'Ewen, "The Working Methods and the Results in Essex County, New Jersey, of the Work of the Medical Milk Commission," *First Conference*, 39.

22. Emma G. Coit, "Clean Milk," *Bulletin of the Medical Milk Commission of Essex County, New Jersey* 4, no. 2 (1923); Waserman, "Henry L. Coit," 365, 365n20; Rogers, "Henry Leber Coit," 38.

23. Waserman, "Henry L. Coit," 364–65. Francisco later trademarked the term. Waserman, "Henry L. Coit," 365; Parker, *City Milk Supply*, 404.

24. Waserman, "Henry L. Coit," 366–70; Rogers, "Henry Leber Coit," 38; Selitzer, *Dairy Industry*, 132, credits Walker-Gordon Laboratories in Boston with the idea of certified milk.

25. Parker, *City Milk Supply*, 408–23; For an example of debate and deliberation over the standards, see, e.g., "Proceedings of Third Session," in *First Conference*, 98–110.

26. Kerr, "Certified Milk," 613–28; Otto P. Geier, "Report of the Milk Commission of the Academy of Medicine, Cincinnati, Ohio," in *First Conference*, 21, 23; M'Ewen, "Working Methods," 34; Henry E. Tuley, "Report of the Jefferson County Milk Commission of Louisville, Ky.," in *First Conference*, 62; "Program of Second Session," *First Conference*, 70–71; Henry L. Coit, "The Medical Milk Commission, Its Organization, Its Minimum Requirements for Certifica-

tion, Its Scope of Work, and Its Extension," in *Third Annual Conference*, 58–59; Ward, *Pure Milk*, 164. Although the association occasionally appointed joint committees and met in joint session with the Certified Milk Producers' Association to discuss standards and obtain input from industry, the medical milk commissions affirmed their independence from producers when they rebuffed an attempt in 1915 by the latter group to share equal responsibility for developing and promulgating certified milk standards. "Joint Committee Report," in *Third Annual Conference*, 45; Waserman, "Henry L. Coit," 380. Some commissions were established in conjunction with or by civic groups. See, e.g., Ward, *Pure Milk*, 157 (milk commission in California established by a women's club).

27. Parker, *City Milk Supply*, 407; Philip K. Brown, "The Milk Commission of the San Francisco County Medical Society," in *Third Annual Conference*, 28; North, "Milk and Its Relation," 268; Smith-Howard, *Pure and Modern Milk*, 25; Waserman, "Henry L. Coit," 373.

28. David de Sola Pool, "Nathan Straus," *American Jewish Yearbook* 33 (1931–1932): 143; Nathan Straus, *Disease in Milk: The Remedy Pasteurization* (New York: Lina G. Straus, 1913), 53, 139; Julie Miller, "To Stop the Slaughter of the Babies: Nathan Straus and the Drive for Pasteurized Milk, 1893–1920," *New York History* 74, no. 2 (April 1993): 170.

29. Miller, "Stop the Slaughter," 163–64, 172–79; Selitzer, *Dairy Industry*, 133–34. The idea of a milk depot dates back at least to 1872, when temperance activists in Boston established milk bars—selling between one and two hundred gallons a day in the summer—to reduce the consumption of beer and liquor. Selitzer, *Dairy Industry*, 133. Moreover, Straus was not the first to establish an infant milk depot. In 1889, Dr. Henry Koplik opened a milk depot that dispensed milk for children and provided instruction for mothers about infant hygiene. Selitzer, *Dairy Industry*, 133; Kerr, "Certified Milk," 629. At this time, similar institutions were emerging in Europe. Starting in 1890, several clinics in France, known as *consultations de nourrissons* (infant clinics), offered combined obstetric, maternity, and two years of pediatric care that strongly encouraged and supported breastfeeding and provided pasteurized milk for bottle-feeding when mothers were unable to breastfeed their babies. Beginning in 1892, also in France, milk dispensaries, known as *gouttes de lait* (drops of milk), offered pasteurized and modified milk at subsidized prices. Spargo, *Common Sense*, 187–96; Kerr, "Certified Milk," 634; Kerr, "The Relation of the Medical Milk Commission to the Establishment and Conduct of Infants' Milk Depots," in *Third Annual Conference*, 89.

30. Selitzer, *Dairy Industry*, 134–35; Shaftel, "Short History," 286; Parker, *City Milk Supply*, 266; North, "Milk and Its Relation," 279; Kerr, "Relation," 89; Kerr, "Certified Milk," 632; Straus, *Disease in Milk*, 101, 91 Miller, "Stop the Slaughter," 172.

31. Straus, *Disease in Milk*, 89, 171, 173, 135, 79; Miller, "Stop the Slaughter," 172–79. See also Kurlansky, *Milk!*, locs. 2857–2933

32. Selitzer, *Dairy Industry*, 133–35, 157–58; Parker, *City Milk Supply*, 269; Shaftel, "Short History," 286; MacNutt, *Modern Milk Problem*, 108, 113; North, "Milk and Its Relation," 271, 274; Waserman, "Henry L. Coit," 376. In the 1850s, Louis Pasteur had discovered that heating milk would postpone souring, and he applied his findings in the 1860s to develop techniques for preserving wine. In 1887, a German chemist, Franz von Soxhlet, developed a device for home sterilization of milk and advocated the use of boiled milk for infant feeding. American physicians Abraham Jacobi and Rowland Freeman championed the use of Soxhlet's home sterilization method in America. In 1889, Dr. Henry Koplik opened the first infant milk depot in the United States, distributing pasteurized milk. His initiative was admired and followed by Straus, who dramatically scaled up Koplik's modest effort. Selitzer, *Dairy Industry*, 132–33. See also North, "Milk and Its Relation," 270–77; Shaftel, "Short History," 286–87.

33. Smith-Howard, *Pure and Modern Milk*, 33; Waserman, "Henry L. Coit," 373, 376–77, 380, 382–83, 386; North, "Milk and Its Relation," 272–73, 276–77; Parker, *City Milk Supply*, 267; Selitzer, *Dairy Industry*, 157; Straus, *Disease in Milk*, 88, 168; Charles E. North, "The Limitations of Certified Milk," *Fifth Annual Conference*, 32. The contemporary controversy over whether to permit the sale of raw milk can be traced back to this rivalry between the certified milk movement and advocates of pasteurization. See, e.g., Schmid, *Untold Story*.

34. Kerr, "Certified Milk," 635.

35. Miller, "Stop the Slaughter," 166, 184, 173–74, 181; Straus, *Disease in Milk*, 101, 198–99.

36. Selitzer, *Dairy Industry*, 159–61; Smith-Howard, *Pure and Modern Milk*, 33; John Duffy, *A History of Public Health in New York City 1866–1966* (New York: Sage, 1974), 258, 274, 466–68; North, "Milk and Its Relation," 279, de Sola Pool, "Nathan Straus," 144; Miller, "Stop the Slaughter," 163, 184.

37. Waserman, "Henry L. Coit," 377–89; Schmid, *Untold Story*, loc. 677; Ernest Kelly, "Certified Milk, Past, Present, and Future," in *Proceedings of the Sixth Annual Conference of the American Association of Medical Milk Commissions*, Louisville, KY, April 30–May 1, 1912, 165–66.

38. Spargo, *Common Sense*, 209; Parker, *City Milk Supply*, 370–74; Selitzer, *Dairy Industry*, 126; North, "Milk and Its Relation," 283, 286; Shaftel, "Short History," 282–83; MacNutt, *Modern Milk Problem*, 65; Duffy, *History 1866–1966*, 128; Selitzer, *Dairy Industry*, 129; Marc T. Law and Gary D. Libecap, "The Determinants of Progressive Era Reform: The Pure Food and Drugs Act of 1906," in *Corruption and Reform: Lessons from America's Economic History*, ed. Edward L. Glaeser and Claudia Goldin (Chicago: University of Chicago Press, 2006), 327–29; Peter Barton Hutt and Peter Barton Hutt II, "A History of Government Regulation of Adulteration and Misbranding of Food," *Food Drug Cosmetic Law Journal* 39 (1984): 40; Parker, *City Milk Supply*, 373; Duffy, *Sanitarians*, 140, 153.

39. MacNutt, *Modern Milk Problem*, 68, 88. For a general discussion of the inadequacy of private efforts in the eradication of animal-borne disease, see Olmstead and Rhode, *Arresting Contagion*.

40. Duffy, *History 1866–1966*, 107–8, 132–36; New York City Department of Health and Mental Hygiene, *Protecting Public Health in New York City: 200 Years of Leadership 1805–2005* (New York: Bureau of Communications, Department of Health and Mental Hygiene, 2005), 16, http://www1.nyc.gov/assets/doh/downloads/pdf/bicentennial/historical-booklet.pdf, archived at https://perma.cc/K6R5-KB4F; Dupuis, *Nature's Perfect Food*, loc. 802; Chester L. Roadhouse and James L. Henderson, *The Market-Milk Industry* (New York: McGraw-Hill, 1950), 6–7; Thomas Darlington, "Municipal Regulation of the Production and Sale of Market Milk," in *Third Annual Conference*, 122–23; Selitzer, *Dairy Industry*, 156; Shaftel, "Short History," 285, 287; Dillon, *Seven Decades*, 22–23. "New York's Milk Supply Declared to Be Pure," *New York Times*, December 2, 1906, 1, reports that the New York City Health Department's dairy inspection program began in early 1905. Compare Selitzer, *Dairy Industry*, 156 (stating that the program began in 1906).

41. Darlington, "Municipal Regulation," 122–23; Spargo, *Common Sense*, 283.

42. "New York's Milk Supply"; Selitzer, *Dairy Industry*, 156; Spargo, *Common Sense*, 286.

43. Spargo, *Common Sense*, 284–90; Selitzer, *Dairy Industry*, 161; Shaftel, "Short History," 287; Dupuis, *Nature's Perfect Food*, loc. 1474, 1515.

44. Parker, *City Milk Supply*, 372; Herbert W. Conn, "A Scheme for Organization and Control of the Milk in Small Communities," in *Fifth Annual Conference*, 109; Ward, *Pure Milk*, 171–72; Spargo, *Common Sense*, 205–17; Selitzer, *Dairy Industry*, 159; Smith-Howard, *Pure and Modern Milk*, 31–32; North, "Milk and Its Relation," 276–77; J. H. Mason Knox, "The Recent

Campaign for Clean Milk in Baltimore," in *Proceedings of the Second Annual Conference of the American Association of Medical Milk Commissions*, Chicago, June 1, 1908, 40 (hereafter *Second Annual Conference*).

45. Parker, *City Milk Supply*, 377–78; Duffy, *Sanitarians*, 153–54; Dupuis, *Nature's Perfect Food*, loc. 1525; Conn, "Scheme," 109; D. Steffen, "How Regulation Came to Be: Pasteurization," *Daily Kos*, March 25, 2012, https://www.dailykos.com/stories/2012/03/25/1076932/-How-regulation-came-to-be-Pasteurization#, archived at https://perma.cc/Q4QB-96EF; Alan Czaplicki, "'Pure Milk Is Better Than Purified Milk': Pasteurization and Milk Purity in Chicago, 1908–1916," *Social Science History* 31, no. 3 (Fall 2007), 411–33.

46. Pure Food and Drug Act, 34 Stat. 768 (1906), § 7. For a history of earlier federal efforts to regulate zoonotic disease in cattle, see Olmstead and Rhode, *Arresting Contagion*.

47. *Dade v. United States*, 40 App. D.C. 94 (D.C. Ct. App. 1913); *United States v. Sprague*, 208 F. 419 (E.D.N.Y. 1913); *United States v. Two Hundred Cases of Adulterated Tomato Catsup*, 211 F. 780 (Dist. Ct. Ore. 1914); Mastin G. White and Otis H. Gates, *Decisions of Courts in Cases Under the Federal Food and Drugs Act* (Washington, DC: US Government Printing Office, 1934); Hutt, "History," 58; Harvey W. Wiley, "National Inspection of Milk," in Public Health and Marine Hospital Service, *Milk and Its Relation to the Public Health*, 743.

48. Hutt, "History," 61–62; Parker, *City Milk Supply*, 276–77.

49. Parker, *City Milk Supply*, 173, 247; Ward, *Pure Milk*, 102, 106; MacNutt, *Modern Milk Problem*, 70–75; Edward H. Webster, "Sanitary Inspection and Its Bearing on Clean Milk," in Public Health and Marine Hospital Service, *Milk and Its Relation to the Public Health*, 564–65. By 1914, the dairy scorecard had been adopted by more than two hundred cities and twenty-five states. Parker, *City Milk Supply*, 174; Selitzer, *Dairy Industry*, 157.

50. Selitzer, *Dairy Industry*, 38, 112, 158–59; "H. P. Hood Dairy Mogul & Colonel Stark of Live Free or Die Fame," YouTube (video), 4:37, posted by Larry Seaman, November 11, 2009, https://www.youtube.com/watch?v=29ut6Cv5RqU; North, "Milk and Its Relation," 274; Dupuis, *Nature's Perfect Food*, loc. 318, 1680–1700.

51. Parker, *City Milk Supply*, 231–33, 378; Conn, "Milk Supply," 629–30, 627; Charles C. Johnson, "The Milk Supply as a National Problem," *American Review of Reviews* 36 (November 1907): 588–90; MacNutt, *Modern Milk Problem*, 55; Samuel C. Prescott, "The Production of Clean Milk from a Practical Standpoint," *Charities and the Commons* 16 (April–October 1906), 489; Selitzer, *Dairy Industry*, 158.

52. Prescott, "Production of Clean Milk," 489–90; Parker, *City Milk Supply*, 231; Johnson, "Milk Supply," 590.

53. Johnson, "Milk Supply," 589; MacNutt, *Modern Milk Problem*, 55; Conn, "Milk Supply," 629; Parker, *City Milk Supply*, 378; Prescott, "Production of Clean Milk," 489; Rollin M. Perkins, "Unwholesome Food as a Source of Liability," *Iowa Law Bulletin* (1919–1920): 86.

54. Spargo, *Common Sense*, 287–88.

55. Selitzer, *Dairy Industry*, 166; "Charles E. North Papers," USDA Special Collections, http://specialcollections.nal.usda.gov/guide-collections/charles-e-north-papers, archived at https://perma.cc/M2DA-RZD7.

56. Leslie C. Frank, "A National Program for the Unification of Milk Control," *Public Health Reports (1896–1970)* 41, no. 31 (July 30, 1926): 1583–86.

57. Selitzer, *Dairy Industry*, 159; Dupuis, *Nature's Perfect Food*, loc. 1453; MacNutt, *Modern Milk Problem*, 78.

58. Dupuis, *Nature's Perfect Food*, loc. 1444–1553; North, "Milk and Its Relation," 287. The

commission was disbanded in 1921. Extracts from Reports Commission on Milk Standards, Report, 1936, Charles E. North Papers, Special Collections, National Agricultural Library, Washington, DC, archived at https://perma.cc/7FQ4-37JR.

59. Duffy, *Sanitarians*, 130, 134; Okun, *Fair Play*, x, 90–91; Selitzer, *Dairy Industry*, 182; "History of ASTHO," Association of State and Territorial Health Officials, http://www.astho .org/About/History/, archived at https://perma.cc/9MQT-5KLR; William Horwitz, "The Role of the A.O.A.C. in the Passage of the Federal Food and Drugs Act of 1906," *Food Drug Cosmetic Law Journal* 11 (1958): 77–85; W. B. White, "A.O.A.C. Methods of Analysis," *Food Drug Cosmetic Law Quarterly* 1 (1946): 442–56; Henry Lepper, "Methodology," *Food Drug Cosmetic Law Journal* 7 (1952): 783–92; Joseph Corby, "Association of Food and Drug Officials: Boots on the Ground for Food Safety," *Food Safety Magazine*, December 2013–January 2014, https:// www.foodsafetymagazine.com /magazine-archive1/december-2013january-2014/association -of-food-and-drug-officials-boots-on-the-ground-for-food-safety/, archived at https:// perma.cc/4RZJ-YX9Y; American Dairy Science Association, "History of ADSA," https:// www.adsa.org/AboutADSA /MoreAboutADSA /History.aspx, archived at https://perma.cc/ X5JK-RN3V; International Association for Food Protection, *History 1911–2011* (Des Moines, IA: IAFP, 2011), 5–7, https://www.foodprotection.org/downloads/history-book.pdf https:// perma.cc/5FZK-JNN9; American Veterinary Medical Association, "History of the AVMA," https://www.avma.org/About/ WhoWeAre /Pages/history.aspx, archived at https://perma.cc/ FU9C-2C92.

60. "Dr. Charles E. North (1869–1961), A Register of His Papers in the National Agricultural Library," 5 (unpaginated), https://specialcollections.nal.usda.gov/speccoll/collectionsguide/ north/119PDF.pdf, archived at https://perma.cc/S4J2-7K3X; Selitzer, *Dairy Industry*, 160. Similarly, Nathan Straus led private sector philanthropic efforts to solve the milk problem and served a brief term as president of the New York City Board of Health. Spargo, *Common Sense*, 231; Miller, "Stop the Slaughter," 166. Cornell professor R. A. Pearson started out working in the dairy industry and eventually left academia to become the New York State commissioner of agriculture. "Made a State Commissioner," *Cornell Alumni News* 10, no. 28 (April 22, 1908), 1, https://ecommons.cornell.edu/bitstream /handle/1813/26081/010_28.pdf?sequence=1&is Allowed=y, archived at https://perma.cc/ZR82-9VGT; Schmid, *Untold Story*, loc. 762; Parker, *City Milk Supply*, 385–91.

61. Parker, *City Milk Supply*, 173–74; "Made a State Commissioner"; Webster, "Sanitary Inspection," 564–65; Ward, *Pure Milk*, 102; "Joint Committee Report," in *Third Annual Conference*, 48; Wikipedia, s.v. "American Dairy Science Association," last modified February 1, 2018, https://en.wikipedia.org/wiki/American_Dairy_Science_Association, archived at https://perma .cc/DM7B-QVC4.

62. Parker, *City Milk Supply*, 176, 177; Ward, *Pure Milk*, 94, 103; Raymond Pearson, "The Scoring of Dairies for Raising the Grade of Milk," in *Third Annual Conference*, 79; Webster, "Sanitary Inspection," 569; Henry L. Coit, "An Efficiency Score Card for the Use of the Medical Milk Commission," in *Proceedings of the Eighth Annual Conference of the American Association of Medical Milk Commissions*, Rochester, NY, June 19–20, 1914, 412–22 (hereafter *Eighth Annual Conference*); Parker, *City Milk Supply*, 247; Ward, *Pure Milk*, 106; Smith-Howard, *Pure and Modern Milk*, 25–27; H. A. Harding and J. D. Brew, *The Financial Stimulus in City Milk Production*, New York Agricultural Experiment Station, Bulletin No. 363, April 1913, https:// ecommons.cornell.edu /bitstream /handle/1813/4122/bulletin363.pdf?sequence=1&isAllowed =y, archived at https://perma.cc/3RGL-5Y5G.

63. Webster, "Sanitary Inspection," 569; James D. Brew, *Milk Quality as Determined by Present Dairy Score Cards*, New York Agricultural Experiment Station, Bulletin No. 398, March, 1915, 107, 131, https://ecommons.cornell.edu/bitstream/handle/1813/4845/bulletin398 .pdf?sequence=1&isAllowed=y, archived at https://perma.cc/53H7-G9GN; Parker, *City Milk Supply*, 177–81; MacNutt, *Modern Milk Problem*, 71–76, 78–86; Brainerd and Mallory, "Milk Standards," 6–7.

64. Smith-Howard, *Pure and Modern Milk*, 22–23; Parker, *City Milk Supply*, 177; Brew, "Milk Quality," 110; MacNutt, *Modern Milk Problem*, 85, 105, 161; Brainerd and Mallory, "Milk Standards," 5, 7, 16–17, 19–20; Rosenau, *Milk Question*, 75–78; C. V. Craster, "The Value of Municipal Dairy Inspection," *American City* 23, no. 2 (August 1920): 172–75; Selitzer, *Dairy Industry*, 168–70; Lepper, "Methodology"; White, "A.O.A.C Methods of Analysis"; J. W. Kerr, "The Need of Co-Operation in Securing Pure Milk," in *Eighth Annual Conference*, 373.

65. Frank, "National Program," 1583, 1587; Steffen, "How Regulation Came to Be," 8; "The History and Accomplishments of the National Conference on Interstate Milk Shipments," 1–2, 10, http://ncims.org/wp-content/uploads/2015/02/History-thru-2009-1.pdf, archived at https://perma.cc/U3CU-EZ9B; George R. Taylor, Edgar L. Burtis and Frederick V. Waugh, *Barriers to Internal Trade in Farm Products* (Washington, DC: US Government Printing Office, 1939).

66. FDA, "Grade 'A' Pasteurized Milk Ordinance, 2015 Revision," iii, https://www.fda .gov/downloads/food/guidanceregulation/guidancedocumentsregulatoryinformation/milk/ ucm513508.pdf, archived at https://perma.cc/L884-9CZ6; "History and Accomplishments," 1–3; Steve Ingham (administrator, Division of Food Safety, Wisconsin Department of Agriculture), interview with the author, May 19, 2015; FDA, "Interstate Milk Shippers List," https://www .fda.gov/Food/GuidanceRegulation/FederalStateFoodPrograms/ucm2007965.htm, archived at https://perma.cc/ZMF3-2NMQ.

67. "Who Are We?" National Conference of Interstate Milk Shippers, https://web.archive .org/web/20150303201501/http://www.ncims.org/index.htm; Ingham, interview; "History and Accomplishments," 28; Food and Drug Administration, "Pasteurized Milk Ordinance," iii.

68. Selitzer, *Dairy Industry*, 149–51.

69. Okun, *Fair Play*, xi. For a leading study on the role of experts in regulatory governance, see David Demortain, *Scientists and the Regulation of Risk: Standardising Control* (Cheltenham, UK: Edward Elgar, 2011).

70. Duffy, *Sanitarians*, chaps. 1–6; Dupuis, *Nature's Perfect Food*, loc. 1325; Selitzer, *Dairy Industry*, 161; Shaftel, "Short History," 287. See also Waserman, "Henry L. Coit," 372, on the 1905 Washington, DC, typhoid epidemic traced to milk, which spurred a landmark 1908 study by the Public Health and Marine Hospital Service, *Milk and Its Relation to the Public Health*. On focusing events more generally, see Thomas A. Birkland, *After Disaster: Agenda Setting, Public Policy, and Focusing Events* (Washington, DC: Georgetown University Press, 1997).

71. Lorine Swainston Goodwin, *The Pure Food, Drink, and Drug Crusaders, 1879–1914* (Jefferson, NC: McFarland, 1999), 80; Okun, *Fair Play*, 9, 18, 45; Young, *Pure Food*, chaps. 2 and 8; Selitzer, *Dairy Industry*, 123–24; Dupuis, *Nature's Perfect Food*, loc. 1663.

72. Conn, "Milk Supply," 628. See also Spargo, *Common Sense*, 247; Rosenau, *Milk Question*, 17. On fear of germs and anxiety about milk, see Harvey Levenstein, *Fear of Food: A History of Why We Worry about What We Eat* (Chicago: University of Chicago Press, 2012), chaps. 1 and 2.

73. Young, *Pure Food*, 31; Goodwin, *Crusaders*, 41, 47–49; Duffy, *Sanitarians*, 185–86; Okun, *Fair Play*, ix, 4; Parker, *City Milk Supply*, 278–79, 378; MacNutt, *Modern Milk Problem*, 3–4,

38, 65, 124. See also Levenstein, *Fear of Food*, 1–4; Brainerd and Mallory, "Milk Standards," 3; Parker, *City Milk Supply*, 228–38; Hartley, *Essay on Milk*, 110.

74. Spargo, *Common Sense*, 185–86; Miller, "Stop the Slaughter," 168. See also MacNutt, *Modern Milk Problem*, 3, 31.

75. Young, *Pure Food*, chap. 12; Dupuis, *Nature's Perfect Food*, loc. 1331; Goodwin, *Crusaders*, 11, 87; Okun, *Fair Play*, 37, 45; Selitzer, *Dairy Industry*, 157; Otto Geier, "The American Association of Medical Milk Commissions: Past and Present—What of the Future?" in *Third Annual Conference*, 5; Coit, "Medical Milk Commission," 61; Coit, "Clean Milk," 1; A. W. Myers, "Some of the By-Products of the Work of the Association," in *Proceedings of the Seventh Annual Conference of the American Association of Medical Milk Commissions*, Minneapolis, MN, June 19–20, 1913, 296–97; Miller, "Stop the Slaughter," 170. From the point of view of the early temperance crusaders, there may have been something redemptive about the application of pasteurization—originally developed by Louis Pasteur in the early 1860s as a way to preserve wine—to address the milk problem. Selitzer, *Dairy Industry*, 130.

76. Young, *Pure Food*, chap. 12; Duffy, *Sanitarians*, 129; Okun, *Fair Play*, xi; Dupuis, *Nature's Perfect Food*, locs. 1340, 1415, 1462; Andrew Abbott, *The System of Professions: An Essay on the Division of Expert Labor* (Chicago: University of Chicago Press, 1988), 8–9, 20, 59–60. On the role of professional experts in regulatory governance, see Demortain, *Scientists*. On the influence of political ideology on regulatory culture, see Joseph Rees, *Reforming the Workplace: A Study of Self-Regulation in Occupational Safety* (Philadelphia: University of Pennsylvania Press, 1988), 4–5; Jerry L. Mashaw and David L. Harfst, *The Struggle for Auto Safety* (Cambridge, MA: Harvard University Press, 1990); Ian Ayres and John Braithwaite, *Responsive Regulation: Transcending the Deregulation Debate* (Oxford: Oxford University Press, 1992); Robert Kagan, *Adversarial Legalism: The American Way of Law* (Cambridge, MA: Harvard University Press, 2001).

77. Dillon, *Seven Decades*, 19; MacNutt, 48–51; Duffy, *History 1866–1966*, 107, 432; Okun, *Fair Play*, 18–22, 32, 47, 286; Young, *Pure Food*, chap. 2; Selitzer, *Dairy Industry*, 124, 202–3; 286; Leona Baumgartner, "One Hundred Years of Health: New York City, 1866–1966," *Bulletin of the New York Academy of Medicine* 45, no. 6 (June 1969): 557; Dupuis, *Nature's Perfect Food*, locs. 1565, 1658; Smith-Howard, *Pure and Modern Milk*, 24; George W. Goler, "Municipal Milk Work in Rochester," *Charities in the Commons* 16 (April–October 1906): 484–85; McCleary, *Early History*, 363; Hollis Godfrey, "The City and Its Milk Supply," *Atlantic* 100 (1907): 260; MacNutt, *Modern Milk Problem*, 46, 126–27. On capture, see Peter H. Schuck, "Against (and for) Madison: An Essay in Praise of Factions," in *The Limits of Law* (Boulder, CO: Westview Press, 2000), 204–50.

78. Dupuis, *Nature's Perfect Food*, locs. 1519–59, 1588–98, 1614, 1696; Smith-Howard, *Pure and Modern Milk*, 22–32; Okun, *Fair Play*, xi–xii, 185–87, 289; Young, *Pure Food*, 95; Selitzer, *Dairy Industry*, 164, 177; North, "Milk and Its Relation," 274–77.

79. Geier, "Report," 19; MacNutt, *Modern Milk Problem*, 46, 49, 58 (quoting Conn), 68, 122–51; George Walker, "Why Walker-Gordon Milk Is Not Certified in All Cities," in *Fifth Annual Conference*, 58; Spargo, *Common Sense*, 219; Parker, *City Milk Supply*, 407, 423–24; McCleary, *Early History*, 363; Smith-Howard, *Pure and Modern Milk*, 24–25; Dupuis, *Nature's Perfect Food*, loc. 1565.

80. Goler, "Municipal Milk Work," 485; MacNutt, *Modern Milk Problem*, 126; Walker, "Walker-Gordon Milk," 58.

81. Smith-Howard, *Pure and Modern Milk*, locs. 18–20; "Early Developments in the American Dairy Industry," US Department of Agriculture, Special Collections, https://specialcollections

.nal.usda.gov/dairy-exhibit, archived at https://perma.cc/BB4P-8T7F; MacNutt, *Modern Milk Problem*, 33, 105–7; Selitzer, *Dairy Industry*, 36, 38; Parker, *City Milk Supply*, 424.

82. H. A. Harding, *Publicity and Payment Based on Quality as Factors in Improving a City Milk Supply*, New York Agricultural Experiment Station, Bulletin No. 337, April 1911, 83, http:// hdl.handle.net/1813/4206; Spargo, *Common Sense*, 209, 279–82; Duffy, *History 1866–1966*, 134, 307–9; MacNutt, *Modern Milk Problem*, 92–93; Craster, "Value of Municipal Dairy Inspection"; William C. Woodward, "The Municipal Regulation of the Milk Supply of the District of Columbia," in *Milk and Its Relation to the Public Health*, 783–84.

83. Selitzer, *Dairy Industry*, 149–51; Duffy, *Sanitarians*, 194; Parker, *City Milk Supply*, 425; Webster, "Sanitary Inspection," 570; Woodward, "Municipal Regulation," 751, 770; Coit, "Medical Milk Commission," 59; Young, *Pure Food*, 64–65; Dupuis, *Nature's Perfect Food*, locs. 1529, 3270; Goodwin, *Crusaders*, 72, 81–83, 168; Smith-Howard, *Pure and Modern Milk*, 27; Spargo, *Common Sense*, 288–90; Parker, *City Milk Supply*, 377, 380; Conn, "Scheme for Organizing," 109; Mary H. Abel, "Safe Foods and How to Get Them: Official Milk Inspection," *Delineator* (November 1905), 910–16.

84. Spargo, *Common Sense*, 279–82; Harding, *Publicity*, 89–90; Ward, *Pure Milk*, 97, 380; North, "Milk and Its Relation," 283, 287; White, "A.O.A.C Methods of Analysis"; Parker, *City Milk Supply*, 382, 427; James A. Tobey, *Public Health Law: A Manual of Law for Sanitarians* (Baltimore, MD: Williams & Wilkins, 1926), 99.

85. David W. Horn, "Local Health Boards and Medical Milk Commissions," *American Journal of Public Health* 12, no. 10 (October 1922): 837–38; Coit, "Efficiency Score Card," 415, 421; Webster, "Sanitary Inspection," 570; Woodward, "Municipal Regulation," 771; Duffy, *History 1866–1966*, 264, 307; Okin, *Fair Play*, 54.

86. Duffy, *History 1866–1966*, 133; Coit, "Medical Milk Commission," 59.

87. Spargo, *Common Sense*, 288–90; Parker, *City Milk Supply*, 377, 380, 387, 923, 476; Woodward, "Municipal Regulation," 751; Alice K. Fallows, "A City's Campaign for Pure Milk," *Century* 66 (1903): 565; William A. Northridge, "The Working Methods and Results in the Borough of Brooklyn, New York City, of the Milk Commission of the Medical Society of the County of Kings," in *First Conference*, 43; Abel, "Safe Foods," 914; Goodwin, *Crusaders*, 83, 168; Smith-Howard, *Pure and Modern Milk*, 32; Dupuis, *Nature's Perfect Food*, locs. 318, 1680–1700.

88. MacNutt, *Modern Milk Problem*, 92–93; Kerr, "Certified Milk," 624; Brainerd and Mallory, "Milk Standards," 5; Craster, "Value of Municipal Dairy Inspection."

89. See, e.g., North, "Milk and Its Relation," 269, 278, 280–81; Harding and Brew, *Financial Stimulus*; Parker, *City Milk Supply*, 375, 428, 459–72; "Report of Milk Commissions," in *Third Annual Conference*, 8–37.

90. James Q. Wilson, *Bureaucracy: What Government Agencies Do and Why They Do It* (1989; New York: Basic Books, 2001), loc. 924, Kindle; Selitzer, *Dairy Industry*, 158, 177; Harding, *Publicity*, 109; C. Hampson Jones, "The Present Needs of the Milk Supply in Baltimore," *Charities and the Commons* 16 (April–October 1906): 501.

91. Coit, "Origin," 16; Park, "Report," 26; Tuley, "Report," 62; Ward, *Pure Milk*, 168–69; Kerr, "Certified Milk," 624, 628; Waserman, "Henry L. Coit," 368–70; Horn, "Local Health Boards," 837; Goodwin, *Crusaders*, 63–64, 159, 269–70; Rogers, "Henry Leber Coit," 27, 37; Schmid, *Untold Story*, loc. 672; North, "Milk and Its Relation," 286; Myers, "By-Products," 297; Ward, *Pure Milk*, 102–3; Harding, *Publicity*, 84; Straus, *Disease in Milk*, 199; J. H. Mason Knox Jr., "The Recent Campaign for Clean Milk in Baltimore," *Second Annual Conference*, 40; John W. Kerr, "Federal Recognition of the Work of the Medical Milk Commission," in *Second*

Annual Conference, 73; Kerr, "Need of Co-operation," 372; Ward, *Pure Milk*, 103. As these examples illustrate, hybridization of private and public efforts has long been a feature of food safety governance. For a more detailed analysis of hybridization, see Paul Verbruggen and Tetty Havinga, "Hybridization of Food Governance: An Analytical Framework," in *Hybridization of Food Governance: Trends, Types and Results*, ed. Paul Verbruggen and Tetty Havinga (Cheltenham, UK: Edward Elgar, 2017), 1–27.

92. Tuley, "Report," 61; Parker, *City Milk Supply*, 428.

93. Parker, *City Milk Supply*, 370–74, 389–90, 408; Brainerd and Mallory, "Milk Standards," 6, 12; North, "Milk in Its Relation," 241, 286; White, "A.O.A.C Methods of Analysis"; Selitzer, *Dairy Industry*, 168–70; Rogers, "Henry Leber Coit," 37; "Who Are We?"; Ingham, interview; "History and Accomplishments," 28; FDA, "Pasteurized Milk Ordinance," iii.

94. North, "Milk and Its Relation," 286, 283; Parker, *City Milk Supply*, 408; Brainerd and Mallory, "Milk Standards," 5–7, 19–20; MacNutt, *Modern Milk Problem*, 85; Smith-Howard, *Pure and Modern Milk*, locs. 32–33. On different types of rules in administrative regulation, see Cary Coglianese and David Lazer, "Management-Based Regulation: Prescribing Private Management to Achieve Public Goals," *Law and Society Review* 37 (2003): 691–730.

95. Parker, *City Milk Supply*, 386; Duffy, *Sanitarians*, 151; John E. Sayles, "Clean Milk for New York City," *Charities and the Commons* 17 (October 1906–April 1907), 683; Parker, *City Milk Supply*, 268; Woodward, "Municipal Regulation," 784–86; Henry L. Coit, "Address of the President," in *Second Annual Conference*, 42.

96. Tobey, *Public Health Law*, 99; MacNutt, *Modern Milk Problem*, 161; Spargo, *Common Sense*, 283–84. See also Parker, *City Milk Supply*, 374; Prescott, "Production of Clean Milk," 489–90.

97. Marc T. Law, "How Do Regulators Regulate? Enforcement of the Pure Food and Drugs Act, 1907–38," *Journal of Law, Economics & Organization* 22, no. 2 (October 2006): 478, 483; Milton J. Rosenau, "Address of the President," in *Fifth Annual Conference*, 124–25.

98. MacNutt, *Modern Milk Problem*, 115–16; "The Milk Show in Baltimore," *Charities and the Commons* 16 (April–October 1906): 290–91; "The Cleveland Milk Contest," *Charities and the Commons* 20 (April–October 1908): 128; "Cleveland Milk Exhibit," *Charities and the Commons* 18 (April–October 1907): 180; Geier "Past and Present, in *Third Annual Conference*, 4; Clarence B. Lane, "A Plan for Annual Certified Milk Contests," in *Third Annual Conference*, 81–88.

99. Goodwin, *Crusaders*, 64, 271; Parker, *City Milk Supply*, 379, 453; Ward, *Pure Milk*, 102; Webster, "Sanitary Inspection," 569; Harding, *Financial Stimulus*, 170; Smith-Howard, *Pure and Modern Milk*, loc. 591; MacNutt, *Modern Milk Problem*, 117; Smith-Howard, *Pure and Modern Milk*, 25; North, "Milk and Its Relation," 241, 287.

100. Spargo, *Common Sense*, 182–83; Darlington, "Municipal Regulation," in *Third Annual Conference*, 123; Rowland G. Freeman, "Remarks on the Development of Dairy Hygiene in the United States," in *First Conference*, 17; Johnson, "Milk Supply," 5; Leonard Pearson, "Tuberculosis of Cattle: How It May Be Repressed and Its Relation to Public Health," *Charities and the Commons* 16 (April–October 1906): 498.

101. Smith-Howard, *Pure and Modern Milk*, 21; Dillon, *Seven Decades*, 22–23; Woodward, "Municipal Regulation," 750; Selitzer, *Dairy Industry*, 135; Duffy, *History 1866–1966*, 135–36; Parker, *City Milk Supply*, 391; Knox, "Recent Campaign," 40; Darlington, "Municipal Regulation," 123; Duffy, *History 1866–1966*, 134–36; Law, "How Do Regulators Regulate?" 470–72; Olmstead and Rhode, *Arresting Contagion*, loc. 2292.

102. Woodward, "Municipal Regulation," 780; Johnson, "Milk Supply," 589; William H. Park, "Report of the Milk Commission of the Medical Society of the County of New York," in *First Conference*, 28.

103. Ayres and Braithwaite, *Responsive Regulation*; Spargo, *Common Sense*, 207–8.

104. This and next two paragraphs rely on Lee, "Infant Mortality Decline."

Chapter Three

1. Lori Valigra, "Former NASA Food Coordinator Pioneered the HACCP System," *Food Quality & Safety*, April 2, 2012, 1; Paul A. Lachance, interview by Jennifer Ross-Nazzal, NASA Johnson Space Center Oral History Project, May 4, 2006, https://www.jsc.nasa.gov/history/oral _histories/LachancePA/LachancePA_7-18-07.htm, archived at https://perma.cc/G9HY-5QE3; Paul A. Lachance, "How HACCP Started," *Food Technology* 51, no. 5 (1997): 35; William H. Sperber, "Happy 50th Birthday to HACCP: Retrospective and Prospective," *Food Safety Magazine*, December 2009–January 2010, https://www.foodsafetymagazine.com/magazine-archive1/ december-2009january-2010/happy-50th-birthday-to-haccp-retrospective-and-prospective1/, archived at https://perma.cc/9Z5E-MK86; Jennifer Ross-Nazzal, "'From Farm to Fork': How Space Food Standards Impacted the Food Industry and Changed Food Safety Standards," in *Societal Impact of Spaceflight*, ed. Steven J. Dick and Roger D. Launius (Washington, DC: NASA, 2007), 221.

2. Howard E. Bauman, "The Origin of the HACCP System and Subsequent Evolution," *Food Science & Technology Today* 8, no. 2 (June 1994): 67–68; Lachance, interview, 20; Ross-Nazzal, "From Farm to Fork," 221.

3. Howard Bauman, "HACCP: Concept, Development, and Application," *Food Technology* 44, no. 5 (May 1990): 156; Bauman, "Origin," 68; Lachance, interview, 25; Ross-Nazzal, "From Farm to Fork," 223–24.

4. NASA, "A Dividend in Food Safety," *Spinoff* (1991): 52, https://ntrs.nasa.gov/archive/ nasa/casi.ntrs.nasa.gov/20020086314.pdf, archived at https://perma.cc/KU4S-TNDD; National Academies, *Scientific Criteria to Ensure Safe Food* (Washington, DC: National Academies Press, 2003), 69; Dan Flynn, "HACCP: The Space Program's Contribution to Food Safety," *Food Safety News*, July 1, 2013, http://www.foodsafetynews.com/2013/07/haccp-space-programs -contribution-to-food-safety/#.WnyleejwaUk, archived at https://perma.cc/R8ZC-HVXX.

5. David (Dave) Theno, telephone interview by the author, August 7, 2015.

6. "The Seven Principles of HACCP," Institute of Agriculture and Natural Resources, University of Nebraska–Lincoln, https://food.unl.edu/seven-principles-haccp, archived at https:// perma.cc/6ZTC-654C. For a more detailed overview, see C. A. Wallace, "Hazard Analysis and Critical Control Point System (HACCP): Principles and Practice," in *Encyclopedia of Food Safety*, ed. Yasmine Motarjemi, Gerald Moy, and Ewen Todd (Amsterdam: Elsevier, 2013), 4:226–39.

7. Bauman, "Origin," 70. On the role of experts in mediating between the theory and application of HACCP, see David Demortain, "Standardising through Concepts: The Power of Scientific Experts in International Standard-Setting," *Science and Public Policy* 35, no. 6 (July 2008): 391–402.

8. J. Andres Vasconcellos, *Quality Assurance for the Food Industry: A Practical Approach* (Boca Raton, FL: CRC Press, 2004), 296–97; Edward Dunkelberger, "The Statutory Basis for the FDA's Food Safety Assurance Programs: From GMP, to Emergency Permit Control, to HACCP," *Food and Drug Law Journal* 50, no. 3 (1995): 361; Neal Fortin, "HACCP and Other Regulatory

Approaches to Prevention of Foodborne Illness," in *Foodborne Infections and Intoxications*, ed. J. Glenn Morris Jr. and Morris E. Potter (London: Academic Press, 2013), 508; Consumer Federation of America, *The Promise and Problems of HACCP: A Review of USDA's Approach to Meat and Poultry Safety* (Washington, DC: Consumer Federation of America, 2015), 5, https://consumerfed.org/wp-content/uploads/2010/06/150424_CFA-HACCP_report.pdf, archived at https://perma.cc/UUS4-2FAR; Cary Coglianese and David Lazer, "Management-Based Regulation: Using Private Management to Achieve Public Goals," *Law & Society Review* 37 (2003): 691–730.

9. Bauman, "Origin," 68; Neal Fortin, "The Hang-Up with HACCP: The Resistance to Translating Science into Food Safety Law," *Food and Drug Law Journal* 58, no. 4 (2003), 567–68; National Academies, "Scientific Criteria," 70.

10. Ross-Nazzal, "From Farm to Fork," 220; Bauman, "Origin," 69.

11. Ross-Nazzal, "From Farm to Fork," 224–25.

12. *Oversight of Food Inspection Activities of the Federal Government, Hearings, before the Subcommittee on Public Health and the Environment of the Committee on Interstate and Foreign Commerce, House of Representatives*, 92nd Cong. 55–56 (chronological summary of Bon Vivant soup outbreak), 137 (discussion of FDA enforcement powers), 458–69 (statement of Andrew Paretti, president of Bon Vivant Soup Inc.) (August 3–4, September 10 and 13–14, 1971); Paul L. Montgomery, "Botulism Death in Westchester Brings Hunt for Soup," *New York Times*, July 2, 1971, 35; Paul L. Montgomery, "Bon Vivant Voluntarily Recalls All Vichyssoise from Dealers," *New York Times*, July 4, 1971, 29; "Bon Vivant's Canned Food Is Being Recalled by US," *New York Times*, July 7, 1971, 1; Walter H. Waggoner, "A Victim Recalls Bon Vivant Soup," *New York Times*, July 18, 1973, 41; Joyce Jensen, "Epilogue: A Glance Back at Some Major Stories," *New York Times*, June 9, 1974, 6; Associated Press, "Bon Vivant Files for Bankruptcy," *New York Times*, July 27, 1971, 40; Nancy Ross, "Tracking Down the Soup Can Killer," *Washington Post*, July 18, 1971, G1; Nancy Ross, "FDA Acts to Seize Bon Vivant Foods across the Nation," *Washington Post*, August 14, 1971, E1; Nancy Ross, "More Cans of Soup Suspect," *Washington Post*, July 24, 1971, E3; Nancy Ross, "Remember That Vichyssoise?" *Washington Post*, June 25, 1972, K1; Ross-Nazzal, "From Farm to Fork," 225–28. At the time, the FDA had no legal authority to impose a recall, but it did have authority to seize products that it deemed adulterated or misbranded. The Bon Vivant nationwide seizure is the only nationwide seizure in the history of FDA. It required separate seizures in every federal judicial district, not a single nationwide seizure, and within each judicial district it required separate seizures for each location of the merchandise. According to FDA chief counsel at the time, Peter Barton Hutt, the effort crippled FDA enforcement. Peter Barton Hutt, email message to the author, August 21, 2017. On the FDA's lack of authority to order product recalls before FSMA, see Tina Curatolo, "Pop-Tarts and Elixirs of Death: An Examination of FDA's Recall Authority," Digital Access to Scholarship at Harvard, posted April 27, 2005, https://dash.harvard.edu/handle/1/8963880, archived at https://perma.cc/6YXK-WQLY.

13. Peter Kihss, "Campbell Recalls a Soup after Botulism Detected," *New York Times*, August 23, 1971, 1; Boyce Rensberger, "Campbell Also Recalling Batch of Vegetarian Vegetable Soup," *New York Times*, September 1, 1971, 22; United Press International, "Warning Is Issued on Stokely Beans," *New York Times*, October 30, 1971, 34 (reporting 658 cases recalled); 658 cases, with twenty-four cans per case, totals 15,792 cans.

14. Ross-Nazzal, "From Farm to Fork," 226–29; James S. Turner, *The Chemical Feast* (New York: Grossman, 1970); Grace Lichtenstein, "Bon Vivant's Soup Plant Not Inspected for 4 Years," *New York Times*, July 21, 1971, 1; *Oversight of Food Inspection*, 7, 36 (discussions about frequency of FDA food facility inspection).

15. *Oversight of Food Inspection*, 132 (testimony of Charles Edwards); Dunkelberger, "Statutory Basis," 359–61, 365; Federal Food, Drug, and Cosmetic Act, Pub. L. No. 75-717, § 402(a)(4), 52 Stat. 1040, 1046 (1938); 34 Fed. Reg. 6978 (April 26, 1969).

16. Dunkelberger, "Statutory Basis," 366; Food, Drug, and Cosmetic Act FDCA § 404.

17. Dunkelberger, "Statutory Basis," 366.

18. The NCA guidelines focused specifically on low-acid canned foods. Canning foods, such as pickles, in an acidic liquid, such as vinegar, blocks the growth of botulinum bacteria, which could otherwise multiply in a low-oxygen environment, like a sealed container. By contrast, low-acid canned foods, such as potato soup or meat, are highly susceptible to the proliferation of botulinum bacteria if not properly heated during the canning process. The FDA eventually extended its canning regulations to include acidified foods. 44 Fed. Reg. 30442, 30457 (July 23, 1976); 44 Fed. Reg. 16235 (March 16, 1979). Subsequently, the USDA promulgated similar requirements for canned meat and poultry products. 49 Fed. Reg. 14636 (April 12, 1984); 51 Fed. Reg. 45602 (December 19, 1986). See Peter Barton Hutt, Richard A. Merrill, and Lewis A. Grossman, *Food and Drug Law: Cases and Materials*, 3rd ed. (New York: Foundation Press, 2007), 359.

19. Dunkelberger, "Statutory Basis," 365–70; 36 Fed. Reg. 21688 (November 12, 1971); Ross, "Remember That Vichyssoise?"; *Oversight of Food Inspection*, 240 (testimony of Ira Sommers, director of research laboratories National Canners Association), 251 (NCA low-acid canned foods processing standards); National Canners Association, *The Canning Industry: Its Importance, Organization, Methods, and the Public Service Values of Its Products*, 4th ed. (Washington, DC: National Canners Association, 1959), 35–37, https://catalog.hathitrust.org/Record/009058773, archived at https://perma.cc/VHL3-86WX; National Canners Association, *The Canning Industry: Its Importance, Organization, Methods, and the Public Service Values of Its Products*, 6th ed. (Washington, DC: National Canners Association, 1971), archived at https://perma.cc/8FTT-BV44.

20. Dunkelberger, "Statutory Basis," 365; Edward Dunkelberger, telephone interview by the author, October 22, 2015.

21. Peter Barton Hutt, telephone interview by the author, October 16, 2015; National Academies, "Scientific Criteria," 211–12. The National Canners Association, founded in 1907, established its first research laboratory in 1913 in Washington, DC, and added branch laboratories in Seattle in 1919 and San Francisco in 1926. National Canners Association, *Canning Industry*, 36. In 1923, the NCA developed a standard botulism retort method of cooking, which employs a large pressure cooker that uses steam under pressure to reach temps above 212 degrees Fahrenheit. Robert V. Tauxe and Emilio J. Esteban, "Advances in Food Safety to Prevent Foodborne Diseases in the United States," in *Silent Victories: The History and Practice of Public Health in Twentieth-Century America*, ed. John W. Ward and Christian Warren (Oxford: Oxford University Press, 2006), 24.

22. Dunkelberger, "Statutory Basis," 368; 38 Fed. Reg. 2398 (January 24, 1973); 38 Fed. Reg. 12720 (May 14, 1973); 38 Fed. Reg. 14174 (May 30, 1973); 39 Fed. Reg. 3748 (January 29, 1974); 39 Fed. Reg. 11877 (April 1, 1974).

23. 38 Fed. Reg. 2398 (January 24, 1973); Ross-Nazzal, "From Farm to Fork," 229–30; Sperber, "Happy 50th Birthday," 2.

24. Bauman, "Origin," 69; National Academies, "Scientific Criteria," 212–13; Ross-Nazzal, "From Farm to Fork," 229–31; Dunkelberger, "Statutory Basis," 370; Fortin "Hang-Up," 568; James W. Woodlee, *The Food Safety Modernization Act: A Comprehensive, Practical Guide to the Landmark Legislation* (Washington, DC: Food and Drug Law Institute, 2012), 10.

25. *Oversight of Food Inspection*, 140 (testimony of Virgil Wodicka, director of FDA Bureau

of Foods), 239–40 (testimony of Ira Somers), 251, 256 (NCA standards). Compare Ross, "Remember that Vichyssoise?" (stating fifteen botulism related deaths from commercially prepared foods).

26. Hutt, interview, 7.

27. "Peter Barton Hutt," Covington & Burling, https://www.cov.com/en/professionals/h/peter-hutt, archived at https://perma.cc/52U4-FLE7; "A Tribute to H. Thomas Austern," *Food Drug Cosmetic Law Journal* 39 (1984): 127, 123; Dunkelberger, interview. Obituaries referred to Austern at "the dean of the food and drug bar," a title later conferred upon Hutt. "H. Thomas Austern," *New York Times*, April 19, 1984, B15 (obituary).

28. The account in this and the following paragraphs is based on Paretti's statement in *Oversight of Food Inspection*, 458–73.

29. Associated Press, "Bon Vivant Files"; Jensen, "Epilogue."

30. Ross, "Remember That Vichyssoise?" 2; Ross, "FDA Acts."

31. Ross, "Remember That Vichyssoise?"

32. Quotations from Turner, *Chemical Feast*, 39, 106 and see 75, 203–4, 185, 234. For a more general analysis of aggressive agency responses to health and safety risks motivated by a concern to protect the agency's reputation ("CYA behavior"), see Eugene Bardach and Robert A. Kagan, introduction to *Social Regulation: Strategies for Reform*, ed. Eugene Bardach and Robert A. Kagan (San Francisco: Institute for Contemporary Studies, 1982), 14–17.

33. Turner, *Chemical Feast*, 40.

34. Ross, "More Cans"; Ross, "Tracking Down."

35. Daniel Carpenter and David Moss, eds., *Preventing Regulatory Capture: Special Interest Influence and How to Limit It* (New York: Cambridge University Press, 2014), intro. and chaps. 4–7; Wendy Wagner, "Administrative Law, Filter Failure, and Information Capture," *Duke Law Journal* 59 (2010): 1321–1432; Sidney Shapiro, "Old and New Capture," *Regulatory Review*, June 28, 2016, https://www.theregreview.org/2016/06/28/shapiro-old-and-new-capture/, archived at https://perma.cc/J4XD-5Q6Y. For a detailed analysis and critique of capture theory, see Steven P. Croley, *Regulation and Public Interests: The Possibility of Good Regulatory Government* (Princeton, NJ: Princeton University Press, 2008), chap. 3. See also Peter H. Schuck, *Why Government Fails So Often: And How It Can Do Better* (Princeton, NJ: Princeton University Press, 2014), 109–10, 214; Peter H. Schuck, "Against (and for) Madison: An Essay in Praise of Factions," *Yale Law & Policy Review* 15 (1997): 553–97; David Freeman Engstrom, "Corralling Capture," *Harvard Journal of Law & Public Policy* 36 (2013): 31–39.

36. Turner, *Chemical Feast*, 100, 103.

37. Turner, *Chemical Feast*, 105–6; H. Thomas Austern, "The Regulatory Gospel According to St. Peter," *Food Drug Cosmetic Law Journal* 29 (1974): 316–23; "Peter Barton Hutt"; Carol Ann Eiden, "The Courts' Role in Preserving the Family Farm during Bankruptcy Proceedings Involving FmHA Loans," *Law & Inequality* 11 (1993): 427n59.

38. Turner, *Chemical Feast*, 40; *Oversight of Food Inspection*, 4, 11, 126–27, 134, 139 (testimony of Charles Edwards), 224–25 (testimony of Ralph Nader and Peter Schuck, a junior associate of Mr. Nader); *Hearings on S. 983 to Protect Consumers Against Unreasonable Risk of Injury from Hazardous Products and Other Purposes . . . before the Committee on Commerce*, 92nd Cong. 586 (testimony of Ralph Nader) (July 28–30, 1971).

39. See, e.g., William G. Laffer III, "How Regulation Is Destroying American Jobs," Backgrounder No. 926, Heritage Foundation, February 16, 1993, archived at https://perma.cc/4MLL -QVF4; William A. Niskanen Jr., *Bureaucracy and Representative Government* (New Brunswick, NJ: Aldine Transaction, 1971); Jennifer Bachner and Benjamin Ginsberg, *What Washington Gets*

Wrong: The Unelected Officials Who Actually Run the Government and Their Misconceptions about the American People (Amherst, NY: Prometheus Books, 2016); Dorit Rubenstein Reiss, "The Benefits of Capture," *Wake Forest Law Review* 47 (2012): 595.

40. *Hearings on S. Res. 39, Part 2, before the Subcommittee on Administrative Practice and Procedure of the Committee on the Judiciary*, 89th Cong. 424–31 (testimony of Ellis Arnall) (April 18 and 27–29; May 5–6; and June 7, 1965).

41. Dunkelberger, "Statutory Basis," 368; Dunkelberger, interview; Hutt, interview; Hutt, Merrill, and Grossman, *Food and Drug Law*, 359. For further detail on various differences between the NCA and the FDA and their resolution, see 38 Fed. Reg. 2398 (January 24, 1973); 38 Fed. Reg. 12720 (May 14, 1973); 38 Fed. Reg. 14174 (May 30, 1973); 39 Fed. Reg. 3748 (January 29, 1974); 39 Fed. Reg. 11877 (April 1, 1974). Whereas the GMPs were published as final regulations in January 1973, legal wrangling between the NCA and the FDA delayed publication of the enforcement provisions until April 1974.

42. Derek Bok, *The Trouble with Government* (Cambridge, MA: Harvard University Press, 2001), 120–21; Schuck, *Why Government Fails So Often*, 14, 161–71.

43. Turner, *Chemical Feast*, 217.

44. *Oversight of Food Inspection*, 11; Hutt, Merrill, and Grossman, *Food and Drug Law*, 356. See Bardach and Kagan, introduction, 14–17.

45. Hutt, interview; Hutt, email message to the author.

46. On the theory of sensemaking, see Karl E. Weick, *Sensemaking in Organizations* (Thousand Oaks, CA: Sage, 1995); Mitchel Abolafia, "Narrative Construction as Sensemaking: How a Central Bank Thinks," *Organization Studies* 31, no. 3 (2010): 350–51. For a similar theory of conceptual modeling, see John Braithwaite and Peter Drahos, *Global Business Regulation* (Cambridge: Cambridge University Press, 2000), 581.

47. Peter Barton Hutt, "Food Legislation in Perspective," *Food Drug Cosmetic Law Journal* 34 (1979): 597, 602; Dunkelberger, "Statutory Basis," 370–72; *Joint Hearings on S. 641 to Regulate Commerce and Protect Consumers from Adulterated Food by Requiring the Establishment of Surveillance Regulations for the Detection and Prevention of Adulterated Food, and for Other Purposes and S. 1168 to Regulate Commerce and Protect Consumers by Requiring Improved Safety Assurance Measures in Food Manufacture and Distribution and Registration of Producers of Food before the Subcommittee for Consumers of the Committee on Commerce and the Subcommittee on Health of the Committee on Labor and Public Welfare*, 94th Cong. 90–93 (testimony of Nancy Chasen, Consumers Union of the United States), 97–99 (testimony of Anita Johnson, Health Research Group) (June 4 and 17–18, 1975). The White House Conference on Food, Nutrition, and Health in 1969 discussed many of these reforms. Turner, *Chemical Feast*, 234.

48. *Joint Hearings*, 73, 87.

49. *Joint Hearings*, 125–46 (testimony of Ira Sommers, executive vice president of the NCA, and Edward Dunkelberger, counsel). The hearings contain similar statements by over a dozen food industry associations.

50. Dennis Hevesi, "Paul G. Rogers, 'Mr. Health,' in Congress, Is Dead at 87," *New York Times*, October 15, 2008, A29; Hutt, interview.

Chapter Four

1. A. D. Melvin, *The Federal Meat Inspection Service*, USDA, Bureau of Animal Industry Circular No. 125 (Washington, DC: Government Printing Office, February 28, 1908); Milton J. Rosenau, *Preventive Medicine and Hygiene* (New York: D. Appleton, 1913), 547–48; Federal Meat

Inspection Act, 34 Stat. 672–79 (1906); USDA, *Twenty-Third Annual Report of the Bureau of Animal Industry for the Year 1906* (Washington, DC: Government Printing Office, 1908), 364–65. The 1891 act made pre-slaughter inspection mandatory and post-slaughter inspection discretionary. The 1906 act made pre-slaughter inspection discretionary and post-slaughter inspection mandatory. Congress made pre-slaughter inspection again mandatory in the Wholesome Meat Act of 1967. Pub. L. No. 90-201, 81 Stat. 588 (1967). For a history of the 1891 act and the origins of federal animal inspection, see Alan L. Olmstead and Paul W. Rhode, *Arresting Contagion: Science, Policy, and Conflicts over Animal Disease Control* (Cambridge, MA: Harvard University Press, 2015), chap. 3.

2. Melvin, *Federal Meat Inspection*, 6; Rosenau, *Preventive Medicine*, 540–41, 557.

3. National Academy of Sciences, *An Evaluation of Public Health Hazards from Microbiological Contamination of Foods*, Publication No. 1195 (Washington, DC: National Academy of Sciences, 1964), 34; American Society for Microbiology, "Significant Events in Microbiology 1861–1999," archived at https://perma.cc/D49Q-GNLM; US Department of Health, Education, and Welfare, *Proceedings: National Conference on Salmonellosis*, Public Health Services Publication No. 1262 (Washington, DC: Government Printing Office, 1965), 9–11, 155–56, 188–89; Harrison Wellford, *Sowing the Wind* (New York: Grossman, 1972; rpt., New York: Bantam, 1973), 125. For a more detailed account of how advances in microbiology propelled the evolution of foodborne illness outbreak investigation, see chap. 7.

4. Michael Ollinger and Valerie Mueller, *Managing for Safer Food: The Economics of Sanitation and Process Controls in Meat and Poultry Plants*, USDA, Agricultural Economic Report No. 817 (April 2003), 3–4.

5. Wellford, *Sowing the Wind*, 49, 58, 125, 129–30, 133–36; Diane Sawyer, "1 out of 3," *60 Minutes* 19, no. 28 (March 29, 1987) (television broadcast transcript); Comptroller General of the United States, *Salmonella in Raw Meat and Poultry: An Assessment of the Problem*, US General Accounting Office, B-164031(2) (1974). Alarmed by a rise in the reported incidence of salmonellosis, the Communicable Disease Center (CDC) (later renamed the Centers for Disease Control and Prevention) in Atlanta convened a three-day conference in 1964 that included government officials, industry representatives, and academics. Department of Health, Education, and Welfare, *National Conference on Salmonellosis*.

6. Wellford, *Sowing the Wind*, chap. 1 and p. 125; Pathogen Reduction; Hazard Analysis and Critical Control Point (HACCP) Systems, Proposed Rule, 60 Fed. Reg. 6774–76 (February 3, 1995); Ollinger and Mueller, *Managing for Safer Food*, 3–4; Comptroller General of the United States, *A Better Way for the Department of Agriculture to Inspect Meat and Poultry Processing Plants*, US General Accounting Office, B-163450 (1977), 2–5; Robert K. Somers, "60 Years of Federal Meat Inspection," *Agricultural Marketing* 11, no. 6 (June 1966), 3; *Hearing on S. 2348 to Amend the Federal Meat Inspection Act, the Poultry Products Inspection Act, and the Egg Products Inspection Act [. . .] before the Subcommittee on Agricultural Research and General Legislation of the Committee on Agriculture, Nutrition, and Forestry*, 97th Cong. 5 (testimony of C. W. McMillan, assistant secretary for the USDA Marketing and Inspection Services) (August 11, 1982).

7. USDA, National Agricultural Statistics Service, Quick Stats Ad-Hoc Query Tool, US beef production 1950–1976, survey results archived at https://perma.cc/47ET-BUCK; USDA, National Agricultural Statistics Service, Quick Stats Ad-Hoc Query Tool, US poultry production 1960–1976, survey results archived at https://perma.cc/47ET-BUCK; PR/HACCP Proposed Rule, 60 Fed. Reg. 6775–76; Somers, "60 Years," 5; National Research Council, *Meat and Poultry Inspection: The Scientific Basis of the Nation's Program* (Washington, DC: National Academy

Press, 1985), 29, 121–25; National Academies, *Cattle Inspection* (Washington, DC: National Academy Press, 1990), 17. On the eradication of animal diseases, see Olmstead and Rhode, *Arresting Contagion.*

8. National Academy of Sciences, *Evaluation*, 19, 49, 171–74; Ollinger and Mueller, *Managing for Safer Food*, 5–8; *Hearing on S. 2348 to Amend the Federal Meat Inspection Act*, 4–5; PR/HACCP Proposed Rule, 60 Fed. Reg. 6776–77; Comptroller General, *Better Way*, 3–4; Comptroller General, *Salmonella in Raw Meat and Poultry*, 21; Isadore Rosenthal and Howard Kunreuther, "Roles for Third Parties in Implementing USDA Food Safety and Inspection Service (FSIS)'s Food Safety Process Management Programs" (Working Paper No. 2008-12-16, Wharton Risk Management and Decision Process Center, April 12, 2010), 27, https://riskcenter .wharton.upenn.edu/wp-content/uploads/2014/07/WP2010-04-12_IRHK_FoodSafety_ERS .pdf, archived at https://perma.cc/7J66-AZD5; Processed Products Inspection Improvement Act of 1986, Pub. L. No. 99-641, 100 Stat. 3567 (1986). For an overview of FDA and USDA inspection and enforcement authorities, see Neal Fortin, *Food Regulation: Law, Science, Policy, and Practice*, 2nd ed. (Hoboken, NJ: John Wiley & Sons, 2017), chaps. 16 and 17.

9. National Research Council, *Meat and Poultry Inspection*, 9–10, 124, 135; PR/HACCP Proposed Rule, 60 Fed. Reg. 6783–84; Jennifer Ross-Nazzal, "'From Farm to Fork': How Space Food Standards Impacted the Food Industry and Changed Food Safety Standards," in *Societal Impact of Spaceflight*, ed. Steven J. Dick and Roger D. Launius (Washington, DC: NASA, 2007), 232; Marion Nestle, *Safe Food: The Politics of Food Safety*, rev. ed. (Berkeley: University of California Press, 2010), loc. 1813, Kindle. The National Academy of Sciences report noted that the FSIS had already started experimenting with HACCP principles in some aspects of plant operation. National Research Council, *Meat and Poultry Inspection*, 9–10, 124.

10. David Theno, telephone interview by the author, August 7, 2015; Bill Marler, "Dave Theno—My Food Safety Hero—Has Passed Away," *Marler Blog*, June 21, 2017, http://www .marlerblog.com/lawyer-oped/dave-theno-my-food-safety-hero-has-passed-away/, archived at https://perma.cc/46SZ-8RUE; Sawyer, "1 out of 3," 13; *Recommendations of the National Advisory Committee on Microbiological Criteria for Foods*, January 31, 1990, iii, https://www.fsis .usda.gov/wps/wcm/connect/b408ece9-ea92-482f-af47-f6621b2c3f9c/rec_rte1990.pdf?MOD =AJPERES, archived at https://perma.cc/P9HT-7GBN.

11. "Catherine Adams Hutt," *LinkedIn*, https://www.linkedin.com/in/catherine-adams -hutt-b3a1829, archived at https://perma.cc/UK5P-9PZN; Catherine Adams Hutt, telephone interview by the author, October 23 and 27, 2015; *Recommendations of the National Advisory Committee*, iii, 12; Neal Fortin, "HACCP and Other Regulatory Approaches to Prevention of Foodborne Diseases," in *Foodborne Infections and Intoxications*, ed. J. Glenn Morris Jr. and Morris E. Potter (London: Academic Press, 2013), 498; William H. Sperber, "Happy 50th Birthday to HACCP: Retrospective and Prospective," *Food Safety Magazine*, December 2009–January 2010, https://www.foodsafetymagazine.com/magazine-archive1/december-2009january-2010/ happy-50th-birthday-to-haccp-retrospective-and-prospective/, archived at https://perma.cc/ WC27-8XBZ.

12. Adams Hutt, interview; Nestle, *Safe Food*, loc. 1849.

13. *APHA v. Butz*, 511 F.2d 331 (D.C. Cir. 1974), 4; Nestle, *Safe Food*, loc. 1722.

14. Adams Hutt, interview.

15. Diane Sawyer, "1 out of 3."

16. Wikipedia, s.v. "1993 Jack in the Box E. coli Outbreak," last modified January 11, 2018, https://en.wikipedia.org/wiki/1993_Jack_in_the_Box_E._coli_outbreak, archived at https://

perma.cc/97KK-7GRG; Jeff Benedict, *Poisoned: The True Story of the Deadly* E. coli *Outbreak that Changed the Way Americans Eat* (New York: February Books, 2011) x. For stylistic purposes, the discussion that follows uses the term *E. coli* O157 to refer to *E. coli* O157:H7.

17. Nicols Fox, *Spoiled: Why Our Food Is Making Us Sick and What We Can Do about It* (New York: Penguin, 1997), 219–39; Lee W. Riley et al., "Hemorrhagic Colitis Associated with a Rare Escherichia coli Serotype," *New England Journal of Medicine* 308 (March 24, 1983): 681–85.

18. CDC, "Update: Multistate Outbreak of Escherichia coli O157:H7 Infections from Hamburgers—Western United States, 1992–1993," *Morbidity and Mortality Weekly Report* 42, no. 14 (April 16, 1993): 258–63; Robert V. Tauxe and Emilio J. Esteban, "Advances in Food Safety to Prevent Foodborne Diseases in the United States," in *Silent Victories: The History and Practice of Public Health in Twentieth-Century America*, ed. John W. Ward and Christian Warren (Oxford: Oxford University Press, 2006), 31; Benedict, *Poisoned*, 31; Wikipedia, "1993 Jack in the Box *E. coli* Outbreak"; Nestle, *Safe Food*, loc. 1881; Robert V. Tauxe, interview on *Frontline*, PBS, April 2002, https://www.pbs.org/wgbh/pages/frontline/shows/meat/interviews/tauxe.html, archived at https://perma.cc/WR75-PTBY. A search of the LexisNexis Major US Newspapers database for articles since January 1, 2015, containing a mention of the Jack in the Box *E. coli* outbreak yielded forty articles. Summary of search results, archived at https://perma.cc/ABH2-9HTF.

19. Nestle, *Safe Food*, loc. 2234; Fox, *Spoiled*, 252; Patrick Boyle, interview on *Frontline*, PBS, April 2002, https://www.pbs.org/wgbh/pages/frontline/shows/meat/interviews/boyle.html, archived at https://perma.cc/7KUA-AL8T.

20. Nestle, *Safe Food*, loc. 2051; Glenn Morris, interview on *Frontline*, PBS, April 2002, https://www.pbs.org/wgbh/pages/frontline/shows/meat/interviews/morris.html, archived at https://perma.cc/3NL8-JH48; Michael Taylor, interview by Larry Quinn, October 31, 2000, USDA Oral History, 20, 22–28, http://www.foodsafetynews.com/Taylor%20Oral%20History.pdf, archived at https://perma.cc/L3JF-NQWN.

21. *Hearing on the Need for Changes to Federal Food Inspection Programs to Ensure Meat Is Safe for Consumers before the Subcommittee on Agricultural Research, Conservation, Forestry, and General Legislation*, 103rd Cong. 15 (testimony of Russell Cross), 58 (testimony of James Marsden, American Meat Institute) (February 5, 1993); Tauxe, interview on *Frontline*; Nestle, *Safe Food*, loc. 1919; Theno, interview.

22. Benedict, *Poisoned*, 74–75. On how news organizations shape news stories, see Timothy D. Lytton, *Holding Bishops Accountable: How Lawsuits Helped the Catholic Church Confront Clergy Sexual Abuse* (Cambridge, MA: Harvard University Press, 2008), 85–86.

23. On the framing effects of civil litigation, see Lytton, *Holding Bishops Accountable*, 84–85.

24. Benedict, *Poisoned*, 39–40, 61, 75, 77, 291; Bill Marler, "E. coli Update," Marler Clark, October 31, 1997, https://marlerclark.com/news_events/e-coli-update, archived at https://perma.cc/JDX5-6JL8. Newspaper coverage of the McDonald's outbreak did not appear on the front pages of major newspapers, nor did it appear as frequently or for as long as coverage of the Jack in the Box outbreak a decade later. Pam Brannon (law librarian at Georgia State University College of Law), email message to the author, May 18, 2016, archived at https://perma.cc/8AA7-9BQQ (results of a newspaper search); Pam Brannon, email messages to the author, February 13–14, 2018, archived at https://perma.cc/C46R-U9DD (results of more detailed newspaper search). On litigation as an unfolding drama, see Lytton, *Holding Bishops Accountable*, 98.

25. Benedict, *Poisoned*, 23, 25, 35, 40; Beth P. Bell et al., "A Multistate Outbreak of *Escherichia coli* O157:H7—Associated Bloody Diarrhea and Hemolytic Uremic Syndrome from Hamburgers," *JAMA* 272, no. 17 (November 2, 1994): 1349–53.

26. "History," *STOP Foodborne Illness*, http://www.stopfoodborneillness.org/about-us/history/, archived at https://perma.cc/U2KA-SD57; "Achievements," *STOP Foodborne Illness*, http://www.stopfoodborneillness.org/about-us/achievements/, archived at https://perma.cc/KUV7-NKY5STOP; Benedict, *Poisoned*, 196–99.

27. Rosemary Mucklow, telephone interview by the author, November 10, 2015; *Hearing on the Need for Changes*; Martin Tolchin, "Clinton Orders Hiring of 160 Meat Inspectors," *New York Times*, February 12, 1993, A23; Federal Crop Insurance Reform and Department of Agriculture Reorganization Act, Pub. L. No. 103-354, 108 Stat. 3227, § 261.

28. John Kingdon, *Agendas, Alternatives, and Public Policies*, 2nd ed. (New York: Longman, 2003), 168–69, 201; Benedict, *Poisoned*, 46–47; Adams Hutt, interview. On policy change, see also John Braithwaite and Peter Drahos, *Global Business Regulation* (Cambridge: Cambridge University Press, 2000), 562.

29. Benedict, *Poisoned*, 45–46, 170–71; Ross-Nazzal, "From Farm to Fork," 233; Eric Schlosser, *Fast Food Nation: The Dark Side of the All-American Meal* (New York: Harper Perennial, 2001), 208–10; David Theno, interview on *Frontline*, PBS, April 2002, https://www.pbs.org/wgbh/pages/frontline/shows/meat/interviews/theno.html, archived at https://perma.cc/D4J3-FYQZ; Theno, interview by the author; Lisa White, "A Food Safety Focus: Jack in the Box," *Food Service Equipment & Supplies*, February 28, 2006, http://www.fesmag.com/features/foodservice-issues/1891-a-food-safety-focus-jack-in-the-box, archived at https://perma.cc/SCQ4-RT34.

30. Elise Golan et al., *Food Safety Innovation in the United States: Evidence from the Meat Industry*, USDA Agricultural Economic Report No. 831 (April 2004), 30–36.

31. Russell Cross, telephone interview by the author, November 12, 2015; "Alliance Board Room," International HACCP Alliance, http://www.haccpalliance.org/sub/boardroom.html, archived at https://perma.cc/57GK-RRMZ.

32. Benedict, *Poisoned*, 171; Theno, interview by the author. Theno's were not the first such efforts in response to an outbreak. Following the 1982 *E. coli* O157 outbreak, McDonald's had quietly hired Michael Doyle, a professor of microbiology at the University of Wisconsin, who recommended higher cooking temperatures, the use of clamshell grills, and regular monitoring of suppliers' levels of *E. coli* and *Salmonella*. Michael Doyle, personal communication with the author, February 4, 2016.

33. Bob Hibbert, "Performance Standards: Past, Present and Future," *Food Safety News*, December 1, 2010, http://www.foodsafetynews.com/2010/12/performance-standards-past-present-and-future/#.WoH-IejwaUk, archived at https://perma.cc/J9ZN-FTZV; Pathogen Reduction; Hazard Analysis and Critical Control Point (HACCP) Systems, Final Rule, 61 Fed. Reg. 38,806–814 (July 25, 1996).

34. FSIS, "Pathogen Reduction and HACCP Systems . . . and Beyond," May 1998, https://www.fsis.usda.gov/Oa/background/bkbeyond.htm?redirecthttp=true, archived at https://perma.cc/759S-ZGVG; PR/HACCP Final Rule, 61 Fed. Reg. 38,864–871.

35. National Academies, *Scientific Criteria to Ensure Safe Food* (Washington, DC: National Academies Press, 2003), 14, 17–18, 21, 137; Consumer Federation of America, *The Promise and Problems of HACCP: A Review of USDA's Approach to Meat and Poultry Safety* (Washington, DC: Consumer Federation of America, 2015), 6, https://consumerfed.org/wp-content/uploads/2010/06/150424_CFA-HACCP_report.pdf, archived at https://perma.cc/UUS4-2FAR; Fortin, "HACCP and Other Regulatory Approaches," 501; Neal Fortin, "The Hang-Up with HACCP: The Resistance to Translating Science into Food Safety Law," *Food and Drug Law Journal* 58, no. 4 (2003): 567; Morris, interview on *Frontline*; Elsa Murano, interview on *Frontline*, PBS,

April 2002, https://www.pbs.org/wgbh/pages/frontline/shows/meat/interviews/murano.html, archived at https://perma.cc/7B24-57PJ. For a more theoretical analysis of management-based regulation, see Cary Coglianese and David Lazer, "Management-Based Regulation: Prescribing Private Management to Achieve Public Goals," *Law and Society Review* 37 (2003): 691–730.

36. Wikipedia, s.v. "Michael R. Taylor," last modified June 24, 2017, https://en.wikipedia .org/wiki/Michael_R._Taylor, archived at https://perma.cc/6H9L-4Y4C; NASA, "A Dividend in Food Safety," *Spinoff* (1991): 55, https://ntrs.nasa.gov/archive/nasa/casi.ntrs.nasa.gov/ 20020086314.pdf, archived at https://perma.cc/KU4S-TNDD; Taylor, interview by Quinn; Nestle, *Safe Food*, loc. 2058.

37. Nestle, *Safe Food*, loc. 2081; Mucklow, interview; *Texas Food Industry Assoc. v. Espy*, F. Supp. 143 (W.D. Tex. 1994), 149.

38. Consumer Federation, *Promise and Problems*, 6–9; Mucklow, interview; PR/HACCP Final Rule, 61 Fed. Reg. 38,849–854.

39. *Supreme Beef Processors v. USDA*, 275 F. 3d 432 (5th Cir. 2001); Nestle, *Safe Food*, loc. 2587; Consumer Federation, *Promise and Problems*, 13.

40. Nestle, *Safe Food*, loc. 2340; Consumer Federation, *Promise and Problems*, 20; *AFGE v. Glickman*, 215 F.3d. 7 (D.C. Cir. 2000); GAO, *Weakness in Meat and Poultry Inspection Pilot Should Be Addressed before Implementation*, GAO-02-59, December 2001, 40–41.

41. Consumer Federation, *Promise and Problems*, 14, 21; Daniel Engeljohn to Sarah Klein and Caroline Smith DeWaal, July 31, 2014, rejecting petition by the Center for Science in the Public Interest to classify antibiotic-resistant strains of *Salmonella* as adulterants, https://www.fsis .usda.gov/wps/wcm/connect/73037007-59d6-4b47-87b7-2748edaa1d3e/FSIS-response-CSPI -073114.pdf?MOD=AJPERES, archived at https://perma.cc/B8MD-FMTK.

42. Consumer Federation, *Promise and Problems*, 16–17, Coglianese and Lazer, "Management-Based Regulation," 6, 16, 26; Rosenthal and Kunreuther, "Roles for Third Parties," 30; Rick Young, "The Trouble with Chicken," *Frontline*, PBS, May 12, 2015, https://www.pbs.org/wgbh/ frontline/film/trouble-with-chicken/transcript/, archived at https://perma.cc/ZM5K-QBFS.

43. Consumer Federation, *Promise and Problems*, 18, 19.

44. John Munsell, "*E coli* Confession: Part 2," *Food Safety News*, October 12, 2011, 4, 8, http:// www.foodsafetynews.com/2011/10/1-of-13-parts/#.Wo1Eejwa Uk, archived at https://perma .cc/8XKQ-UAV6; "HACCP—Clear as Mud," International Association for Food Protection, August 4, 2014, https://iafp.confex.com/iafp/2014/webprogram/Session1905.html, archived at https://perma.cc/2F9B-92TR.

45. John Munsell, "*E coli* Confession: Part 3," *Food Safety News*, October 13, 2011, 7, http:// www.foodsafetynews.com/2011/10/after-my-grinder-had-been/#.WoIn2OjwaUk, archived at https://perma.cc/VD9G-MTMS.

46. Michael Ollinger, Danna Moore, and Ram Chandran, *Meat and Poultry Plants' Food Safety Investments*, USDA Technical Bulletin No. 1911, May 2004, 39; Mary K. Muth, "Lessons from USDA's Mandatory HACCP Rule for Meat and Poultry," presentation at the Post-AAEA Workshop, Economic Analysis of Food Safety: The Food Safety Modernization Act, Washington, DC, August 7, 2013, http://www.aaea.org/UserFiles/file/2013am/Lessons%20from%20USDA %27s%20Mandatory%20HACCP%20Rule%20for%20Meat%20and%20Poultry.pdf, archived at https://perma.cc/YB9C-PASB. Small processors have accused the agency of reducing inspection scrutiny of large plants with sophisticated HACCP plans while driving small operations out of business as a result of relentless enforcement demands. They also allege that the agency fears politically powerful large corporations and seeks to establish a reputation for consumer protec-

tion by cracking down on little companies. John Munsell, "HACCP's Disconnect from Public Health Concerns," https://web.archive.org/web/20170226201459/http://johnmunsell.com/articles/HACCP-Disconnect-From-Public-Health-Concerns.html, archived at https://perma .cc/QY5L-XRW6; John Munsell, "*E. coli* Confessions: Part 3."

47. Bennett, *Poisoned*, 171; David Theno, personal communication with the author, February 10, 2016; Ann Marie McNamara (former vice president for food safety at Jack in the Box), email message to the author, February 16, 2016.

48. Alecia L. Naugle et al., "Food Safety and Inspection Service Regulatory Testing Program for *Escherichia coli* O157:H7 in Raw Ground Beef," *Journal of Food Protection* 68, no. 3 (2005): 462–68; Alecia L. Naugle et al., "Sustained Decrease in the Rate of Escherichia coli O157:H7—Positive Raw Ground Beef Samples Tested by the Food Safety Inspection Service," *Journal of Food Protection* 69, no. 3 (2006): 480–81; Stacy M. Crim et al., "Preliminary Incidence and Trends of Infection with Pathogens Transmitted Commonly Through Food—Foodborne Diseases Active Surveillance Network, 10 US Sites, 2006–2014," *Morbidity and Mortality Weekly Report* 64, no. 18 (May 15, 2015):495–99. For similar findings in a more recent CDC study, see Ellyn P. Marder et al., "Preliminary Incidence and Trends of Infection with Pathogens Transmitted Commonly Through Food—Foodborne Diseases Active Surveillance Network, 10 US Sites, 2006–2017," *Morbidity and Mortality Weekly Report* 67, no. 11 (March 23, 2018): 324–28.

49. Naugle, "Food Safety and Inspection Service."

50. Crim, "Preliminary Incidence and Trends." See also Marder, "Preliminary Incidence and Trends."

51. Emma Schwartz, "Can We Get to Zero Salmonella in Poultry," *Frontline*, May 12, 2015, https://www.pbs.org/wgbh/frontline/article/can-we-get-to-zero-salmonella-in-poultry/, archived at https://perma.cc/46ZF-G4NU; Changes in the Salmonella and Campylobacter Verification and Testing Program: Proposed Performance Standards [. . .], Notice and Request for Comments, 80 Fed. Reg. 3946 (January 26, 2015); New Performance Standards for Salmonella and Campylobacter in Young Chicken and Turkey Slaughter Establishments, Notice, 76 Fed. Reg. 15,284 (March 21, 2011); USDA FSIS, "Serotypes Profile of Salmonella Isolates from Meat and Poultry Products: January 1998 through December 2013," https://www.fsis.usda.gov/wps/wcm/connect/c7b5903c-8e8b-4f85-9b5c-12eaf990d2dd/Salmonella-Serotype-Annual-2013 .pdf?MOD=AJPERES, archived at https://perma.cc/S59H-V7EU; USDA FSIS, "A Comparison of Salmonella Serotype Incidence in FSIS-Regulated Products and Salmonellosis Cases," https://www.fsis.usda.gov/wps/wcm/connect/746242e6-e309-4f7c-88e3-74f28721f392/Serotype _Incidence_and_Salmonellosis.pdf?MOD=AJPERES, archived at https://perma.cc/AD6A -E6QE. See also Marder, "Preliminary Incidence and Trends."

52. Ollinger, Moore, and Chandran, *Meat and Poultry Plants*, i, iii, 37–39; Stephen R. Crutchfield et al., *An Economic Assessment of Food Safety Regulations: The New Approach to Meat and Poultry Inspection*, USDA Agricultural Economic Report No. 755, July 1997, 9 (assumptions), 12 (resulting estimates). A 2003 USDA study estimated annual compliance costs at $623 million. Ollinger, Moore, and Chandran, *Meat and Poultry Plants*, 37.

53. Ollinger, Moore, and Chandran, *Meat and Poultry Plants*, iii, 14; Michael Ollinger and Danna Moore, *The Interplay of Regulation and Market Incentives in Providing Food Safety*, USDA Economic Research Report No. 75, July 2009, iii–iv, 37–38.

54. Interview by the author of anonymous food safety manager at poultry processing plant, February 9, 2015; Theno, personal communication with the author, February 10, 2016; Ollinger, Moore, and Chandran, *Meat and Poultry Plants*, iii, 37.

55. Theno, interview by the author; "HACCP—Clear as Mud."

56. Theno, interview by the author; Adams Hutt, interview.

57. Ross-Nazzal, "From Farm to Fork," 234.

58. Frank R. Baumgartner and Bryan D. Jones, *Agendas and Instability in American Politics* (Chicago: University of Chicago Press, 1993).

59. For a model of policy change that includes both patterns of change, see Braithwaite and Drahos, *Global Business Regulation*, 562 (discussing proactive and reactive sequences of policy change).

60. On the influence of political ideology and regulatory culture on regulation, see Joseph Rees, *Reforming the Workplace: A Study of Self-Regulation in Occupational Safety* (Philadelphia: University of Pennsylvania Press, 1988), 4–5; Jerry L. Mashaw and David L. Harfst, *The Struggle for Auto Safety* (Cambridge, MA: Harvard University Press, 1990), 20–26; Robert A. Kagan, *Adversarial Legalism: The American Way of Law* (Cambridge, MA: Harvard University Press, 2001), 3–17.

61. *Oversight of Food Inspection Activities of the Federal Government, Hearings before the Subcommittee on Public Health and the Environment of the Committee on Interstate and Foreign Commerce, House of Representatives*, 92nd Cong. 251, 256 (10th ed. of standards) (August 3–4, September 10 and 13–14, 1971). For a typical account of "sea change" in food safety following an outbreak, see, e.g., James Andrews, "Jack in the Box and the Decline of *E. coli*," *Food Safety News*, February 11, 2013, http://www.foodsafetynews.com/2013/02/jack-in-the-box-and-the-decline-of-e-coli/#.WoLkGOjwaUl, archived at https://perma.cc/VJP6-KC63.

62. Baumgartner and Jones, *Agendas and Instability*. See also Braithwaite and Drahos, *Global Business Regulation*, 28–29, and chap. 24 (discussing forum shifting).

Chapter Five

1. Drew McDonald, telephone interview by the author, June 2, 2016; "The CNN Wire," *CNN*, September 15, 2006, http://www.cnn.com/2006/WORLD/europe/09/14/thursday/index.html, archived at https://perma.cc/WX74-AHL4; "FDA Warning on Serious Foodborne *E. coli* O157:H7 Outbreak: One Death and Multiple Hospitalizations in Several States," FDA News Release, September 14, 2006, https://web.archive.org/web/20100304211313/http://www.fda.gov/NewsEvents/Newsroom/PressAnnouncements/2006/ucm108731.htm; "FDA Statement on Foodborne *E. coli* O157:H7 Outbreak in Spinach," FDA News Release, September 15, 2006, https://web.archive.org/web/20110201045249/http://www.fda.gov/NewsEvents/Newsroom/PressAnnouncements/2006/ucm108732.htm; Cara L. Cuite et al., *Public Response to the Contaminated Spinach Recall of 2006*, Publication No. RR-0107-013, Food Policy Institute, Rutgers University, February 5, 2007, 3; *Hearing on Examining Current Challenges and New Ideas to Safeguard Consumers Relating to Food Safety [. . .] before the Committee on Health, Education, Labor, and Pensions*, 109th Cong. 8 (testimony of Robert Brackett, FDA) (November 15, 2006); Linda Calvin, "Outbreak Linked to Spinach Forces Reassessment of Food Safety Practices," USDA Economic Research Service, *Amber Waves* (June 1, 2007), https://www.ers.usda.gov/amber-waves/2007/june/outbreak-linked-to-spinach-forces-reassessment-of-food-safety-practices/, archived at https://perma.cc/LHX4-WP32.

2. Robert (Bob) Whitaker, telephone interview by the author, June 1, 2016; David Gombas, telephone interview by the author, June 6, 2016; McDonald, interview; Varun Shekhar, "Produce Exceptionalism: Examining the Leafy Greens Marketing Agreement and Its Ability to Improve Food Safety," *Journal of Food Law & Policy* 6 (2010): 279; GAO, *Improvements Needed in FDA Oversight of Fresh Produce*, GAO-08-1047, September 2008, 1. See also *Hearing on Examin-*

ing Current Challenges, 45–46 (testimony of Robert Whitaker, MissionStar Processing), 78 (testimony of Dan Verdelli, Verdelli Farms). For alternative estimates of the industry losses caused by the outbreak, see Linda Calvin, Helen H. Jensen, and Jing Liang, "The Economics of Food Safety: The 2006 Foodborne Illness Outbreak Linked to Spinach," in *Microbial Safety of Fresh Produce*, ed. Xuetong Fan et al. (Ames, IA: Wiley-Blackwell, 2009), 399–418 (hereafter *Microbial Safety*); Carlos Arnade, Linda Calvin, and Fred Kuchler, "Consumers' Response to the 2006 Foodborne Illness Outbreak Linked to Spinach," USDA Economic Research Service, *Amber Waves* 8, no. 1 (March 1, 2010), https://naldc.nal.usda.gov/download/40131/PDF, archived at https://perma.cc/S3JW-C6NS; Jon Seltzer, Jeff Rush, and Jean Kinsey, *Natural Selection: 2006 E. coli Recall of Fresh Spinach, A Case Study by the Food Industry Center*, Food Industry Center, University of Minnesota, October 2009, 20–21, http://ageconsearch.umn.edu/bitstream/54784/2/Natural%20Selection.pdf, archived at https://perma.cc/AQ3P-KXPS.

3. M. Meadows, "How the FDA Works to Keep Produce Safe," *FDA Consumer Magazine* 41, no. 2 (March–April 2007) (reporting 205 cases of illness), https://permanent.access.gpo.gov/lps1609/www.fda.gov/fdac/features/2007/207_foodsafety.html, archived at https://perma.cc/Y5DS-XH79; CDC, "Multistate Outbreak of *E. coli* O157:H7 Infections Linked to Fresh Spinach (Final Update)" (reporting 199 cases of illness), https://www.cdc.gov/ecoli/2006/spinach-10-2006.html, archived at https://perma.cc/GS44-7U33; Seltzer, *Natural Selection*, 16; Bill Marler, "Two More Deaths Tied to Local *E. coli* Outbreak," *Marler Blog*, January 30, 2007 (counting five deaths), http://www.marlerblog.com/legal-cases/two-more-deaths-tied-to-local-e-coli-outbreak/, archived at https://perma.cc/CUB6-9TW2.

4. California Food Emergency Response Team, *Investigation of an Escherichia coli O157:H7 Outbreak Associated with Dole Pre-Packaged Spinach*, March 21, 2007, 3–4, http://www.marlerblog.com/files/2013/02/2006_Spinach_Report_Final_01.pdf, archived at https://perma.cc/N356-SCVS; Gombas, interview; Seltzer, *Natural Selection*, 20–23; Will Daniels, "Nationwide Produce Outbreak: A Moment You Never Forget," *Food Safety Magazine*, December 2011–January 2012, https://www.foodsafetymagazine.com/magazine-archive1/december-2011january-2012/nationwide-produce-outbreak-a-moment-you-never-forget/, archived at https://perma.cc/M8ZA-NXNU; *Hearing on Examining Current Challenges*, 28, 33, 35 (testimony of Kevin Reilly, California Department of Health Services). The outbreak pathogen was *E. coli* O157:H7. For stylistic purposes, here and elsewhere, I have used the shorthand *E. coli* O157.

5. Gombas, interview. For more detail on rise of foodborne illness caused by contaminated fresh produce in the decade before the 2006 outbreak, see *Microbial Safety of Fresh Produce*, chaps. 1, 5, and 20; and Calvin, "Outbreak Linked to Spinach."

6. Gombas, interview; Eric Schwartz (former president of Dole Fresh Vegetables), telephone interview by the author, June 1, 2016.

7. Gombas, interview; Schwartz, interview; Michelle Smith, telephone interview by the author, June 7, 2016; *Hearing on Examining Current Challenges*, 30, 36–37, 92 (discussing food safety challenges of leafy greens); Julie Schmit, "Tainted Spinach: All Bacteria May Not Come Out in the Wash," *USA Today*, October 5, 2006, archived at https://perma.cc/9V52-T2CT; A. Bryan Endres and Nicholas R. Johnson, "Integrating Stakeholder Roles in Food Production, Marketing, and Safety Systems: An Evolving Multi-Jurisdictional Approach," *Journal of Environmental Law & Litigation* 26 (2011): 54; Roy Costa, "The Packinghouse: Safety and Uses of Process-Water," *Food Safety News*, March 18, 2015, http://www.foodsafetynews.com/2015/03/the-packinghouse-safety-and-uses-of-process-water/#.WoMaz-jwaUk, archived at https://perma.cc/Z8GY-96AC; Center for Produce Safety, "Key Learnings," May 20, 2014, 9, https://www.centerforproducesafety.org/amass/documents/document/210/CPS%20Key%20Learnings

%20May%202014_FINAL2.pdf, archived at https://perma.cc/ XZH8-BN89; Seltzer, *Natural Selection*, 7; Marion Nestle, *Safe Food: The Politics of Food Safety*, rev. ed. (Berkeley: University of California Press, 2010), loc. 2846 (irradiation), Kindle; Xuetong Fan, Brendan A. Niemira, and Anuradha Prakash, "Irradiation of Fresh Fruits and Vegetables," *Food Technology* 62, no. 3 (March 2008): 36–43; Neal Fortin, *Food Regulation: Law Science, Policy, and Practice* (Hoboken, NJ: John Wiley & Sons, 2017), 236–39; Michael Booth and Jennifer Brown, *Eating Dangerously* (Lanham, MD: Rowman & Littlefield, 2014), loc. 2282, Kindle; Susan Bach and Pascal Delaquis, "The Origin and Spread of Human Pathogens in Fruit Production Systems," in *Microbial Safety*, 45; Robert B. Gravani, "The Role of Good Agricultural Practices in Produce Safety," in *Microbial Safety*, 109; Brendan Niemira et al., "Research Needs and Future Directions," in *Microbial Safety*, 421; M. F. Lynch, R. V. Tauxe, and C. W. Hedberg, "The Growing Burden of Foodborne Outbreaks Due to Contaminated Fresh Produce: Risks and Opportunities," *Epidemiological Infection* 137 (2009): 307–15; "Food Safety & International Markets," USDA Economic Research Service Background, archived at http://perma.cc/GUN8-RHSW; Staff, "Study: Fresh Produce Bacteria Can Thrive Despite Routine Chlorine Sanitizing," *Food Safety Magazine*, April 24, 2018, https://www.foodsafetymagazine.com/news/study-fresh-produce-bacteria-can-thrive-despite -routine-chlorine-sanitizing/, archived at https://perma.cc/KC8B-ZXW7. Not everyone agrees that consumers would be averse to purchasing irradiated fresh produce. See Suresh D. Pillai and Sohini S. Bhatia, "Electron Beam Technology: A Platform for Safe, Fresh, and Chemical-Free Food," *Food Safety Magazine*, April–May 2018, https://www.foodsafetymagazine.com/ magazine-archive1/aprilmay-2018/electron-beam-technology-a-platform-for-safe-fresh-and -chemical-free-food/, archived at https://perma.cc/78MA-R293.

8. Endres and Johnson, "Integrating Stakeholder Roles," 53–54; Rita Marie Cain, "Salads, Safety and Speech under a National Leafy Greens Marketing Agreement," *Food and Drug Law Journal* 67 (2012): 3; Elliot T. Ryser, Jianjun Hao, and Zhinong Yan, "Internalization of Pathogens in Produce," in *Microbial Safety*, 55–80.

9. Gombas, interview; Vanessa Burrows, *FDA Authority to Regulate On-Farm Activity*, Congressional Research Service, Report RS22939, August 14, 2008, 3; FDA, "Guide to Produce Farm Investigations," November 2005, https://www.fda.gov/ICECI/Inspections/InspectionGuides/ ucm074962.htm, archived at https://perma.cc/2VPQ-C5FP; 21 C.F.R. 110.19; Shekhar, "Produce Exceptionalism," 269, 273; National Academies, *An Evaluation of the Role of Microbiological Criteria for Foods and Food Ingredients* (Washington, DC: National Academies Press, 1985), 257–58.

10. FDA, "Guide to Produce Farm Investigations," 2; Whitaker, interview; Smith, interview; Trevor Suslow (vice president of food safety, Produce Marketing Association), telephone interview by the author, June 1, 2016.

11. Matthew Kohnke, "Reeling in a Rogue Industry: Lethal *E. coli* in California's Leafy Green Produce & the Regulatory Response," *Drake Journal of Agricultural Law* 12 (2007), 499; FDA, "Guidance for Industry: Guide to Minimize Microbial Food Safety Hazards for Fresh Fruits and Vegetables," October 26, 1988, 3–4, https://www.fda.gov/Food/GuidanceRegulation/ GuidanceDocumentsRegulatoryInformation/ucm064574.htm, archived at https://perma.cc/ BFH3-2WHZ; Smith, interview; Whitaker, interview; Gombas, interview; Suslow, interview; "Spoiled Rotten: Food-Borne Illnesses Kill Thousands, Sicken Millions More," *48 Hours*, CBS News Transcripts, July 10, 1997; Lynn Sherr, Hugh Downs, and Barbara Walters, "Fresh Hazards," *20/20*, ABC News, May 11, 1998.

12. IFPA-WGA, *Voluntary Food Safety Guidelines for Fresh Produce*, Summer 1997, iv–v, archived at https://perma.cc/99EF-B25G. The IFPA-WGA Food Safety Initiative was one of a number of such efforts at this time. In the summer of 1995, the National Advisory Committee

on Microbiological Criteria for Foods formed a Fresh Produce Working Group. Concurrently, United Fresh convened the Produce Microbiology Committee to study microbiological food safety. Eventually, this latter committee developed into the United Fresh Food Safety and Technology Council. Before 1995, United Fresh had a science and technology committee focused on agricultural inputs and EPA regulations. Tom Stenzel, president and CEO of United Fresh, email message to author, November 15, 2016.

13. IFPA-WGA, *Voluntary Food Safety Guidelines*; United Fresh Fruit and Vegetable Association, *Industrywide Guidance to Minimize Microbiological Food Safety Risks for Produce*, 1997 (date of publication unclear, might be 1998), archived at https://perma.cc/4FLG-YTGM; Anusuya Rangarajan et al., *Food Safety Begins on the Farm: Reduce Microbial Contamination with Good Agricultural Practices*, Good Agricultural Practices (GAPs) Program, Cornell University, November 2000 (revision of original 1997 GAPs trifold pamphlet), archived at https://perma.cc/GH48-23H3; *Prevention of Foodborne Illness Begins on the Farm*, Agricultural Engineering Information Series No. 649, Michigan State University, August 1997 (1997 version of Cornell GAPs published by MSU) https://msu.edu/~brook/publications/aeis/aeis649.htm, archived at https://perma.cc/L8P2-BF4F; *Prevention of Foodborne Illness Begins on the Farm*, *The Great Lake Fruit Growers News*, January 1998 (explaining that AEIS No. 649 "was adapted . . . from a Cornell University fact sheet"), http://virtualorchard.net/glfgn/january1998/foodsafety.html, archived at https://perma.cc/68DE-PJVX; Michelle Smith, email message to author, August 3, 2016 (recalling the materials she relied on in drafting FDA GAPs guidance). For a more detailed definition of GAPs, see Gravani, "Role of Good Agricultural Practices," 108–9.

14. IFPA-WGA, *Voluntary Food Safety Guidelines*, 1–2.

15. IFPA-WGA, *Voluntary Food Safety Guidelines*, ii, 2–3.

16. IFPA-WGA, *Voluntary Food Safety Guidelines*, ii–iii.

17. White House, "President Clinton Announces Initiative to Ensure the Safety of Imported and Domestic Fruits and Vegetables," October 2, 1997, https://clintonwhitehouse4.archives.gov/WH/New/html/19971002-8886.html, archived at https://perma.cc/Q5GV-J6WV; Smith, interview; Smith, email message; Suslow, interview; FDA, "Guide to Minimize Microbial Food Safety Hazards for Fresh Fruits and Vegetables," October 26, 1998, 1, archived at https://perma.cc/CKG4-FZZ6.

18. FDA, "Guide to Minimize Microbial Food Safety Hazards," 6, 8–10; Endres and Johnson, "Integrating Stakeholder Roles," 61–62.

19. FDA, "Guide to Minimize Microbial Food Safety Hazards," 3–4, 9. In contrast to these early GAPs, Good Manufacturing Practices (GMPs), designed to reduce the risk of microbial contamination in post-harvest processing, offered more specific guidance. By 1997, the International Fresh-Cut Produce Association had already published three editions of its leading GMP manual, *Food Safety Guidelines for the Fresh-Cut Produce Industry*, originally published in 1992, which provided specific methods and metrics for pathogen testing, detailed equipment and plant design suggestions, step-by-step equipment and facility cleaning procedures, and a model HACCP plan to help processors design, implement, and monitor measurable risk reduction routines. During the late 1990s and early 2000s, food processing in other sectors provided expertise and experience that informed the efforts of fresh produce processors to improve their food safety management. For example, Dole drew on experience with HACCP in its canned fruit and juice divisions in the design and operation of its fresh-cut produce plants. David Gombas, hired by the United Fresh Fruit and Vegetable Association in 2005 brought with him two decades of experience working in the processed food sector implementing HACCP. McDonald, interview, 2–4; Gombas, interview; Standards for the Growing, Harvesting, Packing, and

Holding of Produce for Human Consumption, Proposed Rule, 78 Fed. Reg. 3513 (January 16, 2013). While the sophistication of GMPs in fresh produce processing developed, the refinement of GAPs lagged behind. Suslow explains that "very few people had the combined expertise in microbiology, agronomy, horticulture, and practical experience dealing with and thinking about the issues related to contamination and sanitation for those types of products at the farm level, or even awareness of the diversity of sources of irrigation water, the practices related to the use of manure, or the composting process." A 2001 report, *Preventive Control Measures for Fresh & Fresh-Cut Produce*, by the Institute of Food Technologists (IFT), commissioned by the FDA, concluded that "there are no known mitigation strategies that will completely remove pathogens after contamination has occurred while maintaining produce freshness." This meant that, no matter how much processors improved food safety in their own operations, they remained vulnerable to contamination in the field. Suslow, interview; Gombas, interview; IFT, *Analysis & Evaluation of Preventive Control Measures for the Control & Reduction/Elimination of Microbial Hazards on Fresh & Fresh-Cut Produce*, September 30, 2001, chap. 5, § 3, https://web.archive.org/web/20170118085935/http://www.fda.gov/Food/FoodScienceResearch/SafePracticesforFoodProcesses/ucm091363.htm.

20. FDA, "Letter to Firms That Grow, Pack, or Ship Fresh Lettuce and Fresh Tomatoes," February 5, 2004, http://wayback.archive-it.org/7993/20171114022534/https://www.fda.gov/Food/GuidanceRegulation/GuidanceDocumentsRegulatoryInformation/ProducePlantProducts/ucm118896.htm; FDA, "Produce Safety from Production to Consumption: 2004 Action Plan to Minimize Foodborne Illness Associated with Fresh Produce Consumption," October 2004, 3, http://wayback.archive-it.org/7993/20170111013540/http://www.fda.gov/Food/FoodborneIllnessContaminants/BuyStoreServeSafeFood/ucm129487.htm; FDA, "Letter to California Firms That Grow, Pack, Process, or Ship Fresh and Fresh-Cut Lettuce," November 4, 2005, http://web.archive.org/web/20061111103625/http://www.cfsan.fda.gov/~dms/prodltr2.html; Smith, interview.

21. Hank Giclas, telephone interview by the author, August 26, 2016.

22. IFPA et al., *Commodity Specific Food Safety Guidelines for the Lettuce and Leafy Greens Supply Chain*, April 25, 2006, iv, https://www.fda.gov/downloads/Food/GuidanceRegulation/UCM169008.pdf, archived at https://perma.cc/XE65-PWFL.

23. IFPA et al., *Commodity Specific Food Safety Guidelines*, 4; Gombas, interview.

24. Robert Brackett, telephone interview by the author, July 1, 2016; *Hearing on Examining Current Challenges*, 10 (testimony of Robert Brackett); Smith, interview; Calvin, "Outbreak Linked to Spinach," 5; Standards for the Growing, Harvesting, Packing, and Holding of Produce for Human Consumption, Proposed Rule, 78 Fed. Reg. 3512 (January 16, 2013).

25. Devon Zagory (President, Devon Zagory & Associates), telephone interview by the author, August 21, 2013; Tom Chestnut (Vice President, NSF Global), telephone interview by the author, August 15, 2013. For an overview of private food safety governance in the European Union, see Tetty Havinga, "Private Food Safety Standards in the EU" (Nijmegen Sociology of Law Working Papers Series, 2017/01, January 2017), https://papers.ssrn.com/sol3/papers.cfm?abstract_id=3030634.

26. Gale Prince, telephone interview by the author, January 21, 2015; Frank Yiannas (vice president for food safety, Walmart), telephone interview by the author, January 8, 2015; Craig Wilson (vice president for quality assurance and food safety, Costco Wholesale), telephone interview by the author, August 15, 2013; McDonald, interview, 11.

27. Edward W. McLaughlin, Kristen S. Park, and Gerard F. Hawkes, *Produce Industry Pro-*

curement: Changing Preferences and Practices, Food Industry Management Program, Cornell University, No. E.B. 2015-10, September 2015, 6–7; John Hansen, telephone interview by the author, March 17, 2015; Hilary Thesmar (vice president of food safety programs, Food Marketing Institute), telephone interview by the author, December 17, 2014; David Acheson (president and CEO, Acheson Group, former FDA associate commissioner of foods), telephone interview by the author, December 15, 2014; Richard Stier (independent food safety consultant), telephone interview by the author, August 26, 2013; Chestnut, interview; James (Jim) Prevor (editor in chief of *Produce Business* magazine), telephone interview with the author, August 13, 2013.

28. Prevor, interview; McLaughlin et al., *Produce Industry Procurement,* 7–8. According to one industry expert, for brand-name manufactured products, retailers rely on supplier warranty and indemnification, not third-party audits. David (Dave) Theno, telephone interview by the author, September 5, 2014.

29. Roy Costa (founder and owner of Environmental Health Associates), telephone interview by the author, August 12, 2013; Art Davis (vice president of food safety, Vista Institute), telephone interview by the author, August 12, 2013; Theno, interview; Gale Prince, telephone interview by the author, August 6, 2013; Chestnut, interview; James Prevor, email message to the author, September 4, 2014; Spencer Henson and James Northern, "Economic Determinants of Food Safety Controls in Supply of Retailer Own-Branded Products in United Kingdom," *Agribusiness,* 14, no. 2 (1998): 113–26; Linda Fulponi, *Final Report on Private Standards and the Shaping of the Agro-Food System,* OECD JT03212398, July 31, 2006.

30. Wilson, interview; Davis, interview; Prevor, email message; Chestnut; interview.

31. McDonald, interview; Prevor, interview; Prince, interview, August 6, 2013; Ronald Doering (counsel, Gowling WLG, former administrator of the Canadian Food Inspection Agency), telephone interview with the author, September 4, 2014.

32. The term *food facilities* here refers to operations that manufacture, process, pack, or hold food. It does not include retail food establishments that sell directly to consumers—such as restaurants, bakeries, and supermarkets—which are subject to state and local health codes and are inspected primarily by local health department inspectors. For more on restaurant inspections, see Daniel E. Ho, "Fudging the Nudge: Information Disclosure and Restaurant Grading," *Yale Law Journal* 122 (2012): 595; Ho, "Does Peer Review Work? An Experiment of Experimentalism," *Stanford Law Review* 69 (2017): 1; Daniel E. Ho, Zoe C. Ashwood, and Cassandra Handan-Nader, "The False Promise of Simple Information Disclosure: New Evidence on Restaurant Hygiene Grading" (Working Paper No. 17-043, Stanford Institute for Economic Policy Research, December 20, 2017). There are several challenges in estimating the number of government inspections of retail food establishments. A starting point might be that, in 2016, there were 620,000 chain and independent restaurants in the United States. "Number of Restaurants in the United States from 2012 to 2016, by Type," Statista, https://www.statista.com/statistics/374866/number-of-restaurants-by-type-us/, archived at https://perma.cc/5FZN-AQTF. This number does not include other regulated retail food establishments, such as supermarkets and caterers. To further complicate matters, the number of inspections required per year varies by jurisdiction and risk classification of the establishment, as well as the extent to which local and state authorities actually carry out inspections required by law. Daniel Ho, email message to the author, September 28, 2017.

33. FDA, "Annual Report to Congress on Food Facilities, Food Imports, and FDA Foreign Offices," August 2012, https://web.archive.org/web/20150324025558/http://www.fda.gov/Food/GuidanceRegulation/FSMA/ucm315486.htm; USDA, *Fiscal Year 2012 Summary of Performance and Financial Information,* https://web.archive.org/web/20151112064634/http://www

.ocfo.usda.gov/docs/USDA_SPF_508_FINAL.pdf. For more recent data on FDA inspection of food facilities, see *Challenges Remain in FDA's Inspections of Domestic Food Facilities*, Department of Health and Human Services Office of Inspector General, Report No. OEI-02-14-00420, September 2017, 27. The New York State Department of Agriculture and Markets inspects 2,800 food-processing facilities annually. "Inspection," New York Department of Agriculture and Markets, https://www.agriculture.ny.gov/FS/inspection.html, archived at https://perma.cc/JTH4-N2ZY. Food Safety Service Providers, Comments on Proposed Rule for Accreditation of Third-Party Auditors/Certification Bodies . . ." Docket No. FDA-2011-N-0146, January 24, 2014 (stating that "FSSP members conduct more than 200,000 audits and inspections in over 100 countries each year"), https://www.regulations.gov/document?D=FDA-2011-N-0146-0079, archived at https://perma.cc/8BAJ-NVJB; FDA, *Preliminary Regulatory Impact Analysis for the Proposed Rules on Foreign Supplier Verification Programs (Docket No. FDA-2011-N-0143 . . .* , 2011, 139 (estimating "there are 568 accredited auditors/CBs specializing in food safety audits"), https://www.fda.gov/downloads/aboutfda/reportsmanualsforms/reports/economicanalyses/ucm363286.pdf, archived at https://perma.cc/FS2F-72PN. See also Julie A. Caswell et al., "Food Certification Industry Capacity and Ability to Comply with FSMA Final Rule on Accredited Third-Party Certification," unpublished paper presented at the annual meeting of the Agricultural and Applied Economics Association, Chicago, July 30, 2017, 3 (estimating 581 food safety certification bodies internationally), http://ageconsearch.umn.edu/record/258468/files/Abstracts_17_05_24_20_25_18_51__71_192_117_16_0.pdf, archived at https://perma.cc/YS2K-XPK5; US House of Representatives, Committee on Energy and Commerce, Committee Staff, "Report on the Investigation of the Outbreak of *Listeria monocytogenes* in Cantaloupe at Jensen Farms," January 10, 2012, 6 (stating that Primus Labs "conducts approximately 15,000 audits per year . . . for over 3,000 clients worldwide"). The American Institute of Baking, a leading food safety auditing organization, audited 5,954 US food facilities in 2002 and was slated to audit 6697 in 2003. Elise Golan et al., *Traceability in the US Food Supply: Economic Theory and Industry Studies*, USDA Economic Research Service, Agricultural Economic Report No. 830, March 2004, 36. For an overview of FDA and USDA inspection, see Fortin, *Food Regulation*, chap. 17. For an overview of private third-party auditing in meat and poultry production, see Michael Ollinger, Mary K. Muth, Shawn A. Karns, and Zanethia Choice, *Food Safety Audits, Plant Characteristics, and Food Safety Technology Use in Meat and Poultry Plants*, USDA Economic Research Service, Economic Information Bulletin No. 82, October 2011. For a general introduction to private food safety auditing, see Bernd M. J. van der Meulen, ed., *Private Food Law: Governing Food Chains through Contract Law, Self-Regulation, Private Standards, Audits and Certification Schemes* (Wageningen, Netherlands: Wageningen Academic Publishers, 2011).

34. Patricia Wester (vice president, Food Safety Net Services), telephone interview by the author, August 13, 2013; Elanor Starmer and Marie Kulick, *Bridging the GAPs: Strategies to Improve Produce Safety, Preserve Farm Diversity and Strengthen Local Food Systems*, Food & Water Watch and Institute for Agriculture and Trade Policy, September 2009, 3, https://www.iatp.org/files/258_2_106746.pdf, archived at https://perma.cc/5UQW-A9X3.

35. *SQF Code, Edition 8*, SQF Institute, archived at https://perma.cc/CC36-EWZ6; *Criteria for SQF Certification Bodies*, 8th ed., SQF Institute, October 2017, http://www.sqfi.com/wp-content/uploads/Criteria-for-SQF-Certification-Bodies-October-2017.pdf, archived at https://perma.cc/3WBC-VGT3; "GlobalG.A.P. History," https://www.globalgap.org/uk_en/who-we-are/about-us/history/, archived at https://perma.cc/5H85-QGLW; "GlobalG.A.P. Milestones," https://www.globalgap.org/uk_en/who-we-are/about-us/Timeline/, archived at https://perma

.cc/4XXJ-CZTS; Donal Casey, "Structuring Private Food Safety Governance: GLOBALG.A.P and the Legitimating Role of the State and Rule Intermediaries," in *Hybridization of Food Governance: Trends, Types and Results*, ed. Paul Verbruggen and Tetty Havinga (Cheltenham, UK: Edward Elgar, 2017), 31; Starmer and Kulick, *Bridging the GAPs*, 7–8; "History," CanadaGAP, http://www.canadagap.ca/history/, archived at https://perma.cc/AE3Y-YC4V.

36. Wester, interview; Stier, interview; Davis, interview.

37. Linda L. Leake, "Auditing Makes the World Go Round," *Food Quality & Safety*, August 1, 2008, http://www.foodqualityandsafety.com/article/auditing-makes-the-world-go-round/, archived at https://perma.cc/C7YX-WFXJ; GFSI, *Enhancing Food Safety through Third Party Certification*, March 2011, 2, 4, http://www.mygfsi.com/gfsifiles/GFSI_White_Paper_-_Enhancing_Food_Safety_Through_Third_Party_Certification.pdf, archived at https://perma.cc/QG4C-X5NG; GFSI, "General Presentation," 2013, archived at https://perma.cc/9DT8-WWAY; GFSI, "Recognized Certification Programs," http://www.mygfsi.com/certification/recognised-certification-programmes.html, archived at https://perma.cc/R45N-85L4; http://www.mygfsi.com/schemes-certification/recognised-schemes.html; John G. Surak, "GFSI's Role in Harmonizing Food Safety Standards," *Food Safety Magazine*, June–July 2009, https://www.foodsafetymagazine.com/magazine-archive1/junejuly-2009/gfsis-role-in-harmonizing-food-safety-standards/, archived at https://perma.cc/FK9K-6MYS.

38. Megan Chedwick (director of food safety and sustainability, Church Brothers), telephone interview by the author, May 31, 2016; Thesmar, interview; Jim Loseke (plant manager, Sargento Foods), telephone interview by the author, August 6, 2013.

39. David Gombas, "Produce GAPs Harmonization: The Goal Is in Sight," *Food Safety Magazine*, June–July 2013, https://www.foodsafetymagazine.com/magazine-archive1/junejuly-2013/produce-gaps-harmonization-the-goal-is-in-sight/, archived at https://perma.cc/4NDA-5SR3.

40. Gombas, "Produce GAPs Harmonization." For a historical overview of global harmonization efforts, see G. G. Moy and Y. Motarjemi, "International Standards and Harmonization of Food Safety Legislation," in *Encyclopedia of Food Safety*, ed. Yasmine Motarjemi, Gerald Moy, and Ewen Todd (Amsterdam: Elsevier, 2013), 4:39–49.

41. Bill Pursley (vice president of food safety education, AIB, retired), telephone interview by the author, August 8, 2013; William Schwartz (vice president, NSF), telephone interview by the author, August 9, 2013.

42. Pursley, interview; Stier, interview; Gombas, interview; Davis, interview; Costa, interview; Theno, interview. For a critique of checklists in restaurant inspections, see Daniel E. Ho, "Do Checklists Make a Difference? A Natural Experiment from Food Safety Enforcement," *Journal of Empirical Legal Studies* 15 (2018): 242.

43. Schwartz, interview; Gombas, interview; Costa, interview. Consistency is also a problem for government inspections. See Ho, "Fudging the Nudge," 574; Ho, "Does Peer Review Work?" 19, 21; Ho, "Checklists."

44. Wester, interview; Costa, interview; Irwin Pronk, "Is Food Safety Auditing about Safety or Money? GFSI-light," *Barfblog*, May 4, 2011, http://www.barfblog.com/2011/05/is-food-safety-auditing-about-safety-or-money-gfsi-light/, archived at https://perma.cc/48CX-GS5Q; Irwin Pronk, "Third-Party Audits: Missing the Forest for the Trees," *Barfblog*, November 5, 2010, http://www.barfblog.com/2010/11/third-party-audits-missing-the-forest-for-the-trees/, archived at https://perma.cc/VN3S-TJEF; Lena Sun, "Food Inspection Is Often Flawed," *Washington Post*, October 22, 2010, A1; Doug Powell et al., "Audits and Inspections Are Never Enough:

A Critique to Enhance Food Safety," *Food Control* 30 (2012): 686–91. On conflict of interest in private third-party food safety auditing, see Timothy D. Lytton and Lesley K. McAllister, "Oversight in Private Food Safety Auditing: Addressing Auditor Conflict of Interest," *Wisconsin Law Review* (2014): 300–303; Friederike Albersmeier et al., "The Reliability of Third-Party Certification in the Food Chain: From Checklists to Risk-Oriented Auditing," *Food Control* 20 (2009): 927–35. According to one account, audit fees in the fresh produce sector typically range from $500 to $1,500 per audit, and initial costs associated with audits—including training, implementation, and audits—have cost some producers as much as $8,500. Starmer and Kulick, *Bridging the GAPs*, 15. On conflict of interest in private auditing more generally, see Jodi L. Short and Michael W. Toffel, "The Integrity of Private Third-Party Compliance Monitoring" (Working Paper RPP-2015–20, Harvard Kennedy School, December 10, 2016), 1.

45. Whitaker, interview; McDonald, interview; Suslow, interview; Schwartz, interview; Giclas, interview; Scott Horsfall (CEO of the California LGMA), telephone interview by the author, September 15, 2015; Shermain D. Hardesty and Yoko Kusunose, "Growers' Compliance Costs for the Leafy Greens Marketing Agreement and Other Food Safety Programs," UC Small Farm Research Brief, University of California, Davis, September 2009, 2; "Good Agricultural Practices (GAPs)," Western Growers, archived at https://perma.cc/FN9A-XPL3; *California Leafy Green Products Handler Marketing Agreement*, State of California Department of Food and Agriculture Marketing Branch, May 4, 2015, https://www.cdfa.ca.gov/mkt/mkt/pdf/LeafyGreensProductsHandlerMktAgmt.pdf, archived at https://perma.cc/8NQP-ER65.

46. Gombas, interview.

47. McDonald, interview, 3; Giclas, interview.

48. For details, see the discussion and citations in the previous section of this chapter.

49. *Commodity Specific Food Safety Guidelines for the Production and Harvest of Lettuce and Leafy Greens*, LGMA, July 10, 2009, 18, 27, 41, 47, archived at https://perma.cc/K62Q-UV8P; Whitaker, interview; Linda Calvin, "Outbreak Linked to Spinach Forces Reassessment of Food Safety Practices," USDA Economic Research Service, *Amber Waves*, June 1, 2007, 6, archived at https://perma.cc/G3KG-MQ5W.

50. Diana Stuart, "Science, Standards, and Power: New Food Safety Governance in California," *Journal of Rural Social Sciences* 25, no. 3 (2010): 120; Endres and Johnson, "Integrating Stakeholder Roles," 67–72; G. B. Wood, "Marketing Agreements and Orders—Without Production Controls," in *Increasing Understanding of Public Problems and Policies*, conference publication (Chicago: Farm Foundation, 1961), 69–70, http://ageconsearch.umn.edu/record/17627/files/ar610069.pdf, archived at https://perma.cc/PDL7-PE5Q.

51. *California Leafy Green Products Handler Marketing Agreement*, 1–2, 9–10; Horsfall, interview. See also Endres and Johnson, "Integrating Stakeholder Roles"; Stuart, "Science, Standards, and Power"; Hardesty and Kusunose, "Growers' Compliance Costs"; Kohnke, "Reeling in a Rogue Industry"; Shekhar, "Produce Exceptionalism"; Starmer and Kulick, *Bridging the GAPs*.

52. *California Leafy Green Products Handler Marketing Agreement*, 1, 3, 4, 6, 11; Giclas, interview; Endres and Johnson, "Integrating Stakeholder Roles."

53. Horsfall, interview.

54. Gombas, interview; Daniel Cohen, *The History, Politics & Perils of the Current Food Safety Controversy: CAFF Guide to Proposed Food Safety Regulations*, Community Alliance with Family Farmers, January 2008, 9, 11, archived at https://perma.cc/TM8V-PDKB; Endres and Johnson, "Integrating Stakeholder Roles," 48–49; "Good Agricultural Practices (GAPs)," also Western Growers, "Leafy Green Marketing Agreement and Marketing Order Frequently

Asked Questions," January 2, 2007, 3, archived at https://perma.cc/6RYA-ZKY3; Giclas, interview; Kohnke, "Reeling in a Rogue Industry," 509; Shekhar, "Produce Exceptionalism," 285; April Ward, "Canadian Report Opens Dialogue for Improving Food Safety," California LGMA, https://www.caleafygreens.ca.gov/2012/02/canadian-report-opens-dialogue-improving-food-safety/, archived at https://perma.cc/3RE5-D999. The LGMA founders briefly considered developing a marketing order, which would have legally obligated all growers to adopt the new standards, but approval of a marketing order would have required a supermajority of growers, and the founders were doubtful that they could generate sufficient support among the more than one thousand leafy greens growers in the state. "Good Agricultural Practices (GAPs)."

55. Linda Calvin, "Food Safety Practices and Costs under the California Leafy Greens Marketing Agreement," USDA Economic Research Service Economic Information Bulletin No. 173, June 2017, 15–18.

56. McDonald, interview; *Commodity Specific Food Safety Guidelines*, LGMA, 10. For analysis of the complexities of adopting the EPA water standard for agricultural water, see Jennifer McEntire and Jim Gorny, "Fixing FSMA's Ag Water Requirements," *Food Safety Magazine*, August–September 2017, https://www.foodsafetymagazine.com/magazine-archive1/august september-2017/fixing-fsmae28099s-ag-water-requirements/, archived at https://perma.cc/MNM3-RU3L.

57. *Commodity Specific Food Safety Guidelines*, LGMA, 48; Suslow, interview; Gombas, interview.

58. "Committees," California LGMA, February 14, 2018, http://www.lgma.ca.gov/about-us/committees/, archived at https://perma.cc/C78D-U5TK; Suslow, interview; Whitaker, interview; "About CPS," Center for Produce Safety, February 14, 2018, https://www.center forproducesafety.org/about.php, archived at https://perma.cc/6ERD-FJB7.

59. Handling Regulations for Leafy Greens under the Agricultural Marketing Agreement Act of 1937, Advanced Notice of Proposed Rulemaking, 72 Fed. Reg. 56,678 (October 4, 2007); Proposed National Marketing Agreement Regulating Leafy Green Vegetables [. . .], Proposed Rule and Opportunity to File Exceptions, 76 Fed. Reg. 24,292–293 (April 29, 2011).

60. Proposed National Marketing Agreement, 76 Fed. Reg. 24,330–337; USDA, "Proposed National Leafy Greens Marketing Agreement, Summary Points," archived at https://perma.cc/P89R-V6EQ.

61. This and the next two paragraphs rely on David Runsten (director of policy and programs, Community Alliance with Family Farmers), testimony at the USDA hearing on the proposed National Leafy Green Marketing Agreement, Monterey, California, September 22, 2009, http://www.nationalorganiccoalition.org/_literature_113917/David_Runsten,_Director_of _Policy_and_Programs,_Community_Alliance_with_Family_Farmers,_Davis,_CA, archived at https://perma.cc/G4YG-KT2M. See also Cohen, *History, Politics & Perils*.

62. This and the next two paragraphs rely on *Ready-to-Eat or Not? Examining the Impact of Leafy Greens Marketing Agreements, a Hearing before the Subcommittee on Domestic Policy of the Committee on Oversight and Government Reform, House of Representatives*, 111th Cong. 70–85 (July 29, 2009) (testimony of Caroline Smith DeWaal, director of food safety, Center for Science in the Public Interest); Elisa Odabashian, "CU Comments on USDA Proposal to Use Federal Marketing Agreement to Oversee Safety of Leafy Greens," Comments of Consumers Union, http://consumersunion.org/news/cu-comments-on-usda-proposal-to-use-federal-marketing -agreement-to-oversee-safety-of-leafy-greens/, archived at https://perma.cc/6NVV-C7BW.

63. National Marketing Agreement Regulating Leafy Green Vegetables [. . .], Termination of Proceeding, 78 Fed. Reg. 73,111–112 (December 5, 2013).

64. White House, "Weekly Address: President Barack Obama Announces Key FDA Appointments and Tougher Food Safety Measures," March 14, 2009, https://obamawhitehouse.archives.gov/the-press-office/weekly-address-president-barack-obama-announces-key-fda-appointments-and-tougher-fo, archived at https://perma.cc/Z7T4-E5VH.

65. White House, "Obama Admin Delivers on Commitment to Upgrade US Food Safety System," July 7, 2009, https://obamawhitehouse.archives.gov/realitycheck/the-press-office/obama-administration-delivers-commitment-upgrade-us-food-safety-system, archived at https://perma.cc/DG33-B2MQ; Standards for Growing, Proposed Rule, 78 Fed. Reg. 3509–3510, 3516.

66. Standards for Growing, Proposed Rule, 78 Fed. Reg. 3508–3510; IFPA et al., *Commodity Specific Food Safety Guidelines*, ii; Smith, interview; FDA, "Produce Safety from Production to Consumption," 3; FDA, "Guidance for Industry: Guide to Minimize Microbial Food Safety Hazards of Fresh-Cut Fruits and Vegetables," February 2008, https://www.fda.gov/Food/GuidanceRegulation/GuidanceDocumentsRegulatoryInformation/ucm064458.htm, archived at https://perma.cc/9VTV-R446. In a related effort, the Association of Food and Drug Officials, a membership organization for federal, state, and local officials, started work in 2007 on the Model Code for Produce Safety, which it published in November 2009. In developing its model code, AFDO relied heavily on previous industry and FDA guidance and solicited input from industry experts, government officials, academics, and consumer advocates. *Model Code for Produce Safety*, AFDO, November 2009, available at http://www.afdo.org/.

67. Caroline Smith DeWaal, Citizen Petition to FDA on behalf of the Center for Science and the Public Interest, November 15, 2006, archived at https://perma.cc/VFE9-37JL; Michael Jacobson, Caroline Smith DeWaal, and Chris Waldrop, letter to FDA commissioner Andrew C. von Eschenbach, July 3, 2008, archived at https://perma.cc/2MY4-NJ44; *Ready-to-Eat or Not?*, 79; Daniel B. Wood, "*E. coli* Cases Prompt Calls to Regulate Farm Practices," *Christian Science Monitor*, September 18, 2006, 2.

68. Covington & Burling, "The Food and Drug Administration Globalization Act of 2008," Food & Drug E-Alert, April 24, 2008, https://www.cov.com/~/media/files/corporate/publications/2008/04/the-food-and-drug-administration-globalization-act-of-2008.pdf, archived at https://perma.cc/F6QJ-866J; Covington & Burling, "Bipartisan Food Safety Bill Introduced in the Senate," Food & Drug E-Alert, March 6, 2009, https://www.cov.com/-/media/files/corporate/publications/2009/03/bipartisan-food-safety-bill-introduced-in-the-senate.pdf, archived at https://perma.cc/4RB5-EFCB; Covington & Burling, "House Passes New Food Safety Bill," Food & Drug E-Alert, July 31, 2009, https://www.cov.com/-/media/files/corporate/publications/2009/07/house-passes-new-food-safety-bill.pdf, archived at https://perma.cc/J5LJ-329X; Covington & Burling, "Food Safety Bill Clears Senate Committee," Food & Drug E-Alert, November 20, 2009, https://www.cov.com/-/media/files/corporate/publications/2009/11/food-safety-bill-clears-senate-committee.pdf, archived at https://perma.cc/S6R8-KJW6; Bill Marler, "FSMA: The End of My 20-Year Law Practice? Let's Hope So!" *Marler Blog*, March 9, 2014, http://www.marlerblog.com/case-news/fsma-the-end-of-my-20-year-law-practice-lets-hope-so/, archived at https://perma.cc/37GJ-BLQU; CSPI, "President to Sign Historic Food Safety Bill, Reforming FDA," January 3, 2011, https://cspinet.org/new/201101032.html, archived at https://perma.cc/8P5A-QJ4Y.

69. Smith, interview; McDonald, interview; Gombas, interview.

70. FDA Food Safety Modernization Act, Pub. L. No. 111-353, 124 Stat. 3885 (January 4, 2011), § 105(a)(1); Standards for Growing, Harvesting, Packing, and Holding of Produce for Human

Consumption, Final Rule, 80 Fed. Reg. 74,355–356, 74,375, 74,555 (§ 112.44), 74,588 (§ 112.83); 74,373 (future guidance); for problems with FSMA water testing rules, see McEntire Fixing FSMA's Ag Water Requirements

71. Standards for Growing, Final Rule, 80 Fed. Reg. 74,368, 74,370.

72. Smith, interview.

73. *FDA Standards for the Growing, Harvesting, Packing and Holding of Produce for Human Consumption, Final Regulatory Impact Analysis [. . .].* Docket No. FDA-2011-N-0921, 40, archived at https://perma.cc/ZZ4E-F5LF; Ronald Doering, "The Food Safety Modernization Act: Lessons for Canada," *FoodInCanada.com,* September 2011, archived at https://perma.cc/2ZH3-JNDT.

74. FDA, "Operational Strategy for Implementing the FDA Food Safety Modernization Act (FSMA)," May 2, 2014, https://www.fda.gov/Food/GuidanceRegulation/FSMA/ucm395105.htm, archived at https://perma.cc/75BF-4YGW.

75. Michael R. Taylor, "We're Reinventing Ourselves to Keep Your Food Safe," *FDA Voice,* May 2, 2014, https://blogs.fda.gov/fdavoice/index.php/2014/05/were-reinventing-ourselves-to-keep-your-food-safe/, archived at https://perma.cc/A3JP-EEXL; "FDA's Taylor Stresses Industry/Government Cooperation to Enforce FSMA," *Food Safety Magazine,* September 15, 2014, https://www.foodsafetymagazine.com/news/fdas-taylor-stresses-industry-government-cooperation-to-enforce-fsma/, archived at https://perma.cc/GT6Q-SRFL. See also Standards for Growing, Proposed Rule, 78 Fed. Reg. 3608; Standards for Growing, Final Rule, 80 Fed. Reg. 74,519–521, 74,373.

76. Michael Taylor, "Food Safety Collaboration in a Global Food System," remarks at the Global Food Safety Conference, Orlando, FL, February 16, 2012, https://wayback.archive-it.org/7993/20170111074016/http://www.fda.gov/Food/GuidanceRegulation/FSMA/ucm292162.htm, archived at https://perma.cc/64AK-YE2M. For additional comparison between the California LGMA and the FSMA Produce Rule, see Calvin, "Food Safety Practices," 9–11.

77. Similarly, the USDA's Harmonized GAPs audit program relies on government inspectors to audit against private industry standards. USDA, "Harmonized GAP," https://www.ams.usda.gov/services/auditing/gap-ghp/harmonized, archived at https://perma.cc/WCL3-DJNC. For further analysis of FSMA's dependence on private third-party audits, see Caswell et al., "Food Certification Industry Capacity." See also Steven L. Schwarcz, "Private Ordering," *Northwestern University Law Review* 97 (2002): 319–49; "States and FDA Prepare for On-Farm Inspections," *The Packer,* February 22, 2017, https://www.thepacker.com/article/states-and-fda-prepare-farm-inspections, archived at https://perma.cc/GMX3-DCWQ.

78. Standards for Growing, Final Rule, 80 Fed. Reg. 74,373; Kenneth S. Petersen (chief of Audit Services Branch, USDA-AMS Fruit and Vegetable Program), telephone interview by the author, September 2, 2016. On efforts to align the requirements of the USDA Harmonized GAP Audit Program with the FDA's Produce Safety Rule, see USDA, "USDA and FDA Announce Key Step to Advance Collaborative Efforts to Streamline Produce Safety Requirements for Famers," press release 0120.18, June 5, 2018, archived at https://perma.cc/E534-BQ6M.

79. Renee Johnson, *Implementation of the FDA Food Safety Modernization Act (FSMA, P.L. 111-353),* Report No. R43724, Congressional Research Service, August 25, 2015; Standards for Growing, Proposed Rule, 78 Fed. Reg. 3516; Standards for Growing, Final Rule, 80 Fed. Reg. 74,354 (November 27, 2015); "FDA Commissioner Addresses Sate Agriculture Commissioners; Announces New Steps to Enhance Collaboration with States to Ensure Farmers are Prepared for FSMA," FDA Constituent Update, September 12, 2017, https://www.fda.gov/Food/NewsEvents/ConstituentUpdates/ucm575532.htm, archived at https://perma

.cc/QC73-ETNR; Standards for Growing, Harvesting, Packing, and Holding of Produce for Human Consumption, Extension of Compliance Dates for Subpart E, 82 Fed. Reg. 42,963 (September 13, 2017); FDA, "Policy Regarding Certain Entities Subject to the Current Good Manufacturing Practice and Preventive Controls, Produce Safety, and/or Foreign Supplier Verification Programs, Guidance for Industry," 83 Fed. Reg. 598–600 (January 5, 2018) (filed on January 4, 2018 at 8:45 a.m.); FDA, "At This Time, FDA Does Not Intend to Enforce Certain Provisions in Four Regulations Implementing FSMA," Fact Sheet, https://www.fda .gov/downloads/Food/GuidanceRegulation/GuidanceDocumentsRegulatoryInformation/ UCM591242.pdf, archived at https://perma.cc/3528-F7DH; CSPI, "Trump Administration Indefinitely Delays Key Food Safety Protections," January 4, 2018, archived at https://perma .cc/J6FZ-5GBV.

80. FDA, "What to Expect Now that Larger Farms Must Comply with the FSMA Produce Safety Rule," February 1, 2018, archived at https://perma.cc/DN8U-BG6R; "Produce Safety Alliance, Cooperative Agreement," Cornell College of Agriculture and Life Sciences, 2018, archived at https://perma.cc/BUF3-67RP; "States and FDA Prepare for On-Farm Inspections."

81. Bill Marler, telephone interview by the author, May 31, 2016.

82. Marler, interview; "Marler Clark Files Fourth E. coli Lawsuit Against Dole," Marler Clark, February 14, 2006, https://marlerclark.com/news_events/marler-clark-files-fourth-e -coli-lawsuit-against-dole, archived at https://perma.cc/6FNY-44VA; "Dole Lettuce *E. coli* Outbreak Lawsuits—Minnesota, Wisconsin, Oregon (2005)," Marler Clark, April 1, 2008, https:// marlerclark.com/news_events/dole-lettuce-e-coli-outbreak-minnesota-wisconsin-and-oregon, archived at https://perma.cc/YX3F-PBDJ; Bill Marler, "Publisher's Platform: Will the Justice Department Look at Dole's History of Recalls and Outbreaks?" *Food Safety News*, May 2, 2016, http://www.foodsafetynews.com/2016/05/publishers-platform-will-the-justice-department -look-at-doles-history-of-recalls-and-outbreaks/#.WoZIIKjwaUk, archived at https://perma .cc/L93V-VTP9.

83. Marler, interview; "FDA Statement on Foodborne *E. coli* O157:H7 Outbreak in Spinach Update: Wednesday, September 2006," FDA News Release, September 20, 2006, https:// web.archive.org/web/20100304211025/http://www.fda.gov/NewsEvents/Newsroom/ PressAnnouncements/2006/ucm108740.htm; "Dole Sued by Oregon *E. coli* Victim," Marler Clark, September 14, 2006, https://marlerclark.com/news_events/dole-sued-by-oregon-e -coli-victim, archived at https://perma.cc/9JS9-VRSG; Capi Lynn, "Salem Woman Wasn't Expected to Live," *Statesman Journal*, September 10, 2006, https://marlerclark.com/news_events/ salem-woman-wasnt-expected-to-live, archived at https://perma.cc/MK8L-QCES; *Majeska v. Dole Fresh Vegetables, Inc.*, Plaintiffs' First Complaint for Damages, September 2009, http:// www.marlerblog.com/uploads/file/MAJESKA,%20Jane%20-%20Complaint.pdf, archived at https://perma.cc/23TK-DTHR; Seltzer, *Natural Selection*, 5–6; California Food Emergency Response Team, *Investigation*, 3. Marler had filed lawsuits against Dole during the previous winter on behalf of victims sickened by bagged lettuce contaminated with *E. coli* O157. Marler, interview; "Dole Sued by Oregon *E. coli* victim," Marler Clark, September 14, 2006, http://www .foodpoisonjournal.com/food-poisoning-watch/dole-sued-by-oregon-e-coli-victim/, archived at https://perma.cc/526N-RPW4.

84. Tom Baker, "Liability Insurance as Tort Regulation: Six Ways That Liability Insurance Shapes Tort Law in Action," *Connecticut Insurance Law Journal* 12 (2005–2006): 4; Tim Linden, "Liability Insurance: How Much Is Enough?" *Produce News*, May 31, 2012, http://producenews .com/news-dep-menu/test-featured/7945-liability-insurance-how-much-is-enough, archived

at https://perma.cc/376M-GG2D. On the symbiosis of tort law and insurance, see Kenneth S. Abraham, *The Liability Century: Insurance and Tort Law from the Progressive Era to 9/11* (Cambridge, MA: Harvard University Press, 2008), 1–13, 171–97. See also Shauhin Talesh, "Insurance and the Law," in *International Encyclopedia of the Social & Behavioral Sciences*, 2nd ed., ed. James D. Wright (Amsterdam: Elsevier, 2015), 215–20.

85. Ed Mitchell (principal underwriter for product recall insurance, MS Amlin), telephone interview by the author, January 29, 2015; Jack Hipp (vice president for claims, Allianz Global), telephone interview by the author, April 16, 2015; Theno, interview; "Food Contamination Insurance Coverage Issues: An Insurer's Perspective," Cozen O'Connor, March 1, 2008, 25–26, https://www.cozen.com/admin/files/publications/Food_Contamination_Coverage_White _Paper_Current.pdf?embed, archived at https://perma.cc/XK8D-KFCH; Marc S. Mayerson, "Insurance Recovery for Losses from Contaminated or Genetically Modified Foods," *Tort Trial & Insurance Practice Law Journal* 39, no. 3 (Spring 2004): 844, 853–54; Jerry R. Skees, Aleta Botts, and Kimberly A. Zeuli, "The Potential for Recall Insurance to Improve Food Safety," *International Food and Agribusiness Management Review* 4 (2001): 106–8; "New Developments in Product Recall Insurance," *Western Growers*, October 1, 2013, https://www.wga.com/magazine/ 2013/10/01/new-developments-product-recall-insurance, archived at https://perma.cc/AKT5 -F3RY. See also Matt Carpenter, "Case Study: Ingredient Manufacturers and Their Product Recall Insurance Risk," AmWINS Group, June 9, 2016, http://www.amwins.com/insights/article/ case-study-ingredient-manufacturers-and-their-product-recall-insurance-risk_6-15, archived at https://perma.cc/VK2C-ZFT9; Arthur S. Garrett III, "Insurance for Food Recall," *Risk Report* 39, no. 2 (October 2016), archived at https://perma.cc/MY7L-5X6E; Virginia White-Mahaffey, "Coverage Issues Arising from Food Contamination Claims," ABA, March 21, 2014, http://apps .americanbar.org/litigation/committees/insurance/articles/janfeb2014-food-contamination -claims.html, archived at https://perma.cc/YL6L-HGFN; Jonathan Cohen, Adrian Azer, and John Girgenti, "A Primer for Food and Beverage Attorneys on Contamination and Recall Insurance," ABA, December 5, 2013, archived at https://perma.cc/U4TX-HZC8; Bernie Steves, *2017 Emerging Trends in Product Recall and Contamination Risk Management*, Aon Risk Solutions, 2017, http://www.aon.com/attachments/risk-services/2017-Emerging-Trends-Product-Recall -Report%20-USLtr-FINAL.pdf, archived at https://perma.cc/G2YG-8MTB; GMA, Covington & Burling and Ernst & Young, *Capturing Recall Costs: Measuring and Recovering the Losses*, October 2011, https://cdn2.hubspot.net/hub/288450/file-606071909-pdf/Capturing_recall_costs .pdf, archived at https://perma.cc/PLE5-9ASP; Robert Chesler and Janine M. Stanisz, "Bringing Home the Bacon: Emerging Issues in Food Insurance Law," *Metropolitan Corporate Counsel*, April 2016, http://www.advisen.com/tools/fpnproc/fpns/articles_new_1/P/259742038.html, archived at https://perma.cc/SE5-7L2H. One commentator suggests that there is little market demand for recall insurance among fresh produce suppliers. Linden, "Liability Insurance." For evidence of damage to share price of branded foods in the meat and poultry sectors as a result of a recall, see Michael R. Thomsen and Andrew M. McKenzie, "Market Incentives for Safe Foods: An Examination of Shareholder Losses from Meat and Poultry Recalls," *American Journal of Agricultural Economics* 83, no. 3 (August 2001): 526–38.

86. Tom Baker and Rick Swedloff, "Regulation by Liability Insurance: From Auto to Lawyers Professional Liability," *UCLA Law Review* 60 (2012–2013): 1412–50; Kyle Logue and Omri Ben-Shahar, "Outsourcing Regulation: How Insurance Reduces Moral Hazard," *Michigan Law Review* 111 (2012): 197–248. See also Richard V. Ericson, Aaron Doyle and Dean Barry, *Insurance as Governance* (Toronto: University of Toronto Press, 2003); John Rappaport, "How Private Insur-

ers Regulate Public Police," *Harvard Law Review* 130, no. 6 (April 2017): 1541–1614; Tetty Havinga, "The Influence of Liability Law on Food Safety on Preventive Effects of Liability Claims
and Liability Insurance" (Nijmegen Sociology of Law Working Papers Series, 2010/02, February 2010), http://repository.ubn.ru.nl/bitstream/handle/2066/91432/91432.pdf?sequence=2,
archived at https://perma.cc/5DBP-N7FH; Eliza Mojduszka, "Private and Public Food Safety
Control Mechanisms: Interdependence and Effectiveness," paper presented at the 2004 annual
meeting of the American Agricultural Economics Association, Denver, Colorado, August 1–3,
2004, https://www.researchgate.net/publication/23505412_PRIVATE_AND_PUBLIC_FOOD
_SAFETY_CONTROL_MECHANISMS_INTERDEPENDENCE_AND_EFFECTIVENESS, archived at https://perma.cc/N2WG-5DB4.

   87. Hipp, interview; Baker and Swedloff, "Regulation by Liability Insurance," 1419–20;
Logue and Ben-Shahar, "Outsourcing Regulation," 205–8, 209; Mayerson, "Insurance Recovery," 845. For specific examples, see Bernie Steves, *2016 Emerging Trends in Product Recall
and Contamination Risk Management*, AON Risk Solutions, 2016, 25 http://www.aon.com/
attachments/risk-services/product-recall-2016.pdf, archived at https://perma.cc/LAZ8-QN4K;
Elise Golan et al., *Food Safety Innovation in the United States: Evidence from the Meat Industry*, USDA Economic Research Service, Agricultural Economic Report No. 831, April 2004,
28. For evidence that risk pricing reduces environmental accidents, see Haitao Yin, Howard
Kunreuther, and Matthew W. White, "Risk-Based Pricing and Risk-Reducing Effort: Does the
Private Insurance Market Reduce Environmental Accidents" (Working Paper No. 2008-01-31,
Wharton Risk Management and Decision Process Center, January 2008).

   88. Hipp, interview; Mike Johnson, telephone interview by the author, May 21, 2015; Jane
McCarthy (vice president, Liberty International Underwriters), telephone interview by the author, May 22, 2017; Bernie Steves (managing director for National Crisis Management, Aon),
telephone interview by the author, May 15, 2017.

   89. Hipp, interview; James Derr (safety and risk management professional at XL Catlin Insurance), telephone interview by the author, April 9, 2015; Johnson, interview; Alan (Al) Maxwell (attorney at Weinberg Wheeler Hudgins Gunn & Dial, Atlanta), personal communication
with the author, May 26, 2016; Charles Stauber (Hallmark Financial Services, Philadelphia),
telephone interview by the author, August 27, 2013; Mitchell, interview; Prince, interview, January 21, 2015; Giclas, interview; McCarthy, interview.

   90. Douglas Becker, telephone interview by the author, May 21, 2015; Skees, "Potential for
Recall Insurance," 107–8.

   91. Johnson, interview; Derr, interview.

   92. Hipp, interview.

   93. Baker and Swedloff, "Regulation by Liability Insurance," 1421; Logue and Ben-Shahar,
"Outsourcing Regulation,"16; Mitchell, interview; Hipp, interview; McCarthy, interview.

   94. Baker and Swedloff, "Regulation by Liability Insurance"; Logue and Ben-Shahar, "Outsourcing Regulation"; Mayerson, "Insurance Recovery," 846.

   95. Hipp, interview. Hipp explains that these types of terms and conditions appear primarily in policies written by nonadmitted insurance carriers. Jack Hipp, telephone interview by the
author, June 17, 2016. Jane McCarthy suggests that these types of terms and conditions are rare
and that most risk reduction is done through risk selection and preincident services. McCarthy,
interview.

   96. Baker and Swedloff, "Regulation by Liability Insurance," 1421–22; Logue and Ben-
Shahar, "Outsourcing Regulation," 12; Mitchell, interview; XL Group Insurance, "Integrated
Solutions for the Food & Beverage Industry," April 2013, archived at https://perma.cc/XVL3

-T2Q2; XL Group Insurance, "Product Contamination," April 2014, archived at https://perma .cc/3N5N-KUME; XL Group Insurance, "Response XL United States," January 2014, archived at https://perma.cc/7WQB-6FGS; Johnson, interview; Mayerson, "Insurance Recovery," 845; McCarthy, interview; Kristen Markley, *Food Safety and Liability Insurance: Emerging Issues for Farmers and Institutions*, Community Food Security Coalition, December 2010, http://www.cias .wisc.edu/farmertools14/3-prepare-your-business/food-safety-and-liability-insurance.pdf, archived at https://perma.cc/A5B6-457J. For an analysis of the role of insurance loss prevention services in improving environmental safety, see "Larry Collins et al., "The Insurance Industry as a Qualified Third-Party Auditor," *Professional Safety*, April 2002, 31.

97. Hipp, interview, April 16, 2014; Hipp, interview, June 17, 2016; XL Group Insurance, "Response XL United States"; McCarthy, interview.

98. Donella H. Meadows, *Thinking in Systems: A Primer* (White River Junction, VT: Chelsea Green Publishers, 2008), loc. 327, 755–882, Kindle.

99. Meadows, *Thinking in Systems*, locs. 418 and 1435; John H. Holland, *Complexity: A Very Short Introduction* (Oxford: Oxford University Press, 2014), 5.

100. For an early call for an "integrated (systems) analysis of public and private food safety control mechanisms, their interdependence and effectiveness," see Mojduszka, "Private and Public Food Safety Control Mechanisms," 9. See also Klementina Kirezieva and Pieternel Luning, "The Influence of Context on Food Safety Governance: Bridging the Gap between Policy and Quality Management," in *Hybridization of Food Governance: Trends, Types and Results*, ed. Paul Verbruggen and Tetty Havinga (Cheltenham, UK: Edward Elgar, 2017), 156–79. For systems analysis of risk regulation more generally, see Christopher Hood, Henry Rothstein, and Robert Baldwin, *The Government of Risk: Understanding Risk Regulation Regimes* (Oxford: Oxford University Press, 2001), 9; Kernaghan Webb and Andrew Morrison, "The Law and Voluntary Codes: Examining the 'Tangled Web,'" in *Voluntary Codes: Private Governance, the Public Interest and Innovation*, ed. Kernaghan Webb (Ottawa: Carleton University Research Unit for Innovation, Science, and the Environment, 2002): 105. For systems analysis of regulatory governance, see sources cited in chapter 1 of this book.

101. For a systems analysis of professions, see Andrew Abbott, *The System of Professions: An Essay on the Division of Expert Labor* (Chicago: University of Chicago Press, 1988).

102. Meadows, *Thinking in Systems*, locs. 354–71; Gary Grobman, "Complexity Theory: A New Way to Look at Organizational Change," *Public Administration Quarterly* 29, no. 3 (Fall 2005): 360–61; Holland, *Complexity*, 9–10.

103. Mark Granovetter, "The Impact of Social Structure on Economic Outcomes," *Journal of Economic Perspectives* 19, no. 1 (Winter 2005): 33–50; Walter W. Powell, "Neither Market nor Hierarchy: Network Forms of Organization," *Research in Organizational Behavior* 12 (1990): 295–336; John Braithwaite and Peter Drahos, *Global Business Regulation* (Cambridge: Cambridge University Press, 2000), 550.

104. Michael Ferrary and Mark Granovetter, "The Role of Venture Capital Firms in Silicon Valley's Complex Innovation Network," *Economy and Society* 38, no. 2 (May 2009): 332–33; Zachary D. Clopton, "Redundant Public-Private Enforcement," *Vanderbilt Law Review* 69, no. 2 (March 2016): 285–332; Hood, Henry, and Baldwin, *Government of Risk*, 174–75. In a study by a group of USDA economists, the authors found that multiple audits were associated with higher levels of food safety technology in beef and poultry plants. Ollinger et al., *Food Safety Audits*.

105. Granovetter, "Impact of Social Structure," 33–34; Neil Gunningham and Joseph Rees, "Industry Self-Regulation: An Institutional Perspective," *Law & Policy* 19, no. 4 (October 1997). See also Timothy D. Lytton, *Kosher: Private Regulation in the Age of Industrial Food* (Cambridge,

MA: Harvard University Press, 2013), 134–35; Frank Yiannas, *Food Safety Culture: Creating a Behavior-Based Food Safety Management System* (New York: Springer, 2009).

106. Malden C. Nesheim, Maria Oria, and Peggy Tsai Yih, eds., *A Framework for Assessing Effects of the Food System* (Washington, DC: National Academies Press, 2015), 6–7, 233–42; J. B. Ruhl and Daniel Martin Katz, "Measuring, Monitoring, and Managing Legal Complexity," *Iowa Law Review* 101 (2015): 203.

107. Granovetter, "Impact of Social Structure," 34–35. For a related analysis of interfaces where different entities within a complex network meet, see Angie M. Boyce, "Fast but Right: Outbreak Surveillance and Foodborne Knowledge Infrastructure" (PhD diss., Cornell University, 2014), 29.

108. Pierami interview; Pursley, interview; CSPI Petition for GAPs; *Hearing on Examining Current Challenges*; for another example of reputational interdependence, see Calvin, "Economics of Food Safety" (discussing green onions outbreak). Compare Michael R. Thomsen, Rimma Shiptsova, and Sandra J. Hamm, "Sales Responses to Recalls for *Listeria monocytogenes:* Evidence from Branded Ready-to-Eat Meats," *Review of Agricultural Economics* 28, no. 4 (2006): 482.

109. Joseph Rees, *Hostages of Each Other: The Transformation of Nuclear Safety since Three Mile Island* (Chicago: University of Chicago Press, 1996); Daniel Carpenter, *Reputation and Power: Organizational Image and Pharmaceutical Regulation at the FDA* (Princeton, NJ: Princeton University Press, 2010), locs. 981–1000, Kindle.

110. Nesheim, Oria, and Yih, *Framework,* 6–7, 239.

111. Nesheim, Oria, and Yih, *Framework,* 6–7, 239; Susan Leigh Star, "The Ethnography of Infrastructure," *American Behavioral Scientist* 43, no. 3 (November–December 1999): 377–91.

112. Kenneth W. Abbott, David Levi-Faur, and Duncan Snidal, "Theorizing Regulatory Intermediaries: The RIT Model," *Annals, AAPSS* 670 (March 2017): 14–35; Timothy D. Lytton, "The Taming of the Stew: Regulatory Intermediaries in Food Safety Governance," *Annals, AAPSS* 670 (March 2017): 78–92. On informational intermediaries, see Ho, "Fudging the Nudge," 650.

113. This paragraph and the next are drawn from Lytton, "Taming," which, in turn, relies on Abbott, Levi-Faur, and Snidal, "Theorizing Regulatory Intermediaries."

114. Shauhin Talesh, "Legal Intermediaries: How Insurance Companies Construct the Meaning of Compliance with Antidiscrimination Laws," *Law & Policy* 37, no. 3 (July 2015): 209–39. On the intermediary role of "interstitial organizations," see David Demortain, *Scientists and the Regulation of Risk: Standardising Control* (Cheltenham, UK: Edward Elgar, 2011), 15, 34, 181–86.

115. On the implications of network structures, see Nicholas A. Christakis and James H. Fowler, *Connected: How Your Friends' Friends' Friends Affect Everything You Feel, Think, and Do* (New York: Little, Brown & Co., 2011), 30–32. Kathryn Boys et al., "The Business of Safe Food: An Assessment of the Global Food Safety Certification Industry," presentation at the annual meeting of the Agricultural and Applied Economics Association and Western Agricultural Economics Association, San Francisco, CA, July 26–28, 2015, 21, archived at https://perma.cc/GNP3-5MHU.

116. Meadows, *Thinking in Systems,* loc. 2873; Nesheim, Oria, and Yih, *Framework;* J. B. Ruhl, "Law's Complexity: A Primer," *Georgia State University Law Review* 24, no. 4 (2008): 885–911.

117. Ruhl, "Law's Complexity," 893–94n28; J. B. Ruhl, "Managing Systemic Risk in Legal Systems," *Indiana Law Journal* 89 (2014): 565–68; Demortain, *Scientists and the Regulation of Risk,* 35, 167; Harm Schepel, *The Constitution of Private Governance: Product Standards in the Regulation of Integrating Markets* (Oxford, UK: Hart Publishing, 2005), 3–6, 19; Harm Schepel, "Rules of Recognition: A Legal Constructivist Approach to Transnational Private Regulation," in *Private International Law and Global Governance,* ed. Horatia Muir Watt and Diego P. Fernandez Arroyo (Oxford: Oxford University Press: 2014), 201–10; Jody Freeman, "The Private

Role in Public Governance," *New York University Law Review* 75, no. 3 (2000): 571–72, 673; Jody Freeman, "Private Parties, Public Functions and the New Administrative Law," *Administrative Law Review* 52 (2000): 816.

118. On the concept of a rule of recognition, see H. L. A. Hart, *The Concept of Law*, 2nd ed. (Oxford: Oxford University Press, 1994). On acceptance of authority as the basis for authority, see Bruce Lincoln, *Authority: Construction and Corrosion* (Chicago: University of Chicago Press, 1994), 4–10. On the authority of private standards, see Steven Bernstein and Benjamin Cashore, "Can Non-State Global Governance Be Legitimate? An Analytical Framework," *Regulation and Governance* 1 (2007): 347–71; Benjamin Cashore, "Legitimacy and the Privatization of Environmental Governance: How Non-State Market-Driven (NSMD) Governance Systems Gain Rule-Making Authority," *Governance: An International Journal of Policy, Administration, and Institutions* 5, no. 4 (October 2002): 503–29; Schepel, "Rules of Recognition," 207–9.

Chapter Six

1. For an analysis of the need to balance food safety concerns with environmental and small farm sustainability, see Daniel S. Karp et al., "The Unintended Ecological and Social Impacts of Food Safety Regulations in California's Central Coast Region," *BioScience* 65, no. 12 (December 2015): 1173–83; Patrick Baur et al., "Inconsistent Food Safety Pressures Complicate Environmental Conservation for California Produce Growers," *California Agriculture* 70, no. 3: 142–51; Patrick Baur, Christy Getz, and Jennifer Sowerwine, "Contradictions, Consequences and the Human Toll of Food Safety Culture," *Agriculture and Human Values* 34, no. 3 (2017): 713–28; Margot J. Pollans, "Regulating Farming: Balancing Food Safety and Environmental Protection in a Cooperative Governance Regime," *Wake Forest Law Review* 50 (2015): 399–460; Elanor Starmer and Marie Kulick, *Bridging the GAPs: Strategies to Improve Produce Safety, Preserve Farm Diversity and Strengthen Local Food Systems*, Food & Water Watch and Institute for Agriculture and Trade Policy, September 2009, https://www.iatp.org/files/258_2_106746.pdf, archived at https://perma.cc/5UQW-A9X3; Kathryn A. Boys, Michael Ollinger, and Leon L. Geyer, "The Food Safety Modernization Act: Implications for US Small Scale Farms," *American Journal of Law & Medicine* 41 (2015): 395–405; Baylen J. Linnekin, *Biting the Hands that Feed Us: How Fewer, Smarter Laws Would Make Our Food System More Sustainable* (Washington, DC: Island Press, 2016), chap. 1. On trade-offs more generally in the food system, see Malden C. Nesheim, Maria Oria, and Peggy Tsai Yih, eds., *A Framework for Assessing Effects of the Food System* (Washington, DC: National Academies Press, 2015), 2, 14, 266; Emily M. Broad Leib and Margot J. Pollans, "The New Food Safety," *California Law Review* 107 (forthcoming).

2. On the cost of policy information, see Peter Schuck, *Why Government Fails So Often: And How It Can Do Better* (Princeton, NJ: Princeton University Press, 2014), 161–71. On the challenges of assessing the cost-effectiveness of food safety efforts, see Spencer Henson and Bruce Traill, "The Demand for Food Safety: Market Imperfections and the Role of Government," *Food Policy* (April 1993): 159, 162; Nesheim, Oria, and Yih, *Framework*, 10; John M. Antle, *Choice and Efficiency in Food Safety Policy* (Washington, DC: AEI Press, 1995).

3. A survey of 213 New York fruit and vegetable growers in 2002 found that "most growers used surface water for irrigation (76%), but few reported testing for water quality," that "growers commonly washed produce on farm (92%) but rarely added sanitizers to this water," and that "of the 76 respondents (36% of the total) who applied manure or compost, most (88%) used practices that would reduce food safety risks based on federal guidelines ... [but] only 52% of growers identified these practices as reducing food safety risk." Anusuya Rangarajan et al.,

"Focusing Food Safety Training Based on Current Grower Practices and Farm Scale," *Hort Technology* 12, no. 1 (January–March 2002): 126–31. A survey of 297 New England fruit and vegetable growers in 2005 found that a majority employed good agricultural practices with regard to water quality, soil amendments, animal exclusion, worker hygiene, field sanitation, and record keeping. Nancy Cohen et al., "Farm Food Safety Practices: A Survey of New England Growers," *Food Protection Trends* 25, no. 5 (May 2005): 363–70; LGMA, *2016/2017 Annual Report*, 5, http://www.lgma.ca.gov/wp-content/uploads/2017/07/2016-2017-CA-LGMA-Annual-Report-web.pdf, archived at http://perma.cc/MFH6-LSAV; Gregory Astill et al., *Before Implementation of the Food Safety Modernization Act's Produce Rule: A Survey of U.S. Produce* Growers, EIB-194, USDA, Economic Research Service, August 2018, archived at https://perma.cc/Y5V2-QV3V. For a literature review of these and other studies of on-farm food safety practices, see Aaron Adalja and Erik Lichtenberg, "Impacts of the Food Safety Modernization Act on On-Farm Food Safety Practices for Small and Sustainable Produce Growers," presentation at the annual meeting of the Agricultural and Applied Economics Association and Western Agricultural Economics Association, San Francisco, CA, July 26–28, 2015, https://scholarship.sha.cornell.edu/cgi/viewcontent.cgi?article=1006&context=conf, archived at https://perma.cc/5KAP-852Q; Linda Calvin et al., *Food Safety Practices and Costs under the California Leafy Greens Marketing Agreement*, USDA Economic Research Service Bulletin No. 173 (June 2017), 3–4.

4. Shermain D. Hardesty and Yoko Kusunose, "Growers' Compliance Costs for the Leafy Greens Marketing Agreement and Other Food Safety Programs," UC Small Farm Research Brief, University of California, Davis, September 2009; Calvin et al., *Food Safety Practices*. For additional studies, see F. A. Becot et al., "Costs of Food Safety Certification on Fresh Produce Farms in Vermont," *HortTechnology* 22, no. 5 (2012): 705–14; M. S. Paggi et al., "Domestic and Trade Implications of Leafy Green Marketing Agreement Type Policies and the Food Safety Modernization Act for the Southern Produce Industry," *Journal of Agricultural and Applied Economics* 54, no. 3 (2013): 453–64; "Cost of Food Safety: Leafy Greens Food Safety Cost Study Final Report," University of Minnesota, On-Farm GAPs Education Program, http://safety.cfans.umn.edu/links/costs, archived at https://perma.cc/PDX9-27KT; Mollie Woods and Suzanne Thornsbury, *Costs of Adopting Good Agricultural Practices (GAPs) to Ensure Food Safety in Fresh Strawberries*, Agricultural Economics Report No. 624, Department of Agricultural Economics, Michigan State University, December 2005; Dennis Tootelian, "California Leafy Greens Products 2007 Signatory Summary Report of Findings," January 2008, http://www.perishablepundit.com/docs/leafygreens-summary-finalreport.pdf, archived at https://perma.cc/F83J-LCBM. One study calculated the cost-effectiveness of LGMA water-testing prescriptions in terms of the cost per acre of resulting reductions in contamination, with the aim of enabling comparisons between different water testing and, by extension, other food safety measures, prescribed by other approaches. Helen H. Jensen et al., "Development of a Cost-Effectiveness Analysis of Leafy Green Marketing Agreement Irrigation Water Provisions," *Journal of Food Protection* 77, no. 6 (2014): 1038–42.

5. Hardesty and Kusunose, "Growers' Compliance Costs," 5; Adalja and Lichtenberg, "Impacts of the Food Safety Modernization Act"; Calvin, "Food Safety Practices." For a study of influences on food safety managers' decision making, see Bridget Hutter, *Managing Food Safety and Hygiene: Government and Regulation as Risk Management* (Cheltenham, UK: Edward Elgar, 2011).

6. Idecisionsicences, *Expert Panel Review of the Commodity Specific Food Safety Guidelines for the Production and Harvest of Lettuce and Leafy Greens*, November 19, 2015, 6, http://

www.lgma.ca.gov/wp-content/uploads/2016/05/2016-LGMA-Expert-Review.pdf, archived at https://perma.cc/4GQD-8K7H.

7. Scott Horsfall, telephone interview by the author, September 5, 2016; April Ward, "The Leafy Greens Marketing Agreement: 5 Years Later," *Food Safety Magazine* (October–November 2012), https://www.foodsafetymagazine.com/magazine-archive1/octobernovember-2012/category-produce-the-leafy-greens-marketing-agreement-5-years-later/, archived at https://perma.cc/56WD-VKED; Idecisionsicences, *Expert Panel Review*, 7; Bill Marler, telephone interview by the author, May 31, 2016; CDC, "Multistate Outbreak of E. coli O157:H7 Infections Linked to Romaine Lettuce," June 28, 2018, archived at https://perma.cc/VZ2F-FC9G; Bill Marler, "12 Years Later: Seems Like the Same E. coli Nightmare," *Marler Blog*, June 1, 2018, http://www.marlerblog.com/legal-cases/12-years-later-seems-like-to-same-e-coli-nightmare/, archived at https://perma.cc/RE7H-LX6B. For a list of leafy greens outbreaks since 1995, see "Almost 6 Dozen Outbreaks Traced to Leafy Greens Since 1995," *Food Safety News*, April 20, 2018, archived at https://perma.cc/A6WZ-LLLK.

8. *Ready-to-Eat or Not? Examining the Impact of Leafy Greens on Marketing Agreements, a Hearing before the Subcommittee on Domestic Policy of the Committee on Oversight and Government Reform, House of Representatives*, 111th Cong. 78 (testimony of Caroline Smith DeWaal, director of food science, Center for Science in the Public Interest) (July 29, 2009).

9. Alexis Robert, Chet Fenton, and Aylin Sertkaya, *Cost Effectiveness of Practices Intended to Prevent Tomato-Related Illness*, Eastern Research Group, EGR Task No. 0193.16.003.001, March 18, 2009 (report submitted to the FDA), archived at https://perma.cc/7FGE-SQ2N; Alexis Robert, Chet Fenton, and Aylin Sertkaya, *The Effectiveness of Harvest and Post-Harvest Measures for Reducing E. coli on Leafy Green Production*, Eastern Research Group, EGR Task No. 0193.16.002.001, March 20, 2009 (report submitted to the FDA), archived at http://perma.cc/7DYM-4TBM; FDA, *Standards for the Growing, Harvesting, Packing and Holding of Produce for Human Consumption, Final Regulatory Impact Analysis [. . .]*, Docket No. FDA-2011-N-0921, 58, https://www.fda.gov/downloads/AboutFDA/ReportsManualsForms/Reports/Economic Analyses/UCM472330.pdf, archived at https://perma.cc/ZZ4E-F5LF; FDA, *Technical Appendix: Estimation of Contamination Risk Mitigated Based on External Expert Elicitation Studies of Leafy Greens and Tomatoes*, 2, archived at https://perma.cc/LF6C-KE4N; For fuller commentary, see Sofie E. Miller and Cassidy B. West, "Public Interest Comment on The Food and Drug Administration's Proposed Rule: Standards for the Growing, Harvesting, Packing, and Holding of Produce for Human Consumption," Docket ID No. FDA-2011-N-0921, August 12, 2013, 8–12, https://regulatorystudies.columbian.gwu.edu/sites/regulatorystudies.columbian.gwu.edu/files/downloads/FDA_2011_N_0921_Miller_West.pdf, archived at https://perma.cc/L76N-UMY3.

10. FDA, *Final Regulatory Impact Analysis*, 56.

11. For a defense of expert elicitation, see W. P. Aspinall et al., "Evaluation of a Performance-Based Expert Elicitation: WHO Global Attribution of Foodborne Diseases," *PLOS One* 11, no. 3 (March 1, 2016), http://journals.plos.org/plosone/article/file?id=10.1371/journal.pone.0149817&type=printable, archived at https://perma.cc/M2ME-FLWR. For a critique of the FDA's prospective regulatory impact analysis in support of it egg rule, see Randall Lutter, "How Effective Are Federal Food Safety Regulations? The Case of Eggs and *Salmonella* Enteritidis," Resources for the Future, Discussion Paper No. 15-24, June 2015, http://www.rff.org/files/sharepoint/WorkImages/Download/RFF-DP-15-24.pdf, archived at https://perma.cc/EUL5-B88S.

12. FDA Food Safety Modernization Act, Pub. L. No. 111-353, 124 Stat. 3885 (January 4, 2011), § 105 (a), (b); Renee Johnson, *Implementation of the FDA Food Safety Modernization*

Act (FSMA, P.L. 111-353), Report No. R43724, Congressional Research Service, August 25, 2015; Maeve P. Carey, *Cost-Benefit and Other Analysis Requirements in the Rulemaking Process*, Report No. R41974, Congressional Research Service, December 9, 2014; Peter Strauss, *Administrative Justice in the United States* (Durham, NC: Carolina Academic Press, 2016), 455–516. On the challenges of risk analysis in policy making, see David Demortain, *Scientists and the Regulation of Risk: Standardizing Control* (Cheltenham, UK: Edward Elgar, 2011), 2–11.

13. Linda Calvin, personal communication with the author, August 22, 2016; Jim Prevor, "Food Safety Arms War Claimed as WGA Responds to Publix Demand for Enhanced Produce Standards," *Jim Prevor's Perishable Pundit* (blog), November 13, 2007, http://www.perishablepundit.com/index.php?date=11/13/07&pundit=1, archived at https://perma.cc/ZC63-X9CZ.

14. FDA, *Final Regulatory Impact Analysis*, 1.

15. William Nganje et al., "Traceability in Food Systems: An Economic Analysis of LGMA and the 2006 Spinach Outbreak," unpublished paper presented at the 85th Annual Conference of the Agricultural Economics Society, Warwick University, April 18–20, 2011, https://ageconsearch.umn.edu/bitstream/108776/2/79nganje_skilton_jenseoyeahala.pdf, archived at https://perma.cc/6ZEV-DYE6; Carla Mejia et al., "Traceability (Product Tracing) in Food Systems: An IFT Report Submitted to the FDA: Volume 2: Cost Considerations and Implications," *Comprehensive Reviews in Food Science and Food Safety* 9 (2010): 167–69.

16. Jean C. Buzby and Paul D. Frenzen, "Food Safety and Product Liability," *Food Policy* 24 (1999): 637. See also Jean C. Buzby, Paul D. Frenzen, and Barbara Rasco, *Product Liability and Microbial Foodborne Illness*, USDA Economic Research Service Agricultural Economic Report No. 799, April 2001. For other studies on the impact of liability on food safety, see Spencer Henson and Julie Caswell, "Food Safety Regulation: An Overview of Contemporary Issues," *Food Policy* 24 (1999): 589–603 (asserting that liability plays a "secondary role" in promoting food safety); Hutter, *Managing Food Safety*, 98–99 (finding little influence of lawyers or liability exposure on retail food safety decisions in the United Kingdom); Tetty Havinga, "The Influence of Liability Law on Food Safety on Preventive Effects of Liability Claims and Liability Insurance" (Nijmegen Sociology of Law Working Papers Series, 2010/02, February 2010) (modeling the risk reduction effect of liability and calling for further empirical study), http://repository.ubn.ru.nl/bitstream/handle/2066/91432/91432.pdf?sequence=2, archived at https://perma.cc/5DBP-N7FH; Alexia Brunet Marks, "Check Please: Using Legal Liability to Inform Food Safety Regulation," *Houston Law Review* 50, no. 3 (2013): 724 (concluding that foodborne illness litigation sends a "strong signal to firms to increase food safety practices"); Karen Robinson-Jacobs, "Victims of Foodborne Illness Don't Usually Seek Legal Relief," *Dallas Morning News*, May 24, 2015, https://www.dallasnews.com/business/business/2015/05/24/victims-of-food-borne-illness-dont-usually-seek-legal-relief, archived at https://perma.cc/6LAN-H7NN.

17. Denis Stearns, "Contaminated Fresh Produce and Product Liability: A Law-in-Action Perspective," in Xuetong Fan et al., *Microbial Safety of Fresh Produce* (Ames, IA: Wiley-Blackwell, 2009), 397n19; Bill Marler, telephone interview by the author, October 5, 2014. For a similar focus on jury verdicts, see Omchand Mahdu, "Penalties for Foodborne Illness: Jury Decisions and Awards in Foodborne Illness Lawsuits" (master's thesis, Virginia Polytechnic Institute and State University, 2015) (studying reported jury verdicts 1979–2014), https://vtechworks.lib.vt.edu/bitstream/handle/10919/54935/Mahdu_O_T_2015.pdf?sequence=1, archived at https://perma.cc/M9X2-K6K8. For a study based on reported settlements, see Marks, "Check Please."

18. Buzby and Frenzen, "Food Safety and Product Liability," 637. See also Jean C. Buzby,

Paul D. Frenzen, and Barbara Rasco, "Jury Decisions and Awards in Personal Injury Lawsuits Involving Foodborne Pathogens," *Journal of Consumer Affairs* 36, no. 2 (2002): 237.

19. See the discussion of framing effects in chapter 4.

20. Reed Dickerson, *Products Liability and the Food Consumer* (New York: Little, Brown & Co., 1951), quoted in Marc S. Mayerson, "Insurance Recovery for Losses from Contaminated or Genetically Modified Foods," *Tort Trial & Insurance Practice Law Journal* 39, no. 3 (Spring 2004): 846n37; Buzby, Frenzen, and Rasco, *Product Liability and Microbial Foodborne Illness*, 26. See the discussion of the Jack in the Box outbreak in chapter 4.

21. Marler, interview; Bill Marler, keynote address at the annual meeting of the International Association for Food Protection, Indianapolis, IN, August 3, 2014, lecture notes of the author. See also, Melissa Mortazavi, "Tort as Democracy: Lessons from the Food Wars," *Arizona Law Review* 57 (2015): 929–76.

22. John Aloysius Cogan, "The Uneasy Case for Food Safety Liability Insurance," *Brooklyn Law Review* 81 (2016): 1501, 1542–52.

23. James Derr, telephone interview by the author, April 9, 2015; Douglas Becker, telephone interview by the author, May 21, 2015; Marler, interview. For a discussion of how risk perceptions are based on more than just data, see Richard V. Ericson and Aaron Doyle, *Uncertain Business: Risk, Insurance and the Limits of Knowledge* (Toronto: University of Toronto Press, 2003), chap. 1.

24. Jack Hipp, telephone interview by the author, April 16, 2015; Jane McCarthy (vice president, Liberty International Underwriters), telephone interview by the author, May 22, 2017.

25. Cogan, "Uneasy Case," 1551–52; Jerry R. Skees, Aleta Botts, and Kimberly A. Zeuli, "The Potential for Recall Insurance to Improve Food Safety," *International Food and Agribusiness Management Review* 4 (2001): 108–9.

26. Charles Stauber, telephone interview by the author, August 27, 2013; Alan (Al) Maxwell (attorney at Weinberg Wheeler Hudgins Gunn & Dial, Atlanta), personal communication with the author, May 26, 2016, on insurance underwriting; Marler, interview; Tim Linden, "Liability Insurance: How Much Is Enough?" *Produce News*, May 31, 2012, http://producenews.com/news -dep-menu/test-featured/7945-liability-insurance-how-much-is-enough, archived at https:// perma.cc/376M-GG2D.

27. Jack Hipp, telephone interview by the author, June 17, 2016; Hipp, interview, April 16, 2015; Ed Mitchell (principal underwriter for product recall insurance, MS Amlin), telephone interview by the author, January 29, 2015.

28. Timothy D. Lytton and Lesley K. McAllister, "Oversight in Private Food Safety Auditing: Addressing Auditor Conflict of Interest," *Wisconsin Law Review* (2014): 304; Elena Fagotto, "Private Roles in Food Safety Provision: The Law and Economics of Private Food Safety," *European Journal of Law and Economics* 37, no. 1 (February 2014): 83–109; Sam F. Halabi and Ching-Fu Lin, "Assessing the Relative Influence and Efficacy of Public and Private Food Safety Regulation Regimes: Comparing Codex and GlobalG.A.P. Standards," *Food and Drug Law Journal* 72 (2017): 1–34; Catherine E. Rudder, A. Lee Fritschler, and Yon Jung Choi, *Public Policymaking by Private Organizations: Challenges to Democratic Governance* (Washington, DC: Brookings Institution Press, 2016), 108–11; Elisa Odabashian, "CU Comments on USDA Proposal to Use Federal Marketing Agreement to Oversee Safety of Leafy Greens," Comments of Consumers Union, 2, http://consumersunion.org/news/cu-comments-on-usda-proposal-to-use-federal -marketing-agreement-to-oversee-safety-of-leafy-greens/, archived at https://perma.cc/6NVV -C7BW; *Ready-to-Eat or Not?*, 83. On comparative institutional analysis more generally, see

Ross E. Cheit, *Setting Safety Standards: Regulation in the Public and Private Sectors* (Berkeley: University of California Press, 1990), 17, 193; Neil Komesar, *Imperfect Alternatives: Choosing Institutions in Law, Economics, and Public Policy* (Chicago: University of Chicago Press, 1997), 3–13; Peter H. Schuck, *The Limits of Law: Essays on Democratic Governance* (Boulder, CO: Westview Press, 2000), 424; David Vogel, "Taming Globalization?: Civil Regulation and Corporate Capitalism," in *The Oxford Handbook of Business and Government*, ed. David Coen et al. (Oxford: Oxford University Press, 2010), 473; Philip Harter and George Eads, "Policy Instruments, Institutions, and Objectives: An Analytical Framework for Assessing 'Alternatives' to Regulation," *Administrative Law Review* 37 (1985): 221–58.

29. For an initial attempt to create benchmarks for comparative institutional analysis but noting a dearth of empirical data, see John M. de Figueiredo and Edward H. Stiglitz, "Democratic Rulemaking," in *The Oxford Handbook of Law and Economics*, vol. 3, *Public Law and Legal Institutions*, ed. Francesco Parisi (Oxford: Oxford University Press, 2017). See also Stephen M. Maurer, *Self-Governance in Science: Community-Based Strategies for Managing Dangerous Knowledge* (Cambridge: Cambridge University Press, 2017), 156–57.

30. Standards for Growing, Harvesting, Packing, and Holding of Produce for Human Consumption, Final Rule, 80 Fed. Reg. 74,373 (November 27, 2015).

31. On hybridization see Paul Verbruggen and Tetty Havinga, eds., *Hybridization of Food Governance: Trends, Types and Results* (Cheltenham, UK: Edward Elgar, 2017); Eliza Mojduszka, "Private and Public Food Safety Control Mechanisms: Interdependence and Effectiveness," paper presented at the annual meeting of the American Agricultural Economics Association, Denver, CO, August 1–3, 2004, https://www.researchgate.net/publication/23505412_PRIVATE _AND_PUBLIC_FOOD_SAFETY_CONTROL_MECHANISMS_INTERDEPENDENCE _AND_EFFECTIVENESS, archived at https://perma.cc/N2WG-5DB4. See also Axel Marx, "How Relevant is the Public Private Distinction in the Case of Voluntary Sustainability Standards?" (Working Paper No. RSCAS 2915/30, 2015, Robert Schuman Center for Advanced Studies, European University Institute), https://papers.ssrn.com/sol3/papers.cfm?abstract_id= 2631991, archived at https://perma.cc/J527-HGZN; Jody Freeman, "The Private Role in Public Governance," *New York University Law Review* 75, no. 3 (2000): 543–675; Schuck, *Why Government Fails So Often*, 28; Christopher Hood, Henry Rothstein, and Robert Baldwin, *The Government of Risk: Understanding Risk Regulation Regimes* (Oxford: Oxford University Press, 2001), 9; Kernaghan Webb and Andrew Morrison, "The Law and Voluntary Codes: Examining the 'Tangled Web,'" in *Voluntary Codes: Private Governance, the Public Interest and Innovation*, ed. Kernaghan Webb (Ottawa: Carleton University Research Unit for Innovation, Science, and the Environment, 2002): 105; Harm Schepel, *The Constitution of Private Governance: Product Standards in the Regulation of Integrating Markets* (Oxford, UK: Hart Publishing, 2005), 176; Harm Schepel, "Rules of Recognition: A Legal Constructivist Approach to Transnational Private Regulation," in *Private International Law and Global Governance*, ed. Horatia Muir Watt and Diego P. Fernandez Arroyo (Oxford: Oxford University Press: 2014), 201–10.

32. Paul J. DiMaggio and Walter W. Powell, "The Iron Cage Revisited: Institutional Isomorphism and Collective Rationality in Organizational Fields," in *The New Institutionalism in Organizational Analysis*, ed. Walter W. Powell and Paul J. DiMaggio (Chicago: University of Chicago Press, 1991), 65–66. See also Marc A. Olshan, "Standards-Making Organizations and the Rationalization of American Life," *Sociological Quarterly* 34, no. 2 (May 1993): 327–30; Daniel C. Esty, "Good Governance at the Supranational Scale: Globalizing Administrative Law," *Yale Law Journal* 115 (2006): 1490–1562; Errol Meidinger, "Multi-Interest Self-Governance through

Global Product Certification Programmes," in *Responsible Business: Self-Governance and Law in Transnational Economic Transactions*, ed. Olaf Dilling, Martin Herberg, and Gerd Winter (Oxford, UK: Hart Publishing, 2008).

33. See Schepel, *Constitution of Private Governance*, 31, 176. For a related point, see Lawrence Busch, "Standards, Law, and Governance," *Journal of Rural Social Sciences* 25, no. 3 (2010): 73.

Chapter Seven

1. John Guzewich, telephone interview by the author, June 21, 2015; Casey Barton Behravesh et al., "2008 Outbreak of *Salmonella* Saintpaul Infections Associated with Raw Produce," *New England Journal of Medicine* 364 (February 23, 2011): 919; John Cloud, "Salmonella Saintpaul," *Time*, November 3, 2008, http://content.time.com/time/specials/packages/article/0,28804 ,1855948_1864255_1864260,00.html, archived at https://perma.cc/5J5U-PA8T. Throughout this chapter, I use *Salmonella* as a shorthand for *Salmonella enterica*, a class of *Salmonella* bacteria that causes foodborne illness.

2. Behravesh et al., "2008 Outbreak," 919, 924; Guzewich, interview.

3. "FDA Warns Consumers in New Mexico and Texas Not to Eat Certain Types of Raw Red Tomatoes," FDA News Release, June 3, 2008, http://wayback.archive-it.org/7993/2016 1023232522/http://www.fda.gov/NewsEvents/Newsroom/PressAnnouncements/2008/ucm 116904.htm; "FDA Warns Consumers Nationwide Not to Eat Certain Types of Raw Red Tomatoes," FDA News Release, June 7, 2008, http://wayback.archive-it.org/7993/20161023232521/ http://www.fda.gov/NewsEvents/Newsroom/PressAnnouncements/2008/ucm116908.htm.

4. Guzewich, interview; "McDonald's Holds the Tomatoes, Fearing Salmonella," *NPR*, June 9, 2008; Julie Jargon, "Grocers and Restaurants Toss Out Tomatoes: *Salmonella* Scare Delivers a Blow to Crop's Growers," *Wall Street Journal*, June 10, 2008, B1; Jane Zhang and Janet Adamy, "Tomato Probe Targets Florida and Mexico," *Wall Street Journal*, June 14, 2008, A3; Gardiner Harris, "F.D.A. Reports Progress in Tracing *Salmonella*," *New York Times*, June 11, 2008, A17; Annys Shin, "Keeping Produce on the Safe Track," *Washington Post*, July 17, 2008, D1.

5. Annys Shin, "Tomatoes Still Lead List of Suspects in *Salmonella* Probe," *Washington Post*, July 2, 2008, D1.

6. Behravesh et al., "2008 Outbreak," 923; AP, "Pepper Provided Hot Lead in Hunt for *Salmonella*," NBC News, July 23, 2008; Behravesh et al., "2008 Outbreak," Supplementary Appendix 27, http://www.nejm.org/doi/suppl/10.1056/NEJMoa1005741/suppl_file/nejmoa1005741 _appendix.pdf, archived at https://perma.cc/VS7Y-K9CD. For a detailed timeline, see *Breakdown: Lessons to be Learned from the 2008 Salmonella Saintpaul Outbreak* (Washington, DC: Pew Charitable Trusts at Georgetown University), November 17, 2008, 27–28, http://www.pewtrusts.org/~/ media/legacy/uploadedfiles/phg/content_level_pages/reports/psprptlessonssalmonella2008pdf .pdf, archived at https://perma.cc/MD66-DT2K; *Hearing on the Recent* Salmonella *Outbreak: Lessons Learned and Consequences to Industry and Public Health before the Subcommittee on Oversight and Investigations of the Committee on Energy and Commerce, House of Representatives*, 110th Cong. 282–290 (FDA timeline) (July 31, 2008). See also Rajal K. Mody et al., "National Outbreak of *Salmonella* Serotype Saintpaul Infections: Importance of Texas Restaurant Investigations in Implicating Jalapeño Peppers," *PLoS ONE* 6, no. 2 (February 2011): https://doi.org/10.1371/ journal.pone.0016579.

7. Behravesh et al., "2008 Outbreak," 920, 922; 926; Ronald Doering, "Uncertainty and Food Safety Investigations—Part II," *Food Law*, November–December 2011, https://gowlingwlg

.com/en/insights-resources/articles/2011/uncertainty-and-food-safety-investigations-part, archived at https://perma.cc/5YQX-GWK6.

8. *Hearing to Review the Legal and Technological Capacity for Full Traceability in Fresh Produce before the Subcommittee on Horticulture and Organic Agriculture of the Committee on Agriculture, House of Representatives*, 110th Cong. 37 (testimony of David Acheson) (July 30, 2008); "Transcript for FDA Media Briefing on *Salmonella* Outbreak," July 21, 2008, 8, archived at https://perma.cc/PM74-BF74; "Transcript for Media Briefing on *Salmonella* Outbreak," FDA-CDC, August 28, 2008, 10–11, archived at https://perma.cc/4GVH-DS66.

9. On how investigations make outbreaks visible, see Angie M. Boyce, "Fast but Right: Outbreak Surveillance and Foodborne Knowledge Infrastructure" (PhD diss., Cornell University, 2014), 9, 17.

10. "The Produce Traceability Initiative," September 2011, https://www.producetraceability .org/documents/PTI%20Flyer_FNL_v2%202011-10-20.pdf, archived at https://perma.cc/ QTC7-22T7; Jennifer C. McEntire et al., "Traceability (Product Tracing) in Food Systems: An IFT Report Submitted to the FDA: Volume 1: Technical Aspects and Recommendations," *Comprehensive Reviews in Food Science and Food Safety* 9 (2010): 92–158; Carla Mejia et al., "Traceability (Product Tracing) in Food Systems: An IFT Report Submitted to the FDA: Volume 2: Cost Considerations and Implications," *Comprehensive Reviews in Food Science and Food Safety* 9 (2010): 159–75; David Acheson, telephone interview by the author, December 19, 2016; FDA Food Safety Modernization Act, Pub. L. No. 111-353, 124 Stat. 3885 (January 4, 2011), § 204.

11. Robert V. Tauxe, telephone interview by the author, November 23, 2015; Robert V. Tauxe, email message to the author, November 15, 2015; Robert V. Tauxe, "Molecular Subtyping and the Transformation of Public Health," *Foodborne Pathogens and Disease* 3, no. 1 (2006): 4–5; Kimberlee Musser and Nellie Dumas (senior scientists, Wadsworth Center), personal communication with the author during tour of Wadsworth Center bacteriology laboratories, February 10, 2017.

12. Boyce, "Fast but Right," 101; Stephen B. Thacker, Judith R. Qualters and Lisa M. Lee, "Public Health Surveillance in the United States: Evolution and Challenges," *MMWR* 61, suppl. (July 27, 2012): 3; S. Declich and A. O. Carter, "Public Health Surveillance: Historical Origins, Methods and Evaluation," *Bulletin of the World Health Organization* 72, no. 2 (1994): 285; Bernard C. K. Choi, "The Past, Present, and Future of Public Health Surveillance," *Scientifica* (2012) 3; Wikipedia, s.v. "Public Health Reports," last modified September 10, 2017, https://en .wikipedia.org/wiki/Public_Health_Reports, archived at https://perma.cc/U8JZ-M2UK.

13. Robert V. Tauxe and Emilio J. Esteban, "Advances in Food Safety to Prevent Foodborne Diseases in the United States," in *Silent Victories: The History and Practice of Public Health in Twentieth-Century America*, ed. John W. Ward and Christian Warren (Oxford: Oxford University Press, 2006), 26–27; Tauxe, interview; J. C. Geiger, "The Status of Bacterial Food Poisoning in the United States," *American Journal of Public Health* 14, no. 4 (1924): 302, 303; Boyce, "Fast but Right," 102.

14. Geiger, "Status of Bacterial Food Poisoning."

15. Boyce, "Fast but Right," 111–16; Lisa Durso, "Unit Background: Food Borne Illness: Focus on Issues Relating to *E. coli* O157:H7," http://www.math.unl.edu/~jump/Center1/Labs/ DursoUNIT%20background.pdf, archived at https://perma.cc/GLJ9-5MQZ; House of Rep July 31 157

16. Boyce, "Fast but Right," 107–50 (detailed history); Tauxe, interview.

17. Boyce, "Fast but Right," 26–27; *Hearing on the Recent* Salmonella *Outbreak*, 158 (testimony of Lonnie J. King, CDC)

18. Boyce, "Fast but Right," 68–70, 216–22; CDC, "Pulse-Field Gel Electrophoresis (PFGE)," October 24, 2017, https://www.cdc.gov/pulsenet/pathogens/pfge.html, archived at https://perma.cc/9DF7-TLEY.

19. Boyce, "Fast but Right," 221–30; David Boxrud et al., "The Role, Challenges, and Support of PulseNet Laboratories in Detecting Foodborne Disease Outbreaks," *Public Health Reports* 125, suppl. 2 (2010): 57–62; Ban Mishu Allos et al., "Surveillance for Sporadic Foodborne Disease in the 21st Century: The FoodNet Perspective," *Clinical Infectious Diseases* 38, suppl. 3 (2004): 119; Christopher R. Braden, "Foodborne Outbreak Detection and Response: The National Perspective," PowerPoint slides from presentation at the Food Safety Summit, Baltimore, MD, April 29, 2015, archived at https://perma.cc/V327-GTYZ.

20. Boyce, "Fast but Right," 66, 78, 85, 88; CDC, "Epidemic Intelligence Service," January 23, 2018, https://www.cdc.gov/eis/index.html, archived at https://perma.cc/C5F9-KRMJ; Alicia Cronquist (epidemiologist, Colorado Department of Public Health and Environment), telephone interview by the author, January 8, 2015.

21. CDC, "Guide to Confirming an Etiology in Foodborne Disease Outbreak," January 31, 2017, https://www.cdc.gov/foodsafety/outbreaks/investigating-outbreaks/confirming _diagnosis.html, archived at https://perma.cc/H2E7-FJZP; Cronquist, interview; Boyce, "Fast but Right," 75–78.

22. Boyce, "Fast but Right," 75–78; Michelle Smith (senior policy analyst, FDA), telephone interview by the author; Olga L. Henao et al., "Foodborne Diseases Active Surveillance Network—2 Decades of Achievements, 1996–2015," *Emerging Infectious Diseases* 21, no. 9 (September 2015): 1532; CDC, "Foodborne Outbreak Online Database (FOOD Tool)," August 25, 2016, https://wwwn.cdc.gov/foodborneoutbreaks/, archived at https://perma.cc/4UHX-GW77; CDC, "National Outbreak Reporting System (NORS)," https://www.cdc.gov/nors/index.html, archived at https://perma.cc/N9HM-AD2W CDC; Guzewich, interview; CDC, "Safer Food Saves Lives: Stopping Multistate Foodborne Outbreaks," *CDC Vital Signs*, November 2015, https://www.cdc.gov/vitalsigns/foodsafety-2015/index.html, archived at https://perma.cc/U5UX-EWKH.

23. CDC, *Principles of Epidemiology in Public Health Practice*, 3rd ed. (Washington, DC: CDC, May 2012); Boyce, "Fast but Right," 94.

24. Tauxe and Esteban, "Advances in Food Safety," 20; Henao et al., "Foodborne Diseases Active Surveillance Network"; Boyce, "Fast but Right," 224–26; Allos, "Surveillance for Sporadic Foodborne Disease"; Food Safety Modernization Act Surveillance Working Group, Annual Report to the Secretary, Department of Health and Human Services, 2015, 4, https://www .cdc.gov/oid/docs/BSC_OID_FSMA_Surv_WG_2015_Annual_Report.pdf, archived at https://perma.cc/Q5L9-UTKJ. For a related effort to coordinate CDC, FDA, and FSIS efforts, see CDC, "Interagency Food Safety Analytics Collaboration (IFSAC)," https://www.cdc.gov/foodsafety/ifsac/index.html, archived at https://perma.cc/UDP4-EJYK.

25. Robert V. Tauxe, "Molecular Subtyping and the Transformation of Public Health," *Foodborne Pathogens and Disease* 3, no. 1 (2006): 4–8.

26. Boyce, "Fast but Right," 107–50, 243.

27. Tauxe, email message to the author; CDC "Whole Genome Sequencing," February 11, 2016, https://www.cdc.gov/pulsenet/pathogens/wgs.html, archived at https://perma.cc/6F9W -HC7Z; Heather A. Carleton and Peter Gerner-Smidt, "Whole-Genome Sequencing Is Taking Over Foodborne Disease Surveillance," *Microbe* 11, no. 7 (2016): 311–17; Brendan R. Jackson et al., "Implementation of Nationwide Real-Time Whole-Genome Sequencing to Enhance

Listeriosis Outbreak Detection and Investigation," *Clinical Infectious Disease* 63, no. 3 (August 1, 2016): 380–86.

28. Dan Flynn, "CDC Sending States New Outbreak Tool: Launching PulseNet 2.0," *Food Safety News*, May 13, 2016, http://www.foodsafetynews.com/2016/05/cdc-sending-states-new -outbreak-tool-launching-pulsenet-2-0/#.Wo12iqjwaUk, archived at https://perma.cc/W3SM -KUKQ; CDC, "Whole Genome Sequencing"; Tauxe, email message to the author. As of January 2018, the CDC switched PulseNet surveillance of *Listeria* to WGS and is moving to do the same for *E. coli* O157 and *Salmonella*. Robert Tauxe, personal communication with the author, February 4, 2018.

29. FDA, "GenomeTrakr Network," November 16, 2017, https://www.fda.gov/Food/Food ScienceResearch/WholeGenomeSequencingProgramWGS/ucm363134.htm, archived at https:// perma.cc/VTJ9-4VFZ; FDA, "Total Number of Sequences in the GenomeTrakr Database," CDC, 2017, https://www.fda.gov/downloads/Food/FoodScienceResearch/WholeGenomeSequencing ProgramWGS/UCM422244.pdf, archived at https://perma.cc/WUD9-R32Q; "Labs Outside the US Contributing to GenomeTrakr," CDC, 2016, https://www.fda.gov/downloads/Food/ FoodScienceResearch/WholeGenomeSequencingProgramWGS/UCM481650.pdf, archived at https://perma.cc/XL5R-QA5A; CDC, "The PFGE Process," February 14, 2014, https://www.cdc .gov/pulsenet/pathogens/protocol-images.html#pfge, archived at https://perma.cc/99S5-8H3B; Patrick Van Roey (senior scientist, Wadsworth Center), personal communication with the author during tour of Wadsworth Center Core Lab, February 10, 2017; Patrick Van Roey, personal com- munication with the author, July 21, 2017.

30. Ronald Limberger, Kimberlee Musser, William Wolfgang, and Daryl Lamson (senior scientists), group interview by author at Wadsworth Center, New York State Department of Health, February 10, 2017; Musser and Dumas, personal communication with the author; Ai Kataoka and Warren Stone, "Whole Genome Sequencing: A Magic Bullet for Outbreaks?" *Qual- ity Assurance & Food Safety*, December 11, 2015, http://www.qualityassurancemag.com/article/ qa1215-whole-genome-sequencing-technology/, archived at https://perma.cc/DC3A-JM74; Boxrud et al., "Role, Challenges, and Support ," 59; Boyce, "Fast but Right," 72; Braden, "Food- borne Outbreak Detection and Response," 26.

31. Shari Shea et al., "Clinical Microbiology Laboratories Adoption of Culture-Independent Diagnostic Tests Is a Threat to Foodborne-Disease Surveillance in the United States," *Journal of Clinical Microbiology* 55, no. 1 (January 2017): 10–19; CDC, "The Future of PulseNet," February 16, 2016, https://www.cdc.gov/pulsenet/next-generation.html, archived at https://perma.cc/Y5WK -TSFK; CDC, "Timeline for Reporting Cases of *Salmonella* Infection," March 9, 2015, https://www .cdc.gov/salmonella/reporting-timeline.html, archived at https://perma.cc/EW9Y-5YX7; Andy Weisbecker, "CDC: We Need Bacterial Cultures to Catch Foodborne Outbreaks," *Food Poison Journal*, April 17, 2016, http://www.foodpoisonjournal.com/food-poisoning-information/cdc-we -need-bacterial-cultures-to-catch-foodborne-outbreaks/#.WXR4K4jyuUk, archived at https:// perma.cc/6N8A-VV7G; Boyce, "Fast but Right." For the use of emerging metagenomics analysis to rapidly detect and type pathogens, see "Scientist Creates Faster Way to Fingerprint Foodborne Pathogens," *Food Safety News*, April 23, 2018, archived at https://perma.cc/JM2P-ST5X.

32. *Inventory Management and Tracking: Reference Guide*, National Food Service Manage- ment Institute, University of Mississippi, Item No. ET 109-12, 2012, 18; CPMA/PMA Task Force, *Traceability Best Practices*, 2004, 8, http://www.perishablepundit.com/docs/traceability_best _practices.pdf, archived at https://perma.cc/Y6WH-GHGW.

33. Guzewich, interview.

34. Guzewich, interview. It can be especially difficult to identify the source of outbreaks caused by fresh produce. Because fresh produce is perishable, outbreak victims are likely to have discarded any leftovers by the time investigators show up seeking samples of contaminated food. The absence of brand labels on much fresh produce and the mixing of items from different sources by retailers, distributors, and processors, may make it impossible to identify the origin of a contaminated head of lettuce or a tomato. In those instances where investigators do manage to identify the origin of contaminated produce, the fields in which it was grown are typically harvested and may already be replanted with a different crop by the time they arrive, leaving no direct evidence of contamination during cultivation. *Hearing on Food Safety: Current Challenges and New Ideas to Safeguard Consumers before the Committee on Health, Education, Labor, and Pensions, United States Senate*, 109th Cong. 32 (testimony of Kevin Reilly, California Department of Health Services) (November 15, 2006); GAO, "Highlights," in *Improvements Needed in FDA Oversight of Fresh Produce*, GAO-08-1047, September 2008.

35. Douglas Karas, "Traceback Investigations: Mapping the Maze," *Food Safety Magazine*, October–November 2014, 5, archived at https://perma.cc/P52Q-UCNW; McEntire et al., "Traceability," 111; Elise Golan et al., "Traceability in the US Food Supply: Economic Theory and Industry Studies," USDA Economic Research Service Agricultural Economic Report No. 830, March 2004, 12–15.

36. 21 U.S.C. § 350c; Establishment and Maintenance of Records under the Public Health Security and Bioterrorism Preparedness and Response Act of 2002, Final Rule, 69 Fed. Reg. 71,653 (December 9, 2004); McEntire et al., "Traceability," 111; Jennifer McEntire and Tejas Bhatt, *Pilot Projects for Improving Product Tracing Along the Food Supply System—Final Report*, August 2012, 232, https://www.fda.gov/downloads/Food/GuidanceRegulation/UCM341810.pd, archived at https://perma.cc/AEP2-JUNC, 232; *Traceability in the Food Supply Chain*, Office of the Inspector General, Department of Health and Human Services, OEI-02-06-00210, March 2009, 22.

37. 21 U.S.C. § 350f; McEntire et al., "Traceability," 111; IFT, August 2012, 232, https://www.fda.gov/downloads/Food/GuidanceRegulation/UCM341810.pdf, archived at https://perma.cc/AEP2-JUNC.

38. Golan et al., "Traceability in the US Food Supply," 12–21.

39. The 1997 United Fresh Fruit and Vegetable Association GAPs guidance had earlier highlighted the importance of supply chain tracing for containing outbreaks, limiting liability, and curtailing the reputational damage to an industry sector, stating that "the organizations producing this document support the concept of traceback and encourage industry associations and operators to engage in thoughtful consideration of means to provide traceback capability." Following a series of outbreaks in the 1980s and 1990s, the California Cantaloupe Advisory Board, in 2000, required detailed traceback information on field-packed boxes—including packing date, field, and packing crew—as part of a marketing order. United Fresh Fruit and Vegetable Association, Industrywide Guidance to Minimize Microbiological Food Safety Risks for Produce, 1997 (date of publication unclear, might be 1998), 17–18, archived at https://perma.cc/4FLG-YTGM; Golan et al., "Traceability in the US Food Supply," 15; CPMA/PMA Task Force, *Traceability Best Practices*, 4.

40. In developing traceability standards, the Produce Traceability Initiative relied on earlier pilot studies and standards developed by CAN-Trace, a coalition of Canadian trade associations representing different sectors of the food industry and different parts of the supply chain, with input from Canadian government agencies, academics, and consumer advocates. CAN-Trace's pilot studies in food traceability were, in turn, informed by earlier traceability pilot studies

involving a variety of products by the Uniform Code Council and the European Article Numbering Association, which later merged to become GS1. The CPMA/PMA Task Force *Traceability Best Practices* also borrowed from preexisting ISO and EAN traceability standards. CPMA/PMA Task Force, *Traceability Best Practices*; PMA/CPMA, *Fresh Produce Traceability: A Guide to Implementation, Version 2*, October 2006, http://www.cpma.ca/pdf/IndustryTech/CPMA_PMA_Traceability_Guide_to_Implementation_Oct_2006.pdf, archived at https://perma.cc/BU2K-YPA4; Ed Treacy (vice president, supply chain efficiencies, Produce Marketing Association), email message to the author, March 6, 2017; Ed Treacy, *Produce Traceability Initiative*, MP4 video, PMA (no longer available online, on file with the author).

41. CPMA/PMA Task Force, *Traceability Best Practices*, 5.

42. "PMA, CPMA, United Fresh Appoint Steering Committee of the Produce Traceability Initiative," press release, Produce Traceability Initiative, November 28, 2007, https://www.producetraceability.org/press-contact/details/pma-cpma-united-fresh-appoint-steering-committee-of-the-produce-traceabilit, archived at https://perma.cc/H5VJ-BFGG; "Produce Traceability Initiative Steering Committee's First Meeting Begins Laying Groundwork for Industry-Wide Standards Program," press release, Produce Traceability Initiative, January 15, 2008, https://www.producetraceability.org/press-contact/details/produce-traceability-initiative-steering-committees-first-meeting-begins-la, archived at https://perma.cc/TA87-2A27.

43. "Produce Industry Already Enhancing Traceability on Its Own, PMA's Silbermann Tells Congress," press release, Produce Traceability Initiative, June 30, 2008, https://www.producetraceability.org/press-contact/details/produce-industry-already-enhancing-traceability-on-its-own-pmas-silbermann, archived at https://perma.cc/M78J-7GEK; *Hearing to Review the Legal and Technological Capacity*, 71–75 (testimony of Parker Booth, president of Delta Pre-Pack Inc. and Ace Tomato Co. Inc.); "34 Supply Chain Leaders Endorse Plan for Chain-Wide Electronic Produce Traceability," press release, Produce Traceability Initiative, October 7, 2008, https://www.producetraceability.org/press-contact/details/34-supply-chain-leaders-endorse-plan-for-chain-wide-electronic-produce-trac, archived at https://perma.cc/DF3S-84C8.

44. "Produce Traceability Initiative Survey Finds Widespread Progress toward All Milestones," press release, Produce Traceability Initiative, May 3, 2012, https://www.producetraceability.org/press-contact/details/produce-traceability-initiative-survey-finds-widespread-progress-toward-all, archived at https://perma.cc/T9ZG-9MGU.

45. This paragraph and the next draw from McEntire et al., "Traceability," 122–23, 142–43. See also Golan et al., "Traceability in the US Food Supply," 32–34.

46. Caroline Smith DeWaal, Citizen Petition to FDA on behalf of the Center for Science and the Public Interest, November 15, 2006, 3, archived at https://perma.cc/VFE9-37JL; Michael Jacobson, Caroline Smith DeWaal, and Chris Waldrop, letter to FDA commissioner Andrew C. von Eschenbach, July 3, 2008, archived at https://perma.cc/2MY4-NJ44.

47. *Traceability in the Food Supply Chain*, ii–v.

48. *Hearing to Review the Legal and Technological Capacity*, 71–80 (testimony of Bryan Silbermann), *Hearing on the Recent* Salmonella *Outbreak*, 260 (testimony of Robert Brackett); Jim Prevor, "Consumer Watchdogs Ignore Current Outbreak in Pursuit of Predetermined Agenda," *Jim Prevor's Perishable Pundit* (blog), July 10, 2008, http://www.perishablepundit.com/index.php?article=1848, archived at https://perma.cc/T78Z-YRQU; Jim Prevor, "Senator Harkin Calls for Reform of FDA's Food Safety System," *Jim Prevor's Perishable Pundit* (blog), July 17, 2008, http://www.perishablepundit.com/index.php?article=1856, archived at https://

perma.cc/T4W4-NERC; Jim Prevor, "Dr. Michael Osterholm, Esteemed Authority on Public Health Speaks Frankly about the FDA . . ." *Jim Prevor's Perishable Pundit* (blog), June 24, 2008, http://www.perishablepundit.com/index.php?article=1808, archived at https://perma.cc/S6CG-CMEC; Jim Prevor, "State Health Departments Need Increased Level of Competence," *Jim Prevor's Perishable Pundit* (blog), July 30, 2008, http://www.perishablepundit.com/index.php?article=1882, archived at https://perma.cc/D6RK-D38X; CDC, "Timeline for Reporting Cases."

49. McEntire et al., "Traceability"; Mejia et al., "Traceability." Oddly, these reports fail to cite the earlier 2004 study of Golan et al., "Traceability in the US Food Supply," which covers fresh produce, meat, and grains and oils.

50. FDA Food Safety Modernization Act, §204; McEntire and Bhatt, *Pilot Projects*, 15–16; *Report to Congress on Enhancing Tracking and Tracing of Food and Recordkeeping*, FDA, November 16, 2016, https://www.fda.gov/downloads/Food/GuidanceRegulation/FSMA/UCM540940.pdf, archived at https://perma.cc/JXJ8-KSKT; "Comments to FDA in Response to IFT Traceability Recommendations in Support of the Food Safety Modernization Act," Docket No. FDA-2012-N-1153, July 1, 2013, https://www.producetraceability.org/documents/CPMA_GS1US_PMA_UFPA_Comment_docket_to_FDA_07012013pdf.pdf, archived at https://perma.cc/AU64-F6XS.

51. Tauxe, "Molecular Subtyping," 5, 7; Robert Whitaker, telephone interview by the author, June 1, 2016. A recent study estimated the illness reduction attributable the CDC's PulseNet surveillance system and offered an assessment of its costs and benefits. Based on data from fifteen outbreaks of *E. coli* O157 associated with ground beef and five outbreaks of *Salmonella* associated with various foods in 2007 and 2008, the study claimed that faster outbreak identification attributable to PulseNet resulted in earlier recalls of contaminated products, thereby reducing their consumption and directly averting between 2,480 and 6,943 cases of *E. coli* illness and between 3,750 and 33,021 cases of *Salmonella* illness, saving between $1 million and $37 million, which translates into a net cost savings of between $0.20 and $5 for every $1 invested by public health agencies. On the basis of state illness reports between 1994 and 2009, the study further claimed that PulseNet generated information that incentivized food companies to implement new food safety measures, thereby indirectly averting between 266,522 and 737,845 cases of *Salmonella* illness, between 8,096 and 69,755 cases of *E. coli* illness, and between 56 and 316 cases of *Listeria* illness in 2009, saving between $491 and $645 million, which translates into a cost savings of between $3 and $90 for every $1 invested by public health agencies. Robert L. Scharff et al., "An Economic Evaluation of PulseNet: A Network for Foodborne Disease Surveillance," *American Journal of Preventive Medicine* 50, no. 5 (2016): S66–S73. For additional evidence that advances in outbreak investigation have reduced the size of foodborne listeriosis outbreaks and prevented illness, see Robert Tauxe, "Whole Genome Sequencing and the Transformation of Public Health Surveillance (for Enteric Infections)," conference presentation slides, Georgia Emerging Infections Program Annual Conference, Atlanta, March 24, 2017, slide 16, archived at https://perma.cc/K9RM-J8RY. Multistate outbreaks have played a disproportionate role in honing the tools of outbreak investigation. Of the 4,198 foodborne illness outbreaks reported to the CDC between 2008 and 2012, 93 percent were contained within a single county and another 4 percent spread to multiple counties within a single state. Only 2.5 percent were multistate. However, these multistate outbreaks accounted for 11 percent of outbreak illnesses, 34 percent of hospitalizations, and 51 percent of deaths. Moreover, federal agencies tend to focus on multistate outbreaks. Local and state health departments typically identify the causes of single-county or

single-state outbreaks quickly and with little, if any, federal involvement. By contrast, multistate outbreaks require federal agency coordination of more extensive, complex, and expensive investigations. In addition, large multistate outbreaks—such as the Jack in the Box ground beef outbreak (1993), the Dole baby spinach outbreak (2006), and the Mexican hot peppers outbreak (2008)—generate months of national media coverage, which fuels public pressure on the federal government to improve food safety. The resulting new initiatives and additional funding generally focus on improvements in multistate outbreak investigation. For all these reasons, multistate outbreaks have motivated relatively large federal government investments in advances such as more extensive surveillance via PulseNet and FoodNet, more precise pathogen typing using PFGE and WGS, and more reliable traceability through data standardization and barcoding. Braden, "Foodborne Outbreak Detection and Response"; Samuel J. Crowe et al., "Vital Signs: Multistate Foodborne Outbreaks—United States, 2010–2014," *MMWR* 64, no. 43 (November 6, 2015): 1221–25.

52. On identifying and using leverage points to steer or guide a system, see Christopher Koliba, Lasse Gerrits, Mary Lee Rhodes, and Jack W. Meek, "Complexity Theory and Systems Analysis," in Handbook on Theories of Governance, ed. Christopher Ansell and Jacob Torfing (Cheltenham, UK: Edward Elgar, 2016), 372.

53. National Academies, *An Evaluation of the Role of Microbiological Criteria for Foods and Food Ingredients* (Washington, DC: National Academies Press, 1985), 257; James Gorny, telephone interview by the author, August 8, 2016; David Gombas (vice president, food safety and technology, United Fresh Produce Association, retired), telephone interview by the author, June 6, 2016; John A. Painter et al., "Attribution of Foodborne Illnesses, Hospitalizations, and Deaths to Food Commodities by Using Outbreak Data, United States, 1998–2008," *Emerging Infectious Diseases* 19, no. 3 (March 2013): 410; CDC, "Attribution of Foodborne Illness: Findings," July 16, 2016, https://www.cdc.gov/foodborneburden/attribution/attribution-1998-2008 .html, archived at https://perma.cc/S7UZ-BDZJ. A subsequent report by the Center for Science in the Public Interest similarly found that produce was responsible for more outbreaks and illnesses, and more illnesses per outbreak on average, than any other food category between 2004 and 2013. Nils Fischer, Ariel Bourne, and David Plunkett, *Outbreak Alert! 2015: A Review of Foodborne Illness in the US from 2004–2013*, Center for Science in the Public Interest, November 2015, 7, https://cspinet.org/sites/default/files/attachment/outbreak-alert-2015.pdf, archived at https://perma.cc/DW32-WB2Y; Tauxe, "Molecular Subtyping," 4; Boyce, "Fast but Right," 8.

54. Gorny, interview; "The Fundamentals of Food Traceability," Global Food Traceability Center, IFT, 2014, PowerPoint slides, 7, archived at https://perma.cc/96XK-YNW8; Robert B. Gravani, "The Role of Good Agricultural Practices in Produce Safety," in *Microbial Safety of Fresh Produce*, ed. Xuetong Fan et al., 106–7; Tauxe, "Molecular Subtyping," 7; Whitaker, interview.

55. David Theno, telephone interview with the author, September 5, 2014; Gray Mackenzie, "If You Can't Measure It, You Can't Improve It," *Guava Box*, http://www.guavabox.com/blog/if -you-cant-measure-it-you-cant-improve-it, archived at https://perma.cc/E4XD-62RK.

56. Bill Marler, telephone interview by the author, October 5, 2014.

57. Jack Hipp (vice president for claims, Allianz Global), telephone interview by the author, April 16, 2015.

58. Tauxe, "Molecular Subtyping," 5.

59. Tauxe, "Molecular Subtyping," 4–5; Tauxe, email message to the author. For examples of feedback and learning in the *Salmonella* Saintpaul outbreak, see "Transcript for Media Briefing," August 28, 2008, 6–7; and Jim Prevor, "Can We Avoid This Mess in the Future?" *Jim*

Prevor's Perishable Pundit (blog), June 28, 2008, http://www.perishablepundit.com/index.php ?article=1816, archived at https://perma.cc/6W4Z-ECVD; Golan et al., "Traceability in the US Food Supply," Traceability 7.

60. FDA, *FDA's Core: A Food Safety Network 2011–2012*, https://www.fda.gov/downloads/ Food/RecallsOutbreaksEmergencies/Outbreaks/UCM349231.pdf, archived at https://perma .cc/DR7J-4BH7; Travis Goodman, "Integrating Response: Past, Present, and Future: How the Rapid Response Team (RRT) Program and the Partnership for Food Protection are Integrating Response," (PowerPoint presentation, Food Safety Summit, Baltimore, MD, April 28, 2015), archived at https://perma.cc/T4A6-AQZR; USDA, "California Food Protection Rapid Response Team (RRT)," USDA National Agricultural Library, https://www.nal.usda.gov/fsrio/research _projects//printresults.php?ID=12302, archived at https://perma.cc/34RP-HEMY; CDC "About FoodCORE," September 26, 2014, https://www.cdc.gov/foodcore/about.html#video, archived at https://perma.cc/8LTN-FVQY.

61. CDC, "About the Integrated Food Safety Centers for Excellence," September 23, 2015, https://www.cdc.gov/foodsafety/centers/about.html, archived at https://perma.cc/36WD-WRJC.

62. CDC, "Interagency Food Safety Analytics Collaboration (IFSAC)," https://www.cdc .gov/foodsafety/ifsac/index.html, archived at https://perma.cc/DA42-2VAN; "IRAC Charter," *FoodRisk.org*, February 28, 2011, http://foodrisk.org/irac/charter, archived at https://perma.cc/ 8KXF-3MJT; *The Federal Food Safety Working Group Progress Report*, White House, December 2011, archived at https://perma.cc/T874-LCH2; "Welcome," CIFOR, archived at https://perma .cc/YR59-RZR3.

63. "Our Leadership," IFT, February 21, 2018, http://www.ift.org/about-us/our-leadership .aspx, archived at https://perma.cc/D4WZ-ZGR2; *Report to Congress*, 23.

Chapter Eight

1. Alvina Chu, "Foodborne Illness Outbreaks in Maryland" (PowerPoint presentation, Food Safety Summit, Baltimore, MD, April 29, 2015), archived at https://perma.cc/U6FT-4YXF; *Summary Report: Outbreak 2014-119*, Office of Infectious Disease Epidemiology and Outbreak Response Prevention and Health Promotion Administration, Maryland Department of Health and Mental Hygiene, September 2014, https://health.maryland.gov/docs/Outbreak%202014 -119%20FINAL_with%20Attachments_v3.pdf, archived at https://perma.cc/KJ8D-QXV5.

2. Jenni Spinner, "The Plot Sickens: More Than 100 Food Safety Summit Attendees Fall Ill," *FoodQualityNews.com*, April 23, 2014, https://www.foodqualitynews.com/Article/2014/04/23/ Foodborne-illness-strikes-attendees-at-a-food-safety-event, archived at https://perma.cc/2GA7 -L9MD; JoNel Aleccia, "Side of Irony? Meal Sickens People at Food Safety Summit," NBCNews .com, April 18, 2014, archived at https://perma.cc/5FNF-4XYS; Jonathan Vankin, "This Is Exactly What Is Not Supposed to Happen at the National Food Safety Summit," *Inquisitr*, April 29, 2014, archived at https://perma.cc/3VLD-XWTQ.

3. Chu, "Foodborne Illness Outbreaks in Maryland"; *Summary Report*.

4. Chu, "Foodborne Illness Outbreaks in Maryland." Microbial contamination of food during preparation—by restaurant workers, caterers, and home cooks—is a major source of concern in efforts to prevent foodborne illness. There are an estimated 620,000 restaurants in the United States, not including caterers, food trucks, grocery stores, school lunch programs, and food service providers in hospitals and nursing homes. State and local health codes, informed by a model FDA food code, govern these operations. State and local officials inspect restaurants and food service operations to monitor their compliance. Of the 902 foodborne

illness outbreaks identified by the CDC in 2015, 60 percent were traced back to restaurants and 14 percent to catering or banquet facilities. Nine percent were traced back to private homes. However, none of these data indicate whether contamination originated during preparation or at some earlier stage of production. Eighty-six percent of the outbreaks were traced back to a single location, from which one might infer contamination during preparation, as contamination earlier in the production process would be, arguably, more likely to result in multiple location outbreaks. But again, even a single location outbreak could owe its root cause to, for example, a chicken breast originally contaminated during processing with a pathogen, such as *C. perfringens*, from the intestines of the chicken, which then cross contaminated other chicken breasts or other foods during preparation. CDC, *Surveillance for Foodborne Disease Outbreaks, United States, 2015, Annual Report* (Atlanta: US Department of Health and Human Services, 2017), 1, 9; Statista, https://www.statista.com/statistics/374866/number-of-restaurants-by-type-us/, archived at https://perma.cc/5FZN-AQTF; FDA, *Food Code 2017*, 9th ed.; CDC, "Clostridium perfringens," January 10, 2017, https://www.cdc.gov/foodsafety/diseases/clostridium-perfringens.html, archived at https://perma.cc/V8MT-BLAC; David Gombas, email message to the author, February 1, 2018. On restaurant inspection, see Daniel E. Ho, "Fudging the Nudge: Information Disclosure and Restaurant Grading," *Yale Law Journal* 122 (2012): 595; Daniel E. Ho, "Does Peer Review Work? An Experiment of Experimentalism," *Stanford Law Review* 69 (2017): 1; Daniel E. Ho, Zoe C. Ashwood, and Cassandra Handan-Nader, "The False Promise of Simple Information Disclosure: New Evidence on Restaurant Hygiene Grading" (Working Paper No. 17-043, Stanford Institute for Economic Policy Research, December 20, 2017).

5. Lydia Zuraw, "Groups Want Increased Funding to Support CDC's PulseNet Database," *Food Safety News*, June 4, 2015, http://www.foodsafetynews.com/2015/06/groups-want-increased-funding-to-support-cdcs-pulsenet/#.Wo6Xy6jwaUl, archived at https://perma.cc/D5MP-PEET; Isadore Rosenthal and Howard Kunreuther, "Roles for Third Parties in Implementing USDA Food Safety and Inspection Service (FSIS)'s Food Safety Process Management Programs" (Working Paper No. 2008-12-16, Wharton Risk Management and Decision Process Center, April 2010), 38–40, https://riskcenter.wharton.upenn.edu/wp-content/uploads/2014/07/WP2010-04-12IRHKFoodSafetyERS.pdf, archived at https://perma.cc/7J66-AZD5; Bill Marler, "Liability of Private Outside Food Safety Auditors for Injuries to Consumers," *Marler Blog*, November 13, 2010, archived at https://perma.cc/993J-CTJQ.

6. FDA Food Safety Modernization Act, Pub. L. No. 111-353, 124 Stat. 3885 (January 4, 2011); FDA, "The Context and History of FSMA Funding," December 15, 2017, https://www.fda.gov/Food/GuidanceRegulation/FSMA/ucm436160.htm, archived at https://perma.cc/3THX-878H; FDA, "Reports and Studies," December 29, 2017, archived at https://perma.cc/WYQ2-BF96; For a progress report up to 2017, see GAO, *A National Strategy Is Needed to Address Fragmentation in Federal Oversight*, GAO-17-74, January 2017.

7. FDA Food Safety Modernization Act, § 201; Standards for Growing, Harvesting, Packing, and Holding of Produce for Human Consumption, Proposed Rule, 78 Fed. Reg. 3608–9; Michael Taylor, "Food Safety Collaboration in a Global Food System," remarks at the Global Food Safety Conference, Orlando, FL, February 16, 2012, https://wayback.archive-it.org/7993/20170111074016/http://www.fda.gov/Food/GuidanceRegulation/FSMA/ucm292162.htm, archived at https://perma.cc/64AK-YE2M. For an assessment of FDA's performance in fulfilling FSMA inspection mandates, see *Challenges Remain in FDA's Inspections of Domestic Food Facilities*, Department of Health and Human Services Office of Inspector General, Report

No. OEI-02-14-00420, September 2017. For a description of the FDA's approach to inspecting food processing facilities under FSMA, see Steve Armstrong, "The Food Safety Modernization Act, After One Year: Advancing and Building Food Safety Systems for the 21st Century," *Update Magazine,* January–February 2018, archived at https://perma.cc/Z6C8-LG8J.

8. Nils Fischer, Ariel Bourne, and David Plunkett, *Outbreak Alert! 2015: A Review of Foodborne Illness in the US from 2004–2013,* CSPI, November 2015, iv, 2, https://cspinet.org/sites/default/files/attachment/outbreak-alert-2015.pdf, archived at https://perma.cc/DW32-WB2Y; Caroline Smith DeWaal et al., *All over the Map: A 10-Year Review of State Outbreak Reporting,* CSPI, 2015, https://cspinet.org/sites/default/files/attachment/all-over-the-map-report-2015.pdf, archived at https://perma.cc/GBF5-4VW3; Olga L. Henao et al., "Foodborne Diseases Active Surveillance Network—2 Decades of Achievements, 1996–2015," *Emerging Infectious Diseases* 21, no. 9 (September 2015): 1534; Robert Tauxe, personal communication with the author, February 5, 2018.

9. Robert V. Tauxe, "Molecular Subtyping and the Transformation of Public Health," *Foodborne Pathogens and Disease* 3, no. 1 (2006): 4–8; Henao et al., "Foodborne Diseases Active Surveillance Network." For an example of using foodborne illness surveillance data to evaluate the efficacy of restaurant grading, see Daniel E. Ho, Zoe C. Ashwood, and Cassandra Handan-Nader, "The False Promise of Simple Information Disclosure: New Evidence on Restaurant Hygiene Grading," 31–32. For evidence that recent advances in outbreak investigation have reduced the size of outbreaks and prevented illness, see Robert Tauxe, "Whole Genome Sequencing and the Transformation of Public Health Surveillance (for Enteric Infections)," conference presentation slides, Georgia Emerging Infections Program Annual Conference, Atlanta, March 24, 2017, slide 16, archived at https://perma.cc/K9RM-J8RY; Robert L. Scharff et al., "An Economic Evaluation of PulseNet: A Network for Foodborne Disease Surveillance," *American Journal of Preventive Medicine* 50, no. 5 (2016): S66–S73.

10. *Challenges Remain in FDA's Inspections,* 27. FSIS similarly lacks sufficient staff resources to regularly evaluate the adequacy of HACCP programs in the meat and poultry facilities under its jurisdiction. Isadore Rosenthal and Howard Kunreuther, "Roles for Third Parties"; "States and FDA Prepare for On-Farm Inspections," *The Packer,* February 22, 2017, https://www.thepacker.com/article/states-and-fda-prepare-farm-inspections, archived at https://perma.cc/GMX3-DCWQ.

11. Douglas Powell, "Killer Cantaloupe Facility Got Big Thumbs Up from Auditor Days Before Outbreak," *Barfblog,* October 20, 2011, http://www.barfblog.com/2011/10/killer-cantaloupe-facility-got-big-thumbs-up-from-auditor-days-before-outbreak-what-retailers-relied-on-those-audits-25-dead-123-sick-means-more-required-than-faith-based-food-safety/, archived at https://perma.cc/B5LK-LC7Z; Elizabeth Weise, "Food Safety Auditors Are Often Paid by the Firms They Audit," *USA Today,* October 4, 2010, https://usatoday30.usatoday.com/yourlife/food/safety/2010-10-01-foodaudits01_ST_N.htm, archived at https://perma.cc/HS96-3A9Q; Bill Marler, telephone interview by the author, October 5, 2014.

12. Jim Prevor, "Auditing and Food Safety: California Agencies Weigh In on Cantaloupe Crisis," *Jim Prevor's Perishable Pundit* (blog), January 4, 2012, http://www.perishablepundit.com/index.php?article=2695, archived at https://perma.cc/WU9C-4PGC. The FDA has experience with regulated industry paying for government oversight in a number of areas, including approvals for human and animal drugs, medical devices, and tobacco products. For example, the Prescription Drug User Fee Act of 1992 (PDUFA) authorized the FDA to collect fees from drug companies to pay for the review of certain new drug and biological license applications. As

required, to maintain the FDA's prescription-drug-user fee program, PDUFA has been reauthorized every five years since 1992. For analysis of the program, see Margaret Gilhooley, "Drug User Fee Reform: The Problem of Capture and a Sunset, and the Relevance of Priorities and the Deficit," *New Mexico Law Review* 41 (2011): 327.

13. The AMS developed the GAP and GHP Audit Program in response to requests from growers and state officials. Standards for Growing, Proposed Rule, 78 Fed. Reg. 3513; USDA AMS, *Good Agricultural Practices and Good Handling Practices Audit Verification Program: User's Guide*, April 2011, 1–2, http://www.canr.msu.edu/foodsystems/uploads/files/Good -practices-audit.pdf, archived at https://perma.cc/HXX9-H8JN; A. Bryan Endres and Nicholas R. Johnson, "Integrating Stakeholder Roles in Food Production, Marketing, and Safety Systems: An Evolving Multi-Jurisdictional Approach," *Journal of Environmental Law & Litigation* 26 (2011): 60–61; USDA AMS, "Harmonized GAP," archived at https://perma.cc/UQ7D -ULQ2; Ken Petersen (chief of Audit Services Branch, USDA-AMS Fruit and Vegetable Program), telephone interview by the author, September 2, 2016. Earlier, in 1996, the AMS had launched a similar program—Qualified through Verification (QTV)—at the request of the International Fresh-Cut Produce Association to provide fee-for-service audits to evaluate HACCP programs in fresh-cut produce processing plants. Plants that satisfied AMS standards and submitted themselves to periodic unannounced audits earned the right to use a QTV certification symbol in advertising and on packaging to promote their products. Before the QTV program, AMS inspectors enforcing USDA grading standards in fruit and vegetable processing plants verified that the plants operated in accordance with the FDA's GMP regulations. Request for Comments on the Qualified through Verification Program for the Fresh-Cut Produce Industry, 63 Fed. Reg. 47,220–221 (September 4, 1998). For more on USDA and state agriculture department audits in the fresh produce sector, see Elanor Starmer and Marie Kulick, *Bridging the GAPs: Strategies to Improve Produce Safety, Preserve Farm Diversity and Strengthen Local Food Systems*, Food & Water Watch and Institute for Agriculture and Trade Policy, September 2009, 3–4, 19, https://www.iatp.org/files/258_2_106746.pdf, archived at https://perma.cc/ 5UQW-A9X3.

14. The estimate for the number of farms that grow fresh produce for sale is from FDA, *Standards for the Growing, Harvesting, Packing and Holding of Produce for Human Consumption, Final Regularity Impact Analysis [. . .]*. Docket No. FDA-2011-N-0921, 40, archived at https:// perma.cc/ZZ4E-F5LF. The number of USDA audits in 2016 is from Ken Petersen, email message to author, May 11, 2017. Data on the California LGMA is from LGMA, *2015/2016 Annual Report*, http://www.lgma.ca.gov/wp-content/uploads/2016/09/2016-LGMA-Annual-Report_web.pdf, archived at https://perma.cc/E4ZF-RGWV, and on the Arizona LGMA is from Arizona Leafy Greens Marketing Agreement, *Annual Report 2015/2016*, archived at https://perma.cc/7EFT -7H4N. Audit volume for Primus Labs is from US House of Representatives, Committee on Energy and Commerce, Committee Staff, "Report on the Investigation of the Outbreak of *Listeria monocytogenes* in Cantaloupe at Jensen Farms," January 10, 2012, 6.

15. Petersen, interview.

16. Petersen, interview.

17. Scott Horsfall, telephone interview by the author, September 15, 2016; Petersen, interview; GFSI, *Guidance Document*, version 6.3, October, 2013, pt. II, §§ 2.4.6 and 3.3.2, http:// www.mygfsi.com/images/mygfsi/gfsifiles/information-kit/GFSI_Guidance_Document.pdf, archived at https://perma.cc/5TEJ-8PAT.

18. David (Dave) Theno, telephone interview by the author, September 5, 2014; Prevor, "Au-

diting and Food Safety"; James (Jim) Prevor, telephone interview by the author, January 28, 2014. For evidence of political and social pressure on government inspectors in restaurant and food service inspection, see Daniel E. Ho, "Fudging the Nudge: Information Disclosure and Restaurant Grading," *Yale Law Journal* 122 (2012): 595; Ho, "Does Peer Review Work?" 58n355. See also, Jodi L. Short and Michael W. Taffel, "The Integrity of Private Third-Party Compliance Monitoring" (Working Paper RPP-2015–20. Harvard Kennedy School, December 10, 2016), 2.

19. Patricia Wester (food safety consultant), telephone interview by the author, August 13, 2013; Patricia Wester, telephone interview by the author, March 2, 2015; Keith Schneider (professor of food science, University of Florida), telephone interview by the author, August 2, 2013; FSSP, "Every Company Deserves Professional Audits: Members of FSSP Strive to Improve and Enhance," 2013, archived at https://perma.cc/84PL-6FZC; Nancy A. Finney, "NEHA Credential Creates a Professional Pathway for Food Safety Auditors," *Food Safety Magazine*, August–September 2016, archived at https://perma.cc/EP2Y-FJH8; Coral Beach, "Auditor Credential Program Added to Food Safety Summit," *Food Safety News*, April 3, 2017, http://www.foodsafetynews.com/2017/04/auditor-credential-program-added-to-food-safety-summit/#.Wo85nKjwaUk, archived at https://perma.cc/RJ6U-VJMY; NEHA, "New Food Safety Auditing Credentials," *Food Safety Magazine*, May 2, 2017, https://www.foodsafetymagazine.com/enewsletter/new-food-safety-auditing-credentials/, archived at https://perma.cc/6556-UYU4.

20. Private food safety auditing is just one example of a widespread industrial practice known as conformity assessment. For a general introduction to conformity assessment, accreditation, and the ISO/IEC standards governing them, see ISO and UN Industrial Development Organization, *Building Trust: The Conformity Assessment Toolbox*, https://www.iso.org/files/live/sites/isoorg/files/archive/pdf/en/casco_building-trust.pdf, archived at https://perma.cc/N7YH-CUHH. For a more detailed account of the conformity assessment infrastructure in food safety auditing, see Timothy D. Lytton and Lesley K. McAllister, "Oversight in Private Food Safety Auditing: Addressing Auditor Conflict of Interest," *Wisconsin Law Review* (2014): 289–335.

21. Dan B. Dobbs, Paul T. Hayden, and Ellen M. Bublick, *The Law of Torts*, 2nd ed. (St. Paul, MN: West, 2011), §§ 405 and 412; Restatement (Second) of Torts §§ 314 and 324A (1965). For more detailed analysis of these doctrinal issues, see Timothy D. Lytton, "Exposing Private Third-Party Food Safety Auditors to Civil Liability for Negligence: Harnessing Private Law Norms to Regulate Private Governance," *European Review of Private Law* 27 (forthcoming).

22. Order Re: Primus Group, Inc.'s Amended Motion to Dismiss, Case No. 2011CV1891, District Court, Arapahoe County, State of Colorado (October 28, 2014), archived at https://perma.cc/H3VH-237S; Bill Marler, "Publisher's Platform: Three Years since People Died from Cantaloupe," *Food Safety News*, July 22, 2014, archived at https://perma.cc/FS7F-92KK. For additional details of the Jensen Farms cantaloupe melon *Listeria* outbreak, see chapter 1. For a survey of court opinions in this litigation, see Timothy D. Lytton, "Exposing Private Third-Party Food Safety Auditors to Civil Liability for Negligence," *European Review of Private Law* 27 (forthcoming 2019).

23. Order Re: Primus Group, 4–6.

24. The public record of the litigation against Primus ends with court orders denying Primus's motion to dismiss, which suggests that it quietly settled the litigation. For discussion of the liability exposure of third-party inspectors in the regulation of occupational safety and health, see Isadore Rosenthal and Howard Kunreuther, "Roles for Third Parties." For an analysis of insurers' liability for negligent inspection, see Kyle D. Logue, "Encouraging Insurers to Regulate: The Role (If Any) for Tort Law," *UC Irvine Law Review* 5 (2015): 1358, 1368–89.

25. On standards of reasonable care in negligence claims, see Rick Friedman and Patrick Malone, *Rules of the Road: A Plaintiff Lawyer's Guide to Proving Liability,* 2nd ed. (Portland, OR: Trial Guides, 2010); Dobbs, Hayden, and Bublick, *The Law of Torts,* §§ 178–81.

26. Wester, interview, August 13, 2013.

27. On the impact of the litigation process on risk regulation, see Timothy D. Lytton, "Using Tort Litigation to Enhance Regulatory Policy Making: Evaluating Climate-Change Litigation in Light of Lessons from Gun-Industry and Clergy-Sexual-Abuse Lawsuits," *Texas Law Review* 86 (2008): 1837–76.

28. For evidence of this effect of liability on public financial accountancy partnerships, see Lee Berton and Joann S. Lublin, "Seeking Shelter: Partnership Structure Is Called in Question as Liability Risk Rises," *Wall Street Journal,* June 10, 1992, A1; Lee Berton, "Big Accounting Firms Weed out Risky Clients," *Wall Street Journal,* June 26, 1995, B1.

29. Tom Baker, *The Medical Malpractice Myth* (Chicago: University of Chicago Press, 2005), chap. 5; Joanna C. Schwartz, "A Dose of Reality for Medical Malpractice Reform," *New York University Law Review* 88 (2013): 1224–1307. Compare David M. Studdert et al., "Relationship between Quality of Care and Negligence Litigation in Nursing Homes," *New England Journal of Medicine* 364 (March 31, 2011): 1243–50; Michelle M. Mello et al., "Who Pays for Medical Errors? An Analysis of Adverse Event Costs, the Medical Liability System, and Incentives for Patient Safety Improvement," *Journal of Empirical Legal Studies* 4, no. 4 (2007): 835–60; Y. Tony Yang el al., "Does Tort Law Improve the Health of Newborns, or Miscarry? A Longitudinal Analysis of the Effect of Liability Pressure on Birth Outcomes," *Journal of Empirical Legal Studies* 9, no. 2 (2012): 217–45.

30. Carl Liggio (attorney specializing in accounting and securities law), telephone interview by the author, May 10, 2017; Joanna C. Schwartz, "What Police Learn from Lawsuits," *Cardozo Law Review* 33 (2012), 841–94. See also Rick Swedloff and Tom Baker, "Insurers as Bumblebees in the Garden of Law Firm Norms," unpublished manuscript on file with Harvard Law School Library, 2016; Joanna C. Schwartz, "Introspection through Litigation," *Notre Dame Law Review* 90, no. 3 (2015): 1055–1104; Margo Schlanger, "Operationalizing Deterrence: Claims Management (in Hospitals, a Large Retailer, and Jails and Prisons)," *Journal of Tort Law* 2, no. 1 (2008): 1; John Rappaport, "How Private Insurers Regulate Public Police," *Harvard Law Review* 130 (2017): 1539–1614. See also Charles Epp, *Making Rights Real: Activists, Bureaucrats, and the Creation of the Legalistic State* (Chicago: University of Chicago Press, 2009); Timothy D. Lytton, *Holding Bishops Accountable: How Lawsuits Helped the Catholic Church Confront Clergy Sexual Abuse* (Cambridge, MA: Harvard University Press, 2008); Jeb Barnes and Thomas F. Burke, "The Diffusion of Rights: From Law on the Books to Organizational Rights Practices," *Law & Society Review* 40 (2006): 493–524; Jeb Barnes and Thomas F. Burke, "Making Way: Legal Mobilization, Organizational Response, and Wheelchair Access," *Law & Society Review* 46 (2012): 167–198.

31. For an example of insurance underwriters' reliance on audit scores, see Bernie Steves, *2016 Emerging Trends in Product Recall and Contamination Risk Management,* Aon Risk Solutions, 2016, 25, http://www.aon.com/attachments/risk-services/product-recall-2016.pdf, archived at https://perma.cc/LAZ8-QN4K.

32. Consumer Reports, "Food Fights, Fouls & Victories," *Consumer Reports,* March 31, 2016, https://www.consumerreports.org/food-safety/food-fights-fouls-and-victories/, archived at https://perma.cc/674C-2H29; *Study on Federal Regulation Prepared Pursuant to S. Res. 71 to Authorize a Study of the Purpose and Current Effectiveness of Certain Federal Agencies for the*

Committee on Governmental Affairs, US Senate, 95th Cong., vol. 5 (December 1977); Richard A. Merrill and Jeffrey K. Francer, "Organizing Federal Food Safety Regulation," *Seton Hall Law Review* 31 (2000): 66.

33. Lisa Heinzerling, "Divide and Confound: The Strange Allocation of US Regulatory Authority over Food," in *Food and Drug Regulation in an Era of Globalized Markets*, ed. Sam F. Halabi (Amsterdam: Elsevier, 2015), 125–34; Stephanie Tai, "Whole Foods: The FSMA and the Challenges of Defragmenting Food Safety Regulation," *American Journal of Law & Medicine* 41 (2015): 447–58.

34. Merrill and Francer, "Organizing Federal Food Safety Regulation," 78–92; Heinzerling, "Divide and Confound"; Tai, "Whole Foods." As a result of this history, funding for the FDA comes through congressional agriculture committees, not health committees. Marion Nestle, *Safe Food: The Politics of Food Safety*, rev. ed. (Berkeley: University of California Press, 2010), loc. 5877, Kindle.

35. Merrill and Francer, "Organizing Federal Food Safety Regulation," 115–25; National Academies, *Ensuring Safe Food: From Production to Consumption* (Washington, DC: National Academy Press, 1998), 98, 115–60; GAO, *A National Strategy*, 3n8. For a recent unsuccessful legislative attempt, see Safe Food Act of 2015, S. 287, 114th Cong. § 102, January 28, 2015. Executive Office of the President of the United States, *Delivering Government Solutions in the 21st Century: Reform Plan and Reorganization Recommendations*, released on June 21, 2018, and, archived at https://perma.cc/2B9A-T3Z4.

36. Merrill and Francer, "Organizing Federal Food Safety Regulation," 164–67, 150–55, 168–70; Jody Freeman and Jim Rossi, "Agency Coordination in Shared Regulatory Space," *Harvard Law Review* 125 (2012): 1151–55; Alejandro E. Camacho and Robert L. Glicksman, *Reorganizing Government: A Functional and Dimensional Framework* (New York: New York University Press, 2019), chap. 3.

37. GAO, "Highlights," in *Experiences of Seven Countries in Consolidating Their Food Safety Systems*, GAO-05-212, February 2005, 1–5.

38. Merrill and Francer, "Organizing Federal Food Safety Regulation," 115–18; National Academies, *Enhancing Food Safety: The Role of the Food and Drug Administration* (Washington, DC: National Academy Press, 2010), 16; GAO, *Opportunities to Reduce Potential Duplication in Government Programs, Save Tax Dollars, and Enhance Revenue*, GAO-11-318SP, March 2011, 10; Camacho and Glicksman, *Reorganizing Government*, chap. 3.

39. White House, "President Clinton Announces Initiative to Ensure the Safety of Imported and Domestic Fruits and Vegetables," October 2, 1997, https://clintonwhitehouse4 .archives.gov/WH/New/html/19971002-8886.html, archived at https://perma.cc/Q5GV -J6WV; "Breakdown: Lessons to be Learned from the 2008 *Salmonella Saintpaul* Outbreak," Produce Safety Project, Pew Charitable Trusts at Georgetown University, November 17, 2008, 4– 5, http://www.pewtrusts.org/~/media/legacy/uploadedfiles/phg/content_level_pages/reports/ psprptlessonssalmonella2008pdf.pdf, archived at https://perma.cc/MD66-DT2K; Federal Food Safety Working Group Progress Report, White House, December 2011, 1, 18, archived at https:// perma.cc/T874-LCH2; GAO, *Food Safety Working Group Is a Positive First Step but Governmentwide Planning Is Needed to Address Fragmentation*, GAO-11-289, March 2011; GAO, *High Risk Series: An Update*, GAO-15-290, February 2015, 263–64; Dan Flynn, "FSIS, FDA Leadership Does Yearly Lounge Act before IAFP," *Food Safety News*, July 11, 2017, http://www.foodsafety news.com/2017/07/fsis-fda-leadership-does-yearly-lounge-act-before-iafp/#.WpBSiajwaUk, archived at https://perma.cc/AH7U-JGJ7; Food Safety Modernization Act Surveillance Work-

ing Group, Annual Report to the Secretary, Department of Health and Human Services, 2015, 4, https://www.cdc.gov/oid/docs/BSC_OID_FSMA_Surv_WG_2015_Annual_Report.pdf, archived at https://perma.cc/Q5L9-UTKJ. Information about the disappearance of the Federal Food Safety Working Group is from Robert Brackett (professor of food science and nutrition, Illinois Institute of Technology and former FDA official), email to the author, May 17, 2017, and David Acheson (food safety consultant and former FDA official), email to the author, May 17, 2017. On interagency coordination, see Freeman and Rossi, "Agency Coordination," 1155–81.

40. Jeff Farrar, *History of the Integrated Food Safety System* (PowerPoint presentation, Food Safety Summit, Baltimore, MD, April 28, 2015), archived at https://perma.cc/LU4P-AFUV; FDA, "Working Groups," June 8, 2016, https://www.fda.gov/ForFederalStateandLocalOfficials/ProgramsInitiatives/PartnershipforFoodProtectionPFP/ucm404634.htm, archived at https://perma.cc/MJP4-ALRH; Travis Goodman, "Integrating Response: Past, Present, and Future: How the Rapid Response Team (RRT) Program and the Partnership for Food Protection are Integrating Response," (PowerPoint presentation, Food Safety Summit, Baltimore, MD, April 28, 2015), archived at https://perma.cc/T4A6-AQZR; USDA, "National Integrated Food Safety Initiative," https://nifa.usda.gov/program/national-integrated-food-safety-initiative, archived at https://perma.cc/9VZN-R35M; USDA National Integrated; FDA Food Safety Modernization Act, §§ 203, 209, 210.

41. "Welcome," CIFOR, archived at https://perma.cc/YR59-RZR3.

42. Blayne Davis, "Big Peanut Gets Cracked," *Huffington Post*, October 2, 2016, https://www.huffingtonpost.com/entry/big-peanut-gets-cracked_b_8236482.html, archived at https://perma.cc/RV9V-7RLQ.; Wikipedia, s.v. "Peanut Corporation of America," last modified April 4, 2018, archived at https://perma.cc/7TZE-UQPY.

43. Wikipedia, "Peanut Corporation of America"; Dan Flynn, "Path to Illnesses and Death Began Five Years before *Salmonella* Outbreak," *Food Safety News*, February 22, 2013, http://www.foodsafetynews.com/2013/02/practices-that-ended-with-illnesses-deaths-started-much-earlier/#.WpKWt6jwaUk, archived at https://perma.cc/J5FX-CER3; Elina Tselepidakis Page, *Trends in Food Recalls: 2004–13*, USDA Economic Research Service, Economic Information Bulletin No. 191, April 2018.

44. Wikipedia, "Peanut Corporation of America." For a more detailed account, see Rena Steinzor, *Why Not Jail? Industrial Catastrophes, Corporate Malfeasance, and Government Inaction* (Cambridge: Cambridge University Press, 2015), 183–90.

45. Department of Justice, *Former Officials and Broker of Peanut Corporation of America Indicted: Related to Salmonella-Tainted Peanut Products*, press release, February 21, 2013, https://www.justice.gov/opa/pr/former-officials-and-broker-peanut-corporation-america-indicted-related-salmonella-tainted, archived at https://perma.cc/CRL3-JHTY. See also Steinzor, *Why Not Jail?*, 188–90.

46. Flynn, "Path to Illness"; Gretchen Goetz, "Peanut Corporation of America from Inception to Indictment: A Timeline," *Food Safety News*, February 22, 2013, http://www.foodsafetynews.com/2013/02/peanut-corporation-of-america-from-inception-to-indictment-a-timeline/#.WpKdWajwaUk, archived at https://perma.cc/4B52-W2QJ; Dallas Carter, "Ex-PCA Plant Manager Testifies against His Former Associates," *Food Safety News*, August 8, 2014, http://www.foodsafetynews.com/2014/08/former-blakely-peanut-plant-manager-testifies-against-his-former-associates/#.WpKdyqjwaUk, archived at https://perma.cc/75GT-MHLQ.

47. Bill Marler, "Publisher's Platform: A Bit(e) of History of Outbreak Criminal Prosecutions," *Food Safety News*, May 3, 2016, http://www.foodsafetynews.com/2016/05/125984/

#.WpKfUKjwaUk, archived at https://perma.cc/5XJ2-7FPH; Fisher Broyles, "Former Peanut Corp. of America Executive Receives 28-Year Prison Sentence," https://www.fisherbroyles .com / former-peanut-corp-of-america-executive-receives-28-year-prison-sentence/, archived at https://perma.cc/29FP-K8T6; Moni Basu, "28 Years for *Salmonella*: Peanut Exec Gets Groundbreaking Sentence," *CNN.com*, September 22, 2015, https://www.cnn.com /2015/09/21/us/ salmonella-peanut-exec-sentenced/index.html, archived at https://perma.cc/737B-ZR3Q; Dan Flynn, "Circuit Court Denies All Peanut Corp. of America Criminal Appeals," *Food Safety News,* January 23, 2018, archived at https://perma.cc/QVB3-V973; Philip J. Hilts, "Tobacco Chiefs Say Cigarettes Aren't Addictive," *New York Times,* April 15, 1994, A1.

48. Joanne S. Eglovitch, "FDA Resurrects Park Doctrine in Enforcement of Pharmaceutical GMPs," *The Gold Sheet,* April 2011, https://files.skadden.com /sites%2Fdefault%2Ffiles %2Fentity_pdf%2FFDA_Resurrects_Park_Doctrine_in_Enforcement_of_Pharmaceutical _GMPs.pdf, archived at https://perma.cc/8X2P-WE44; Shawn Stevens, "The Food Police are Coming: DOJ and FDA Say Criminal Prosecution of Food Companies is a Priority," *FoodIndustry Counsel,* September 29, 2016, archived at https://perma.cc/A9XU-7TKD; 21 USC. 342(a)(1); *United States v. Park,* 421 U.S. 658 (1975).

49. Eglovitch, "FDA Resurrects," 16; Andrew C. Baird, "The New Park Doctrine: Missing the Mark," *North Carolina Law Review* 91, no. 3 (2013): 964–65.

50. Eglovitch, "FDA Resurrects," 16; Baird, "The New Park Doctrine," 968; FDA, *Regulatory Procedures Manual,* December 2017, chap. 6, 50–51, https://www.fda.gov/downloads/ICECI/ ComplianceManuals/RegulatoryProceduresManual/UCM074317.pdf, archived at https:// perma.cc/XC64-893U.

51. Bill Marler, "PCA, Conagra, DeCosters, Jensen Farms Prosecuted, Blue Bell Under Investigation, But Glass Onion, Townsend, Bidart, Andrew & Williamson Not—Yet?" *Food Poison Journal,* January 2, 2016, http://www.foodpoisonjournal.com /foodborne-illness-outbreaks/pca -conagra-decosters-jensen-farms-prosecuted-blue-bell-under-investigation-but-glass-onion -townsend-bidart-andrew-williamson-not-yet/, archived at https://perma.cc/ZLC8-FKVW; PritzkerLaw, "Jensen Brothers Face Charges for Selling Cantaloupe Contaminated with Listeria," *Food Poisoning Law Blog,* September 26, 2013, archived at https://perma.cc/Z946-QGGV; James Andrews, "Farmers in Cantaloupe Outbreak Sentenced to Probation, House Arrest, Fines," *Food Safety News,* January 29, 2014, http://www.foodsafetynews.com /2014/01/farmers-in -cantaloupe-listeria-outbreak-sentenced-to-probation-house-arrest-fines/#.WpKpMKjwaUk, archived at https://perma.cc/D8FD-RK8K; Bill Marler, email message to the author, September 8, 2017; CDC, "Multistate Outbreak of Human *Salmonella enteritidis* Infections Associated with Shell Eggs (Final Update)," December 2, 2010, https://www.cdc.gov/salmonella/2010/shell -eggs-12-2-10.html, archived at https://perma.cc/D9BM-BAJJ; Dan Flynn, "Supreme Court Will Not Review DeCoster Sentences in Egg Cases," *Food Safety News,* May 23, 2017, http:// www.foodsafetynews.com /2017/05/supreme-court-will-not-review-decoster-sentences-in-egg -cases/#.WpKuOajwaUk, archived at https://perma.cc/2APX-82HF.

52. Marler, "PCA, Con Agra." See also Josh Long, "Food Crimes: Making Sense of DOJ Prosecutions," *Food Law Blogger,* May 28, 2015, archived at https://perma.cc/UL9N-LXGK.

53. Chris Chechin-De La Rosa, "Food Crimes"; "PB & Jail," *Food Crimes,* September 16, 2015, YouTube video, 11:20, posted by Food Republic, written by Chris Chechin-De La Rosa, https://youtu.be/rzYtI9xEmyg, archived at https://perma.cc/F3LV-GCTV; Dave Theno, "A Sarbanes-Oxley Act for Food Safety Could Save Lives," *Food Safety News,* August 26, 2013, http://www.foodsafetynews.com /2013/08/a-sarbanes-oxley-act-for-food-safety-could-save

-lives/#.WpK02qjwaUk, archived at https://perma.cc/NKT3-D4ZP. See also Steinzor, *Why Not Jail*, 47, 64, 67, 76 (asserting that criminal prosecution of corporate executives has a deterrent effect on wrongdoing but noting that "empirical data on the subject is sparse"). On the use of criminal prosecution and the threat of criminal prosecution as a regulatory strategy more generally, see Anthony S. Barkow and Rachel E. Barkow, eds., *Prosecutors in the Boardroom: Using Criminal Law to Regulate Corporate Conduct* (New York: New York University Press, 2011).

54. "What Is the Number of SKUs in a Typical Supermarket, Grocery Store, Fashion Retailer, and an Electronics Store," *Quora*, April 11, 2014, https://www.quora.com/What-is-the-number-of-SKUs-in-a-typical-Supermarket-grocery-store-Fashion-retailer-and-an-electronics-retailer, archived at https://perma.cc/9DUT-5PX7; Theno, interview; James (Jim) Prevor, telephone interview by the author, October 25, 2013; David Acheson (food safety consultant), telephone interview by the author, December 15, 2014; Gale Prince (food safety consultant), telephone interview by the author, January 21, 2015.

55. "CoInspect," 2017, https://coinspectapp.com/, archived at https://perma.cc/YAX4-HPBV; Manik Suri (founder and CEO of CoInspect), telephone interview by the author, May 26, 2017.

56. "Azzule," 2016, http://www.azzule.com/pages/wf_Home.aspx, archived at https://perma.cc/E94A-HFGV.

57. See, e.g., TandD, 2018, http://www.tandd.com/about/index.html, archived at https://perma.cc/34D3-CKVY; PIMM, 2014, http://procuro.com/, archived at https://perma.cc/A27Y-TDJ9.

58. Julie Sobowale, "How Artificial Intelligence Is Transforming the Legal Profession," *ABA Journal*, April 2016, archived at https://perma.cc/35WZ-P6L4; Krista Garver, "6 Examples of Artificial Intelligence in the Food Industry," *Food Industry Executive*, April 11, 2018, archived at https://perma.cc/2NP7-M44C; Kate Brown, "Food & Tech: Using AI and Automation to Improve Food Safety," *Risk & Insurance*, May 1, 2018, archived at https://perma.cc/H4TP-P8RB.

59. Ryan Fothergill (in-house counsel, Primus Labs), telephone interview with the author, May 19, 2017.

60. IBM, "Walmart, IBM and Tsinghua University Explore the use of Blockchain to Help Bring Safer Food to Dinner Tables Across China," news release, October 19, 2016, https://www-03.ibm.com/press/us/en/pressrelease/50816.wss, archived at https://perma.cc/AD2H-DDHX; Roger Aitken, "IBM Forges Blockchain Collaboration with Nestle & Walmart in Global Food Safety," *Forbes*, August 22, 2017, https://www.forbes.com/sites/rogeraitken/2017/08/22/ibm-forges-blockchain-collaboration-with-nestle-walmart-for-global-food-safety/#6a689d253d36, archived at https://perma.cc/V7LZ-FN9R; Jenny McTaggart, "Grocers Embrace Blockchain in New Era of Transparency," *Progressive Grocer*, February 16, 2018, archived at https://perma.cc/U52S-AE3X; Ed Treacy, "How Will Blockchain Work with PTI and Trellis?" Produce Marketing Association, archived at https://perma.cc/U8K2-EWE7; Marco Iansiti and Karim R. Lakhani, "The Truth about Blockchain," *Harvard Business Review*, January–February 2017, 118–27; Michele D'Aliessi, "How Does the Blockchain Work?" *Medium*, June 1, 2016, https://medium.com/@micheledaliessi/how-does-the-blockchain-work-98c8cd01d2ae, archived at https://perma.cc/HD4N-N9TZ.

61. This and the following paragraphs are drawn from Timothy D. Lytton, "Competitive Third-Party Regulation: How Private Certification Can Overcome Constraints That Frustrate Government Regulation," *Theoretical Inquiries in Law* 15 (2014): 539–70, which relies on the account of the history of urban fires and government responses in Scott G. Knowles, *The Disas-*

ter Experts: Mastering Risk in Modern America (Philadelphia: University of Pennsylvania Press, 2011), chaps. 1–2.

62. UL, "By the Numbers," 2014, archived at https://perma.cc/MZ47-53JD; Julie Wernau, "Underwriters Laboratories Sets New Standards for Self, Testing Giant Broadens Scope with Green Goods, More Global Outlook" *Chicago Tribune,* June 30, 2011, C4; NFPA, "About NFPA," 2018, https://www.nfpa.org/About-NFPA, archived at https://perma.cc/UL7Q-AWQ6; NFPA, "List of NFPA Codes & Standards," 2018, https://www.nfpa.org/Codes-and-Standards/All-Codes-and-Standards/List-of-Codes-and-Standards, archived at https://perma.cc/T8WU-B5YB. A company's level of fire safety can influence its eligibility for coverage and their premiums. Chip Pecchio (vice president of underwriting, RSUI Group), personal communication with the author, June 5, 2017; Darrell Pippin (senior vice president, First Specialty Insurance Corp.), email message to the author, May 30, 2017.

63. Kyle Logue and Omri Ben-Shahar, "Outsourcing Regulation: How Insurance Reduces Moral Hazard," *Michigan Law Review* 111 (2012): 223–25; ISO, "What Is the PPC Program?" ISO Mitigation, 2018, https://www.isomitigation.com/ppc/iso-s-public-protection-classification-ppc-program.html, archived at https://perma.cc/KAU7-5QSV.

64. For other examples of risk regulation through insurance, see Logue, "Encouraging Insurers to Regulate" (workers' compensation, products liability, commercial property, boiler, and machinery coverage); Rosenthal and Kunreuther, "Roles for Third Parties," 4–5 (boilers); Rappaport "How Private Insurers Regulate" (police conduct).

65. For doubts about the capacity of fire insurance to generate useful loss control data, see David Hemenway, "Private Insurance as an Alternative to Protective Regulation: The Market for Residential Fire Insurance," *Policy Studies Journal* 15, no. 3 (March 1987): 433.

66. Jane McCarthy (vice president, Liberty International Underwriters), telephone interview by the author, May 22, 2017; *Food Safety in a Globalized World,* 13; Steves, *2016 Emerging Trends,* 16; Cookson Beecher, "Recall Insurance Can Benefit Consumers by Helping Business," *Food Safety News,* October 23, 2017, http://www.foodsafetynews.com/2017/10/recall-insurance-can-benefit-consumers-by-helping-businesses/#.WqmLXujwaUl, archived at https://perma.cc/H9PU-ZYEP.

67. Jerry R. Skees, Aleta Botts, and Kimberly A. Zeuli, "The Potential for Recall Insurance to Improve Food Safety," *International Food and Agribusiness Management Review* 4 (2001): 106; Bernie Steves, *2017 Emerging Trends in Product Recall and Contamination Risk Management,* Aon Risk Solutions, 2017, 22, 23, 26, http://www.aon.com/attachments/risk-services/2017-Emerging-Trends-Product-Recall-Report%20-USLtr-FINAL.pdf, archived at https://perma.cc/T53M-R2GB.

68. McCarthy, interview. Compare Tim Linden, "Liability Insurance: How Much Is Enough?" *Produce News,* May 31, 2012, http://producenews.com/news-dep-menu/test-featured/7945-liability-insurance-how-much-is-enough, archived at https://perma.cc/376M-GG2D, with Western Growers, "United Fresh and WG Team up to Provide Recall Insurance to Fresh Produce Industry," September 18, 2017, https://www.wga.com/press-releases/united-fresh-and-wg-team-provide-recall-insurance-fresh-produce-industry, archived at https://perma.cc/8GMX-L94G.

69. For a relevant analysis of mandatory insurance supported by private inspections to manage safety and environmental risks, see Howard Kunreuther, Shelley Metzenbaum, and Peter Schmeidler, "Mandating Insurance and Using Private Inspections to Improve Environmental Management," in *Leveraging the Private Sector: Management-Based Strategies for Improving En-*

vironmental Performance, ed. Cary Coglianese and Jennifer Nash (Washington, DC: Resources for the Future, 2006), 137–66.

Chapter Nine

1. Interview by the author of anonymous food safety manager at poultry processing plant, February 9, 2015; Megan Chedwick (director of food safety and sustainability, Church Brothers), telephone interview by the author, May 31, 2016.

2. Ken Petersen (chief of Audit Services Branch, USDA-AMS Fruit and Vegetable Program), telephone interview by the author, September 2, 2016; Robert Brackett (professor of food science and nutrition, Illinois Institute of Technology, former director of the FDA Center for Food Safety and Applied Nutrition), telephone interview by the author, July 1, 2016.

3. Bill Marler, interview by the author, October 5, 2014.

4. Bernie Steves (managing director for National Crisis Management, Aon), telephone interview by the author, May 15, 2017; Jane McCarthy (vice president, Liberty International Underwriters), telephone interview by the author, May 22, 2017. On underwriters and uncertainty more generally, see Richard V. Ericson and Aaron Doyle, *Uncertain Business: Risk, Insurance and the Limits of Knowledge* (Toronto: University of Toronto Press, 2004), 15–19.

5. For more general accounts of the role of nongovernmental entities in regulation, see Jody Freeman, "The Private Role in Public Governance," *New York University Law Review* 75, no. 3 (2000): 543–675; Julia Black, "Critical Reflections on Regulation," *Australian Journal of Legal Philosophy* 27, no. 1 (2002): 1–36; Catherine E. Rudder, A. Lee Fritschler, and Yon Jung Choi, *Public Policymaking by Private Organizations,* (Washington, DC: Brookings Institution, 2016).

6. On the theory of punctuated equilibrium more generally, see Frank R. Baumgartner and Bryan D. Jones, *Agendas and Instability in American Politics* (Chicago: University of Chicago Press, 1993).

7. For a successful example of feedback and learning arising out of a listeria outbreak associated with bagged salads, see Robert Tauxe, "Whole Genome Sequencing and the Transformation of Public Health Surveillance (for Enteric Infections)," conference presentation slides, Georgia Emerging Infections Program Annual Conference, Atlanta, March 24, 2017, slide 19, archived at https://perma.cc/K9RM-J8RY.

8. See David Demortain, *Scientists and the Regulation of Risk: Standardising Control* (Cheltenham, UK: Edward Elgar, 2011).

9. On the concept of layering, see Angie M. Boyce, "Outbreaks and the Management of 'Second-Order Friction': Repurposing Materials and Data from the Health Care and Food Systems for Public Health Surveillance," *Science and Technology Studies* 29, no. 1 (2016): 52–69.

10. On hybridization of food safety governance, see Paul Verbruggen and Tetty Havinga, eds., *Hybridization of Food Governance: Trends, Types and Results* (Cheltenham, UK: Edward Elgar, 2017). On the blurring of the public-private distinction in regulatory governance more generally, see Axel Marx, "How Relevant Is the Public Private Distinction in the Case of Voluntary Sustainability Standards?" (Working Paper RSCAS 2015/30, Robert Schuman Center for Advanced Studies, European University Institute), https://papers.ssrn.com/sol3/papers.cfm?abstract_id=2631991, archived at https://perma.cc/J527-HGZN; Jody Freeman, "The Private Role in Public Governance," *New York University Law Review* 75, no. 3 (2000): 543–675; Jody Freeman, "Private Parties, Public Functions and the New Administrative Law," *Administrative Law Review* 52 (2000): 813–58; Peter Schuck, *Why Government Fails So Often: And How*

It Can Do Better (Princeton, NJ: Princeton University Press, 2014), 28; Christopher Hood, Henry Rothstein and Robert Baldwin, *The Government of Risk: Understanding Risk Regulation Regimes* (Oxford: Oxford University Press, 2001), 9; Kernaghan Webb and Andrew Morrison, "The Law and Voluntary Codes: Examining the 'Tangled Web,'" in *Voluntary Codes: Private Governance, the Public Interest and Innovation*, ed. Kernaghan Webb (Ottawa: Carleton University Research Unit for Innovation, Science, and the Environment, 2002): 105; Harm Schepel, *The Constitution of Private Governance: Product Standards in the Regulation of Integrating Markets* (Oxford, UK: Hart Publishing, 2005), 3–4, 19–20, 34–35, 176; Harm Schepel, "Rules of Recognition, A Legal Constructivist Approach to Transnational Private Regulation," in *Private International Law and Global Governance*, ed. Horatia Muir Watt and Diego P. Fernandez Arroyo (Oxford: Oxford University Press: 2014), 201–10: Liora Salter, *Mandated Science: Science and Scientists in the Making of Standards* (Dardrecht, Netherlands: Kluwer Academic Publishers, 1988), 179.

11. On the formalization of risk management generally, see Bridget Hutter, *Managing Food Safety and Hygiene: Governance and Regulation as Risk Management* (Cheltenham, UK: Edward Elgar, 2011): 6–9; Demortain, *Scientists and the Regulation of Risk*; Marc A. Olshan, "Standards-Making Organizations and the Rationalization of American Life," *Sociological Quarterly* 34, no. 2 (1993): 319–35.

12. See Harold L. Wilensky, "The Professionalization of Everyone?" *American Journal of Sociology* 70, no. 2 (September 1964): 137; Andrew Abbott, *The System of Professions: An Essay on the Division of Expert Labor* (Chicago: University of Chicago Press, 1988); Demortain, *Scientists and the Regulation of Risk*.

13. Scott Horsfall (CEO of the California LGMA), telephone interview by the author, September 15, 2015. Idecisionsicences, Expert Panel Review of the Commodity Specific Food Safety Guidelines for the Production and Harvest of Lettuce and Leafy Greens, November 19, 2015, 6, archived at https://perma.cc/4GQD-8K7H.

14. Ericson and Doyle, *Uncertain Business*, 6. On institutional logics, see Patricia H. Thornton, William Ocasio, and Michael Lounsbury, *The Institutional Logics Perspective: A New Approach to Culture Structure and Process* (Oxford: Oxford University Press, 2012).

15. For additional studies not reviewed in these chapters, see Sami L. Gottlieb et al., "Multistate Outbreak of Listeriosis Linked to Turkey Deli Meat and Subsequent Changes in US Regulatory Policy," *Clinical Infectious Diseases* 42 (2006): 29–36; Michael Ollinger et al., *Food Safety Audits, Plant Characteristics, and Food Safety Technology Use in Meat and Poultry Plants*, USDA Economic Research Service, Economic Information Bulletin No. 82, October 2011; *FDA NARMS Retail Meat Interim Report for Salmonella Shows Encouraging Early Trends Continue; Includes Whole Genome Sequencing Data for the First Time*, April 28, 2016, archived at https://perma.cc/XE58-U7RX; Randall Lutter, "How Effective Are Federal Food Safety Regulations? The Case of Eggs and *Salmonella enteritidis*," Resources for the Future, Discussion Paper No. 15–24, June 2015, archived at https://perma.cc/EUL5-B88S. For a discussion of the limits of data regarding the health impact of the FDA's agricultural water requirements under FSMA, see Jennifer McEntire and Jim Gorny, "Fixing FSMA's Ag Water Requirements," *Food Safety Magazine*, August–September 2017, archived at https://perma.cc/PV7B-FBS3. The United States is not alone in lacking sufficient data to evaluate the efficacy and efficiency of food safety policies. See GAO, *Selected Countries' Systems Can Offer Insights into Ensuring Import Safety and Responding to Foodborne Illness*, GAO-08-794, June 2008, 29–34.

16. This claim about decision making in the food safety system is consistent with numerous

studies demonstrating that both ordinary people and professional experts routinely make decisions about risk based not on economically rational probability and cost calculations but rather on emotions, such as fear fueled by media stories and personal experiences that increase the salience of certain risks. Ericson and Doyle, *Uncertain Business*, 6–15. See also Spencer Henson and Julie Caswell, "Food Safety Regulation: An Overview of Contemporary Issues," *Food Policy* 43 (1999): 593. Hutter, *Managing Food Safety and Hygiene*, 5.

17. The actual wording is "what does not kill me makes me stronger." Friedrich Nietzsche, *Twilight of the Idols: Or How to Philosophize with a Hammer* (London: Penguin, 1990), 33.

18. On the experimental nature of governance, see Charles F. Sabel and Jonathan Zeitlin, "Experimentalist Governance," in ed. David Levi-Faur, *The Oxford Handbook of Governance* (Oxford: Oxford University Press, 2011), 169-183.

Appendix A

1. Elaine Scallan et al., "Foodborne Illness Acquired in the United States—Unspecified Agents," *Emerging Infectious Diseases* 17, no. 1 (January 2011): 17; Elaine Scallan et al., "Foodborne Illness Acquired in the United States—Major Pathogens," *Emerging Infectious Diseases* 17, no. 1 (January 2011): 7, 13.

2. Scallan et al., "Unspecified Agents," 7–15.

3. Scallan et al., "Unspecified Agents," 16–22.

4. Scallan et al., "Major Pathogens"; Scallan et al., "Unspecified Pathogens."

5. Sandra Hoffmann and Tobenna D. Anekwe, *Making Sense of Recent Cost-of-Foodborne-Illness Estimates*, USDA Economic Research Service Economic Information Bulletin No. 118, September 2013, 10, 14; Robert L. Scharff, "Economic Burden from Health Losses Due to Foodborne Illness in the United States," *Journal of Food Protection* 75, no. 1 (January 2012): 123–31; Sandra Hoffmann, Michael Batz, and J. Glenn Morriss Jr., "Annual Cost of Illness and Quality-Adjusted Life Year Losses in the United States Due to 14 Foodborne Pathogens," *Journal of Food Protection* 75, no. 7 (January 2012): 1291–1302. Additional studies on the burden of foodborne illness can be found at USDA, "Publications, Food Safety," February 26, 2018, https://www.ers.usda.gov/publications/?topicid=14835, archived at https://perma.cc/ER3Q-95GH. See also World Health Organization, *WHO Estimates of the Global Burden of Foodborne Diseases*, 2015, http://apps.who.int/iris/bitstream/10665/199350/1/9789241565165_eng.pdf?ua=1, archived at https://perma.cc/GVV9-9RBQ.

Appendix B

1. In addition, nine states have "pass-through" statutes that exempt nonmanufacturing sellers from strict liability where they had no knowledge or reason to know of the contamination. Three states do not follow the rule of strict liability, requiring proof of seller negligence in all cases. Denis Stearns, "Chain of Distribution Liability: Tag, You're It," September 2, 2009, https://marlerclark.com/pdfs/chain-of-distribution-liability.pdf, archived at https://perma.cc/M8KJ-PUXS; Denis Stearns, "Product Distributor Liability: Some Different Scenarios," Marler Clark, September 2, 2009, https://marlerclark.com/pdfs/distributor_liability.pdf, archived at https://perma.cc/HLK9-YPY9. For a general introduction to strict liability for the sale of defective products and the liability of wholesalers, distributors, and retailers, see David G. Owen, *Products Liability Law*, 3rd ed. (St. Paul, MN: West Academic Publishing, 2015), §§ 5.1–5.10, 15.2.

2. Stearns, "Chain of Distribution Liability"; Stearns, "Product Distributor Liability"; Denis

Stearns, "Indemnification, Contribution, and Allocation of Fault: Shifting the Blame," Marler Clark, September 2, 2009, https://marlerclark.com/pdfs/Indemnification.pdf, archived at https://perma.cc/D6DP-PGQR.

3. Eric Schwartz (CEO, United Vegetable Growers Cooperative), telephone interview by the author, June 1, 2016; Charles Stauber (Hallmark Financial Services, Philadelphia), telephone interview by the author, August 27, 2013; Jack Hipp (vice president for claims, Allianz Global), telephone interview by the author, April 16, 2015; Bill Marler, telephone interview by the author, October 5, 2014; Alan (Al) Maxwell (attorney at Weinberg Wheeler Hudgins Gunn & Dial, Atlanta), telephone interview by the author, June 1, 2016; James (Jim) Prevor (editor in chief of *Produce Business* magazine), telephone interview with the author, August 13, 2013; James Derr (safety and risk management professional, XL Catlin Insurance), telephone interview by the author, April 9, 2015; Denis Stearns, "Contaminated Fresh Produce and Product Liability: A Law-in-Action Perspective," in Xuetong Fan et al., *Microbial Safety of Fresh Produce* (Ames, IA: Wiley-Blackwell, 2009); Kristen Markley, *Food Safety and Liability Insurance: Emerging Issues for Farmers and Institutions*, Community Food Security Coalition, December 2010, http://www.cias.wisc.edu/farmertools14/3-prepare-your-business/food-safety-and-liability-insurance.pdf, archived at https://perma.cc/A5B6-457J.

4. Hipp, interview; Ed Mitchell (principal underwriter for product recall insurance, MS Amlin), telephone interview by the author, January 29, 2015; Douglas Becker (director of risk management, Nationwide), telephone interview by the author, May 21, 2015; David Acheson (president and CEO, Acheson Group, former FDA associate commissioner for foods), telephone interview by the author, December 15, 2014.

5. Maxwell, interview. On coverage limits for growers, see Tim Linden, "Liability Insurance: How Much Is Enough?" *Produce News*, May 31, 2012, http://producenews.com/news-dep-menu/test-featured/7945-liability-insurance-how-much-is-enough, archived at https://perma.cc/376M-GG2D.

6. Bradley Sullivan (managing attorney, Borton Petrini, Sacramento, CA), telephone interview by the author, August 15, 2013; Maxwell, interview; Stearns, "Chain of Distribution Liability"; Stearns, "Product Distributor Liability."

7. Marler, interview; James Andrews, "Jensen Farms Files for Bankruptcy," *Food Safety News*, May 26, 2012, http://www.foodsafetynews.com/2012/05/jensen-farms-files-for-bankruptcy/#.Wng9u6inGUk, archived at https://perma.cc/6MAF-ESXR. See also Bill Marler, "Why Retailers in Colorado are Ultimately Responsible for Selling *Listeria*-Tainted Cantaloupe that Sickened 40—Killing Nine," *Marler Blog*, April 28, 2013, http://www.marlerblog.com/legal-cases/why-a-retailer-in-colorado-is-ultimately-responsible-for-listeria-tainted-cantaloupe-that-sickened-40-killing-nine/, archived at https://perma.cc/7UYD-JJBC.

8. Kurt Niland, "Jensen Farms Cantaloupe Victims Reach Settlement with Walmart," *Righting Injustice*, May 15, 2014, http://www.rightinginjustice.com/news/2014/05/15/jensen-farms-cantaloupe-victims-reach-settlement-with-walmart/, archived at https://perma.cc/Y7S4-KHX7; Coral Beach, "Victims Settle with Kroger, Frontera; Dismiss Primus," *The Packer*, February 11, 2015, archived at https://perma.cc/8YXQ-MHAR; Marler, interview.

9. Maxwell, interview; Marler, interview; Bill Marler, "Dole Lettuce *E. coli* Outbreak Lawsuits—Minnesota, Wisconsin, Oregon (2005)," April 1, 2008, Marler Clark, https://marlerclark.com/news_events/dole-lettuce-e-coli-outbreak-minnesota-wisconsin-and-oregon, archived at https://perma.cc/QJG7-4B3G.

10. Maxwell, interview; Bill Marler, telephone interview by the author, May 31, 2016.

11. Maxwell, interview; Hipp, interview; Sullivan, interview; Becker, interview.

12. Marler, interview, May 31, 2016; Jack Hipp, telephone interview by the author, June 17, 2016; Maxwell, interview; *Majeska v. Dole Fresh Vegetables*, Plaintiffs' First Complaint for Damages, September, 2009, http://www.marlerblog.com/uploads/file/MAJESKA,%20Jane%20-%20Complaint.pdf, archived at https://perma.cc/8JFH-RKEN.

Appendix C

1. Bill Pursley, "AIB's Mission: Identify, Control and Eliminate (ICE)," *AIB* (Fall 2003): 4–7; Bill Pursley (vice president of food safety education, AIB, retired), interview by the author, August 8, 2013; Ronald L. Wirtz, "Education and Training for the Baking Industry of the World: A History of the American Institute of Baking from Its Origins to the Present Day" (PhD diss., Kansas State University, 1994), 101–5; Michelle R. Ranville, "Legitimacy of Private Governance: Private Food Safety Standards in the United States," unpublished paper presented at the annual conference of the Southern Political Science Association, January 9, 2009, 9–12, archived at https://perma.cc/P4Z3-T5W4. Third-party audits generally refer to audits of a supplier conducted by an outside auditor other than a buyer. The auditor is a third party to the supplier-buyer relationship. Second-party audits are audits of a supplier conducted by a buyer. First-party audits, also known as internal audits, are audits of a supplier conducted by the supplier itself. Mark Hammer, "First-, Second- & Third-Party Audits, What Are Differences?," ISO 9001 Blog, February 24, 2015, archived at https://perma.cc/MA9F-AZ5K.

2. Art Davis (vice president of food safety, Vista Institute), telephone interview by the author, August 12, 2013; Gale Prince (president and founder, SAGE Food Safety Consultants, former corporate director of regulatory affairs at Kroger), telephone interview by the author, January 21, 2015; Drew McDonald (vice president of quality and food safety, Taylor Fresh Foods), telephone interview by the author, June 2, 2016; Charles Cook (managing partner, Country Fare Consulting, founder of Cook and Thurber), personal communication with the author, November 23, 2016. In 1999, Davis Fresh provided food safety audits of produce suppliers for Safeway. Kenneth S. Petersen, "Third-Party Audit Programs for the Fresh-Produce Industry," in *Microbial Safety of Fresh Produce*, ed. Xuetong Fan et al. (Ames, IA: Wiley-Blackwell, 2009), 322; Devon Zagory (president, Devon Zagory Associates), telephone interview by the author, August 21, 2013; Devon Zagory, personal communication with the author, November 18, 2016.

3. Rena Pierami (vice president of technical services, Merieux NutriSciences), telephone interview by the author, September 9, 2013; Jim Wagner (former director of supply chain and certification services, Steritech), telephone interview with the author, August 21, 2008; Tom Huge (president, ASI Food Safety Consultants), personal communication to the author, August 4, 2014; Charles Cook, telephone interview by the author, August 13, 2013; David Acheson (president and CEO, Acheson Group, former FDA associate commissioner for foods), telephone interview by the author, August 6, 2013.

4. Gary Huge (vice president, ASI Food Safety Consulting), email message to the author, August 16, 2013; Tom Huge, personal communication with the author.

5. Tom Chestnut (senior vice president, Global Food Division of NSF International), telephone interview with the author, August 15, 2013; Zagory, interview; NSF International, "Mission, Values and History," 2018, http://www.nsf.org/about-nsf/mission-values-history, archived at https://perma.cc/3P56-AZXX.

Appendix D

1. Brandon Bailey, "After Hearing, Lawmaker Says Grower-State Cooperation Has Failed," *Mercury News*, October 12, 2006, B1; Rong-Gong Lin II, "Senator Seeks New Oversight of Greens," *Los Angeles Times*, October 12, 2006, B1; Frank D. Russo, "Package of Major Food Safety Bills Introduced by California State Senator Dean Florez," *California Progress Reports*, February 1, 2007, 1–2, http://www.californiaprogressreport.com/site/print/4963, archived at https://perma.cc/2MUE-YZLA; California Senate Bill 200, Introduced by Senator Florez, February 7, 2007, http://www.leginfo.ca.gov/pub/07-08/bill/sen/sb_0151-0200/sb_200_bill _20070207_introduced.pdf, archived at https://perma.cc/SY59-MHQ3; California Senate Bill 201, Introduced by Senator Florez, February 7, 2007, http://www.leginfo.ca.gov/pub/07-08/bill/ sen/sb_0201-0250/sb_201_bill_20070207_introduced.pdf, archived at https://perma.cc/4ZR5 -VYEJ; California Senate Bill 202, Introduced by Senator Florez, February 7, 2007, http://www .leginfo.ca.gov/pub/07-08/bill/sen/sb_0201-0250/sb_202_bill_20070207_introduced.pdf, ar- chived at https://perma.cc/TM57-2HWM; Varun Shekhar, "Produce Exceptionalism: Examin- ing the Leafy Greens Marketing Agreement and Its Ability to Improve Food Safety," *Journal of Food Law & Policy* 6 (2010): 281–82.

2. WGA, "Leafy Greens Marketing Agreement and Marketing Order, Frequently Asked Questions," January 2, 2007, archived at https://perma.cc/J8UW-HZQ2; Jerry Hirsch, "State Oks Certification Program for Leafy Crops," *Los Angeles Times*, February 8, 2007, C2; Hank Giclas (senior vice president for strategic planning, science, and technology, Western Growers), telephone interview by the author, August 26, 2016; California Department of Food and Agri- culture, "Leafy Greens Marketing Agreement Sets Compliance Audit Start Date," Press Release No. 07-054, https://www.cdfa.ca.gov/egov/Press_Releases/Press_Release.asp?PRnum=07-054, archived at https://perma.cc/MDA8-JM8M; Shekhar, "Produce Exceptionalism," 281–82.

3. Jim Prevor, "Buyer-led Food Safety Initiative Recap," *Jim Prevor's Perishable Pundit* (blog), http://www.perishablepundit.com/index.php?hot=buyer-led, archived at https://perma.cc/ KQ9B-LZ44; Jim Prevor, "Buyer-Led Food Safety Effort Leaves Open Question of Buyer Com- mitment," *Jim Prevor's Perishable Pundit* (blog), October 30, 2006, http://www.perishablepundit .com/index.php?article=1580, archived at https://perma.cc/9RNF-AU3V; Jim Prevor, "NRA Forms Produce Safety Working Group," *Jim Prevor's Perishable Pundit* (blog), November 7, 2006, http://www.perishablepundit.com/index.php?article=1472, archived at https://perma.cc/QAF4 -TLRP; Elanor Starmer and Marie Kulick, *Bridging the GAPs: Strategies to Improve Produce Safety, Preserve Farm Diversity and Strengthen Local Food Systems*, Food & Water Watch and Institute for Agriculture and Trade Policy, September 2009, 6, https://www.iatp.org/files/258_2_106746.pdf, archived at https://perma.cc/5UQW-A9X3; Diana Stuart, "Science, Standards, and Power: New Food Safety Governance in California," *Journal of Rural Social Sciences*, 25, no. 3 (2010): 120.

4. Jim Prevor, "Food Safety Arms War Claimed as WGA Responds to Publix Demand for Enhanced Produce Standards," *Jim Prevor's Perishable Pundit* (blog), November 13, 2007, http:// www.perishablepundit.com/index.php?date=11/13/07&pundit=1, archived at https://perma .cc/ZC63-X9CZ.

5. Prevor, "Food Safety Arms War"; Jim Prevor, "Coalition of Associations Seeks Dialog with Food Safety Leadership Council," *Jim Prevor's Perishable Pundit* (blog), November 15, 2007; http://www.perishablepundit.com/index.php?article=104, archived at https://perma.cc/5M5E -AE9Y.

6. Starmer and Kulick, *Bridging the GAPs*, 6; David Runsten (Director of Policy and Pro- grams, Community Alliance with Family Farmers), testimony at the USDA hearing on the pro-

posed National Leafy Green Marketing Agreement, Monterey, CA, September 22, 2009, 4–5, http://www.nationalorganiccoalition.org/_literature_113917/David_Runsten,_Director_of _Policy_and_Programs,_Community_Alliance_with_Family_Farmers,_Davis,_CA, archived at https://perma.cc/G4YG-KT2M; Zagory, interview.

Index

Acheson, David, 112, 133, 179, 207
activists. *See* consumer advocates
Adams, Catherine, 92, 112
agendas, 52
Agricultural Marketing Service (AMS), 138–41, 208–9
American Institute of Baking (AIB), 251
American Meat Institute, 95–96, 103
American Public Health Association (APHA), 69, 92–93, 114
American Public Health Association v. Butz, 92, 103
apprehension, 241
ASI Food Safety, 252
assessment. *See* policy evaluation
Association of Food and Drug Officials (AFDO), 220
audits: accreditation and oversight of auditors, 159–60; audit fatigue, 145; audit schemes, 129–30; checklists, 111, 132; civil liability of, 211–16; consultative audits, 42; criticism of, 132, 207; dairy inspection, 33, 42–43, 57, 59; estimated scope of, 129, 206, 208; funding of, 203, 207–10; harmonized standards, 131; history of third-party audits, 251–52; improving reliability of, 202, 207–16; LGMA, 207–8; reasons for reliance on third-party audits, 208–10; redundancy, 58, 130, 132, 137; scores and ratings, 16–18, 47, 58, 132; second-party, 207; standards of, 17; third-party, 2, 127–30, 195, 237, 238, 240. *See also* Global Food Safety Initiative (GFSI); hybridization; inspection; Jensen Farms cantaloupe outbreak; LGMA; Primus Labs; scorecards for dairy inspection
Austern, Thomas, 74, 80, 83

bacterial typing, 9, 88; advances in, 182–83, 238. *See also* National Salmonella Surveillance Program (NSSP); pulsed-field gel electrophoresis (PFGE); PulseNet; whole genome sequencing (WGS)
bankruptcy: Bon Vivant, 77; Jensen Farms, 11, 249; Marler litigation strategy, 250
barcode, 192, 227, 239
Bauman, Howard, 66, 69, 73, 91, 112, 114
Becker, Doug, 150, 172
beef inspection: HACCP-Based Inspection Models Project (HIMP), 105; history of, 87–90, 237, 286n1; patrol system, 90; streamlined inspection systems, 90, 114. *See also* Meat Inspection Act, Federal; poultry inspection
benchmarking, 130. *See also* Global Food Safety Initiative (GFSI)
big business, 241. *See also* capture, theories of
big government, 81, 241
Bioterrorism Act, 190
blockchain, 227
Bon Vivant vichyssoise outbreak, 70, 74–84, 113–15. *See also* recalls
Borden, 46
botulism, 70, 73, 115, 182. *See also* Bon Vivant vichyssoise outbreak
Brackett, Robert, 194
brand competition, 43, 55. *See also* reputation
brand sensitivity. *See* reputation
breastfeeding, 31, 62
burden of foodborne illness, in United States, 3, 163, 243–44; compared to other sources of injury and illness, 4–7; on elderly, 6, 31; root causes, 264n9. *See also* cost of foodborne illness